CHARLESTON
HOSPITALITY

RECIPES FROM

JOHNSON & WALES UNIVERSITY

AT CHARLESTON

Printed in the USA by
WIMMER
The Wimmer Companies, Inc.
Memphis • Dallas

History of the University

Johnson & Wales University was founded as a business school in 1914 in Providence, Rhode Island, by two women, Gertrude I. Johnson and Mary T. Wales. From its origins as a school devoted to business education, Johnson & Wales has grown from a junior college, to a senior college, and ultimately to university status. A private, nonprofit, coeducational institution, Johnson & Wales is accredited by the Accrediting Council for Independent Colleges and Schools of the Career College Association.

Over time the University has grown to become the largest foodservice and hospitality educator in the world. This growth is due to the implementation of new degree programs and the addition of new campus locations, the first being in Charleston, South Carolina, in 1981. One of America's oldest and most beautiful cities, Charleston is famous for its historic homes and plantations, museums, fine restaurants, and miles of wide, sandy beaches. This "grand dame of southern port cities" has proven to provide an excellent setting for a campus known today as "The Hospitality College of the South."

In the early beginnings of the Charleston campus, an associate degree program in culinary arts was offered to military personnel stationed in the area. This evening and weekend program was one calendar year in length. Along with a high school diploma, several years of documented foodservice experience and successful completion of the University's advanced placement test were required for admission.

With minimal recruiting efforts, the University enrolled 30 students and provided training at local schools and existing military facilities. With the birth of this program came community support, recognition, and opportunity.

As the enrollment in this program plateaued two years later, community leaders encouraged Johnson & Wales' opening of a permanent Charleston campus. Several factors convinced school administrators that this was a worthwhile vision. In the early to mid-1980's, explosive growth occurred in the hospitality industry from Hilton Head Island through Charleston and the barrier islands. Attractive to thousands of visitors, this area was also attractive to students. Recreational and employment opportunities coupled with an intensive, proven degree program were the school's biggest assets.

In 1983, Johnson & Wales University requested a license by the South Carolina Commission of Higher Education to operate a two-year Associate in Occupational Science Degree program in Culinary Arts, as well as a 12-month advanced standing program. When a five-year license was granted, nationwide recruiting by the University's admissions representatives began. As federal funds became available, the University established its campus in downtown Charleston's Business & Technology Center (today known as the Port City Center) for its facilities. Apartments were also leased in a nearby apartment complex, and approximately 88 students enrolled in the first official class. Later months saw enrollment mushroom beyond expectations. One year later, over 200 students became a part of the growing Johnson & Wales University at Charleston.

History of the University

Through the next few years, the University steadily grew in enrollment, degree offerings, and physical facilities. The South Carolina Commission on Higher Education granted approval for the University to implement five additional associate degree programs in the foodservice and hospitality areas. By 1990, almost 600 students were enrolled. Clubs and organizations, both professional and recreational, also flourished.

In the following years, the Charleston campus has continued to achieve monumental successes with the approval and implementation of four Bachelor of Science Degree programs and an additional associate level program in Travel-Tourism Management. The administrative and campus facilities today are still located in the Port City Center, and nearby Student Housing accommodates over 400 students. Nineteen clubs and organizations as well as numerous intramural sports activities enhance the educational experience of over 1,000 students. These students, from 41 states and five foreign countries, historically enjoy a 98% placement rate within 90 days of graduation.

While this Charleston campus grows so does the entire University system. Today, Johnson & Wales also maintains campuses in Norfolk, Virginia; North Miami, Florida; Worcester, Massachusetts; and Vail, Colorado. Extension programs with the IHM Business School in Gothenburg, Sweden, and with the University of St. Martin, St. Maarten, NA, are also now a part of the the University system.

Purpose and Dedication

It is with heartfelt thanks that the faculty and staff of Johnson & Wales University at Charleston dedicate this recipe book to those who have made our success possible - our students. These students include those enrolled in our associate and baccalaureate degree programs - both day school and continuing education - and those in our Elderhostel programs, chef's club programs, retraining programs, and other special programs.

This book is also dedicated to our loyal alumni who continuously support the Charleston campus through their recruitment and career development efforts and financial donations.

Special Thanks

Now in its second printing, <u>Charleston Hospitality</u> continues to bring special recipes, commentaries, and nutritional information to thousands of kitchens. Sincere thanks and gratitude from the administration at Johnson & Wales are extended to those who have made <u>Charleston Hospitality</u> possible.

RECIPES/CULINARY COMMENTARIES

Instructors **David Hendricksen, Louis Leichter, Dan Polasek, Kathy Hawkins, William Edwards Wilroy III, Stephen Nogle, Victor Smurro, Marcel Massenet, Armin Gronert, Donna Leventhal,** and **Susan Wigley**

Alumni **Sharon Santos Lawrence, Karen Heist,** and **Michael Speranza**

Student **Helen Taylor**

Pillsbury Bake-Off Winner **Gladys Fulton**

Director of Culinary Education **Karl J. Guggenmos**

Former Charleston Campus President **Paul Wm. Conco**

Local restauranteurs representing **A.W. Shuck's, Charleston Crab House, East Bay Trading Company, 82 Queen, Louis's Charleston Grill, Robert's of Charleston, Shem Creek Bar & Grill, The Colony House,** and **The Mills House**

RECIPE ANALYSES

Students **Melissa Antley, Philip Benton, John Broyles, Jason Evans, Gwen Jackson, John Lynch, Cassandra McKoy, Amy Milford, Jonathan Nelson, Jason Reed, Randy Stubstad, Kiona Swinton, Jude Tauzin, Scott Thomason, Meredith Tomlinson, Daniel Trawick, John Varanese, Akil Washington, David Weikert, Clifford Wilder, Brandon Williams, Michelle Williams,** and **Andrew D. Wood**

COORDINATION/DESIGN

Mim L. Runey, Director of Public Relations

Natalie P. Manning, Director of Publications (Providence, RI campus)

HEALTHFUL HINTS

Rose Anderson, Lowcountry Nutrition Council

Barry L. Gleim

Barry L. Gleim, Ed.D.
President
Johnson & Wales University at Charleston

Table of Contents

BEVERAGES

Beverages

Contents

Beverages

Culinary Commentary

Kathy Hawkins has almost 15 years of experience in such positions as wine sommelier, maitre d'hotel and restaurant manager. She is a maitre d'hotel instructor at the University.

WINE AND FOOD

Although wine consumption in the United States has doubled in the past decade, the average citizen of France or Italy drinks ten times as much wine as his American counterpart. We lack a tradition that encourages people to expect a bottle of wine with lunch and evening meals. In Europe, there is no fuss made about drinking wine. In America, however, many people feel intimidated by wine and often only serve it, with great trepidation, on special occasions.

One reason for our national anxiety over wine is the fear of breaking the rules of wine. In reality, there are no rules. People who follow the axiom, "Drink red wine with meat and white wine with fish," are sure to miss the pleasure of a bottle of Jordan Chardonnay served with Veal Cordon Bleu.

One of the great joys of drinking wine is experimentation. It is fun to discover a new wine that delights the senses. It is even more fun to match that wine with the dish that perfectly complements the flavors. The choosing of a wine to match a type of food is a matter of personal taste and preference. If a person feels he has reached nirvana by drinking a young Cabernet Sauvignon with poached Dover sole, let no man tear them asunder.

While there are no set wine rules, there are certain guidelines which can make easier the task of choosing the correct wine to complement a meal. The primary goal is to establish a balance between the wine and the food so that neither dominates the other. Instead of worrying about red with meat and white with fish, concentrate on choosing a light flavor wine to accompany light flavor foods and a stronger flavor wine to accompany hearty flavor foods. It is important to remember when selecting a wine to accompany a particular dish that the primary concern is not the basic ingredient, but how it is prepared. For example, chicken and veal may be prepared in ways so varied that the appropriate wine can range from a light wine to a mature red.

Though matching wine and food can initially be a bit intimidating, it should not be looked on as a dreaded chore. Through trial and error, you will discover some combinations that turn an ordinary evening meal into a memorable feast. You will very likely also discover a few combinations that simply do not work. But with time your successes will be greater than your failures, and your enjoyment of wine will grow and grow.

Culinary Commentary

Daniel Polasek is a certified T.I.P.S. (Training for Intervention Procedures by Servers of Alcohol) educator. He teaches all mixology classes at Johnson & Wales University at Charleston.

TODAY'S FIVE MOST POPULAR DRINKS

It seems just yesterday that the Harvey Wallbanger, Sloe Gin Fizz, and Tom Collins were the common drinks for party-goers pursuing social activities at their local tavern. But as times change, so does taste. Recently, people have begun to change their drinking practices toward lighter drinks in an attempt to build on moderation.

The popularity of drinks is mostly defined by a particular region and its surroundings. In the Northeast, the focus still seems to be on dark liquors whereas in the South, the light clear spirits are favored due to the long hot summers. A gin and tonic with lime or a "Cape Codder" (vodka and cranberry juice) can quench even the most parched throats.

Many professional mixers pride themselves on their ability to be creative in designing drinks which they feel will get the best response from their customers. But people have grown tired of the paper umbrellas and fancy glassware that are used as a marketing strategy in lieu of taste.

Yes, times have changed. Many once-famous cocktails and mixed drinks are finding new popularity out of old bartending manuals. People have begun to blow the dust off these old favorites and re-introduce them into society. It should not surprise you to find some of these "classics" listed among the 5 most popular drinks of today.

The Bloody Mary — For years, this classic has brought life to many searching for a hangover cure. Today, it's a definite for Sunday brunch.

As each bartender has a recipe for the "best" Bloody Mary, each also has a story of its origination. This bartender recalls the story of a young maiden being courted by her Swedish lover. During the time of the phylloxera (Grape Aphis) that almost destroyed the vines native to Europe, an attempt to make wine from the juice of tomatoes led our fair maiden "Mary" to the vats to begin her repetitive circular journey. Shortly after, her dear love came to court and, as expected, a chase did begin. As they traveled the circumference of the vat, tomatoes under foot, Mary slipped and settled down on the bottle of vodka which had fallen from her lover's hip.

Hence, The Bloody Mary.

2 ounces vodka	dash hot sauce
4 to 6 ounces tomato juice	pinch pepper
1 wedge lemon, squeezed	pinch celery salt
dash worcestershire sauce	

Culinary Commentary

Mix well with ice, and serve in chilled glass. Garnish with any fresh vegetable.

The Margarita — With the popularity of tequila in the United States, the margarita has turned the taco into a fiesta grande. When prepared properly, the flavors will enhance each other.

1-1/2 ounces gold tequila   Juice of 1 large lime
3/4 ounce triple sec

Rim a cocktail glass with a lime wedge, and invert onto a plate of salt. Combine liquid ingredients in mixing glass with plenty of ice. Shake well, and strain into glass. Garnish with slice of lime.

Strawberry Daiquiri — Look beyond the "Rum and Soda" and you will find the Daiquiri. Today, rum is a very popular spirit and is widely used as a base in many cocktails that are enjoyed during the summer and even the winter months.

The traditional lime daiquiri sparked the beginning of a fashionable drink trend as consumers added fresh fruit to their old favorite. As with most popular drinks, the following recipe can be changed to your liking by replacing the strawberries with any fresh or frozen fruit such as raspberries, peaches, banana or kiwi (Yes, kiwi).

1-1/2 ounces light rum   1/2 ounce simple syrup*
1/2 ounce lime juice   6 large fresh strawberries

Combine all ingredients in blender with crushed ice. Blend until smooth. Serve in a tall glass garnished with strawberry or fruit of your choice.

*Simple Syrup — 2 cups of sugar to 1 cup water. Heat to dissolve. Boil 6 to 7 minutes. Cool.

The Whiskey Sour — During Prohibition, the whiskey sour grew in popularity as an attempt to find a way to cut the harshness of bootleg whiskey so the ladies could consume right along with the men. To it, they would add lemon juice, sugar, and egg white, and shake until it turned creamy white. Bartenders in industry today use a prepared sour mix. These mixes can now be found in any grocery or specialty store in the beverage section.

1-1/2 ounces blended whiskey   3 ounces whiskey sour mix

Culinary Commentary

Prepare in mixing glass with ice and shake until frothy. Strain into prechilled cocktail glass or into old fashioned glass with ice. Garnish with orange slices and cherry.

Spritzers and Coolers — Appetites for lighter drinks have once again found their way back to wine spritzers. In the mid 1980's, people were introduced to the wine cooler craze that swept the country. But, like most fads that fade, so be it with most of the pre-packed wine coolers. Today bartenders have resorted back to the "best way" of preparing the light, refreshing coolers.

To make a wine spritzer: Fill a tall Collins glass with ice, squeeze lime wedge into glass, and add 4 to 5 ounces of dry white wine. Fill to top with club soda. Garnish with lemon or lime slice.

To make a wine cooler: Fill glass with ice. Add 4 to 5 ounces of red or white table wine. Fill glass with lemon-lime soda. Garnish with lime, orange slice, cherry or all three!

Beverages

After 5

1/3 ounce coffee liqueur
1/3 ounce Irish cream

1/3 ounce peppermint liqueur

Ice down. Pour into rocks glass.

A Judy Gibson

1-1/2 ounces dry vermouth
1 ounce bourbon whiskey

1 ounce cream de nouyaux
Pineapple juice to 1/4 inch rim

Speed shake. Pour into hi-ball glass. Garnish with cherry.

Almond Kicker

1-1/2 ounces vodka

3/4 ounce amaretto

Ice down. Pour into rocks glass. Garnish with cherry.

Almond Mint

1-1/2 ounces vodka
1/2 ounce amaretto

1/2 ounce white menthe
1 ounce club soda

Ice down. Pour into rocks glass.

Beverages

Almond Tea

4 cups water
3/4 to 1 cup sugar
1/4 cup lemon juice
1-1/2 cups hot strong tea
2-2/3 cups pineapple juice

1/4 cup instant orange
  breakfast drink mix
3/4 teaspoon almond extract
3/4 teaspoon vanilla extract

Combine water, sugar and lemon juice in a Dutch oven. Simmer 5 minutes. Add remaining ingredients. Cook until thoroughly heated.
Yield: 2 quarts.

Apricot Colada

1-1/2 ounces dark rum
1-1/2 ounces apricot brandy

2 scoops ice cream

Blend in blender for 30 seconds. Pour into hurricane glass, and garnish with orange wedge and cherry.

B52

1/3 ounce coffee liqueur
1/3 ounce Irish cream

1/3 ounce orange liqueur

Ice down. Pour into rocks glass.

Beverages

Blue Fish

1 ounce blue curacao

1 ounce vodka

1 ounce orange juice

Shake, and strain. Pour in coupe glass.

Brandied Coffee

2 egg yolks, slightly beaten

1-1/2 cups milk

1 cup half-and-half

2 tablespoons light corn syrup

1 tablespoon plus 1 teaspoon instant coffee

1/3 cup brandy

1/4 cup light corn syrup

1/4 cup water

2 egg whites

Combine the first 5 ingredients in a large saucepan. Cook over medium heat, stirring constantly, until mixture thickens. Remove from heat. Stir in brandy. Set aside. Combine 1/4 cup corn syrup and water in a small saucepan. Cook, uncovered, over high heat until boiling. Reduce heat, and simmer 2 minutes. Beat egg whites (at room temperature) until peaks form. Gradually add the hot syrup to egg whites, beating until stiff peaks form. Whisk egg whites into coffee mixture. Serve immediately.

Yield: 6 cups.

Brandy Alexander

1 ounce brandy

1 ounce dark cacao

1 ounce cream

Serve up in champagne coupe glass. Garnish with nutmeg.

Beverages

Butterfinger

1 ounce butterscotch liqueur   1 ounce dark creme de cacao

Serve straight up or shake, and strain in shot or rocks glass.

Chocolate Milk Cooler

1 cup skim milk   1 teaspoon vanilla
1/3 cup instant nonfat dry milk powder 2 to 3 teaspoons sugar
1 tablespoon unsweetened cocoa   5 to 6 ice cubes

Place milk, milk powder, cocoa, vanilla and sugar in blender. Cover, and blend at high speed until smooth. Add ice cubes, one at a time, blending until each is thoroughly crushed. Serve immediately in hurricane glass.
Servings: 2.

Coastal Twist

1/2 ounce raspberry liqueur   3 scoops of strawberry ice cream
1/2 ounce cream de banana   1 tablespoon whipped cream
1/2 ounce cream de pineapple

Blend for 30 seconds. Pour into goblet. Garnish with half a banana, pineapple wedge and strawberry.

Beverages

Crangrenale

1-1/2 cranberry juice   Fill rest with ginger ale
1/4 ounce grenadine

Stir in sling glass. Garnish with orange or cherry.

Creamy Brandy

3/4 ounce coffee liqueur   3/4 ounce brandy
3/4 ounce Irish cream

Speed shake. Pour into rocks glass. Garnish with cherry.

Eclipse

1-1/2 ounces vodka   Cola
2 ounces lemon mix

Speed shake. Pour into hi-ball glass. Float cola.

Beverages

Eggnog

12 eggs, separated
1 cup sugar
1 cup milk
1 cup bourbon

1 cup cognac
1/2 teaspoon salt
6 cups whipping cream, whipped
Ground nutmeg

Combine egg yolks, sugar and milk, beating until thick and frothy. Gradually stir in bourbon and cognac. Chill several hours. Combine egg whites (at room temperature) and salt, beating until stiff peaks form. Gently fold whites and whipped cream into egg yolk mixture. Chill at least 1 hour. Sprinkle with nutmeg before serving.
Yield: about 30 servings.

Fruity Beginnings

1 ounce vodka
1-1/2 ounces raspberry liqueur

2 ounces sweet and sour mix
2 ounces pineapple

Speed shake. Pour into hi-ball glass. Garnish with pineapple wedge.

Fuzzy Navel

1-1/2 ounces peach liqueur

Orange juice to 1/4 inch rim

Speed shake. Pour into hi-ball glass.

Beverages

Gator Bite

2 ounces grain alcohol
4 ounces thirst quencher energy drink

4 ounces citrus cola

Stir. Pour into sling glass.

Gin and Tonic

1-1/2 ounces gin
1/2 ounce grenadine

Tonic to 1/4 inch rim
1/4 ounce lime juice

Ice down, and pour into hi-ball glass.

Golden Dream

1 ounce
1/2 ounce triple sec

1/2 ounce orange juice
1/2 ounce cream or milk

Shake. Pour into coupe glass.

Grape Ape

2 ounces grape juice
2 ounces orange juice

3 ounces lemon-lime cola

Mix orange and lemon-lime cola. Use grape as float. Pour into hi-ball glass.
Garnish with orange or cherry.

Beverages

In The Pink

1 ounce gin
1 ounce cherry-flavored additive

1 ounce milk

Shake. Pour in coupe glass.

Little Cherry

1-1/2 ounces bourbon
4 ounces cherry cola

1/4 ounce grenadine

Mix, and pour into hi-ball glass.

Long Island Iced Tea

1/2 ounce gin
1/2 ounce rum
1/2 ounce tequila

1/2 ounce triple sec
3/4 ounce sour mix

Speed shake. Pour into zombie/sling glass. Float with cola. Garnish with lemon wheel.

Lowcountry Comfort

1-1/2 ounces bourbon

4 ounces orange juice

Speed shake ingredients. Pour into hi-ball glass.

Beverages

Malibu Dive

1-1/2 ounces coconut rum
3/4 ounce light rum

Papaya juice to 1/4 inch rim

Speed shake. Pour into hi-ball glass. Garnish with orange wedge and cherry.

Melon Ball Cooler

1/4 cup honeydew melon liqueur
1/4 cup vodka
1/4 cup pineapple juice
1/4 cup orange juice
1 cup ginger ale

Crushed ice
Watermelon or honeydew melon balls
  (optional)
Fresh mint sprigs

Combine first 5 ingredients. Stir well. Pour over crushed ice. Garnish with melon balls and mint sprigs, if desired.
Yield: 2 cups.

Midnight Milk

1 ounce Irish cream
1/2 ounce peppermint liqueur

2 ounces cream or milk
1/2 ounce amaretto

Shake. Pour into coupe glass. Garnish with peppermint leaf.

Beverages

Milk-n-Cookies

1 ounce peppermint
1/2 ounce dark cacao

Cream or milk to 1/4 rim

Speed shake ingredients. Pour into hi-ball glass.

Mint Julep

For each cold goblet use:
Several mint leaves
Sugar syrup (See desserts.)
  (2 or 3 teaspoons)

Crushed dry ice
2 ounces bourbon
1 sprig mint

Crush leaves, and let stand in syrup. Put this into a cold, silver julep cup or glass, and add ice, which has been crushed and rolled in a towel to dry. Pour in whiskey. Stir, not touching the glass, and add sprig of mint. Serve immediately.

Mud Slide

3/4 ounce vodka
3/4 ounce coffee liqueur

3/4 ounce Irish cream

Speed shake. Pour into rocks glass.

Beverages

Nutty Irishman

1 ounce hazelnut liqueur   1 ounce Irish cream

Straight pour or shake, and strain into shot or rocks glass.

Opening Cocktail

2 ounces rye whiskey   1/2 ounce grenadine
1 ounce lemon mix

Shake. Pour into cocktail glass.

Peach Refresher

1 (16 ounce) can peach slices   2 teaspoons honey
  in extra light syrup, drained   1/2 teaspoon vanilla extract
1-2/3 cups skim milk

Freeze peach slices 2 hours or until partially frozen. Combine peaches and remaining ingredients in container of an electric blender. Process until smooth. Serve immediately in poco grande glass.
Yield: 5 cups (about 10 calories per 1 cup serving).

Beverages

Peppermint-Eggnog Punch

1 quart peppermint ice cream, softened   4 bottles (12 ounces) ginger ale, chilled
1 quart dairy eggnog   Peppermint sticks

Combine first 3 ingredients in a punch bowl, stirring until blended. Serve immediately with peppermint sticks.
Yield: 4-1/2 quarts.

Pina Colada

1 ounce coconut oil/milk   2 ounces golden rum
3 ounces pineapple juice

Speed shake, and pour over ice into hurricane glass.

Pineapple Fiz

2 ounces rum   1 ounce pineapple
1 teaspoon sugar   Club soda

Shake. Pour into hi-ball glass. Add club soda to taste.

Pineapple Monkey

1-1/2 ounces creme de banana   Crushed ice
4 ounces pineapple juice

Blend ingredients. Pour into grande glass. Garnish with whipped cream and strawberry.

Beverages

Pink Lemonade

2 ounces whiskey
1 ounce triple sec
1/2 ounce grenadine

2 ounces sour mix
Lemon-lime cola to 1/4 inch rim

Speed shake; then add lemon-lime cola in sling glass. Garnish with lemon wheel and cherry.

Plantation Toddy

1 lump sugar
2 cloves

Small piece lemon skin
1-1/2 ounces whiskey

Pour into toddy glass with a little cracked ice. Add a shake of nutmeg.

Planters Punch

1 ounce lemon mix
1/2 ounce grenadine
1 ounce orange juice

1-1/2 ounces light rum
1/2 ounce sugar

Speed shake. Pour into hi-ball glass.

Prairie Fire

1-1/2 ounces rum

Dash of hot sauce to taste

Pour into shot glass.

Beverages

Raspberry Lime Rickey

1/4 to 1/2 ounce of raspberry syrup   Fill rest with club soda

Mix, and garnish with several lime wedges in hi-ball glass.

Rum Gum Lime

2 ounces light rum   2 ounces fresh lime juice
2 ounces of simple syrup

Speed shake. Pour into hi-ball glass. Garnish with orange wheel and cherry.

Side Car

1 ounce brandy   1-1/2 ounces lemon mix
1/2 ounce triple sec

Speed shake. Pour into rocks glass.

Sloe Gin Fizz

1-1/2 ounces sloe gin   1-1/2 ounces club soda
1-1/2 ounces lemon mix

Speed shake. Pour into hi-ball glass. Garnish with cherry and orange.

Beverages

Southern Sangria

1/3 cup sugar
1/3 cup lemon juice
1/3 cup orange juice

1 bottle (25.4 ounces) sparkling red
grape juice, chilled

Combine first 3 ingredients in a large pitcher, stirring until sugar dissolves. Add grape juice, and gently stir to mix well. Serve over crushed ice.
Yield: 5 cups.

Stars and Stripes

1/3 ounce grenadine
1/3 ounce cream

1/3 ounce blue curacao

Build. Pour into cocktail glass.

Strawberry Shrub

12 pounds fruit
2 quarts water

5 ounces tartaric acid
1-1/2 pounds powdered sugar
to each pint juice

Acidulate water with tartaric acid. Place fruit in jar, cover with the acidulated water, and let remain 48 hours. Strain without bruising fruit. Measure juice, and add sugar proportionately. Stir to dissolve sugar, and leave a few days. Bottle and cork lightly. If slight fermentation takes place, leave cork out a few days. Process all cold. Stand bottles erect.

Beverages

Summer Rum Freeze

1-1/2 ounces light rum
2 scoops lime sherbet

3 ounces pineapple juice
3/4 ounce cream or milk

Speed shake ingredients. Pour into hi-ball glass. Garnish with pineapple spear or lime wheel.

Sunset

1-1/2 ounces tequila
1/2 ounce sweet vermouth

2 ounces lemon mix

Shake. Pour into hi-ball glass.

Sunshine

1-1/2 ounces rum
1 ounce cranberry juice

1 ounce orange juice

Mix, and pour into hi-ball glass.

Superman

1 ounce vodka
1/2 ounce rum
2 ounces orange juice

1 ounce cranberry juice
1 ounce pineapple juice

Shake. Pour into hi-ball glass.

Beverages

Tasty Freeze

1 ounce cherry brandy
1 ounce amaretto
1 ounce coffee liqueur

Vanilla ice cream (2 scoops)
1 ounce cream

Blend 1 minute in blender. Pour into hurricane glass. Garnish with orange wedge and cherry.

Tequila Sunrise

1-1/2 ounces tequila
4 ounces orange juice

1/2 ounce grenadine

Ice down. Pour into hi-ball glass.

The Dog

1-1/2 ounces light rum
1/2 ounce blue curacao

4 ounces of orange juice
Splash of soda

Speed shake. Garnish with orange wheel in zombie/sling glass.

The Southern Gentleman

1-1/2 ounces whiskey
Equal parts of apricot and pineapple juice to 1/4 inch rim

Speed shake. Pour into a hi-ball glass. Garnish with cherry.

Beverages

Tropical Storm

1/2 ounce light rum
1/2 ounce vodka
1/2 ounce amaretto

1/2 ounce bourbon
pineapple juice to 1/2 inch rim
orange juice to 1/4 inch rim

Speed shake. Pour into hi-ball glass. Garnish with cherry and pineapple.

Wassail

2 quarts apple cider
1/2 cup sugar
1/4 cup firmly packed brown sugar
2 (3 inch) sticks cinnamon

12 whole cloves
4 cups grapefruit juice
4 cups orange juice
1 cup pineapple juice

Combine first 5 ingredients in a Dutch oven. Bring to a boil, and cook until sugar dissolves. Reduce heat, and simmer 5 minutes. Add remaining ingredients, and heat just until hot without boiling. Strain, and discard spices. Serve hot. Yield: about 4-1/2 quarts.

Whiskey Sour

1/2 ounce whiskey

2 ounces lemon mix

Speed shake. Pour into rocks glass. Garnish with cherry.

Beverages

White Russian

1-1/2 ounces vodka

1/2 ounce coffee liqueur

1/2 ounce cream or milk

Speed shake. Pour into hi-ball glass.

Wild Mint Julep

3 ounces whiskey

Crushed fresh mint

1/4 ounce simple syrup (See desserts.)

Club soda to rim

Put sugar in first with mint, pour in liquids, and stir. Pour into a collins glass, and garnish with mint leaves.

APPETIZERS

Appetizers

Contents

Appetizers

Culinary Commentary

Paul Wm. Conco, C.C.E., C.F.E., is a former President of Johnson & Wales University at Charleston. He has more than 25 years of experience in the foodservice industry and is actively involved in such organizations as the American Culinary Federation, the Council on Hotel, Restaurant and Institutional Education and the International Food Service Executives Association. He is currently pursuing a Ph.D. in Higher Education at the University of South Carolina.

THE POWER OF THE KITCHEN

In early 1990, I published an article on the never-ending subject of food trends. The article addressed several trends that I and many others had observed. These trends included such things as increased nutritional awareness, Pacific Rim cuisine influences, and the impatience with fast food. Another item I so glibly stated was that this was the last generation to remember Mom in the kitchen. With the two-income family of this modern age, home delivery pizza, microwave ovens, and supermarket catering of the traditional Thanksgiving Dinner was becoming the norm. The image of Mom baking bread or cooking a pot roast was lost. Some have even complained that this traditional image was sexist, anyway!

As I reflected on these concerns, I began to realize the power and influence of that room in our house we fondly refer to as "the kitchen." This is not because I am a professional in the business of food and hospitality, or because I have earned my livelihood by its toil, but because I have grown up in a setting where the kitchen was the center of all activity and the place where most of the important conversations I can remember occurred.

How did this room come to yield such influence and power? What is its history? The first formal kitchens were in Europe and possessed by the nobility. Many of these kitchens were separate from the main house because of the smell, heat and fear of fire. Almost all of the cooks and servants who labored in these kitchens were male, because the heat, smoke and the weight of the heavy pots made the work very strenuous.

When the early settlers came to the new world, the "kitchen" was the part of the single-room cabin that had the fireplace. The pioneer woman became the symbol of hard work as she helped to plow the fields, salted and smoked meats, stored grain, and prepared the daily food. The rapid success in the new world brought the beginning of the colonial kitchens. These kitchens and dining rooms contained fine furniture, silver and china that today we revere as fine antiques. Imagine the gracious entertaining that took place in these rooms!

The succeeding years saw the Americans back on the adventurous road to discovery. The wagon trains rolled West, and the pioneer woman again emerged as a symbol of strength and innovation. She brought West with her the iron bake oven, a cauldron, and the indispensable spider - a frying pan with legs - which cooked most of the meals on the journey. Her ingenuity and creativity for the day's meals rivals that of any great chef.

The Industrial Revolution brought significant changes in the kitchen

Culinary Commentary

and its equipment, as well as changes in our cooking and eating habits. Items such as black cast-iron gas stoves, plate warmers, apple peelers and ice boxes emerged. In the mid-nineteenth century, prosperous middle-class houses were staffed with a hierarchy of servants working to prepare daily meals, as well as the necessary high teas, constant banquets and generous entertaining. It was a recognized feat and skill to manage the busy kitchen.

The well-run and well-stocked kitchens at the turn of the century saw a drastic change as World War I broke out. The supply of female servants (a mainstay in the new modern kitchens) dwindled as many found work in the factories. The middle-class wife now found herself trying to manage and cook the meals. This brought a revolution in modernizing the kitchen. Every "modern" convenience was desired, from gas ovens to refrigerators to kitchen cabinets.

The second World War brought food rationing and a shortage of building materials and resources. The wife again was at the head of the kitchen using ingenuity to prepare balanced diets. The 1950's and 60's saw a boom in modernization and convenience in the kitchen. The 1970's and 80's saw the emergence of fast-paced, two-income families. Have we seen the last of Mom in the kitchen? Or more importantly, is the kitchen still the center of life in the home? Do we now gather around the home computer with the same warmth and stimulating conversation as we did when Mom baked her famous cookies?

Today's kitchen in the home contains many modern conveniences from frost-free refrigerators, and self-cleaning ovens to microwave/convection oven combinations and amazingly quiet dishwashers. Have these modern conveniences made the kitchen any less important? I don't think so. Last year, I made a promise to myself that no matter how busy my career may be, I would bake Christmas cookies with my family. This will become a tradition I will faithfully follow. The quality of time spent, the humor and smiles produced, the retelling of memories, and the important conversations, otherwise unshared, have made me a believer in the power of the kitchen.

I am blessed that my mother was an excellent cook and baker. But I learned more in her kitchen than just cooking. I hope my kids will learn more than cooking from me. The kitchen should remain a place where we gravitate whenever we have a large gathering in our home. It is the place where we should feel the most comfortable. The warmth of the kitchen comes from more than its oven.

Conean, Terena. (1977). <u>The Kitchen Book</u> New York. Crown.

Appetizers

Alligator Bites

2 pounds alligator tail, ground
2 teaspoons salt
1 teaspoon red pepper
1 egg, beaten
1/4 cup milk
1/2 cup bread crumbs

Juice of lemon
1/2 cup onion, chopped
2 tablespoons parsley, chopped
1 cup flour
1 cup corn meal
Fat for deep frying

Mix alligator with salt, pepper, egg, milk, bread crumbs, lemon juice, onion and parsley. Shape into small balls. Mix flour and cornmeal. Roll balls in mixture, and fry in deep fat at 350 degrees until brown.
Servings: 4-6.

Appetizer Spreads

Pepperoni Mustard Spread:
3-1/2 ounces sliced pepperoni
  (3/4 cup)
1 teaspoon fresh lemon juice
  or to taste

2 tablespoons fresh dill
1 tablespoon coarse grain mustard
2 ounces cream cheese, softened

In food processor, blend pepperoni with mustard, lemon juice, cream cheese and dill, scraping down sides until mixture is smooth. Use to fill mushroom caps or black bread.
Yield: 1-1/4 cups.

Appetizers

Cheddar and Dried Apple Spread:
1/4 pound sharp cheddar, grated (1 cup)
2 tablespoons bottled chutney, minced
1 tablespoon mayonnaise
2 teaspoons snipped fresh chives
3/4 cup dried apples, finely chopped
3 tablespoons plain yogurt

In bowl, combine cheddar and dried apples. In small bowl, combine chutney, mayonnaise, yogurt and chives, and stir mixture into cheddar mixture. Fill celery. Yields: 1-1/4 cups.

Feta and Red Pepper Spread:
6 ounces feta, crumbled
2 tablespoons olive oil
1/3 cup red bell pepper, coarsely chopped

In food processor, blend feta and bell pepper, scraping down sides until mixture is smooth. With processor on, add oil, and blend mixture until smooth. Yield: 1 cup.

Swiss Cheese and Carraway Spread:
6 ounces Swiss cheese or gueyere, cut into chunks
2 tablespoons softened unsalted butter
2 tablespoons mayonnaise
1 teaspoon carraway seeds
2 tablespoons coarse grained mustard

In food processor, blend cheese, mayonnaise, butter, mustard and carraway seeds, scraping down sides until mixture is smooth. Yield: 1-1/4 cups.

Appetizers

Artichoke Bottoms with Shrimp

6 cooked artichoke bottoms
1-1/2 tablespoons wine vinegar
1/3 cup mayonnaise
Salt and pepper to taste
1 cup cooked shrimp, cut into
  small pieces

3 tablespoons olive oil
1/2 green pepper, finely diced
2 teaspoons lemon juice
Paprika to taste
6 whole shrimp, cooked

Prepare artichoke bottoms, as for stuffed artichoke. Marinate artichoke bottoms in mixture of olive oil, wine vinegar, salt and pepper to taste for 1 hour. Mix cut shrimp, green pepper and mayonnaise seasoned with lemon juice and paprika. Drain artichoke bottoms, and place on individual serving plates. Pile shrimp on artichoke bottoms. Cover with thin layer of mayonnaise, and garnish each with whole shrimp.
Servings: 6.

Appetizers

Baked Stuffed Clams

1 stick (1/4 pound) unsalted butter
1 small onion, minced
1/2 pound fresh mushrooms, minced
1/4 cup dry white wine
1 pound lump crabmeat, flaked
12 fresh medium clams, shucked and
  minced, shells rinsed and reserved

1/2 cup fresh bread crumbs
1/4 cup Italian flat leaf parsley,
  minced
1 teaspoon salt
1/4 teaspoon fresh pepper
Paprika

Preheat oven to 375 degrees. In medium skillet, melt butter. Add onions, and cook over moderate heat until softened, but not browned, about 3 minutes. Add mushrooms, and cook until softened, about 4 minutes. Stir in wine, crabmeat, minced clams, bread crumbs, parsley, salt and pepper. Remove from heat, and stir well to combine. Fill all 24 reserved shells with clam mixture, and sprinkle lightly with paprika. Place on baking sheet, and bake for 12 minutes or until heated.
Servings: 6 (24 total).

Appetizers

Canapes

Crab:

2 packages (3 ounces) cream cheese, room temperature

2 tablespoons dry white wine

1 teaspoon lemon juice

1/2 teaspoon seasoned salt

1 teaspoon onion, grated

1/8 teaspoon dried dill weed

1 can (6 ounces) crabmeat

In small bowl, beat cream cheese, wine, lemon juice, seasoned salt, onion and dill weed. Set aside. Drain, and flake canned crabmeat. Stir crabmeat into cheese mixture. Refrigerate 3 to 4 hours. Garnish with fresh dill.
Yield: 1 cup.

Swedish Open Face:

3 eggs, hard cooked

1 can (2 ounces) flat anchovy fillets, drained

1/4 cup butter, room temperature

1 tablespoon dijon mustard

1 tablespoon dried dill weed

1 tablespoon parsley, finely minced

1 tablespoon fresh chives, minced

1/8 teaspoon pepper

Slice hard cooked eggs. Set aside. In small bowl, use fork to mash anchovies. Stir in butter until blended. Stir in mustard, dill, parsley, chives and pepper. Spread about 1 teaspoon anchovy mixture evenly over each bread piece. Top with 1 slice egg and 1 small strip pimento.
Yield: 24.

Appetizers

Caviar Mosaic

6 Belgian endives
1 pint sour cream
3 ounces golden caviar

2 ounces imported black caviar
(or 1/2 cup minced chives or
green onions)

Trim bottom 1 inch off the root end of endives. Separate heads into 2 piles of leaves, one with large outside leaves; the other, small inner leaves. Spread the sour cream evenly over an 8 inch round platter. Cut out strips of waxed paper, and arrange in the desired design over sour cream. Spoon golden caviar over all exposed areas, and smooth gently. Remove the waxed paper cut outs, and carefully top the exposed sour cream with black caviar (or greens) to cream contrasting design. Place small platter in middle of 14 inch round platter. Arrange Belgian endive around larger platter like petals with larger leaves underneath. Chill. Serve.
Servings: 12.

Appetizers

Caviar Roulade

4 tablespoons unsalted butter
1/2 cup all purpose flour, sifted
2 cups hot milk
4 eggs, separated

Pinch of salt
3 ounces cream cheese, softened
1 cup sour cream
4 ounces caviar

Preheat oven to 425 degrees. Lightly butter 10x15 jelly roll pan. Line pan with parchment or waxed paper. Lightly butter the paper, dust with flour, and tap out any excess. In medium saucepan, melt the butter over low heat. Stir in flour, increase heat to moderately high, and cook for 1 minute. Pour in hot milk, and cook, whisking constantly until mixture is thick and smooth, about 1 minute. Remove from heat, and beat in egg yolks 1 at a time, beating well after each addition. In large bowl, beat egg whites with salt until stiff but not dry. Gently fold beaten whites into base until no streaks remain. Pour into pan, spread evenly, and bake for about 15 minutes, or until cake rebounds to touch and is golden brown on top. Let cool for 10 minutes, and unmold onto kitchen towel. In small bowl, combine cream cheese with 3 tablespoons sour cream. Spread over cake, starting with short side. Roll cake up jelly roll fashion. To serve, carefully slice off rough ends of roll with serrated knife. Serve each slice with heaping spoonful of remaining sour cream, and top with dollop of caviar. Serve warm or room temperature.
Servings: 8-12.

Appetizers

Charleston Baked Oysters

1 pint shucked oysters
  with their liquid
4 tablespoons olive oil
4 tablespoons shallots, chopped
4 tablespoons parsley, chopped
1 garlic clove, minced

1 cup dry white wine
1/2 teaspoon salt
1/2 teaspoon freshly ground pepper
Dash of hot sauce
2 tablespoons flour

Preheat oven to 300 degrees. Drain oysters, reserving the liquid. Spoon 2 tablespoons olive oil into a shallow baking dish. Add the oysters, and then the remaining oil. Add the herbs, seasoning, wine and about half of the oyster liquid. Sift a little flour over the top, and dot with butter. Bake for 15 to 20 minutes, or until brown on top. Serve with crusty French bread.
Servings: 4-6.

Chicken Liver Mousse

1 pound of chicken livers
1/2 cup shallots

1/4 cup brandy
1/2 pound of butter
Salt and pepper to taste

Clean the livers, and remove all the membranes. Place a cast iron skillet over medium heat, and add 4 tablespoons of butter. Saute livers until cooked 3/4 of the way, and add shallots. Season with salt and pepper, and add brandy. Let it ignite, and cook for a brief minute once all the alcohol has burned off. Remove from heat, and place the livers in a blender or food processor. Puree, mixing with butter until a smooth or desired consistency is reached. Adjust seasonings, and chill. Serve.
Servings: 8.

Appetizers

Chilled Corn and Crab Flan

5 eggs
3/4 cup milk
1/2 cup heavy cream
1/4 cup fresh bread crumbs
1/2 teaspoon salt
1/4 teaspoon black pepper
*Spicy tomato vinaigrette

Dash of cayenne
Dash of nutmeg
3 cups corn kernels
   from 4 to 5 ears corn or package
   (12 ounces) frozen, defrosted
8 ounces lump crabmeat

Preheat oven to 325 degrees. In large bowl, beat together eggs, milk, cream, bread crumbs, salt, pepper, cayenne and nutmeg until blended. Stir in corn and crabmeat. Pour into well-buttered shallow 2 quart baking dish, and cover with aluminum foil. Place baking dish in larger roasting pan, and pour enough hot water to reach about 2/3 up sides of dish. Bake for 35 to 40 minutes until flan is firm. Remove flan from water bath, and cool slightly. Unmold onto platter, cover, and refrigerate overnight. Serve chilled, cut into wedges, and accompanied with tomato vinaigrette.
Servings: 6-8 (first course) or 4 (main course).

Spicy Tomato Vinaigrette:

1 can (8 ounces) Italian tomatoes,
   peeled, juices reserved
1 garlic clove
1/2 teaspoon salt

1/4 teaspoon hot pepper sauce
Dash of black pepper
2 tablespoons olive oil
1/4 cup fresh coriander, minced

In blender or food processor, combine tomatoes and juices, garlic, salt, hot sauce and black pepper. Puree until smooth. With machine on, slowly add olive oil. Pour into serving bowl. Cover, and refrigerate up to 2 days. Just before serving, stir in minced coriander.
Yield: 2 cups.

Appetizers

Coconut Fried Frog Legs

12 small frog legs
6-1/4 cups flour
2-1/2 tablespoons double action
  baking powder
2-1/2 tablespoons salt

5 cups milk
5 whole eggs
15 tablespoons butter, melted
*Large bag long shredded coconut

Sift flour with baking powder and salt, adding milk, egg and melted butter to make batter. Beat well. Dip each frogleg in batter, holding by very end, and let excess drain off. Roll in shredded coconut, and deep fry at 375 degrees until golden. Serve immediately.

Servings: very small froglegs - 4 per person, large froglegs - 2 per person.

Appetizers

Cold Shrimp
with Four-Herb Mayonnaise

2-1/4 teaspoons salt
1 egg yolk
1/4 teaspoon dijon mustard
1 tablespoon dry white wine
Pinch of sugar
3/4 cup safflower or vegetable oil
1 tablespoon warm water
2 tablespoons parsley, minced
2 tablespoons fresh basil, minced

3-1/2 pounds large shrimp, shelled
  with last section of tail intact
1-1/2 tablespoons lemon juice
5 to 6 drops hot pepper sauce
1 teaspoon anchovy paste
1/4 cup extra virgin olive oil
3 tablespoons chives, minced
3 tablespoons fresh tarragon, minced
  or 2 teaspoons dried

Bring large pot of water to boil with 2 teaspoons salt. Add shrimp, and cook until shrimp are loosely curled and just opaque throughout, 2 minutes for medium shrimp, 2 to 3 minutes for large. Drain under cold running water, and pat dry with paper towels. Cover with damp towel, and refrigerate until serving time. Shrimp can be peeled up to 5 hours ahead. In medium bowl, combine egg yolk, mustard, lemon juice, wine, hot sauce, sugar, anchovy paste and remaining 1/4 teaspoon salt. Whisk until thoroughly blended. Gradually whisk in safflower and olive oil, drop by drop at first, then in thin stream. When all has been incorporated, whisk in 1 tablespoon warm water. Stir in fresh herbs. Serve immediately or cover, and refrigerate up to 6 hours.
Servings: 5 dozen.

Appetizers

Crab and Artichoke Bottom Canapes

1/2 cup Russian dressing
1/4 teaspoon dry mustard
1 can (6 ounces) crabmeat,
  picked well

1 can (10 ounces) artichoke bottoms,
  drained
2 tablespoons parsley, chopped
Lemon wedges

Combine Russian dressing and mustard, and fold in crabmeat, mixing lightly, but thoroughly. Pile mixture on artichoke bottoms. Just before serving, brown the canapes in preheated broiler, and sprinkle with chopped parsley. Garnish with lemon wedge, and serve.
Servings: 8-10.

Crab Cakes

10 ounces bread crumbs
7 ounces mayonnaise
1 teaspoon dry mustard
2 teaspoons parsley, chopped
1-1/2 ounces worcestershire

2 eggs
1 teaspoon cracked black pepper
2-1/2 pounds crab meat
2 ounces salsa fria

Combine all ingredients except the crab meat. Blend thoroughly. Fold in the crab meat. Form into 3 ounce balls; then flatten into cakes. Saute in clarified butter over medium heat, 3 to 4 minutes on each side. Serve on warm salad plate with heated salsa.
Servings: 5.

Appetizers

Crab Zucchini Bites

4 small zucchini,
  cut into 3/4 inch thick pieces
1/4 cup fresh mushrooms, chopped
1-1/2 tablespoons butter or margarine
1 tablespoon all purpose flour
1/4 cup milk
1/4 cup green onions, chopped

1/4 teaspoon paprika
1/8 teaspoon salt
1/8 teaspoon white pepper
2-3 dashes hot sauce
1 can (6 ounces) crabmeat,
  drained and rinsed

Scoop out each zucchini center halfway down on one end. Set aside. Reserve zucchini centers for other recipes. Combine mushrooms and butter in casserole. Cook for 5 minutes, and stir in flour. Stirring constantly, add milk, and cook until smooth. Stir in remaining ingredients, except crabmeat. Cook until thick. Stir in crabmeat, and let stand for 2 to 3 minutes. Spoon 1 to 1-1/2 teaspoons crabmeat mixture into each zucchini piece. Place on cookie sheets, and bake in 325 degree oven until hot and lightly browned. Serve.
Servings: 20.

Appetizers

Crispy Chinese Chicken Wings

2 pounds chicken wings, wing tips
  cut off
3 garlic cloves, crushed with flat
  side of cleaver
3 slices of peeled ginger root, each size
  of quarter, flattened with
  flat side of cleaver

1 tablespoon scotch
1 tablespoon soy sauce
3/4 cup cornstarch
Vegetable shortening or vegetable oil
  for deep frying
Scallions and szechwan peppercorn salt
  for accompaniment

In bowl, toss wings with garlic, ginger root, scotch and soy sauce, and let marinate at room temperature for 30 minutes or covered and chilled for up to 8 hours. Discard garlic and ginger root, and in bowl, dredge wings in small batches in cornstarch, transferring to racks to dry. In deep fryer at 375 degrees, cook in small batches for 5 minutes. Transfer to paper towel to drain. When all wings are fried, heat oil to 425 degrees, and fry wings in batches, 2 minutes more or until golden and crisp. Transfer with slotted spoon to paper towel to drain again. Serve with scallions and peppercorn salt for dipping.

Szechwan Peppercorn Salt:
1 teaspoon peppercorns   1 tablespoon salt

In dry small skillet, toast the szechwan peppercorns over moderately low heat, swirling skillet for 4 to 5 minutes or until they are fragrant. Transfer the peppercorns to mortar, and crush with pestle or grinder. Combine peppercorns with salt. Servings: 6.

Appetizers

Curried Lamb Balls

3 tablespoons raisins
1/2 cup apple juice
2-1/2 pounds lean ground lamb
2 large eggs
1 cup fresh whole wheat bread crumbs
2 teaspoons salt
1-1/4 teaspoon cumin, ground
3/4 teaspoon cinnamon
1/2 teaspoon pepper

1/4 cup vegetable oil
2 onions, chopped
2 garlic cloves, minced
2 teaspoons curry powder
2 tablespoons flour
1 cup chicken stock or
  canned chicken broth
1/2 cup canned tomato vegetable juice
2 tablespoons orange marmalade

In small bowl, let raisins soak in the apple juice for 30 minutes. In a bowl, combine well the lamb, eggs, bread crumbs, salt, cumin, cinnamon and pepper, and form mixture into one inch balls. In large skillet brown the balls in batches of 2 tablespoons of oil over high heat, transferring to plates as they are browned and adding more to skillet as necessary. In skillet, cook onions over moderate heat, stirring for 2 minutes. Add garlic, and cook the mixture for 1 minute. Add curry powder, and cook, stirring for 30 seconds. Stir in the stock, tomato-vegetable juice, raisins, apple juice and marmalade, and bring liquid to a boil. Simmer the mixture for 1 minute. Return lamb balls to skillet, and simmer them, covered for 25 minutes. Cook mixture uncovered for 5 minutes. Transfer to heated serving dish or chafing dish, and serve.
Servings: 8.

Appetizers

European Veal Meatballs

1 pound ground veal
1/2 cup dry fine bread crumbs
1/4 cup milk
1 egg, beaten
2 tablespoons fresh parsley, chopped
1 clove garlic, minced
1 teaspoon pepper
3/4 teaspoon salt
2 tablespoons vegetable oil

2 tablespoons all purpose flour
4 ounces mushrooms, sliced
1-1/2 cups commercial sour cream
1 teaspoon browning and seasoning sauce
1/4 teaspoon salt and pepper
1/2 to 3/4 cup of milk
6 ounces egg noodles
1 tablespoon poppy seeds

Combine first 8 ingredients in large bowl. Mix well. Shape mixture into 1-1/2 inch balls. Brown in 2 tablespoons oil 5 to 6 minutes in large skillet. Remove meatballs, reserving pan drippings in skillet. Add flour to pan drippings. Stir until blended. Reduce heat. Add next 5 ingredients, stirring constantly. Gradually stir in milk. Return meatballs to skillet, and cook over low heat 10 minutes. Cook noodles according to package directions. Drain. Sprinkle with poppy seeds. Serve meatballs and sauce over noodles. Add salt and pepper to taste.
Servings: 6.

Flavored Popcorn

Pop corn without using oil. Season to taste with any of the following items: Chili powder, onion powder, garlic powder, grated parmesan cheese, or cinnamon. If the popcorn is sprayed with a non-stick vegetable coating while hot, the seasonings will adhere more easily.

Appetizers

Fried Alligator

1 cup sherry
1/4 cup lemon juice
1 teaspoon seasoned salt
1 tablespoon lemon pepper
1/2 cup Italian salad dressing

Flour to dredge
1 pound alligator meat,
  cut into small pieces
Oil for deep frying

Combine first 5 ingredients, and marinate alligator for 2 hours. Drain meat, and dredge in flour. Fry pieces in hot oil for about 15 minutes, turning often until brown. Drain, and serve hot.
Servings: 4.

Frog Legs Polonaise

1/4 cup light cream
8 small frog legs
3 tablespoons butter
1/4 teaspoon salt

1 tablespoon parsley, chopped
1 hard cooked egg, diced
1/2 teaspoon lemon juice
Paprika

Frog Legs:
Put light cream into bowl. Dip in small frog legs. Next, dip in flour, and coat evenly. In skillet, heat butter. Saute frog legs for about 10 minutes browning on both sides. Sprinkle with salt. Remove from heat, and keep warm and uncovered so they stay crisp.

Sauce:
Pour off used butter, and add parsley, egg and lemon juice to skillet. Cook over high heat for 1 minute. Pour the hot sauce over frog legs. Decorate with lemon, dip in chopped parsley and paprika.
Servings: 2.

Appetizers

Leek and Bacon Roulade

*1 egg sponge recipe (recipe on following page)

Filling:

1/2 pound sliced lean bacon, chopped
2 tablespoons unsalted butter
1/2 cup heavy cream
1/2 cup parmesan cheese
2 tablespoons fresh parsley leaves, minced
1 tablespoon softened unsalted butter

1-1/4 pound leeks, green tops discarded, white halves lengthwise, washed well and chopped
1 teaspoon caraway seeds
1 tablespoon dijon mustard
1 tablespoon parmesan cheese, grated

Prepare egg sponge beforehand. While egg sponge is baking, make filling. In skillet, cook bacon over moderate heat, stirring occasionally until crisp. Transfer with slotted spoon to paper towel to drain, and pour off all but 1 tablespoon fat. Cook leeks in fat and butter over moderate low heat, stirring until softened. Stir in cream, and bring to boil. Simmer mixture, stirring occasionally, until thickened and cream is absorbed. Remove skillet from heat. Stir in parmesan, caraway seeds, parsley, mustard, bacon, salt and pepper to taste. Spread filling over warm sponge in even layer, leaving border 1 inch all around. Roll jelly roll fashion, beginning with long side, and trim ends on diagonal with aid of towel and wax paper. Transfer roulade seam side down to ovenproof platter, spread gently with butter, sprinkle with parmesan, and bake in preheated 350 degree oven for 10 minutes or until heated through.
Servings: 4-8.

Appetizers

Egg Sponge:

3 tablespoons unsalted butter
1-1/4 cups milk
4 large egg whites, separated,
   at room temperature

6 tablespoons all purpose flour
Nutmeg to taste
1/2 cup parmesan cheese, grated
Pinch of cream of tartar

In saucepan, melt butter over low heat. Stir in flour, and cook roux. Stir for 3 minutes. Remove pan from heat, and add milk. Heat mixture to a simmer, whisking occasionally for 5 minutes. Add nutmeg, salt and pepper to taste, and transfer mixture to large bowl. Whisk in egg yolks, one at time, whisking well after each addition. Whisk in parmesan. In bowl with electric mixer, beat egg whites with pinch of salt until frothy, and add cream of tartar. Beat whites until they hold stiff peaks. Stir 1/3 of whites into mixture, and fold in remaining whites gently but thoroughly. Spread sponge batter evenly in buttered 15x10 pan lined with butter and floured wax paper. Bake in preheated 350 degree oven for 25 minutes or until golden and firm to touch. Cover sponge with sheet of buttered wax paper, buttered side down. Invert baking sheet over towel, and invert sponge onto baking sheet. Remove jelly roll pan and wax paper carefully, and trim 1/4 inch from short sides of egg sponge. Fill with filling while still warm and flexible.
Makes: 1.

Appetizers

Marinated Salmon Strips with Green and Pink Peppercorns

2 tablespoons dry white wine
2 tablespoons white wine vinegar
1/4 cup olive oil
2 tablespoons pink peppercorns
Toast points or black bread fingers

2 tablespoons fresh lemon juice
1/4 cup vegetable oil
2 tablespoons green peppercorns, drained
1-1/4 pounds piece of salmon fillet, skinned
   and cut in julienne strips following
   the grain

In large bowl, combine wine, lemon juice, vinegar, salt and pepper to taste. Add oils in stream. Whisk the marinade until emulsified. Add peppercorns, and let marinade stand, covered loosely for 2 hours. Whisk the marinade, add the salmon, tossing it to coat with the marinade, and chill mixture, covered for at least 3 hours to overnight. Toss salmon mixture and divide among 6 chilled dishes. Serve with toast points.
Servings: 6.

Appetizers

Miniature Scallion Crepes with Salmon Caviar and Sour Cream

Scallion Crepes:

1 tablespoon butter
1/4 teaspoon salt
1 scallion
3/4 cup milk, or more
3 ounces salmon caviar

1/2 cup flour
1/8 teaspoon pepper
2 eggs
2/3 cup sour cream

Melt butter. In bowl, combine the flour and salt and pepper. Cut scallion into thin slices. Lightly beat eggs, add to flour, and whisk until smooth. Gradually add milk, whisking until batter is free of lumps. Stir in melted butter and scallions. Cover, and let batter rest at least 45 minutes. If made more than 1-1/2 hours ahead, add scallions at end of resting time. Heat crepe pan or small nonstick frying pan. Butter the pan very lightly. Thin batter with milk, if necessary, so that it is the consistency of heavy cream. Use about 1/2 tablespoon batter for each crepe. Spread to 2 inch circle with back of spoon. Cook about 1 minute on first side, then turn, and cook 30 seconds. Stack crepes with plastic wrap between them. Put crepes on work surface. Put about 3/4 teaspoon sour cream on each, and spread to within 1/4 inch of edge. Cover with 3/4 teaspoon caviar, and fold in half.
Yield: 40 (2 inch crepes).

Mixed Bag

2 cups soy nuts
2 cups raw peanuts roasted in oven

1 cup raisins or other dried fruit

Combine ingredients in a large bowl. Mix thoroughly, and serve or store in an airtight container.

Appetizers

Mozzarella Rice Sticks

1-1/2 cups rice, cooked
3 ounces mozzarella cheese, grated
1/4 cup half and half
2 cups Italian-style bread crumbs

2 eggs
Hot pepper sauce, to taste
Oil for deep frying
Marinara dipping sauce (optional)

Cook 1/2 cup rice in one cup water with 1/2 teaspoon salt. While rice is still hot, toss with grated mozzarella cheese until cheese is melted. Mixture will get firm as it cools. Stir in half and half, as needed, to moisten mixture slightly. Roll out mixture between two sheets of waxed paper to 1/2 inch thickness. Shape into rectangle 3 inches wide using spatula to square off edges and corner. Cut rice mixture into finger lengths measuring approximately 1/2x1/2x3 inches. Beat eggs slightly, and season with a few drops of red pepper sauce. Dip each rice stick in egg mixture, and roll in bread crumbs. Repeat the breading again with egg mixture and bread crumbs. Deep fry sticks in hot oil until lightly browned. Serve hot with dipping sauce, if desired.
Yield: about 1 dozen.

Appetizers

Mushroom Caps

1/2 pound crabmeat, picked over
Juice of 1 lemon
2 tablespoons shallots, finely chopped
1 tablespoon unsalted butter
1/2 cup dry vermouth
2 tablespoons flour
3/4 cup low-fat milk
Grated nutmeg
1/2 cup parmesan cheese,
  freshly grated

2 tablespoons unsalted pistachio nuts,
  crushed
1-1/2 cups fish stock
36 large mushrooms (about 2-1/2
  pounds wiped clean, stems carefully
  removed and finely chopped)
2 teaspoons fresh thyme, or
  1/2 teaspoon dried thyme leaves
1/8 teaspoon salt
White pepper to taste
1/4 cup fresh basil, coarsely chopped

In a large nonreactive skillet, heat 1 cup of the stock and the lemon juice over medium heat. Add the mushroom caps, and toss them gently to coat them with the liquid. Cover the skillet, and poach the mushrooms, turning them occasionally to ensure even cooking, until they are cooked through, 6 to 7 minutes. With a slotted spoon, transfer the mushrooms to a platter lined with paper towels. Add the shallots to the skillet along with the chopped mushroom stems, the vermouth and the thyme. Bring the liquid to a boil, then reduce the heat to medium, and cook the mixture at a brisk simmer, stirring occasionally, until all but 2 tablespoons of the liquid has evaporated, about 15 minutes. Set the mushroom mixture aside. Melt the butter in a small saucepan over medium heat. Whisk in the flour to form a paste, and cook the paste for three minutes. Stirring constantly to prevent lumps from forming, slowly pour in the milk, then the remaining 1/2 cup of stock. Add the salt, and sprinkle in some nutmeg and white pepper. Simmer the sauce until it thickens, about 3 minutes. Stir in the cheese and the basil. Preheat the broiler. To complete the filling, combine the crabmeat with the mushroom mixture in a bowl. Slowly pour the sauce into the bowl, and stir gently to coat the stuffing. Mound 3/4 tablespoon of stuffing in the hollow of

Appetizers

each mushroom cap. Broil the stuffed mushrooms 3 inches below the heat source until the crab begins to brown, about 3 minutes. Sprinkle the pistachios over the top of the mushrooms, and serve them hot.
Servings: 12 (as hors d'oeuvres).

Mushrooms Stuffed with Snails and Scallops

16 large mushrooms, stemmed
16 canned snails, rinsed and patted dry
16 bay scallops, rinsed and patted dry
1 stick butter, softened (1/2 cup)

3 slices bacon, cooked until crisp, drained and crumbled
1 tablespoon shallots, minced
1 tablespoon fresh parsley leaves, minced
1 teaspoon garlic, minced

In buttered baking dish, arrange mushroom caps hollow side up in one layer, and put 1 snail and scallop in each cap. In bowl, combine butter, bacon, shallots, parsley, garlic, salt and pepper to taste. Divide mixture among the mushrooms, mounding it slightly, and bake stuffed mushrooms in preheated oven 350 degrees for 20 to 25 minutes or until butter is bubbling.
Servings: 4.

Appetizers

New Orleans Crab Cakes

1 tablespoon butter
1 onion, finely chopped
1 pound crab meat
1 garlic clove, minced
1 bay leaf, crushed
1 thyme sprig, chopped

2 parsley sprigs, chopped
Pinch of cayenne
1/2 teaspoon salt
1 cup wet bread, squeezed
Lard

Melt the butter in a heavy skillet, and saute onion. Mix together the crab meat, garlic, bay leaf, thyme, parsley, cayenne and salt. Stir into the skillet with the onion, and add the moistened bread. Fry for about 3 minutes. Remove from heat, and cool. Form into 4 flat cakes, and fry in hot lard until golden on both sides. Servings: 4.

Orange Fun Pops

6 ounces orange juice concentrate
6 ounces water

1 cup plain lowfat yogurt
1 teaspoon vanilla

Blend all ingredients, and pour into ice cube trays. Put a drinking straw (which has been cut in half) into each cube. Freeze several hours.

Appetizers

Pears with Curried Crab Filling

3 large firm ripe pears
3/4 cup fresh lemon juice
7/8 cup mayonnaise
1 large egg yolk
2 teaspoons curry powder or to taste
6 ounce lump crab meat, picked apart

1/4 cup cucumber, peeled,
  seeded and chopped
3 scallions, sliced thin
1 tablespoon fresh ginger root, minced
Watercress for garnish

Peel the pears. Halve them lengthwise, and core them. Place them in a bowl of cold water, acidulated with 1/4 cup lemon juice. Remove pears with slotted spoon, reserving water. In large sauce pan of simmering water acidulated with 1/4 cup of remaining lemon juice, poach pears for 2 to 3 minutes or until tender. Return pears to reserved bowl of water, and let cool for 5 minutes. Brush the pears with remaining 1/4 cup lemon juice, and drain on paper towels. In bowl, whisk together the mayonnaise, egg yolk, curry powder, salt and pepper to taste. In another bowl, combine crab meat, cucumber, scallions and ginger root, and fold in half the mayonnaise mixture. Fill the pears with crab mixture, mounding it, and broil them under preheated broiler about 4 inches from heat for 30 seconds to 1 minute, or until filling is golden. Transfer pears to platter, and garnish with watercress. Serve remaining mayonnaise separately.
Servings: 6.

Appetizers

Pistachio Stuffed Mushrooms

20 medium size fresh mushrooms
1/4 cup butter or margarine, melted
1/4 cup pistachios, chopped
1/4 teaspoon whole thyme, chopped
2 tablespoons butter or margarine, melted

3 tablespoons onion, minced
1/3 cup dry fine bread crumbs
2 tablespoons pimento, drained and diced
1/8 teaspoon salt

Clean mushrooms with damp paper towel. Remove, and chop stems. Set caps aside. Saute mushroom stems and onion in 1/4 cup butter until tender. Stir in remaining ingredients, except butter. Spoon mixture into mushroom caps, and place in lightly greased baking pan. Drizzle 2 tablespoons butter over top. Bake at 350 degrees for 10 minutes.
Servings: 20 appetizers.

Prosciutto Radish Toasts

2 tablespoons unsalted butter, softened
Fresh ground pepper and salt to taste
4 thin slices of prosciutto

4 thin diagonal slices of French or Italian bread, toasted lightly
5 radishes, sliced paper thin

Spread butter on toasts, and sprinkle with pepper and salt to taste. Reserving 12 radish slices, cover toasts with remaining radish slices. Arrange prosciutto decoratively on them, and top each toast with reserved radish slices.
Yield: 4 toasts.

Appetizers

Radishes Stuffed with Ricotta

1/4 cup whole milk ricotta or
  small curd cottage cheese, drained
1 teaspoon fresh lemon juice

1/2 teaspoon dijon style mustard
2 teaspoons scallion greens, minced
6 large radishes

In small bowl, combine ricotta, lemon juice, mustard and minced scallion greens, salt and pepper to taste. Cut 1/4 inch from tops of radishes, reserving tops, if desired. Scoop out insides of radishes with small melon ball cutter. Fill radishes with ricotta mixture. Garnish with slice of scallion green or replace top, if desired.
Servings: 2 (as hors d'oeuvres).

Roast Pork Strips

1/2 cup soy sauce
1/4 cup bourbon
1/2 teaspoon ground ginger

3 tablespoons honey
1 clove garlic, minced
1 (3 pound) pork tenderloin

Combine soy sauce, bourbon, ginger, honey and garlic. Place pork in shallow glass dish, and pour marinade over. Cover, and refrigerate overnight, turning meat occasionally. Place meat on rack in open shallow pan, and bake at 300 degrees for about 1-1/2 hours, spooning marinade over it from time to time. To serve, allow meat to cool, cut into thin slices about 1/8 inch thick. Cut slices into strips, and spear each with wooden pick. Arrange on bed of parsley.
Servings: 12.

Appetizers

Roquefort Stuffed Shrimp

2 quarts salted water
24 jumbo shrimp
3 ounces cream cheese
1 ounce roquefort or
   Danish blue cheese

1/2 teaspoon prepared mustard
1 teaspoon scallion or green onions,
   finely chopped
1 cup parsley, finely chopped

Bring water to boil in saucepan. Add shrimp, and when water returns to boil, cook 3 to 5 minutes. Drain shrimp, shell and devein. Split shrimp down spine about halfway through. Chill. Meanwhile, blend cream cheese, roquefort cheese, mustard and green onions. Using knife or small spatula, stuff the cheese mixture into split backs of shrimp. Roll the cheese side of shrimp in parsley, and serve chilled.
Servings: 6 (x2).

Sauteed Chicken Livers

1/2 pound chicken livers
1 cup flour

Salt and pepper
4 tablespoons of oil

Mix salt and pepper to taste with flour. Clean livers, and remove membrane. Roll in flour, and shake dry. Heat pan, preferably a cast iron skillet, over medium high heat. When hot, add the oil and the livers. Saute the livers until brown on both sides seasoning lightly with salt and pepper. Remove to a plate, and serve warm with sauteed onions sprinkled with red wine vinegar, if desired.
Servings: 4.

Appetizers

Scallops in Fermented Black-Bean Sauce

1 pound bay scallops
1/4 cup fresh lime juice
1-1/2 tablespoons fermented black
  beans, rinsed
1 tablespoon fresh ginger, chopped

1-1/2 tablespoons safflower oil
2 tablespoons apricot preserves or
  orange marmalade
1/4 cup fresh lime juice
Freshly ground black pepper

To prepare the sauce, combine the preserves or marmalade, lime juice, black beans, ginger and some pepper in a small bowl. Set the sauce aside. Rinse the scallops under cold running water. Heat the oil in a large, heavy-bottomed skillet over high heat. When the oil is hot, add the scallops, and cook them, stirring constantly, for one minute. Add the sauce, and continue cooking, stirring all the while, for one minute more. With a slotted spoon, transfer the scallops to a heated platter. Cook the sauce, stirring, until it is reduced by half, 1 to 2 minutes. Pour the sauce over the scallops, and serve immediately.
Servings: 4.

Smothered Alligator

2 onions, finely chopped
1/4 cup cooking oil
1 bell pepper, finely chopped
1/2 cup celery, finely chopped
2 pounds alligator meat, cut into chunks

1 bay leaf
Salt and pepper to taste
1/4 cup shallots, finely chopped
1/4 teaspoon dried basil
1/4 cup parsley, finely chopped

Saute onions in oil until golden brown. Add bell pepper and celery, and saute until tender. Add meat and seasoning, and simmer for 40 minutes. Add parsley and shallots about 5 minutes before serving.
Servings: 6-8.

Appetizers

Sole Triangles

Vegetable Garnish:

1/4 pound snow peas, (24)

2 tablespoons butter

2 carrots

Salt and pepper to taste

White Wine Sauce:

3 carrots

2 cups white wine

1 bay leaf

1 clove

5 sprigs parsley

1 pound butter

2 onions

1/2 cup vinegar

1 tablespoon fresh thyme, chopped

  or 1 teaspoon dried

15 peppercorns

1/4 cup chives, minced

Salt and pepper to taste

Broiled Sole:

1-1/2 pounds fillets of sole

Salt and pepper to taste

3 tablespoons coarse grain mustard

For garnish, trim snow peas. Cut into diamond shapes. Cut carrots in thin strips and then at angle into diamond shapes. Blanch snow peas in boiling, salted water, until tender, about 2 minutes. Drain, and cool under cold running water. Blanch carrots in boiling, salted water until tender, about 3 minutes. Drain cool under cold running water. For sauce, chop carrots and onions. In large pan, put carrots, onions, white wine, vinegar and 1 quart water. Tie bay leaf, thyme, clove, peppercorns and parsley in cheesecloth for bouquet garnish, and add to pan. Simmer over low heat for one hour, partially covered. Discard bouquet. Strain liquid, and press solids through sieve. In shallow pan, cook over medium high heat, and reduce to about 1/2 cup. For fish, butter a broiler pan. Cut sole in 2 inch triangles, and put in single layer in prepared pan. Brush pieces with mustard; season with salt and pepper. Heat broiler, and broil fish until done, about 5 minutes. Meanwhile, warm vegetable garnish in butter. Season with salt and

Appetizers

pepper. Gently reheat sauce, and whisk in butter tablespoon by tablespoon so that it softens to creamy sauce, but does not melt completely. Taste for seasoning. Put sauce on warm plate. Sprinkle with minced chives. Put triangles of fish on top. Sprinkle with vegetable diamonds.
Servings: 8.

Spicy Beef Ball

1 package (8 ounces) cream cheese,
  room temperature
1/4 cup mayonnaise
2 green onions, finely chopped

1-1/2 teaspoons prepared mustard
1-1/2 teaspoons prepared horseradish
1/8 teaspoon garlic salt
3 ounces roast beef, minced

In bowl, beat cream cheese and mayonnaise until smooth. Stir in onions, mustard, horseradish, roast beef and garlic salt. Stir into the cream cheese mixture. Roll into a ball. Refrigerate 3 to 4 hours.
Yield: 2 cups.

Veggie Dunk

1 cup plain lowfat yogurt
3 green onions, chopped
1/4 teaspoon dill weed

1/8 teaspoon garlic powder
Dash of pepper

Combine all ingredients in bowl or blender. Refrigerate several hours. Makes 1 cup of dip. Good with all raw vegetables.

SOUPS, SALADS
&
DRESSINGS

Soups, Salads, & Dressings

Contents

Soups, Salads & Dressings

SALADS

Soups, Salads, & Dressings

Soups, Salads & Dressings

Culinary Commentary

William Edwards Wilroy, III, is a graduate of Johnson & Wales University at Charleston. He currently teaches at the University's Vail, Colorado campus.

PERFECTION IN THE KITCHEN?

As cooking would have it, we often find ourselves falling victim to various culinary mistakes whenever we set foot into the kitchen. A well-seasoned chef might have the experience and know how to make sure that few mistakes are made, if any. But mishaps will happen and oftentimes get the best of us. Sometimes these mistakes lead to complications which could make the simplest recipe into an unpalatable dish not even fit to bio-degrade.

Being the patron chef of misfortune, I find myself falling prey more often than not. Perfection, though unattainable, has often been my goal, only under the pretenses that the less you fall short of it, the closer you are to it. Ridding ourselves or lessening the impact of these potential pitfalls would be a wise approach in pursuing perfection.

Unfortunately, these problems are recurring. Their repetitive nature reveals how common certain misfortunes are. Being a chef instructor, there are ample opportunities to witness these occurrences. They occur daily, sometimes in excessive numbers and often accompanied with frustration on behalf of the student and the instructor.

In an effort to minimize our losses, retain our respect, and prevent stress which could lead to heart disease, I have found an approach to the solution. Problems will always exist. As we said, some of our problems occur more often than others. If we eliminate the most commonly occurring problems, then the battle is close to being won. Though we may never defeat the monster, our efforts will subdue it for a period of time. After the big mistakes have been handled, only the simpler mistakes remain.

With this in mind, let me present my list of most commonly occurring cooking mistakes. Here are the top five: 1. The Magic Stove Theory, 2. The Universal Standard and Montage Principle; 3. The Mickey Mouse Syndrome; 4. The No Taste Waste; 5. The Mess in Place Motto.

First, there is The Magic Stove Theory. A stove is designed to apply heat in order to cook foods. Turn it on, set the temperature, and cook the product. This is about all it can do for you. It cannot read someone's mind. It does not cook for itself. Simple as this may seem, this is where the problem occurs. The "it'll take care of itself" slogan is the culprit most of the time, and the result is usually overcooking and worst of all, burning. Avoid putting food in and forgetting about it. Check it from time to time to monitor the progress. It might need rotating or a little bit of stirring.

Culinary Commentary

Here is a good example. The recipe reads, "350 degrees for 20 minutes." The translation would be, "around 350 degrees or so until it is done!" Not all ovens are calibrated the same. Natural occurrences will affect a product such as atmospheric pressure, humidity and extremely high doses of radioactivity. Then, there is the convection oven which tends to be 50 degrees higher in actual temperature as opposed to set temperature. Certain mediums or vessels conduct heat better than others and, for this reason, cooking times may vary.

The solution is to check the progress regularly in order to make up for these differences. Though a 20 minute cook time is likely a good approximation, it really is just a guideline. The product is finished cooking only after it is done, not after 20 minutes. You use the oven as a tool to produce the finished product.

The second mistake is called The Universal Standard and Montage Principle. Here are two concepts rolled into one, both of which refer to recipe interpretation. Measurements and amounts are confusing at times and may require extra attention in order to prevent ill fate. What is the subtle difference in tsp. and tbsp.? The difference is that one is three times the size of the other by volume. What is the difference between a cup of flour, a cup of sifted flour, and a cup of flour sifted? We all lose it when the recipe reads "as needed." Heaven forbid the use of metric measurements. Why, just the thought of converting them means enrollment in a remedial math skills class for some people. What if the recipe is twice what is needed? Doing half the recipe sounds simple but converting the amounts can be as big of a task as developing a cure for cancer.

If the ingredients and their amounts are not enough, there are always the directions to have to deal with. They could be too simple, "blend and bake" or "incorporate all ingredients and cook." Some people require extensive step by step elementary instructions such as "insert tab A into slot B." Others find directions to be a simple guideline, a basis for their own interpretation. Some people follow directions word-for-word, taking them for their literal meaning. This can be especially disastrous with such things as "beat the eggs," "whip vigorously," or "stir by hand."

The solution is that there is no Universal Standard. The recipe itself will be as different in the interpretation as will be the final product. Take some extra time to understand the ingredient measures or the conversions. If you are a strict disciplinarian and follow recipes faithfully, then it is best to familiarize yourself with basic culinary jargon. If recipes are simple, then their construction can be interpreted as being simple. If the directions are complex, then the

Culinary Commentary

construction, in turn, will be complex.

Number three is The Mickey Mouse Syndrome. This mistake deals with time, not cooking times but more so with timing. How many times has today's roast been ready at a perfect medium rare, but today's baked potato is still in Idaho? How many times has the perfectly grilled swordfish been ready only to find the honey glazed carrots still in a plastic bag with a "twisty tie" inside the crisper drawer of the refrigerator. One item overcooks while another is being made. One item gets cold while another is heating up.

The solution is to look ahead in time a little before it is already upon us. If we do this, then there should be an idea of when things should be done. If they are all to be done at once, then stagger the starting times of each dish in order to yield that result. If the meal is in courses, then the appetizer is first, and the dessert is last. It is up to the cook to see to it that it comes out like that.

Our fourth problem is No Taste Waste, the problem of blandness in food. This is one of the unpardonable crimes in cooking. To put time and effort into preparation, and the end result be boring and bland is a pity. Meats begin to taste like wood, vegetables taste like wax, starches, like plastic or paste. We might as well eat straight tofu. If we do not watch ourselves in this respect, food may well come in pill form one day. What about glorifying the food itself? Many times good products are masked with other items when they are perfectly fine alone. The addition of fat, herbs, excessive ingredients, and too much liquid all contribute to covering up the product's natural flavor. There is the baked potato stuffed with broccoli, cheese, bacon, butter, sour cream, chives, mushrooms, and onions. What happened to the baked potato?

The solution is to keep it simple. Creating a quality, tasty food product is often an art. The taste is perceived prior to the preparation in the mind of the cook and constructed with taste as a final goal. Though we sometimes do not know what a recipe tastes like until we make it, the effort comes from within to make it good. A cook can be taught all the fundamentals of cooking, but they cannot be taught pride, desire, or affection. This may very well decide the difference between a cook and a great chef.

The last problem is The Mess in Place Motto. How often does the pasta become one big starch ball while the sauce is being made? Perhaps the sauteed flounder is becoming a crispy critter while you search for some white wine. We find ourselves helplessly watching our hamburger brown and shrink into a stone-like projectile because we did not have the spatula already on hand to flip it.

Culinary Commentary

The solution lies in the problem. The Mess in Place Motto comes from a French term, "Mise en Place" which when translated means that everything should be in its place in a constant state of readiness. It means thinking ahead, anticipation of need before the need exists. It means reading a recipe through before beginning to use it. This type of preventive thinking can eliminate a rash of mistakes in the kitchen.

The highest percentage of mistakes come from the top five cooking mistakes: The Magic Stove, The Universal Standard and the Montage Principle, The Mickey Mouse Syndrome, The No Taste Waste, and The Mess in Place Motto. If we work hard to overcome these mistakes then we eliminate most of our problem. Who knows? Maybe the world will be a better place to eat in.

Soups, Salads & Dressings

Apple and Cabbage Slaw

4 cups cabbage, finely shredded
1 cup carrots, grated
1 apple, diced

2 tablespoons raisins
1/4 cup celery, sliced
2 tablespoons fresh parsley

Dressing:
1/4 cup lemon juice
1 tablespoon honey
1 tablespoon onions, grated

2 teaspoons prepared mustard
1 tablespoon sesame seeds
1 tablespoon cinnamon/clove vinegar

In a large salad bowl, combine cabbage, carrots, apples, raisins, celery and parsley. In a separate bowl, mix together lemon juice, honey, onion, mustard, sesame seeds and vinegar. Pour the dressing over the salad mixture, and toss to mix.
Servings: 7 (1 cup serving).

Apple-Carrot Salad

2 medium apples, diced
1-1/2 cups carrots, grated
1/3 cup raisins

1/4 cup walnuts, chopped
1/2 cup plain lowfat yogurt
1 tablespoon honey

Combine apples, carrots, raisins and walnuts. Blend the yogurt with the honey, and pour over the other ingredients, mixing thoroughly.
Servings: 4.

Soups, Salads, & Dressings

Artichoke Rice Salad

1 package (6 ounces) long grain and
  wild rice mix
1 can (14 ounces) artichoke hearts,
  drained and chopped
1 jar (2 ounces) chopped pimento,
  chopped
12 pimento stuffed olives, chopped

3 green onions with tops,
  chopped
1 cup celery, chopped
1/2 cup mayonnaise
1 teaspoon curry powder
Tomato wedges (optional)

Cook rice according to package directions, omitting butter, and cool. Add remaining ingredients except tomato wedges, and mix well. Cover, and chill thoroughly. Garnish with tomato wedges. Serve.
Servings: 8.

Balsamic Vinaigrette

1 tablespoon mustard (dijon)
1/3 cup of Balsamic vinegar

1 cup of virgin or extra virgin olive oil
Salt and pepper to taste

Place mustard and vinegar in a bowl, and add 1/2 teaspoon of salt. Mix with whisk. Slowly drizzle in olive oil whisking constantly or after each addition. The finished product should be emulsified.

Soups, Salads & Dressings

Banana Nut Slaw

4 cups cabbage, finely shredded
1/4 cup carrots, shredded
1/2 cup mayonnaise
1 teaspoon sugar
1/4 teaspoon celery salt

1/8 teaspoon ground white pepper
1-1/2 teaspoons milk
1 tablespoon vinegar
3 tablespoons salted peanuts
1 medium banana, sliced

Combine cabbage and carrots in medium bowl, and stir well. Combine mayonnaise and next 5 ingredients in small bowl. Add to cabbage mixture, stirring well. Cover, and chill 2 hours. Add peanuts and bananas; toss gently to mix. Serve. Serving: 6.

Basil and Bean Salad

1 cup cooked pinto beans*
1/4 cup onion, chopped

1 cup cherry tomatoes, halved
1/2 cucumber, chopped

Dressing:
1/4 cup parsley, chopped
1 tablespoon basil, chopped
1-1/2 teaspoons olive oil
1 tablespoon white wine vinegar

1 tablespoon lemon juice
1/4 teaspoon black pepper
1 teaspoon sugar

*May substitute kidney or black beans.

In a mixing bowl, combine the beans, onion, cherry tomatoes and cucumber. Combine the parsley, basil, oil, vinegar, lemon juice, pepper and sugar in a blender. Blend until smooth. Mix with the bean and vegetable mixture. Serve on a lettuce leaf.
Servings: 4 (1/2 cup serving).

Soups, Salads, & Dressings

Bean, Corn and Rice Salad with Chili Vinaigrette

3-1/2 cups cooked converted rice, cooled
1 can (16 ounces) pink beans, rinsed and drained
1-1/2 cup cooked corn kernels or 1 can (12 ounces) corn niblets
1/3 cup scallions, chopped

1/3 cup safflower or corn oil
2 tablespoons fresh lime juice
1 tablespoon cider vinegar
1 tablespoon packed brown sugar
1 tablespoon chili powder
1 teaspoon salt
1/2 teaspoon ground cumin

2 pickled jalapeno peppers, stemmed, seeded, deribbed and minced

In large bowl, combine rice, beans, corn, scallions and jalapeno peppers. Toss to mix. In small bowl, combine oil, lime juice, vinegar, brown sugar, chili powder, salt and cumin. Whisk until sugar dissolves and mixture is well blended. Pour dressing over salad, and toss to coat. Let stand at room temperature, tossing occasionally for up to 4 hours before serving or cover and refrigerate for up to 3 days.
Servings: 6.

Soups, Salads & Dressings

BBQ Sauce with Apples

1/2 pound butter
1 onion, diced
1 garlic clove
1 bottle ketchup
4 tablespoons brown sugar
1 tablespoon worcestershire sauce

1 tablespoon wine vinegar
1 teaspoon lemon juice
2 cups red wine
1 can dark cola
4 apples, roughly diced
1 tablespoon pickling spice
   in cheesecloth

Melt butter, and add onion, garlic, sugar, worcestershire sauce, vinegar, lemon juice and spices. Simmer for 10 minutes. Add wine, ketchup and apples. Simmer for 10 minutes. Add dark cola, and simmer for 15 minutes. Puree, and strain. Ready to serve.
Servings: 4.

Blueberry Soup

2 cups blueberries
3/4 cup apple juice
1/4 cup orange juice

1 drop lemon extract
Dash of nutmeg, freshly grated

Place the blueberries, juices and lemon extract in a small saucepan. Bring to a boil over medium heat. Reduce heat, and simmer for 1 minute. Add nutmeg. Pour the soup into a blender, and process until smooth. Chill the soup. Garnish with orange, kiwi or apple slices.
Servings: 3 (1/2 cup serving).

Soups, Salads, & Dressings

Brines for Smoking

Chicken or Pork:

2 cans light beer
1/2 bunch parsley
1 rib celery
4 ounces peach preserves
1/2 cup sugar

1 teaspoon kosher salt
1 teaspoon ginger
1/4 cup lemon juice
1 teaspoon sage

Seafood:

3 cups white wine
1 teaspoon salt
2 ribs celery
1 teaspoon celery seed

1 clove garlic
1 teaspoon dill seed
1 fresh bunch basil

Dark Meat:

3 cups red wine
1 teaspoon salt
1 teaspoon black pepper
1 teaspoon paprika
1 dash cayenne pepper
1 teaspoon cloves

1 teaspoon thyme
1/2 bunch green onion
1 cup sugar
1/4 cup prune juice
1/2 bunch parsley

Mix well.

Soups, Salads & Dressings

Brown Rice and Lentil Salad with Pepperoni

1 cup long grain brown rice
1 cup lentils, picked over,
  rinsed and drained
3/4 cup sliced pepperoni
  (3-1/2 ounces) chopped thinly
2/3 cup celery, finely chopped

1/2 cup red onion, finely chopped
2 cloves garlic, cooked in boiling water
  for 10 minutes, drained and peeled
1/4 cup red wine vinegar or to taste
1 tablespoon dijon style mustard
1/3 cup olive oil

In large saucepan of boiling salted water, add rice, stirring. Cook 25 minutes or until just tender. In colander, drain rice, refresh under cold water, and let drain until cool. In saucepan, combine lentils and 4 cups water. Bring water to boil, and simmer lentils covered for 15 to 20 minutes or until tender. Drain lentils, and in bowl, combine with rice, pepperoni, celery and onion. In a blender or food processor, puree garlic with vinegar, mustard and salt and pepper to taste. Add oil in stream, and blend into dressing until emulsified. Drizzle salad with the dressing, toss well, and add salt and pepper to taste. This may be made one day in advance. Serve at room temperature.
Servings: 4-6.

Soups, Salads, & Dressings

Bulgur Salad

1-1/2 cups bulgur, raw
3 cups boiling water
1/2 cup onion, finely chopped

2 tablespoons parsley, chopped
1 tablespoon horseradish, grated

Place the bulgur in a large heatproof mixing bowl. Stir in the boiling water. Soak 2 hours. Stir occasionally. Chill in the refrigerator. Add onion, parsley and horseradish to bulgur.

Dressing:
2 teaspoons sesame oil
2 tablespoons rice wine vinegar
  or herbal vinegar

2 tablespoons lemon juice
1/2 teaspoon pepper
1/4 teaspoon dry mustard

In a small cup, whisk together the oil, vinegar, lemon juice, pepper and mustard. Fold the dressing into the bulgur salad. Serve chilled or room temperature. Servings: 7 (1-1/2 cup serving).

Soups, Salads & Dressings

Catfish Gumbo

1 pound catfish meat,
  diced (about 4 fillets)
1/2 cup okra
1/2 cup celery, diced
1/2 cup onions, diced
1/2 cup peppers, diced
1-1/2 cups whole tomatoes
1 clove garlic, minced
Gumbo Filo to taste

Salt, paprika to taste
Pepper, cayenne pepper to taste
3 ounces olive oil
3 ounces flour
Thyme to taste
Basil to taste
Marjoram to taste
6 cups chicken stock

Make a roux with oil and flour. Add all vegetables, herbs and spices, and saute. Add stock and catfish. Simmer for 40 minutes.

Note: Gumbo Filo must be cooked in same oil before adding to soup.
Servings: 4.

Cauliflower and Carrot Salad

2 cups cauliflower, chopped
1 cup carrots, sliced
1/2 cup bell pepper, chopped
1/2 cup lemon juice

1/4 cup parsley, chopped
2 cloves garlic, finely minced
1 shallot, chopped (2 tablespoons)

In a covered pot, steam the cauliflower, carrot and bell pepper until tender-crisp. Cool, and drain. Combine the lemon juice, parsley, garlic and shallot in a small bowl. Mix the vegetables and dressing together in a large bowl. Chill, and serve.
Servings: 4 (3/4 cup serving).

Soups, Salads, & Dressings

Celery Beet Salad

2 hard cooked egg yolks
1 raw egg yolk
5 tablespoons olive oil
1-1/2 tablespoons wine vinegar

2 cups celery, diced and chilled
Salt and pepper
1 cup cooked beets,
  sliced and chilled

Sieve hard cooked yolks into bowl. Beat in raw yolk, oil and vinegar. Add celery, toss, and season to taste. Mound mixture in the center of round platter, and circle with beets. Additional oil and vinegar may be dribbled over beets, if desired.
Servings: 6.

Champagne Vinaigrette

1 egg yolk
1/3 cup champagne vinegar

1-1/2 cups vegetable oil
Salt and pepper to taste

Mix egg yolk, vinegar and salt in a bowl. Drizzle oil into mixture, whisking constantly or after each addition. Season to taste with more salt and pepper, if necessary. Will last up to one week in the refrigerator.
Servings: 4.

Soups, Salads & Dressings

Chicken and Braised Leek Salad

3 leeks
Salt and pepper to taste
3 tablespoons butter
1/2 cup white wine

1 (4 pound) chicken
1 tablespoon oil
1-1/2 cups chicken stock
1/2 cup sour cream

Trim leeks, halve lengthwise, and rinse. Cut leeks in half, crosswise, dividing the green and white parts. Dice green leaves. Heat oven to 450 degrees. Season cavity and outside of chicken with salt and pepper. Heat oil in roasting pan. Sear chicken over high heat until golden on all sides, about 10 minutes. Remove chicken, and set aside. Add 2 tablespoons butter and white part of leeks to pan. Season with salt and pepper, and cook until leeks start to brown, 2 minutes. Pour in stock. Return chicken to pan. Roast chicken in preheated oven until juices run clear when thigh is pierced by fork, about 35 minutes. Stir leeks, occasionally. Transfer chicken and leeks to rack over container, and cool to room temperature. Meanwhile, degrease pan juice, and add white wine. Bring to simmer, scraping bottom of pan with wooden spoon to deglaze. Simmer over medium heat until reduced to 2/3 cup, about 10 minutes. Remove from heat, and pour into large bowl. Add remaining tablespoon of butter to pan, and saute leek greens over medium high heat for 1 minute. Add 1/4 cup water, and cook until liquid evaporates, 2 minutes. Set aside. When chicken is cool enough to handle, remove meat from bones, and cut into bite size pieces. Chop leek bulbs. Whisk sour cream into cooled pan juices. Add chicken and any juices and all leeks. Toss together, and season to taste with salt and pepper. Serve at room temperature, or slightly chilled.
Servings: 4.

Soups, Salads, & Dressings

Chicken and Ham Salad with Toasted Pecans

6 whole boneless chicken breasts with
  skin (4-1/2 pounds)
2 teaspoons cumin
2 pounds Canadian bacon or lean ham,
  cut 1/2 inch dice
2 cups scallions, thinly sliced
1-1/2 cups sour cream
2 tablespoons salt
3 tablespoons peanut oil

1/2 pound pecan halves (2-1/3 cups)
2 packages (10 ounces each) frozen
  baby peas
2 pounds mushrooms,
  cut 1/2 inch dice
1/3 cup fresh lemon juice
1-1/2 cups plain yogurt
1/4 cup dijon mustard
2 teaspoons pepper

Place chicken breasts in large wide saucepan or heatproof casserole with water to cover. Bring to simmer over moderate heat. Reduce heat to very low, and poach chicken at bare simmer until firm to touch, about 45 minutes. Remove from heat, and let cool in poaching liquid. Drain chicken, remove skin, and cut meat in 1/2 inch cubes. Meanwhile, in large skillet, heat oil. Add pecans, sprinkle with cumin, and saute over moderately high heat, tossing constantly until aromatic and lightly toasted, 4 minutes. Transfer to paper towel to drain. Blanch peas in boiling salted water for 30 seconds. Drain, and let cool. In large bowl, combine chicken, pecans, Canadian bacon and mushrooms. Add lemon juice, and toss until coated. Add scallions and all but 1/3 cup of peas. In medium bowl, combine yogurt, sour cream, mustard, salt and pepper, and mix well. Pour dressing over salad, and toss to coat. Transfer salad to larger decorative serving bowl or platter, and garnish with remaining peas. Serve at room temperature.
Servings: 12-16.

Soups, Salads & Dressings

Chicken Gumbo

3 chicken breast halves, skinned
2 cloves garlic, minced
1 tablespoon safflower oil
6 cups water
1 canned jalapeno, chopped
  (or to taste)
2 cups fresh tomatoes, peeled
  and chopped

2 cups fresh okra, washed, and sliced
1/2 cup onion, chopped
1/4 cup long-grain brown rice, raw
1 tablespoon water
1-1/2 teaspoons gumbo file
1/4 teaspoon coriander

Heat oil in a large nonstick saucepan over medium heat. Add chicken and garlic, and brown lightly. Add water, and bring to a boil. Reduce heat, and cover. Simmer 45 minutes or until chicken is tender. Remove chicken. Reserve broth. Chill, and skim off excess fat. Remove meat from bone. Chop into bite-size pieces. In a large saucepan, combine cubed chicken, jalapeno, tomatoes, okra, onion and rice, and reserve chicken broth. Bring to a boil; then reduce heat. Cover, and simmer 30 minutes, adding water if mixture begins to stick. Mix gumbo and water to make a smooth paste. Add to saucepan with coriander, stirring constantly. Simmer until slightly thickened. Serve warm.
Servings: 4 (1-1/4 cup serving).

Soups, Salads, & Dressings

Chicken-Mango Salad

1/3 cup mayonnaise
2 teaspoons chives (optional)
2 cups ripe mango, chopped
1 medium size green pepper,
  chopped
1 tablespoon lemon juice

2 green onions, chopped
2 cups cooked chicken, chopped
1 large tomato, chopped
1/3 cup vegetable oil or olive oil
1 tablespoon vinegar
1 teaspoon sugar

Combine mayonnaise, onion, and if desired, chives, and chill. Combine chicken, mango, tomato and green pepper in large bowl. Combine oil, vinegar, lemon juice and sugar in jar. Cover, and shake vigorously. Pour over chicken mixture, and chill at least 30 minutes. Top with mayonnaise mixture, and serve.
Servings: 8.

Chicken Salad Tarts

2-1/4 cups all purpose flour
1/2 teaspoon salt
1/2 cup shortening
1/4 cup margarine
1/2 to 2/3 cup milk
4 cups cooked chicken,
  finely chopped

1/2 cup slivered almonds, toasted
2/3 cup mayonnaise
2 tablespoons steak sauce
1/2 teaspoon curry powder
1/2 teaspoon salt
1/4 teaspoon garlic salt
Pimento strips

Combine flour and salt. Cut in shortening and margarine in blender until mixture resembles coarse meal. Sprinkle milk (1 tablespoon at time) evenly over surface, and stir with fork just until dry ingredients are moistened. Shape dough into 60 (3/4 inch) balls. Place in ungreased 1-3/4 inch muffin pans, and shape each ball into a shell. Bake at 400 degrees for 10 to 12 minutes. Cool. Combine next 7 ingredients, and mix well. Cover, and chill at least 1 hour. Spoon into tart shells. Garnish with pimento strips.
Yield: 5 dozen.

Soups, Salads & Dressings

Chicken Salad
with Walnut and Lime Mayo

3 cups canned chicken broth
4 parsley sprigs
1 large egg, room temperature
5 teaspoons fresh lime juice
1 cup vegetable oil
1/2 cup toasted walnuts, chopped
1/4 teaspoon fresh lime rind,
  finely grated

1 bay leaf
2 whole chicken breasts,
  (1-1/2 pounds) boneless, skinless
1 teaspoon prepared mustard
1/4 teaspoon salt
1-1/2 cups celery, sliced crosswise
1/4 cup fresh parsley leaves, minced

In skillet, bring broth to boil with bay leaf, parsley sprigs, salt and pepper to taste. Add chicken, and cook to light simmer for 7 minutes, turning once. Remove skillet from heat, and let chicken cook in broth for 20 minutes. Transfer chicken to cutting board, pat dry, and cut into bite sized pieces. In food processor or blender with motor on high, blend egg, lime juice, mustard and salt. Add oil in stream, and blend mayonnaise until emulsified. In large salad bowl, combine chicken, celery, salt and pepper to taste. Add mayonnaise, and stir salad until combined.
Servings: 4-6.

Chilled Melon Soup

2 cups cantaloupe, chopped
2 cups honeydew melon, chopped
1/2 cup fresh orange juice

2 tablespoons fresh lime juice
1/2 cup champagne

Puree melon in a blender with orange juice and lime juice. Chill for 30 minutes. Add chilled champagne, and serve.
Servings: 6 (3/4 cup serving).

Soups, Salads, & Dressings

Chunky Tomato Soup

1 tablespoon olive oil
1 cup scallion, minced
2 cloves garlic, crushed
1/4 teaspoon cumin (optional)
Black pepper to taste

3 cans (28 ounces each) tomatoes,
  plus their juice
2 medium tomatoes, diced
2 tablespoons fresh parsley,
  minced

Heat the olive oil in a large saucepan over medium heat. Add the onion and garlic. Cover, and saute, stirring occasionally. Add a little water, if necessary, to keep the ingredients from sticking. Add the cumin and pepper, turn heat to low, and cover. Drain the canned tomatoes, and reserve the juice. In a blender or food processor, mix the canned tomatoes until smooth. Add tomatoes to the onion mixture, along with the reserved juice and the fresh tomatoes. Cover, and let simmer over low heat for about 45 minutes. Sprinkle with parsley, and serve. Servings: 6 (2 cups).   Nutritional Analysis: page 436.

Soups, Salads & Dressings

Cibreo's Italian Salad

1-1/2 pounds all purpose potatoes,
  (6 medium) peeled, quartered
  lengthwise and cut crosswise
  into 1/4 inch slices
1/3 cup parsley, minced
1 large red onion, coarsely chopped
1/4 cup olive oil
2-1/2 tablespoons red wine vinegar

2 tablespoons fresh basil, minced
  or 2 teaspoons dried
1 teaspoon salt
1/2 teaspoon pepper
1-1/2 pounds cooked beef,
  cut into 1/2 inch dice (4 cups)
Boston or romaine lettuce
  for garnish

Bring medium pot of salted water to boil over high heat. Add potatoes, and cook until tender, about 15 minutes. Drain, and transfer to serving bowl. Meanwhile in small bowl, combine parsley, onion, olive oil, vinegar, basil, salt and pepper, and stir until blended. Add cooked beef to bowl with potatoes. Pour dressing on top, and toss to coat well. Let marinate at room temperature, tossing occasionally for 30 minutes to 1 hour. Season with additional salt and pepper to taste. To serve, arrange a bed of lettuce on platter. Mound beef salad in center.
Servings: 4-6.

Soups, Salads, & Dressings

Codfish & Potato Chowder "Southern Style"

4 ounces smoked ham
1-1/2 cups onion, chopped
1 cup carrots, chopped
1/2 cup celery, chopped
2 cups potatoes, peeled and diced
6 cups fish stock or clam juice

Pepper
Cayenne
1/4 cup flour
2 pounds skinless, boneless cod,
  tilefish, sea trout or grouper
3 cups half and half

Saute vegetables with ham and fish. Dust vegetables with flour. Add fish stock. Cook until tender. Finish with half and half.
Servings: 4.

Corn Chowder

1/8 pound salt pork
1/2 cup onion, finely diced
1/4 cup celery, finely diced
1-1/4 cups corn kernels,
  fresh or frozen

1/4 cup flour
3 quarts hot chicken stock
1 cup potatoes, in 1/4 inch dice
Salt and white pepper to taste
1/2 pint heavy cream

Make incisions in salt pork, and melt down the fat over low heat. Saute finely diced onions, celery and corn. Dust with flour, toss lightly, and cook for 5 minutes. Add 3 quarts of chicken stock, bring to boil, and simmer until tender. Puree in a blender or food processor. Return puree to soup pot, add diced potatoes, and cook just until tender. Season to taste with salt and white pepper. Place the heavy cream in a large mixing bowl, add a few ladles of hot chowder to the cream to equalize the temperature, and then add this tempered mixture back into the chowder. Keep soup warm until served, but do not boil. Garnish with finely diced fresh dill.
Servings: 10.

Soups, Salads & Dressings

Cous Cous Salad

2 cups quick-cooking cous cous
1-1/2 cups boiling water
1/2 bunch parsley, chopped
Toasted sesame seeds or pine nuts

1/3 to 1/2 cup each, finely diced
  green peppers
  red or yellow peppers
  celery
  cucumbers, peeled
  tomatoes, peeled and seeded

Soak cous cous in boiling water for 30 minutes. Fluff with a fork. Add diced vegetables, parsley and nuts, and toss. Pour dressing over salad, toss, and let stand 15-20 minutes.

Dressing:
1/2 cup cider or rice wine vinegar
1 cup peanut oil
2 tablespoons sesame oil
2 tablespoons lemon juice

1 teaspoon honey
1 clove garlic, minced
1 teaspoon fresh ginger, minced
Soy sauce and black pepper to taste

Put vinegar in a small bowl, and slowly add oil while whisking. Add the rest of the ingredients, and whisk to combine.
Servings: 6.

Soups, Salads, & Dressings

Crabmeat-Shrimp Seashell Salad

3 cups water
1 pound unpeeled shrimp, medium
6 ounces seashell macaroni
1 cup celery, thinly sliced
1/2 medium size green pepper, finely chopped
1/2 medium size red pepper, finely chopped
1/2 small purple onion, chopped
2 green onions, chopped

1 tablespoon fresh parsley, chopped
1/4 cup mayonnaise
1/4 cup commercial Italian salad dressing
1 tablespoon lemon juice
1/2 teaspoon dried whole oregano, crushed
1/4 teaspoon salt
Dash of pepper
8 ounces crabmeat, drained

Bring water to boil, add shrimp, and cook 3 to 5 minutes. Drain well. Rinse with cold water. Chill. Peel and devein shrimp; set aside. Cook macaroni according to package directions, omitting salt. Drain. Rinse with cold water, and drain again. Add next 6 ingredients; blend well. Combine mayonnaise and next 5 ingredients. Add to macaroni mixture. Stir in crabmeat and shrimp. Chill before serving. Servings: 7.

Soups, Salads & Dressings

Crab Soup with Lemon Egg Sauce

3 tablespoons unsalted butter
1/2 cup celery, chopped
3 tablespoons flour
4 cups milk
2 cups light cream
1 pound fresh white crabmeat,
  broken into bits

Salt and white pepper to taste
2 tablespoons dry sherry
2 lemons, sliced into 12 to 16 slices
2 hard-cooked eggs,
  sliced into 12 to 16 slices

In heavy saucepan, melt butter, and saute celery over medium heat until soft but not colored, about 4 minutes. Stir in flour to make a smooth paste. Cook 2 to 3 minutes, stirring. In another saucepan, heat milk and cream to scalding. Slowly add to roux, stirring constantly until bubbly, slightly thickened and smooth, 5-6 minutes. Add crabmeat, and season to taste with salt and pepper. Cook over low heat until crabmeat is hot, about 3 minutes. Stir in sherry. Place 2 lemon slices and egg slices in bottom of each soup bowl. Ladle soup over, and serve.
Servings: 6-8.

Cranberry Holiday Salad

1 package (12 ounces) fresh cranberries
2 cups sugar
1 pound seedless red grapes, halved

1 cup pecans, chopped and toasted
1 cup whipping cream, whipped

Position knife blade in food processor bowl. Add cranberries. Cover with top. Process until cranberries are coarsely chopped. Combine all ingredients and mold.
Servings: 6.

Soups, Salads, & Dressings

Cream of Celery

1 cup regular rice, uncooked
2 stalks celery, thinly sliced
1 quart milk
1 cup chicken broth

1 teaspoon salt
1/4 teaspoon pepper
Croutons (optional)
Green pepper rings (optional)

Combine rice, celery and milk in a medium saucepan. Bring to a boil, stirring frequently. Cover. Reduce heat, and simmer 5 minutes. Gradually stir in chicken broth, salt and pepper. Continue to cook until thoroughly heated. Do not boil. Garnish with croutons or green pepper rings, if desired.
Servings: 6.

Cream of Pea

1 package (10 ounces) frozen
  green peas
2 cups boiling water
2 cups whipping cream

1 tablespoon butter or margarine,
  melted
1/2 teaspoon salt
1/8 teaspoon pepper
Whipped cream

Combine peas and water in a medium saucepan. Cover, and cook 10 minutes or until peas are tender. Pour half of mixture into electric blender. Process until smooth. Pour into a large bowl. Repeat procedure with remaining pea mixture. Stir in whipping cream, butter, salt and pepper. Cover, and chill for several hours. Serve with a dollop of whipped cream.
Yield: about 5-1/2 cups.

*Note: Soup may be served warm with croutons.

Soups, Salads & Dressings

Cream of Scallop Soup
with Watercress

1 pound of scallops
2 cups dry white wine
2 teaspoons champagne vinegar
1/2 cup shallots, chopped
1 quart of heavy cream

1/2 cup watercress leaves, freshly snipped
3 tablespoons butter
Salt and pepper to taste
1/8 pound raw scallop slices

Place scallops, shallots, vinegar and wine in a saucepan, and bring to a boil. Reduce until liquid is almost dry, and add cream. Reduce by one fourth, and remove from heat. Season with salt and pepper, and strain through a fine mesh sieve. Stir in butter, watercress leaves and scallop slices. Ladle into bowls, and serve.
Servings: 4-5.

Soups, Salads, & Dressings

Cream of Tortilla Soup

2 cans (14-1/2 ounces) chicken broth
1/4 cup (1/2 stick) butter
1 medium onion, diced
1/2 cup celery, diced
2 garlic cloves, minced
1 medium tomato, chopped
2 tablespoons fresh chives, minced
1-1/2 cups unsalted tortilla
  chips, crushed

1 tablespoon all purpose flour
1/4 cup whipping cream
1 cup Monterey Jack cheese, grated
  (about 4 ounces)
1 cup cheddar cheese, grated
  (about 4 ounces)
2 teaspoons chili powder
2 teaspoons ground cumin
Unsalted tortilla chips, crushed

Bring chicken broth to boil in small saucepan over medium heat. Meanwhile, melt butter in heavy medium saucepan over medium heat. Add onion, celery and garlic, and saute until onion is translucent, about 4 minutes. Reserve 1 tablespoon chopped tomato and 1 tablespoon chives for garnish. Add remaining tomato, chives and 1-1/2 cups tortilla chips to saucepan, and saute 2 minutes. Reduce heat to low. Sprinkle 1 tablespoon flour over, and stir mixture for 2 minutes. Stir chicken broth into tortilla mixture. Cover, and bring to boil. Reduce heat. Stir in whipping cream. Add grated Jack and cheddar cheese, and stir mixture until cheese is melted and well blended. Add chili powder and cumin. Season to taste with salt and pepper. (Can be prepared 1 day ahead. Cover tightly and refrigerate. Rewarm soup over low heat, stirring frequently.) Ladle into bowls. Sprinkle each with some of reserved tomato and chives and crushed tortilla chips, and serve.
Servings: 6.

Soups, Salads & Dressings

Creamy Potato Soup

3 medium potatoes (about 1 pound), peeled and thinly sliced
1 medium onion, thinly sliced
1 large stalk celery, thinly sliced
Minced chives

3 packets low-sodium chicken broth or bouillon (3 tablespoons)
6 cups water
1/4 teaspoon black pepper

Combine all ingredients except chives in a saucepan. Bring to a boil. Cover, and reduce heat. Simmer 30 minutes or until potatoes are tender. Remove from heat, and allow mixture to cool. Process mixture, 1/2 batch at a time, in electric blender until smooth. Return to saucepan, and cook until thoroughly heated. Garnish with chives.
Servings: 8 (1 cup serving).

Crunchy Marinated Bean Salad

4 ribs celery, sliced
1 can (17 ounces) small English peas, drained
1 can (16 ounces) cut green beans, drained
1 can (8-1/2 ounces) baby lima beans, drained
1 jar (4 ounces) diced pimento, drained
1 medium size green pepper, chopped

1 medium onion, chopped
1 cup vegetable oil or olive oil
1 cup vinegar
1/2 cup sugar
1 teaspoon paprika
1/4 teaspoon garlic powder
1/4 teaspoon salt
1/4 teaspoon pepper

Combine first 7 ingredients in large bowl; set aside. Combine remaining ingredients in jar. Cover tightly, and shake vigorously. Pour over vegetable mixture, cover, and chill overnight.
Servings: 8-10.

Soups, Salads, & Dressings

Cucumber Salad

2 cucumbers, peeled and sliced thin
1 medium onion, sliced thin
1 teaspoon salt

1 teaspoon sugar
1 teaspoon dill weed
1 cup white vinegar

Mix cucumbers and onion together in a ceramic or glass bowl. Add salt, sugar and dill weed to vinegar, and pour over cucumbers and onion. Chill 1 hour. Servings: 6 (20 calories each).

Curried Broccoli Salad

1-1/2 pounds fresh broccoli
1/4 cup milk
1/4 teaspoon seasoned salt
Dash of pepper

1 cup commercial sour cream
1/2 teaspoon curry powder
1/4 teaspoon dry mustard

Trim off large leaves of broccoli. Remove tough ends of lower stalk, and wash broccoli thoroughly. Cut flowerets and stems in bite size pieces. Steam broccoli 8 to 10 minutes or until crisp tender; cool. Place in serving dish. Combine remaining ingredients in small bowl. Pour over broccoli, toss gently to coat, cover, and chill 2 to 3 hours.
Servings: 6.   Nutritional Analysis: page 436.

Soups, Salads & Dressings

Double Apple Salad

1 large red delicious apple,
  unpeeled and diced
1 large golden delicious apple,
  unpeeled and diced
1 can (8 ounces) pineapple chunks,
  drained
1/2 teaspoon ascorbic citric powder

1 cup miniature marshmallows
2/3 cup flaked coconut
1/2 cup pecans, chopped
1/4 cup raisins
2 tablespoons celery, chopped
1/4 cup mayonnaise

Sprinkle diced apples with ascorbic citric powder. Add remaining ingredients, and mix well. Cover, and chill.
Servings: 6-8.

Soups, Salads, & Dressings

Duck and Apple Salad

2 tablespoons rice vinegar
1 tablespoon ginger root, grated
  and peeled
1 bunch watercress, coarse
  stems discarded and dried
1/2 red apple, sliced thin
1/4 cup red bell pepper, julienned

3 tablespoons apple juice
1/2 cup peanut oil
2 roasted duck legs, boned, skinned
  and meat shredded
1/2 green apple, sliced thin
2 tablespoons almonds, sliced

In blender, mix together the vinegar, apple juice, ginger root, salt and pepper to taste. With motor running, add oil in stream, and blend the dressing until emulsified. In bowl, toss watercress with 1/4 cup dressing, and divide between 2 plates. In bowl, toss duck with 2 tablespoons remaining dressing, and arrange on watercress. Arrange half apple slices on each plate, and sprinkle with bell pepper strips and almonds. Drizzle salads with remaining dressing to taste.
Servings: 2.

Egg Drop Soup

4 cups chicken broth, defatted
3 tablespoons cold water
1 tablespoon cornstarch
2 green onions with tops, chopped

4 egg whites, beaten until frothy
1 teaspoon coarse ground pepper
1 teaspoon soy sauce
1 teaspoon dry cooking sherry

In a 3 quart saucepan, bring broth to a boil. In a small mixing bowl, add water and cornstarch. Mix until smooth. Add to boiling broth, stirring constantly until slightly thick and smooth. Add onions. Drizzle in beaten egg whites, stirring constantly. Remove from heat. Add pepper, soy sauce and sherry. Serve immediately.
Servings: 4 (1 cup serving).   Nutritional Analysis: page 436.

Soups, Salads & Dressings

Fennel Salad with Pecans

1/2 head Boston or Bibb lettuce
1/2 head radicchio, escarole or
  other lettuce
1/2 medium fennel bulb
2 tablespoons pecan pieces
3 tablespoons red wine vinegar
2 tablespoons vegetable oil

1 tablespoon water
1 teaspoon mustard seed, ground
  with mortar and pestle
1/4 teaspoon dried tarragon
1/4 teaspoon salt
1/4 teaspoon pepper

Wash, and dry the lettuce. Tear the leaves into bite-size pieces, and place in a large salad bowl. Trim the tough outer leaves of the fennel. Wash, and core the bulb. Dice, and add to the bowl. Add the pecans. Combine the remaining ingredients in a jar. Cover, and shake; then pour into the salad. Toss, and serve. Servings: 4 (1-1/2 cups).

Soups, Salads, & Dressings

French Onion Soup

2 medium onions, sliced in rounds
1 tablespoon butter or margarine
4 cups beef stock
1 bay leaf
1 teaspoon dried basil
1/2 teaspoon dried thyme

1/2 teaspoon black pepper
Dash of cognac or dry sherry (optional)
4 slices whole-wheat french bread
4 slices Swiss cheese, 1/2 ounce each
2 tablespoons grated parmesan
   or romano cheese

Saute the onions in the butter or margarine until they are translucent, stirring occasionally. Add a little water, if necessary, to keep the onions from sticking. Add the bouillon, seasonings and the cognac, if desired, and bring to a low boil. Reduce heat, and let simmer for 30 minutes. Meanwhile, toast the bread on a foil-covered baking sheet under the broiler until crisp. Top each slice of bread with a slice of Swiss cheese, and broil for several minutes more, until cheese is melted. (Keep your eye on it!) Place 1/2 tablespoon of grated parmesan or romano cheese in each of four soup bowls. Pour 1 cup of onion soup in each bowl, and float the bread slices on top.
Servings: 4 (1-1/2 cups).

Soups, Salads & Dressings

Fresh Citrus Vinaigrette

2/3 cup fresh citrus juice from
  oranges, grapefruits, lemons, limes
  or pineapples

1-1/2 cups high quality
  vegetable oil
Salt and pepper to taste

Mix all ingredients in a bowl until well-blended. Season to taste with salt and pepper. Note that this dressing is not emulsified and must be mixed thoroughly before each use. This vinaigrette will keep for up to three weeks in an air tight container in the refrigerator.

Fresh Herbal Vinaigrette

1 tablespoon dijon mustard
1/3 cup red wine vinegar
1 cup virgin or extra virgin olive oil

2 to 3 tablespoons of fresh herbs such
  as tarragon, thyme, basil,
  chervil or a mixture of any or all
Salt and white pepper to taste

Mix mustard, vinegar and half the herbs in a bowl. Let sit for ten minutes. Add 1 teaspoon of salt, and mix again. Slowly drizzle in oil mixing constantly or after each addition. Season to taste with white pepper, and add the rest of the herbs. This dressing will not keep as the acid in the vinegar will attack the chlorophyll in the herbs. It must be used the same day.

Soups, Salads, & Dressings

Fruited Chicken Salad

Dressing:

1/4 cup grapefruit juice
2 tablespoons red wine vinegar
1 tablespoon vegetable oil

1 teaspoon poppy seeds
2 teaspoons honey
1/2 teaspoon dijon mustard

Salad:

2 chicken filets, trimmed and
   cut crosswise into 1/8 inch strips
Vegetable cooking spray
1 small head green leaf lettuce

2 small red grapefruit, peeled, sectioned
1-1/2 cups green seedless grapes
1 cup fresh strawberries

To prepare dressing, place all dressing ingredients in jar with tight-fitting lid. Shake well. Let stand 15 minutes; shake again. Set aside.
To prepare salad, spray large skillet with non-stick cooking spray. Heat over medium heat. Add chicken strips. Cook about 3 minutes or until chicken is tender, stirring frequently. Cover, and remove from heat. Line 4 individual salad plates with lettuce. Place warm cooked chicken strips in center of each lettuce-lined plate. Arrange grapefruit sections, grapes and strawberries around chicken. Spoon dressing over salads.
Servings: 4.

Soups, Salads & Dressings

Garlic Soup

2 large onions, sliced
10 cloves garlic, peeled and
  thinly sliced (about 1 bulb)
1 tablespoon cooking oil
2 medium tomatoes, peeled, seeded,
  and chopped

1/4 teaspoon dried oregano, crushed
1-1/2 cups water
1/2 teaspoon instant beef
  bouillon granules

In a medium saucepan, cook onions and garlic in hot oil over medium low heat for 15 to 20 minutes or until onions begin to brown, stirring occasionally. Stir in tomatoes and oregano. Cover, and cook over low heat for 30 minutes, stirring occasionally. Stir in water and bouillon. Bring to boil. Reduce heat. Simmer, uncovered, for 10 minutes.
Servings: 4.

Garlic and Shallot Vinaigrette

2 tablespoons dijon mustard
1/3 cup red wine vinegar
1 cup virgin or extra virgin olive oil
2 teaspoons garlic, minced

1 tablespoon shallots, finely minced
1/2 teaspoon fresh peppercorns
1/2 teaspoon salt to taste

Mix mustard, 1/2 teaspoon salt, vinegar, garlic, shallots and peppercorns. Slowly drizzle olive oil into mixture, whisking constantly or after each addition. Season to taste with more salt, if desired. This vinaigrette will keep in an air tight container in the refrigerator for two to three weeks.

Soups, Salads, & Dressings

Gazpacho

Serve this chilled soup in bowls with one of the following garnishes: chopped hard-boiled egg, finely chopped scallions, chives, croutons, or avocado (1 tablespoon per serving; the avocado will add more fat and calories than the other choices).

1 large tomato
1/2 small onion
1/2 medium cucumber
1/2 medium green pepper
1 celery stalk
2 teaspoons fresh parsley,
  finely chopped
2 cloves garlic, minced or
  crushed

2 cups tomato juice
3 tablespoons red wine vinegar
1/2 cup white wine
2 tablespoons basil
1 tablespoon lemon juice
1 teaspoon salt
1/2 teaspoon white pepper
1 teaspoon worcestershire sauce
Dash of hot sauce

Finely chop all vegetables. (A food processor is ideal for this.) Combine all remaining ingredients, and refrigerate for 24 hours.
Servings: 6 (3/4 cup).

Greek Black-Eyed Pea Salad

3 cups black-eyed peas, cooked
1/2 cup bell pepper, diced
  (red or yellow is attractive)
1/2 cup scallions, diced
1 small clove garlic, crushed
1/2 teaspoon dried oregano

3 tablespoons olive oil
4 tablespoons red wine vinegar
1 teaspoon lemon juice
2 tablespoons fresh parsley, minced
1/4 teaspoon salt

Combine all ingredients in a large bowl. Marinate 6 to 8 hours in the refrigerator, stirring occasionally.
Servings: 8 (1/2 cup).

Soups, Salads & Dressings

Green Turtle Soup

1 pound turtle meat
1 large onion
1 cup celery tops, chopped
2 cloves
1 sprig thyme
Lemon, juiced

3 veal tails
1 large clove garlic
1 bay leaf
Pinch allspice, pounded
2 eggs, hard boiled and sliced
1 glass white wine

Put all ingredients except thyme, eggs, lemon and wine into 3 quarts cold water. Season with black pepper, salt and very little cayenne. Simmer 7 to 8 hours. Half an hour before serving put in sprig of thyme, and hard boiled eggs. Remove from heat and add white wine, lemon and 1 flat teaspoon parsley on top of lemon in bowl.
Yield: 3 quarts.

Hazlenut or Walnut Vinaigrette

1 tablespoon dijon mustard
1/4 cup sherry wine vinegar

1 cup walnut or hazlenut oil
Salt and pepper to taste

Mix vinegar, mustard and 1/2 teaspoon of salt in a bowl. Drizzle in oil whisking constantly or after each addition. Season to taste with salt and pepper, if necessary. Will keep in the refrigerator for two to three weeks in an air tight container.

Soups, Salads, & Dressings

Herbed Tomato and Crouton Salad

1-1/4 cups olive oil or vegetable oil
5 cups 1/2 inch cubes of country
  or Italian bread
3 pounds firm ripe tomatoes,
  chopped
1/2 cup fresh parsley leaves, minced

3 garlic cloves, minced
3 tablespoons red wine vinegar
1-1/2 teaspoons dijon style mustard
  to taste
1/2 cup mint leaves, finely chopped
1/2 cup scallion greens, finely chopped

In small bowl, combine oil and garlic. Let mixture stand for 30 minutes, and strain oil into bowl, discarding garlic. Toast bread cubes in one layer on baking sheet in preheated 350 degree oven. Turn occasionally for 15 minutes or until golden brown. Drizzle 1/2 cup garlic flavored oil over croutons. Toss mixture well, and let cool to room temperature. In another small bowl, whisk together vinegar, mustard, salt and pepper to taste. Add remaining 3/4 cup garlic flavored oil in stream, whisking until it emulsifies. In large bowl, toss together croutons, tomatoes, mint, scallion, parsley, salt and pepper to taste. Drizzle mixture with dressing, and toss salad well. For crunchy croutons, serve immediately. The longer the croutons stand, the softer they become.
Servings: 8-10.

Honeydew Salad
with Apricot Cream Dressing

1 carton (8 ounces) sour cream
1/4 cup pecans or walnuts, chopped
1/4 cup coconut, flaked

2 tablespoons apricot preserves
3 to 4 cups honeydew balls, chilled

Combine first 4 ingredients. Stir well. Spoon melon balls into sherbert or champagne glasses. Top with dressing. Serve.
Servings: 4.

Soups, Salads & Dressings

Horseradish Chive Sauce

1 cup fresh horseradish
1/3 cup semi-sweet white wine
1 quart bechamel
1/2 cup heavy cream

Salt to taste
Cayenne pepper
Fresh chives, finely chopped

Place horseradish in water overnight. Before use, peel, grate and place in russe. Add wine to horseradish, and simmer until all liquid is gone. Add bechamel to horseradish, and bring to a boil. Add in heavy cream. Add chives. Season.

Hot Swiss Potato Salad

3 cups cooked potatoes, sliced
1 cup Swiss cheese, julienned
1/2 cup green onions, minced
   including green parts
1/4 cup fresh dill weed, minced
   or 1 tablespoon dried
1 teaspoon salt

1/4 cup peanuts, chopped
Butter or margarine
1 cup sour cream
1/4 cup Swiss cheese, grated
2 to 3 tablespoons fine bread crumbs
2 to 3 tablespoons butter or margarine,
   melted

Toss lightly together the julienned cheese, scallions, dill weed, salt and peanuts. In medium casserole, arrange layers of potatoes, cheese mixture, dabs of butter and sour cream to cover. Repeat layers ending with potatoes. Blend the grated cheese, crumbs and melted butter together, and spread on top. Bake at 375 degrees for 30 to 45 minutes or until well browned.
Servings: 6.

Hungarian Potato Salad

2 pounds boiling potatoes
2 tablespoons olive oil
2 tablespoons vegetable oil
1 tablespoon dill vinegar or
  white wine vinegar
1 teaspoon dijon style mustard
1/2 teaspoon sweet paprika

1/2 teaspoon salt
1/4 teaspoon white pepper
1/2 cup green bell pepper
3/4 cup onion, minced
1-1/2 cups sour cream
2 hard boiled eggs, chopped
Dill sprig for garnish

In pot, cover potatoes with salted cold water. Bring water to boil, and simmer for 25 minutes or until tender. Drain potatoes, let cool, and then peel. Cut potatoes into 1/2 inch slices, and put in large bowl. In small bowl, whisk together olive oil, vegetable oil, vinegar, mustard, paprika, salt and white pepper. Pour dressing over potatoes. Add bell pepper and 1/2 cup onion. Toss mixture, and let marinate, covered loosely for 1 hour. Stir in sour cream, egg, remaining 1/4 cup onion, salt and pepper to taste, and chill salad, covered for at least 2 hours or overnight. Serve salad at room temperature, garnished with dill sprigs and pimento slices.
Servings: 6.

Soups, Salads & Dressings

Jambalaya Salad

1 large egg plus 2 egg yolks
1/3 cup sherry wine vinegar
3 tablespoons whole grain mustard
1-1/2 teaspoons salt
2 teaspoons black pepper
2-1/4 cups olive oil
1 medium onion, finely chopped
1/2 teaspoon crushed hot red pepper
1 teaspoon thyme
2 imported bay leaves
2 cups chicken stock or canned broth
1 cup whole long grain white rice
3 celery ribs, cut crosswise
   on diagonal into 1/2 inch pieces

1 small red bell pepper,
   cut into 1 inch pieces
1 small green bell pepper,
   cut into 1 inch pieces
4 scallions, thinly sliced
1-1/2 cups cooked ham, diced
1 large head iceberg lettuce,
   coarsely shredded (6 cups)
2 ripe medium tomatoes, cut into
   6 wedges each or
   12 cherry tomatoes
18 large cooked shrimp, peeled and
   deveined with tails left on

In food processor, combine whole egg, egg yolks, vinegar, mustard, 1/2 tea-spoon salt and black pepper. Process for 1 minute. With machine on, pour in 2 cups of olive oil in steady stream. Cover, and refrigerate until serving time. In medium saucepan, heat 3 tablespoons olive oil. Add onion, and cook, stirring over medium heat until tender, but not brown, about 5 minutes. Add hot pep-pers, thyme and bay leaves, and cook stirring for 2 to 3 minutes until fragrant. Stir in stock, remaining 1 teaspoon salt and rice. Increase heat to moderate high, and bring to boil. Reduce heat to low, cover pan, and cook undisturbed for 20 minutes or until rice is tender and all liquid is absorbed. Remove from heat, and let stand, covered for 5 minutes. Place rice into large bowl, remove bay leaves and let stand, stirring occasionally until cool. Add celery, green and red bell peppers, scallions, chicken, ham and remaining 1 tablespoon olive oil. Toss well to mix. Let return to room temperature. To serve, mound lettuce and rice, and garnish with tomato wedges and shrimp. Drizzle with some dressing, and serve with additional pepper.
Servings: 6.

Soups, Salads, & Dressings

Layered Cranberry Salad

4 envelopes unflavored gelatin
3/4 cup sugar
1-1/2 cups boiling water
1 cup ginger ale
1-1/2 cups fresh cranberries, ground
3 tablespoons sugar

1/2 cup plus 2 tablespoons
  boiling water
1-1/2 cups sour cream
1-1/4 cups pineapple sherbet, softened
3/4 cup walnuts or pecans, chopped

Combine 2 envelopes gelatin and 3/4 cup sugar in bowl. Add 1-1/2 cups boiling water, and stir until gelatin is dissolved. Stir in ginger ale and cranberries. Pour into lightly greased 8 cup mold. Chill. Combine 2 envelopes gelatin and 3 tablespoons sugar in bowl, add 1/2 cup plus 2 tablespoons boiling water, and stir until gelatin is dissolved. Add sour cream and sherbet. Beat until blended. Cool. Fold in nuts. Pour sour cream mixture over cranberry layer. Chill.
Servings: 10-12.

Leek Soup

1-1/2 cups fresh leeks, with greens,
  minced
1 cup onion, chopped
1 clove garlic, minced
1 quart chicken stock, defatted

2 cups raw potatoes, diced
1 cup skim evaporated milk
1/2 teaspoon white pepper

Saute leeks, onion and garlic in 1 cup stock for 5 minutes. Add remaining stock and potatoes. Bring to a boil, reduce heat, and simmer 20 minutes. Add milk. Remove from heat, and allow mixture to cool. Puree half of soup in blender, and return to saucepan. Serve warm. Garnish with chopped green onion.
Servings: 10 (1/2 cup serving).

Soups, Salads & Dressings

Lemon and Pepper Vinaigrette

1 teaspoon of dijon mustard
1 egg yolk
1/2 cup fresh squeezed lemon juice
1-1/2 cups virgin or extra virgin olive oil

1-1/2 teaspoons freshly cracked
 black pepper to taste
Salt to taste

Mix mustard, lemon juice, cracked pepper and 1 teaspoon of salt in a bowl. Slowly drizzle olive oil into mixture whisking constantly or after each addition. Season to taste with more salt and pepper, if desired. The finished product should be thoroughly emulsified; however, mix again before using.

Lentil-Rice Salad

2/3 cup lentils (uncooked)
2 teaspoons olive oil
2-1/2 tablespoons lemon juice
1/4 cup green onions, chopped
1 cup brown rice, cooked

1/2 teaspoon dried oregano
 or 1 teaspoon fresh
1/3 cup nonfat yogurt
1/2 teaspoon black pepper

Place lentils in saucepan with 2 cups water. Bring to boil, reduce heat, and simmer just until tender (about 40 minutes). Drain. Toss immediately with oil, lemon juice, onions, rice and oregano. Chill. Just before serving, stir in yogurt and pepper.
Servings: 5 (1/2 cup serving).

Soups, Salads, & Dressings

Lentil Soup

2 quarts vegetable stock
1 cup dried lentils
1/2 cup onion, chopped
1/4 cup celery, chopped
1 bay leaf

1/2 teaspoon dried oregano
3 tablespoons tomato paste
2 tablespoons white wine vinegar
   or herbal vinegar

Bring the stock to a boil in a large saucepan. Rinse the lentils, and add to boiling stock. Add all the remaining ingredients except the vinegar. Reduce the heat, cover and simmer, until the lentils are very soft, about 1-1/2 hours. Remove the soup from the heat, and add the vinegar. Discard the bay leaf. Puree half of the soup. Return the puree back to the saucepan, and reheat.
Servings: 5 (1-1/2 cup serving).

Lima Bean Soup

2 cups dried lima beans
1/2 cup onion, finely chopped
1 carrot, peeled and thinly sliced
4 cloves garlic, chopped
1 stalk celery, thinly sliced

8 ounces crushed tomatoes with puree
1/4 cup fresh parsley, chopped
2 tablespoons low-sodium soy sauce
8 cups water

Place all the ingredients in a 2 quart saucepan, and cover. Bring to a boil. Reduce the heat, and simmer for 1-1/2 hours or until the beans are tender. Add water, if necessary. Puree 1/2 of bean mixture. Return to saucepan, and reheat.
Servings: 7 (1 cup serving).

Soups, Salads & Dressings

Lobster Bisque

1 quart lobster stock
1-1/2 cups of cream
1 tablespoon water mixed with
  1 tablespoon of cornstarch

1-1/2 cups lobster meat
Fresh tarragon for garnish
3 tablespoons butter
Salt and cayenne pepper

Place lobster stock in a large saucepan, and bring to a boil. Reduce by half, and add the cream. Reduce by a third, and add cornstarch mixture. Simmer for 5 minutes, whisk in butter, and season with salt and cayenne pepper, as desired. Place lobster meat pieces in bowls, and ladle soup on top. Garnish with freshly snipped tarragon.
Servings: 6.

Macadamia Rum Chicken Salad

8 medium size tomatoes
3 cups chicken, cooked and diced
3/4 cup mayonnaise
1 cup celery, finely diced
Salt and white pepper to taste

Crisp lettuce leaves
Asparagus, carrot sticks, fresh
  pineapple slices, halved cooked egg,
  ripe olives
1/4 cup macadamia nuts, chopped

Mix chicken with 1/4 cup mayonnaise. Chill about 2 hours. Toss chicken with remaining mayonnaise and celery. Season to taste with salt and pepper. Cut each tomato about 3/4 through into 6 equal sections. Fill each with chicken salad. Place in lettuce cup, and garnish with asparagus, etc...
Servings: 8.

*Note: On this recipe you do not have to use stuffed tomato. You may put chicken salad on lettuce cup and garnish, also using tomato wedges.

Macadamia Rum Dressing:
1/4 cup pineapple juice
3/4 cup mayonnaise

1 teaspoon rum extract

Combine all dressing ingredients. Mix well, and chill. Pour over salad.

Soups, Salads, & Dressings

Minestrone

1 onion, finely chopped
1/4 cup vegetable stock
1-1/2 cups celery, chopped
14-1/2 to 16 ounce can tomatoes
  with juice
3 cups vegetable stock
1/4 cup parsley, chopped
3 cups water
Dash of pepper
2 bay leaves
1 teaspoon oregano
2 teaspoons basil

1/2 teaspoon rosemary
1 clove garlic, minced
1/2 cup carrot, chopped
1/2 cup zucchini, diced
1/2 cup potato, diced
1/4 cup green pepper, chopped
1/4 cup frozen or fresh corn
1 cup mushrooms, sliced
1 cup cooked garbanzo beans
1/2 cup broken whole wheat
  spaghetti, uncooked
1/2 cup cooked barley

Saute the onion and celery in stock until soft. Add the tomatoes, 3 cups stock, water, parsley, seasonings and vegetables. Simmer soup 30 minutes. Add spaghetti, garbanzos and cooked barley. Continue cooking over medium heat for 10 minutes.
Servings: 11 (3/4 cup serving).

Soups, Salads & Dressings

Minted Zucchini, Apple and Cheese Salad

1/2 cup currants
2 pounds zucchini, cut
   3x1/4 inch strips
1/4 cup fresh lemon juice
1 pound jarlsberg cheese,
   cut 3x1/4 inch strips
1/2 cup virgin olive oil
1-1/2 tablespoons salt

1/4 cup ruby port or sweet vermouth
3 pounds granny smith apples,
   unpeeled, cut into
   3x1/4 inch strips
2 medium red onions, minced
1/4 cup sherry wine vinegar
1/4 cup fresh mint, minced

In small bowl, soak currants in port for at least 2 hours, or overnight, and drain.
In large bowl, toss zucchini and apple strips with lemon juice. Add cheese and
onions, and toss well to combine. In medium bowl, whisk together oil, vinegar
and salt. Stir in currants and mint, and pour this dressing over salad. Toss gently
but thoroughly. Serve at room temperature.
Servings: 12-16.

Mozzarella and Tomato Salad

1 pound tomatoes, cut crosswise
   into 1/8 inch cubes or slices
1/2 pound mozzarella, sliced thin
1/4 cup packed fresh basil leaves, minced

1 tablespoon wine vinegar
1 small garlic clove, minced
1/3 cup olive oil

On platter, arrange tomato slices, alternately with mozzarella overlapping them.
In small bowl, stir together basil, vinegar, garlic oil, salt and pepper to taste.
Spoon the dressing over the salad, and let stand at room temperature covered
loosely for 30 minutes. Serve.
Servings: 4.

Soups, Salads, & Dressings

Mushroom Soup

1 tablespoon reduced-calorie margarine
1 pound fresh mushrooms,
   washed, drained and sliced
1/2 cup onion, minced
1/2 cup celery, minced

1 garlic clove, minced
5 cups beef or chicken broth, defatted
1 teaspoon white pepper
1 tablespoon dry cooking sherry

In a 3 quart saucepan, melt margarine over medium heat. Add mushrooms, onion, celery and garlic. Saute 3 to 5 minutes or until brown. Add broth and pepper. Bring to a boil. Reduce heat, cover, and simmer 15 minutes or until vegetables are tender. Remove from heat, and add sherry. Serve warm.
Servings: 5 (1-1/4 cup serving).

Mussel Soup with Saffron

4 cups mussel juice
2 cups heavy cream
1 egg yolk mixed with
   1 tablespoon cream
1 tablespoon of cornstarch

Salt and pepper to taste
Fresh chives for garnish
Cooked and shelled mussels
   for garnish
Dash saffron

Place mussel juice and saffron in a saucepan, and bring to a boil. Reduce by half, and add cream. Reduce by a fourth, and remove from heat. Whisk in yolk mixture, and return to heat. Sauce will thicken, but do not allow to boil as it will curdle. Season to taste with salt and pepper, and garnish with mussels and chives.
Servings: 4.

Soups, Salads & Dressings

Okra, Tomato and Mushroom Salad

2 large tomatoes, chopped
1/4 pound mushrooms, sliced thin
2 tablespoons fresh basil, minced

1/3 cup vegetable oil, combined
  with 2 tablespoons cider vinegar
1/2 pound okra

In salad bowl, combine tomatoes, mushrooms and basil. Toss the mixture with oil and vinegar mixture. Add salt and pepper. Just before serving, trim and slice okra 1/8 inch thick. Add to salad, and toss well. Serve.
Servings: 4.

Orange-Onion Salad

3 large navel oranges, peeled,
  pits discarded, sliced thin
3 small red onions, sliced thin
1/2 cup olive oil
2 tablespoons fresh orange juice

1 tablespoon fresh lime juice
1-1/2 teaspoons fresh rosemary, minced,
  or 1/2 teaspoon crumbled, dried
1/4 teaspoon salt
1/4 teaspoon pepper

In salad bowl, combine the oranges and onions. In blender, blend the oil, orange juice, lime juice, the rosemary, salt and pepper until the dressing is smooth. Pour the dressing over the oranges and onions, and toss salad.
Servings: 6.

Soups, Salads, & Dressings

Oriental Spinach-Sesame Salad

1/4 cup water

1-1/2 pounds fresh spinach, washed thoroughly and trimmed

3 tablespoons toasted sesame seeds, ground with mortar and pestle

1 tablespoon honey

2 tablespoons tamari sauce or soy sauce

Bring water to a boil in a saucepan. Toss in the spinach, cover, and cook about 30 seconds, until wilted. Drain the spinach, and rinse with cold water in a colander. Drain well, and transfer to a serving bowl. In a small bowl, combine the honey, tamari sauce and sesame seeds. Pour dressing over the spinach, toss, and serve.

Servings: 4 (1 cup).

Soups, Salads & Dressings

Oxtail and Okra Gumbo

Stock:

4 pounds oxtails, cut into 2-inch
  sections and trimmed
1 carrot
2 teaspoons salt

2 cups canned beef broth
1 onion, halved
1 rib celery
8 cups water

Gumbo:

1/3 cup vegetable oil
2 cups onion, chopped
2 cups celery, chopped
1/2 teaspoon white pepper,
  or to taste
1/2 teaspoon cayenne or to taste
1 pound smoked sausage, cut crosswise
  into 1/2 inch slices
*Cooked rice to accompany

Hot sauce to taste
1/2 cup all purpose flour
2 cups green bell pepper, chopped
10 ounces pack frozen okra,
  thawed and chopped
1/2 teaspon black pepper or to taste
1 bay leaf

To make stock: In pot, combine oxtails, broth, 8 cups water, onion, carrot, celery and salt, and bring liquid to boil, skimming froth. Simmer oxtails covered for 3-1/2 hours or until they are very tender. Transfer oxtails with slotted spoon to bowl, and let cool. Discard bones and fat, reserving meat, and strain stock through fine sieve into bowl. Spoon off fat. To make gumbo: In heavy skillet, heat oil over moderately high heat until hot, but not smoking. Add flour gradually, whisking, and cook roux, whisking constantly for 2 to 5 minutes or until the color of peanut butter. Scrape the roux immediately into heavy pot. Add onion, bell pepper and celery, and cook mixture over moderate heat, stirring until vegetables are softened slightly. Add okra, and cook mixture, stirring for 5 minutes. Stir in white pepper, black pepper, cayenne, oxtail and bay leaf. Bring liquid to boil, stirring, and simmer mixture covered for 30 minutes. In skillet, saute sausage in batches over moderately high heat, turning it, until it has released its fat and is golden brown. Transfer to paper towel to drain, and add

sausage to mixture. Simmer, covered, for 15 minutes. Add reserved oxtail meat, and simmer gumbo, covered for 15 minutes. Discard bay leaf, and season gumbo with salt and hot sauce. Serve over rice.
Serves: 6-8 (makes 12 cups).

Oyster Bisque

4 dozen oysters + 6 for garnish
2 cups mussel juice
1 quart heavy cream

4 tablespoons butter
Fresh snipped chives
Fresh croutons

Shuck the oysters reserving all the liquid. Place three dozen oysters and the liquid into a saucepan with mussel juice. Bring to a boil over high heat for 10 minutes or until reduced by half. Add cream, and cook over medium heat until reduced by 1/3. Strain mixture through a fine sieve, and then place in a blender. Add 1 dozen oysters, and puree. Add four tablespoons of butter, and adjust seasoning with salt and pepper. Place a raw oyster in each bowl, and ladle hot bisque on top. Garnish with fresh chives and croutons.
Servings: 6.

Oyster Stew

1 quart milk
1 cup cream
1 quart oysters
1 tablespoon butter
1-1/2 teaspoons salt

1/2 teaspoon pepper
8 saltines, crumbled
1 cup celery, steamed and diced
Whole mace, if desired

Heat milk, cream, butter, saltine crumbs, soft celery and seasonings in top of double-boiler. Add oysters, and cook until they curl on the edges.
Servings: 6.

Soups, Salads & Dressings

Oyster Stew

1-1/2 cups onion, chopped
2 stalks celery, sliced
2 cloves garlic, minced
2 sprigs fresh parsley, chopped
1/4 teaspoon dried whole thyme
1/4 cup plus 2 tablespoons butter
  or margarine
4-1/2 cups half and half

2 containers (12 ounces) large fresh
  oysters, undrained
1/4 cup plus 2 tablespoons
  golden sherry
3/4 teaspoon salt
1/4 teaspoon pepper
1/4 teaspoon worcestershire sauce
1/8 teaspoon hot sauce

Saute onion, celery, garlic, parsley and thyme in butter in a large Dutch oven until tender. Gradually add half and half, stirring constantly. Drain oysters, reserving liquid. Add liquid to vegetable mixture. Heat thoroughly without boiling. Stir in oysters, sherry, salt, pepper, worcestershire sauce and hot sauce. Continue cooking over low heat, stirring constantly, until mixture is heated and oyster edges curl. Serve warm.
Yield: 10 cups.

Parsley Parmesan and Mushroom Salad

1 tablespoon fresh lemon juice
2 tablespoons olive oil
1/4 pound (4) large mushrooms,
  sliced thin lengthwise

1/2 teaspoon fresh lemon rind, grated
2 cups firmly packed flat leaf parsley
2 tablespoons fresh parmesan cheese,
  grated

In small bowl, whisk together lemon juice, the rind, oil, salt and pepper to taste. Combine parsley, mushrooms and parmesan. Add dressing, and toss the salad until combined.
Servings: 2.

Soups, Salads, & Dressings

Peach Slaw

8 cups cabbage, coarsely shredded
1/2 cup onion, diced
2 teaspoons prepared mustard
1/3 cup vegetable oil, divided
1 tablespoon fresh parsley, chopped

1 can (29 ounces) peach slices, drained
1 tablespoon sugar
1/2 teaspoon salt
1/4 cup vinegar
1 teaspoon celery seeds

Combine oil, mustard, sugar, salt and vinegar. With electric mixer, beat at medium speed until well blended. Add cabbage, onions, peaches, parsley and celery seed. Mix with wooden spoon until thoroughly blended. Chill one hour. Servings: 10.

Pineapple Orange Salad

1 cup canned pineapple chunks,
  unsweetened and drained
1 cup canned mandarin orange slices,
  unsweetened and drained
1 cup nonfat yogurt

1/4 teaspoon coconut extract
2 teaspoons coconut, unsweetened,
  shredded
1 teaspoon vanilla extract
2 teaspoons honey

Combine all ingredients, and toss to mix well. Chill to blend flavors. Serving: 5 (1/2 cup serving).

Soups, Salads & Dressings

Pineapple Slaw

4 cups cabbage, shredded
1 cup (4 ounces) cheddar cheese, shredded
1/3 cup pimento, diced and drained
1/4 cup mayonnaise
1 tablespoon lemon juice

1 can (8 ounces) pineapple tidbits, drained
1/2 cup pimento stuffed olives, sliced
1/4 cup onion, diced
1/8 teaspoon pepper
1/4 cup whipping cream, whipped

Combine cabbage, pineapple, cheese, olives, pimento and onion in large mixing bowl. Chill at least 1 hour. Just before serving, combine mayonnaise, lemon juice and pepper. Stir well. Fold in whipped cream. Pour over slaw. Toss gently to coat.
Servings: 6-8.

Piquant Carrot Salad

8 medium carrots, peeled and cut into strips
1 medium onion cut into rings
1 small bell pepper, cut into rings
1/4 cup white wine vinegar
3 tablespoons sugar

1/2 teaspoon dijon mustard
3 tablespoons salad oil
1 tablespoon catsup
1/2 teaspoon salt
1/2 teaspoon celery seed
1/2 teaspoon worcestershire sauce

Cook carrots covered in 1 inch boiling, salted water, about 5 minutes or until tender. Drain thoroughly. In bowl, layer carrots, onions and pepper rings. In small jar, combine remaining ingredients, shake well, and pour over carrot mixture. Cover, and chill at least 4 hours. Serve.
Servings: 4-6.

Soups, Salads, & Dressings

Poppy Seed Dressing I

1 cup nonfat yogurt
1 tablespoon honey

4 teaspoons lemon juice
1 teaspoon poppy seeds

Combine all ingredients, mixing well. Chill.
Yield: 1 cup.

Poppy Seed Dressing II

1/2 cup nonfat yogurt
1/2 cup lowfat cottage cheese
2 teaspoons lowfat buttermilk
2 tablespoons chives, chopped

2 teaspoons poppy seeds
1/4 teaspoon salt
2 teaspoons sugar
2 tablespoons strawberry vinegar

Place all ingredients in a blender, and process until smooth. Chill. Excellent on
fruit or spinach salad.
Yield: 1-3/4 cups (1 tablespoon serving).

Soups, Salads & Dressings

Potato and Chicken Salad with Shredded Zucchini

*Great with leftover chicken, but remove skin first.

6 cups baked red potatoes, about
  2 pounds uncooked,
  cut into 1/2 inch dice
3 cups cooked chicken, shredded
4 small zucchini, shredded (4 cups)
6 hard cooked eggs, coarsely chopped

1/4 cup fresh tarragon or parsley, minced
3/4 teaspoon salt
1/4 teaspoon pepper
3/4 cup mayonnaise
1/4 cup chicken stock or canned broth
1 tablespoon white wine vinegar

*If not using leftover baked potatoes, cook diced raw potatoes in large pot of boiling, salted water until tender when pierced with fork, approximately 15 minutes. Drain, and let cool to room temperature. In large bowl, toss together the potatoes, chicken, zucchini, eggs, tarragon, salt and pepper. In small bowl, whisk together the mayonnaise, chicken stock and vinegar until blended. Pour over salad. Toss well, and serve at room temperature.
Servings: 10-12.

Soups, Salads, & Dressings

Potato Radish Salad
with Russian Dressing

3/4 pound potatoes, boiled, peeled
  and cut in 1/2 inch pieces
1/4 teaspoon worcestershire sauce
1/2 teaspoon horseradish
3 radishes, sliced thin

1/3 cup mayonnaise
1/2 teaspoon onion, finely grated
2-1/2 teaspoons ketchup
2 tablespoons sweet gherkin,
  finely chopped

In large saucepan of simmering water, cook potatoes for 6 to 8 minutes, or until tender. Drain in colander. Refresh potatoes under cold water, and drain well. Transfer to bowl. In small bowl, whisk together mayonnaise, onion, worcestershire sauce, ketchup, horseradish, gherkin, salt and pepper to taste. Add dressing and radishes to potatoes, and stir mixture gently until combined. Servings: 2.

Potato Salad

2 cups potatoes, diced, cooked
1 tablespoon pimento, chopped
1/2 cup celery, diced
2 tablespoons onion, chopped
4 teaspoons parsley, minced
1-1/2 teaspoons vinegar

1 teaspoon dry mustard
2 tablespoons reduced-calorie mayonnaise
2 tablespoons nonfat yogurt
2 tablespoons fresh dill, minced
1 tablespoon dill or salad vinegar

Combine all ingredients. Toss lightly and chill.
Servings: 5 (1/2 cup serving).

Soups, Salads & Dressings

Potato Salad
with Olives and Boiled Dressing

1 teaspoon salt
1 tablespoon all purpose flour
4 large egg yolks,
  beaten lightly
4 pounds boiling potatoes
2/3 cup pimento-stuffed olives,
  chopped and drained
Cayenne to taste

1-1/2 tablespoons sugar
1/2 cup cider vinegar
1/2 stick unsalted butter,
  cut in pieces
3 cups celery, including
  leaves, chopped
1/2 teaspoon paprika, Hungarian
1/2 cup well chilled heavy cream

In metal bowl, whisk together salt, sugar and flour. Whisk in 1/4 cup water, vinegar and egg yolks. Add butter. Set bowl over saucepan of boiling water, and cook mixture, whisking until very thick. Let cool to room temperature covered with buttered round of wax paper. Peel potatoes, cut into 3/4 inch pieces. In pot of simmering salted water, simmer potatoes for 6 to 8 minutes or until tender. Drain in colander, and refresh under cold water. Drain potatoes well, and in large salad bowl, combine with celery, olives, paprika and cayenne. In chilled bowl, beat cream until it just holds stiff peaks, and fold into yolk mixture until dressing is combined. Pour dressing over potato mixture. Add salt to taste, and toss. Servings: 10-12.

Soups, Salads, & Dressings

Quick Clam Soup

2 cans (6-1/2 ounces each) clams,
  with juice
2 cups vegetable or chicken
  stock

1 bay leaf
1/2 teaspoon dried thyme
Salt and pepper to taste
4 teaspoons chopped chives

Combine the clams with their juice, the stock, bay leaf, thyme, salt and pepper in a saucepan, and heat throughly. Pour into 4 serving bowls, and top each with a teaspoon of chives.
Servings: 4 (1 cup).

Quill Macaroni Salad with Salami and Basil Caper Dressing

1 pound penne (quill mac) macaroni
1/2 cup pimento, drained and chopped
1/4 cup scallion greens, thinly sliced
2 teaspoons dried hot red pepper
1/2 cup olive oil
Sliced genoa salami (1/4 pound)
  cut in 1x1/2 inch strips (1 cup)

1/3 cup fresh parsley leaves, minced
2-1/2 tablespoons drained bottled
  capers
2 tablespoons white wine vinegar
1-1/2 cups loosely packed fresh basil

In pot of boiling, salted water, boil penne for 13 to 15 minutes, or until tender. Drain in colander, and refresh under cold water. Drain well. In a large bowl, combine penne with salami, pimento, parsley and scallion. In blender, blend capers, vinegar, red pepper flakes, basil and salt to taste. With motor running, add oil in stream, and blend dressing until emulsified. Pour over penne mixture, season with salt, and toss well.
Servings: 6-8.

120

Soups, Salads & Dressings

Red Bliss Potato Salad

2 pounds small red potatoes
  (skins on)
1/2 cup onions, chopped
1 cup prepared ranch salad dressing
  mix made from envelope

Cooked bacon crumbled or
  bacon bits from jar
  (use desired amount)
Salt
Black pepper to taste
Chives

Boil potatoes about 30 minutes. They should not be too soft. After they have cooled, cut into 1 inch cubes. Whisk the next three ingredients together; then pour over the potatoes. Add the seasonings. Combine thoroughly. Refrigerate in a covered glass bowl overnight.
Servings: 6.

Rice and Bean Salad

1 can (16 ounces) red kidney beans,
  drained
3 hard cooked eggs, chopped
1 cup regular cooked rice
1/2 cup sweet pickles, chopped

1/4 cup green peppers, chopped
1/4 cup onion, chopped
1/4 cup celery, chopped
1/2 cup mayonnaise

Combine all ingredients, and toss gently to mix. Cover, and chill 1 to 2 hours. Serve.
Servings: 6.

Soups, Salads, & Dressings

Rice and Black Bean Salad

3 cups cooked rice
1 can (16 ounces) black beans
1 medium red bell pepper, minced
1 medium green bell pepper, minced
4 green onions, minced
1/4 cup fresh cilantro, minced

1/3 cup peanut oil
1/4 cup fresh lime juice
Salt and freshly ground pepper
1 avocado, peeled and sliced
1 papaya, peeled, seeded and
  sliced

Combine first 6 ingredients in large bowl. Whisk together oil and lime juice in small bowl. Pour over rice mixture, and toss to coat. Season with salt and pepper. Garnish with sliced avocado and papaya.
Servings: 6.

Rosemary New Potato Salad with Roquefort

2 pounds small new potatoes,
  rinsed well
1/4 cup plus 1 tablespoon white
  wine vinegar
1-1/2 tablespoons fresh rosemary leaves,
  minced or 1-1/2 teaspoon dried, crumbled

1 tablespoon dijon mustard
1/2 cup olive oil
1/4 pound roquefort, crumbled

In saucepan, cover potatoes with cold salted water, and bring water to boil. Simmer potatoes for 15 minutes or until tender. Drain potatoes, and transfer to large bowl. Add 1/4 cup vinegar and minced or crumbled rosemary. Toss mixture, and let potatoes cool until lukewarm. In a bowl, whisk together remaining 1 tablespoon vinegar, mustard, salt and pepper to taste. Add oil in stream, whisking dressing until emulsified. Add dressing and roquefort to potatoes. Toss salad, and transfer to container. Garnish with rosemary sprigs, if desired.
Servings: 6.

Soups, Salads & Dressings

Russian Dressing

6 tablespoons nonfat yogurt
2 tablespoons tomato paste
1/4 cup reduced-calorie mayonnaise
3 tablespoons white wine vinegar

1/4 teaspoon salt
1/4 teaspoon paprika
1/4 teaspoon mustard powder

Combine all ingredients in blender, and process until smooth.
Yield: 1 cup (1 tablespoon serving).

Sauce Mornay

1 quart bechamel
1/4 cup gruyere cheese, grated

1/4 cup parmesan cheese, grated
1/2 cup heavy cream

Bring bechamel to a boil. Add cheeses to bechamel slowly. Simmer until cheese is melted.
Yield: 1-1/2 quarts.

Scallop Soup with Cilantro

1 pound scallops
1 quart chicken stock (clear)

Salt and pepper to taste
1 tablespoon fresh cilantro

Place chicken stock and scallops in a saucepan, and bring to a boil. Simmer for 15 minutes, and add 1 tablespoon cilantro. Simmer 3 more minutes, and remove from heat. Strain, and season with salt and pepper. Ladle into bowls with the raw scallop slices. Garnish with fresh cilantro, and serve.
Servings: 4.

Soups, Salads, & Dressings

Seafood Delight Salad

4-1/2 cups water
1 package (16 ounces) linguini
1 package (6 ounces) frozen snow peas,
  thawed and drained
3/4 cup olive oil
1/4 cup fresh parsley, chopped
1 teaspoon dried whole oregano
1/2 teaspoon garlic salt

1-1/2 pounds medium size shrimp
6 green onions, chopped
4 medium tomatoes, peeled,
  chopped and drained
1/3 cup vinegar
1-1/2 teaspoon dried whole basil
1/2 teaspoon coarsely ground
  black pepper

Bring water to boil, add shrimp, and cook 3 to 5 minutes. Drain well. Rinse with cold water, and chill. Peel, and devein shrimp; set aside. Cook linguini according to instructions, omitting salt, and drain. Rinse with cold water, and drain. Combine shrimp, linguini and remaining ingredients, and toss gently. Cover, and chill at least 3 hours.
Servings: 10.

Shrimp and Cucumber Soup

2 cups onion, chopped
2 to 3 tablespoons butter
1 quart chicken stock
1 cup potatoes, peeled and chopped
1/2 teaspoon salt

1/4 teaspoon pepper
2 small cucumbers
1/2 pound shrimp, cooked
  shelled and deveined
1 cup cream

Saute onion in butter. Add stock and potatoes. Cook until potatoes are tender, and season with salt and pepper. Puree in blender or food processor, and chill. In blender, or food processor, coarsely chop shrimp and cucumber. Add to chilled soup, and mix in cream to desired consistency. Taste for seasoning. Serve in frozen cups, and make rosette of whipped cream on top as garnish.
Servings: 7.

Soups, Salads & Dressings

Shrimp Sauce

Use this as a sauce for fish or add extra shrimp for a pasta sauce. Also good to fill crepes or tiny bouchees for an appetizer.

1/2 cup fresh of frozen shrimp
  in shell
1 scallion, white and green part,
  chopped separately
Enough fish stock and 2 tablespoons
  dry white vermouth
  to poach shrimp in

Desired seasonings for poaching liquid-
  bay leaf, peppercorns, thyme
Salt, cayenne
1 cup bechamel
1 teaspoon tomato paste (optional)
1/4 teaspoon anchovy paste (optional)

Poach the shrimp with the chopped white scallion and seasonings. Shell shrimp, returning shells to poaching liquid. Reduce poaching liquid until nearly evaporated. Add bechamel, season, and strain through chinois mousseline. If the original sauce was a bland bechamel, the fish taste can be pointed up by adding the anchovy paste. The tomato paste will give it a shrimpy color. Return whole or chopped shrimp, and heat through. Add chopped scallion greens as a garnish. Servings: 6.

Soups, Salads, & Dressings

Souffle Cheese Sauce

A cheese sauce with a different texture; beaten egg whites give it its special lightness. It is good with leeks, broccoli or asparagus. May also be used as a gratin sauce for vegetables or fish.

1 cup bechamel
1/2 cup cheddar cheese, grated plus
  1/4 cup parmesan cheese, grated or
  3/4 cup gruyere, emmenthal
  or Swiss cheese, grated

1 medium size egg yolk
Salt and pepper to taste
Cayenne to taste
3 medium-size egg whites

Bring bechamel to a boil (or begin with a mornay). Stir in the cheese, and season. Heat through. Stir in the egg yolk and cayenne off the heat. Beat the whites until stiff, and fold in. Check seasoning, and serve at once.
Servings: 4.

Southern Style Okra Salad

3/4 pound small okra
1/4 cup distilled white vinegar
1 cup vegetable or olive oil

1/2 cup onion, thinly sliced
Fresh pepper to taste

In large saucepan of boiling, salted water, boil okra for 3 to 5 minutes or until tender, and drain. Refresh in bowl of ice and cold water. Drain okra well. Transfer to shallow dish large enough to hold in one layer, and add onion. In small bowl, whisk together, vinegar, pepper and salt to taste. Add oil in stream, whisking. Whisk dressing until emulsified. Pour over okra mixture. Stir carefully until combined well, and chill covered for 1 hour.
Servings: 4-6.

126

Soups, Salads & Dressings

Tahini Dressing

1 cup nonfat yogurt
2 cloves garlic, minced
2 tablespoons tahini (sesame butter)

2 tablepoons green onions, chopped
2 teaspoons lemon juice
1/2 teaspoon black pepper

Put all ingredients in blender, and process until smooth. Chill.
Yield: 2 cups (1 tablespoon serving).

Thousand Island Dressing

2 tablespoons reduced-calorie
  mayonnaise
1/4 cup nonfat yogurt
1 tablespoon ketchup
3 tablespoons skim milk
1 tablespoons onion, chopped

2 tablespoons dill pickle, chopped
1 clove garlic, minced
1/4 teaspoon dried oregano
  or 1/2 teaspoon, minced fresh
1/2 teaspoon dried parsley
  or 1 teaspoon, minced fresh

Combine all ingredients, and chill before serving.
Yield: 1 cup (1 tablespoon serving).

Tomato-Herb Dressing

1/2 cup unsalted tomato juice
1/2 cup red wine vinegar
1 teaspoon dried dill or
  2 teaspoons, minced fresh
1/4 teaspoon dried chervil

1/4 teaspoon dried basil
  or 1/2 teaspoon, minced fresh
1/2 teaspoon dried oregano
  or 1 teaspoon, minced fresh
1/2 clove garlic, minced
1 cup lowfat buttermilk

Combine all ingredients. Keep refrigerated.
Yield: 1-1/2 cups (1 tablespoon serving).

Soups, Salads, & Dressings

Tomato-Pasta Primavera Salad

8 ounces spaghetti
1 small green pepper, cut
  into strips
2 cloves garlic, minced
1 jar (15-1/2 ounces) spaghetti sauce

1-1/2 cup mushrooms, quartered
1 small zucchini, sliced
1 tablespoon vegetable or olive oil
Green onions, chopped

Cook spaghetti according to package directions, omitting salt. Drain. Rinse with cold water, and drain. Set aside. In a large skillet, saute mushrooms, green pepper, zucchini and garlic in oil, about 10 minutes or until tender. Stir in spaghetti sauce. Spoon over spaghetti, toss gently, cover, and chill. Garnish with chopped green onion.

Servings: 4-6.

Nutritional Analysis: page 441.

Soups, Salads & Dressings

Tortellini Chicken Salad

1-1/2 tablespoons white wine vinegar

2 teaspoons dijon mustard

1 clove garlic, minced

1 tablespoon fresh dill, chopped
  or 1/2 teaspoon dried

1 tablespoon fresh basil, chopped
  or 1/2 teaspoon dried

1/2 teaspoon red pepper sauce

1/4 teaspoon salt and pepper

1/4 cup olive oil

1/2 pound cheese tortellini

1/2 cup green onions, sliced

1 tablespoon butter

1 tablespoon olive oil

1 garlic clove, minced fine

2 chicken cutlets (6 ounces each)
  cubed

Salt and pepper to taste

1/2 red pepper, cut into
  thin strips

1 cup green peas, blanched

Chopped parsley

Vinaigrette:

In small bowl, whisk vinegar, mustard, garlic, dill, basil, red pepper sauce, salt and pepper. Whisk in oil in slow steady stream. Cook tortellini according to package directions. In medium bowl, combine green onions and half vinaigrette. In medium skillet, heat butter and oil. Add garlic, and saute over medium heat, 1 to 2 minutes. Season chicken with salt and pepper, saute 3 to 5 minutes, stirring. Drain on paper towels. Add warm chicken to tortellini, and toss. Add red pepper, peas and remaining vinaigrette, and toss again. Sprinkle with parsley. Servings: 4.

Soups, Salads, & Dressings

Turkey Soup with Dumplings

2 tablespoons turkey fat or
  unsalted butter
1 small onion, minced
9 cups turkey stock
Salt and white pepper to taste

1/2 teaspoon thyme
Pinch of grated nutmeg
1 cup all purpose flour
2 eggs

In a large saucepan, melt turkey fat. Add onion, and cook over moderate heat until softened, about 3 minutes. Stir in 8 cups turkey stock, and bring to simmer. Season with salt and white pepper to taste. Meanwhile, in medium saucepan, combine the remaining 1 cup stock with the thyme, nutmeg, 1/2 teaspoon salt and pinch of white pepper. Bring to boil over high heat. Remove from heat, and beat in flour until thoroughly blended. Melt mixture, cool slightly; then beat in eggs, one at a time. Drop tablespoons of the dumpling mixture into the simmering soup, and cook until dumplings begin to firm, about 5 minutes. Remove from heat, cover saucepan, and set aside to steam the dumplings for 3 minutes before serving.
Servings: 6.

Soups, Salads & Dressings

Vegetable Salad
with Mustard Dressing

2 small yellow squash, unpeeled
1 bunch radishes (1/2 pound)
1-1/2 to 2 tablespoons lemon juice
Salt and pepper to taste
1/2 cup olive oil

2 small zucchini, unpeeled
8 scallions
1 egg white
2 tablespoons natural seed dijon mustard
8 outer leaves of Bibb lettuce

Cut unpeeled yellow squash and zucchini into thin julienne strips. Trim, and slice radishes and whole scallions, including green parts. Combine yellow squash, zucchini, radishes and scallions in mixing bowl. Toss well. Whisk or process together lemon juice, egg white and salt until foamy. Add mustard and pepper. With food processor running or while whisking, add oil to mustard mixture in thin stream. Combine to process or whisk until emulsified. Adjust seasoning to taste. Toss mixed vegetables with dressing. Put a Bibb lettuce leaf on each dinner plate, and spoon mixed vegetables onto lettuce, or place in bowl, with lettuce garnish. Servings: 8.

Soups, Salads, & Dressings

Vegetable Soup

1/2 pound margarine
1 bunch celery, diced
2 onions, peeled and diced
4 large carrots, diced
1 head cauliflower, diced
1/2 head green cabbage, diced
4 potatoes, peeled and diced

4 yellow squash, diced
3 ounces chicken base (paste)
1/2 can (10 ounces) crushed tomatoes
3 bay leaves
2 teaspoons pepper
6 quarts stock
2 tablespoons sugar

Peel and dice all vegetables properly. In a large pot, melt margarine, and add vegetables. Saute vegetables for 10 minutes over medium heat. Add crushed tomatoes, bay leaves, stock, sugar and pepper, and simmer for 45 minutes, skimming off any scum that forms on top.
Yield: 10 quarts.

Vinaigrette

1 tablespoon olive oil
1/4 cup lemon juice
2 teaspoons dijon mustard
2 tablespoons shallots, minced

1 tablespoon parmesan cheese, grated
1 tablespoon white wine
  or herbal vinegar

Combine all ingredients in a small jar with a lid. Shake well until thoroughly combined. Store in the refrigerator in a tightly covered container. Return to room temperature before using.
Yield: 1/2 cup (1 tablespoon serving).

Soups, Salads & Dressings

Watercress Salad

1 bunch watercress, tough stems
  removed
1 head Boston lettuce, cored and
  leaves separated

1/4 Bermuda onion, sliced thinly
6 radishes, sliced thinly
3 ounces mushrooms, cleaned
  and sliced thinly

Combine all ingredients. Serve with a variety of vinegars and oils, fresh lemon
and lime wedges and red, white and black pepper (salt optional). Sample of
vinegars: Balsamic, tarragon, white wine, cider, raspberry. Sample of oils: olive,
canola, sesame.
Servings: 4.

ENTREES

Entrees

Contents

Entrees

Entrees

Entrees

Culinary Commentary

Stephen Nogle, Johnson & Wales University at Charleston's first director, is today a chef instructor at the school.

CLASSICAL COOKING

What do the Rolling Stone song "Jumping Jackflash," the Parthenon, and Escalopes de Vea Cordon Bleu have in common? They are all examples of Classicism.

Classical Rock 'n' Roll, Classic Greek architecture, and Classical food presentations all exhibit the same qualities: order, balance, and simplicity. This article recognizes the three concepts as it applies to cooking.

Prior to the 11th century, Europe was in a period where very little transfer of information (learning) occurred. Cooking, a learned skill, was at a low ebb. As the European Renaissance evolved, led by Italy in the 1300's, cooking skills were greatly advanced along with other learned skills. It was in Italy that these skills were established. France later accepted, practiced, and taught them as the Classical concepts known today. After the Renaissance the skills were practiced, but it wasn't until after the French Revolution (Periods of Classicism always follow periods of Romanticism) that the balance and order came to cooking. These concepts were practiced and displayed by cooks of the 18th and 19th centuries, led by Antoine Careme, Prosper Montagne, and Auguste Escofier. These men were adamant in the pursuit for order, balance and simplicity in their chosen skill.

Foods showing Classicism are very orderly in presentation. There are no cutesy or extemporaneous garnishes. In fact, garnish in classicism is always the accompaniment to the entree: the vegetables and starches. There is nothing to take the eye away from the skill arranged on the plate. The food is always balanced in flavor, texture and nutrition; no one aspect is predominate. In traditional Classicism, great care is taken to enhance natural flavor through seasoning. Emphasis is on technique and <u>The Twelve Rudiments of Cookery</u>.

At Classical restaurants, it is the skill of the rudiments that are on display. This is also the reason why Russian service is the form used to serve Classical food presentations. The sauces are subtle and not overbearing, revealing the qualities of a well-made sauce. Roasts must show the exhibition of a roast, depending upon what type of meat is roasted. Sautes must show the reason for the saute. Braises must exhibit succulence and savoriness. Broils and grills exhibit the color and crustiness necessary to capture and retain natural flavor. All the hand skills connected to established concepts, regarding sizes, shapes and cuts, are exhibited. In essence, it is the human skill associated with cooking that is on display.

Culinary Commentary

Who recognizes this skill? The same people who recognize the human skill displayed as music. Beethoven's Fifth Symphony hasn't changed through the years, but various artists practice and then play his arrangement of notes recognized as his "Fifth." The same people recognize the classical "Roast Tenderloin of Beef Richelieu" in the same manner.

Where is the future for this form of cookery? Most of it can be seen through competition, both on a national and international scale. One would only have to view the Culinary Olympic Competition held every few years in Frankfurt, Germany, to see cooks from around the world participate to keep the "Grand Cuisine" alive. It is also found in the home, as a hobby. Many professionals not associated with the food industry as a career now relax and prepare foods in the Classical manner.

The Twelve Rudiments of Cookery, copyrighted 1991.
Stephen Nogle

Culinary Commentary

Karl Guggenmos, a German master chef, is the Director of Culinary Education at Johnson & Wales. He has over 25 years of experience and also serves as the University's Gourmet Club advisor.

EUROPEAN INFLUENCE ON AMERICAN COOKING

Being a European trained chef, it has always been intriguing to learn how European cooking has influenced American cuisine.

The first observation I made is that there really is no such thing as a definite American Cuisine. There are regional Cuisines each with their own unique ingredients, cooking methods and ethnic influence. So let's look at these 3 views of concern, because much of those have European origin in one way or another.

First of all, let's look at ingredients. When the first settlers came to America the only experience of food they had was from the old country. They searched, of course, for the same ingredients they enjoyed in Europe. They searched for the same meats, such as beef, veal, and game; vegetables, such as carrots, celery and cucumbers; starches, such as potatoes, rice and legumes; and various other grain products. Of course, all or most of it was available in great abundance and new items such as corn, various squashes, and new species of game were added to their new diet. There was such an abundance of natural ingredients that most of the settlers wre overwhelmed by it. Seafood especially was in quantity. The basic foods remained just as they were in Europe.

The second area of major European influence was that of cooking methods. The basic cooking methods were well-established during Europe's thousand years of history. In no way were the settlers of the new country either trying or planning to change these ancient methods. Boiling will always be boiling, roasting will always be roasting, and so on. The only difference might come in the alignment of ingredients and cooking methods. For example, in Europe, a certain fish was always poached. It very well could have been baked or sauteed in the new country. New ways of preparing egg dishes that traditionally in Europe were cooked one way were prepared with a different cooking method here. The ingredients never changed, just the methods used.

The third area, which is the most obvious in European influence, is that of ethnic origins. This country was founded predominantly by Europeans. They, of course, brought with them their recipes and sought, as mentioned before, the ingredients they needed to cook those dishes. In the course of this country's development, because of the desire of the people to "melt" into a new nation, old recipes were

Culinary Commentary

changed into new ones. These new recipes are found in all regions. For example, a corn chowder is a derivative of a basic cream soup with potatoes and corn added. The potatoes might have been added from a recipe. The corn, of course, is American.

The American Cuisine has come a long way. One thing it can never deny is its European influence.

Culinary Commentary

Victor Smurro, a graduate of the University's main campus in Providence, RI, teaches such classes as meat cutting, sauce skills and production kitchen at the Charleston campus. In 1991, Smurro was voted Chef Instructor of the Year by the Charleston campus students.

ITALIAN FOOD & CULTURE

Presently Italian food is the most popular ethnic food in this country. It is quite a diverse cuisine. Unfortunately, it has been misrepresented by corporate America. The regions in Italy are as different as the food cooked within them. To most Americans, Italian food is pizza, lasagna, and spaghetti.

First, I would like to explain that Italian cooking is more than cooking; it is an art and a way of life. To shop daily at the market for the highest quality ingredients is a way of life in Italy. Being of Italian heritage, my family holds on to Italian traditions. For example, Christmas Eve conjures up thoughts of an extremely long dinner table seating 20-25 people and a smaller one for the children. There are all sorts of fresh fish prepared in various ways, wonderful aromas of food and much love, not to mention loud conversation. Each time a family member brings a guest, they are in awe. The kitchen is the focal point of the evening. Several hours will pass, and no one leaves the table. The next meal has been discussed and who will prepare it. Perhaps this stems back to the Roman days when a single holiday would last 3 days or longer.

The Italian culture is rich not only in art and history, but also in food. As far back as the Roman Empire, cookbooks were written on how to prepare vegetables. Let us not forget Rome was in power for approximately 500 years. Whenever the army would conquer a region, they would bring back ideas, food items, even seedlings. The army would plant their own gardens where they were. This proved to be an invaluable cultural exchange among civilizations. When Catherine de Medici married the King of France she brought in Northern Italian chefs to prepare the feasts. Italians had a great influence on French cooking.

The contrast in Italian cuisine stems from the availability of certain food as well as the economic status of the people. Northern Italy has long been a mecca for culture, art and wealth. This is reflected in the food, which is very elegant, lighter, and small in portions. Southern Italy is more known for simple living. Food there is hearty and heavy. The paramount ingredient in all Italian cuisine is freshness, from herbs, seafood, meats, vegetables, and poultry. Simplicity meets elegance in Italian cuisine, and the taste is superior even down to the olive oil and cheese.

As I said earlier, it is a way of life and should be preserved from generation to generation.

Entrees

Apple Egg Casserole

4 cooking apples, peeled
 and thinly sliced
2 tablespoons sugar
2 cups (8 ounces) sharp cheddar
 cheese, shredded

1 pound bacon, cooked and crumbled
1-1/2 cups biscuit mix
1-1/2 cups milk
4 eggs, beaten

Combine apples and sugar. Mix well. Spread evenly in lightly greased baking dish. Sprinkle cheese and bacon on top. Combine remaining ingredients. Beat at medium speed with electric mixer, 30 seconds or until smooth. Pour over cheese and bacon. Bake at 375 degrees for 30 to 35 minutes or until golden brown. Serve warm.
Servings: 10.

Artichoke and Oyster Casserole

2 sticks butter
1 quart milk
6 ounces oysters, drained
1 teaspoon black pepper
2 teaspoons worcestershire sauce
8 fresh cooked artichoke hearts,
 finely chopped

Bread crumbs
1 cup flour
1/2 pint breakfast cream
2 teaspoons salt
1 dash hot sauce
1/2 cup sherry

Melt the butter, and blend in flour. Remove from heat. Mix together milk and cream, and heat. Slowly add the mixture. Heat oysters to remove excess liquid, and add to cream sauce. Simmer about 5 minutes, and add seasoning, sherry and artichoke hearts. Pour into casserole dish. If using fresh artichokes, arrange artichoke leaves around edge of dish. Sprinkle casserole with bread crumbs. Bake 10 minutes at 350 degrees.
Servings: 8.

Entrees

Bacon and Egg Delight

3 English muffins, split,
  buttered and toasted
6 slices bacon, cooked and cut in half

6 poached eggs
Parmesan cheese sauce*
Paprika

Top each muffin half with 2 pieces of bacon and a poached egg. Spoon parmesan cheese sauce over eggs, and sprinkle with paprika. Serve.
Servings: 3-6.

Parmesan Cheese Sauce:

2 tablespoons butter or margarine
2 tablespoons instant blending flour
1 cup milk

1/2 cup parmesan cheese, grated
1/4 teaspoon salt
Pepper to taste

Melt butter in heavy saucepan over low heat, add flour, and stir until smooth. Cook 1 minute, stirring constantly. Gradually add milk. Cook over medium heat, stirring constantly until thickened and bubbly. Add parmesan cheese, salt and dash of pepper. Stir until blended. Serve on top of bacon and egg delight.
Yield: 1-1/4 cups.

Entrees

Baked Oysters Nimble

24 large oysters, shucked and drained
*Oyster sauce
2 pounds fresh spinach, blanched,
  squeezed to remove as much moisture
  as possible and chopped

12 strips of bacon, cooked
  until crisp, drained and crumbled
Parmesan cheese, grated
Paprika

Preheat oven to 375 degrees. Grease 6 ovenproof dishes. Place oysters in a single layer, and top with oyster sauce, spinach and crumbled bacon. Liberally sprinkle with parmesan, covering spinach completely. Dust with paprika. Bake uncovered until cheese begins to brown and bubble, about 12 to 15 minutes.

Oyster Sauce:
2 cups mayonnaise
1/4 cup chili sauce
2 tablespoons dijon mustard
1/2 teaspoon paprika

3 to 4 dashes hot pepper sauce
Fresh lemon juice to taste
Salt and pepper to taste

Combine all ingredients.
Servings: 6.

Entrees

Baked Oysters
with Potato Border

1 pint shucked oysters with liquid
2 cups hot mashed potatoes
1/4 cup margarine, melted
4 ounces mushrooms, sliced
1 tablespoon onion, chopped
2 tablespoons green pepper, minced

Light cream
2 tablespoons cornstarch
1/2 teaspoon salt and pepper
1/4 cup pimento, chopped
2 tablespoons dry sherry
1 egg, beaten

Simmer the oysters in their own liquid for 5 minutes. Drain, saving the liquid. In a saucepan, heat the butter, and lightly saute mushrooms, onion and green pepper for 5 minutes. Add enough cream to oyster liquid to make 1-1/4 cups. Mix a little of the oyster liquid with cornstarch. Add the rest to a saucepan, and when it is hot, stir in the cornstarch mixture, continuing to stir until thick and smooth. Season to taste. Add oysters, pimento, and sherry to sauce, and pour into baking pan. Beat egg into mashed potatoes, and make border around top of casserole. Broil 5 minutes or until golden brown, about 4 inches from heat. Servings: 4.

Entrees

Baked Sea Bass Mediterranean

4 fillets (8 ounces) of sea bass
Olive oil
2 tomatoes, peeled, seeded
  and diced
1 red onion, sliced
1 red pepper, cut in strips
1 green pepper, cut in strips

8 black olives
4 bay leaves
4 cloves garlic, peeled
4 fresh basil leaves
2 pints cherry tomatoes
8 tablespoons whole butter
Salt and cayenne pepper to taste

Place the fish fillets in a baking dish, and lightly brush with olive oil. Saute the tomatoes, onion, peppers, olives and garlic in hot oil for 2 minutes. Pour over the fish, and add the basil and bay leaves. Bake in a 425 degree oven for 12 to 15 minutes or until the fish is firm. Meanwhile, puree the cherry tomatoes in a food processor or blender, then strain out the seeds and skin. Heat the puree in a sauce pan until boiling. Remove from heat, and add pieces of butter, one at a time, whisking until incorporated. Season with salt and cayenne. Spoon the sauce onto plates, and place the fish on the sauce. Top with the vegetables. Servings: 4.

Baked Shrimp
with Seasoned Bread Crumbs

2 pounds large shrimp, shelled
  with 1st section of tail left intact
3/4 cup fresh bread crumbs

Approximately 5-1/2 tablespoons
  red pepper and herb butter or
  tarragon pernod butter

Preheat oven to 500 degrees. In large buttered ovenproof serving dish, arrange shrimp with tails in air. Top flat surface of each shrimp with 1 teaspoon bread

Entrees

crumbs and 1/2 teaspoon flavored butter. Bake 5 minutes or until shrimp are opaque throughout.
Servings: 2-1/2 dozen.

Red Pepper and Herb Butter:

1/2 red bell pepper, cut in small pieces
1/2 teaspoon thyme
Pinch cayenne
2 scallions, chopped
1 tablespoon garlic, chopped
1 tablespoon parsley, chopped
1 stick unsalted butter,
  cut in pieces

Combine bell pepper, scallions, garlic, thyme, parsley and cayenne in food processor. Turn machine off and on until ingredients are minced, but not pureed. Add butter pieces, and process until blended. Transfer butter to sheet of plastic wrap, and roll into log shape, about 1-1/2 inches in diameter. Roll up in plastic, and twist ends securely. Freeze butter until firm, about 1-1/2 hours.
Yield: 10 tablespoons.

Tarragon Pernod Butter:

1-1/2 tablespoons shallot, chopped
1-1/2 teaspoons tarragon vinegar
1 teaspoon pernod
1 stick (1/4 pound) butter,
  unsalted cut in pieces
1-1/2 tablespoons fresh tarragon, chopped
  or 2 teaspoons dried
1/2 teaspoon coarsely cracked pepper

Combine shallot, tarragon vinegar, pernod and pepper in food processor. Turn machine off and on until ingredients are minced but not pureed. Add butter, and process until blended. Transfer butter to sheet of plastic wrap, and roll into log, about 1-1/2 inches in diameter. Roll up in plastic, and twist ends securely. Freeze until firm, about 1-1/2 hours.
Yield: 10 tablespoons.

Entrees

Baked Trout in Herb Butter

1/3 cup scallions, minced

2 sticks (1 cup) plus 2 tablespoons unsalted butter, softened

1/2 teaspoon worcestershire sauce

1/2 teaspoon salt

6 trout (6 to 8 ounces), cleaned, leave head and tail intact and pat dry

1 garlic clove, minced

1/2 cup dry white wine

1/2 cup tarragon vinegar

1 tablespoon dried tarragon, crumbled

1/4 teaspoon pepper

1 tablespoon dried rosemary, crumbled

Fresh parsley leaves, chopped

In a saucepan, cook scallions and garlic in 2 tablespoons butter over moderate heat, stirring occasionally until softened. Add wine, vinegar, worcestershire sauce and tarragon, and simmer mixture for 15 minutes or until liquid is reduced to about 2 tablespoons. Let the mixture cool. In a bowl, cream remaining 2 sticks butter, and stir in scallion herb mixture. Add salt and pepper. Spread herb butter in the bottom of a shallow baking pan just large enough to hold trout in one layer, and melt in preheated 375 degree oven. Rub inside of trout with rosemary, and salt to taste. Arrange trout in a pan, and bake in 375 degree oven for 6 minutes. Turn the trout, and bake for 6 to 10 minutes more or until it flakes. Transfer trout to a platter. Spoon the pan juices over, and garnish with parsley and lemon wedges. Serve.

Servings: 6.

Entrees

Beef with Peppers

24 ounces beef tender strips
  (1 inch long, 1/4 inch thick)
1 large onion, sliced
1 red pepper, sliced
1 green pepper, sliced
2 cloves garlic, chopped fine

3 ounces pimento, sliced
8 dashes hot sauce
Salt and pepper to taste
1 cup demi glace or brown sauce
Rice

Saute onions and peppers in small amount of oil. Add garlic, and shake pan. Add beef, and saute until rare, or medium rare. Add pimentos, spices and demi glace. Mix well, and serve over rice.
Servings: 4.

Blackened Fish

1 teaspoon salt
1 tablespoon garlic powder
2 teaspoons thyme
1 tablespoon dried parsley flakes
1 tablespoon basil

1 to 2 teaspoons cayenne pepper
1/4 teaspoon black pepper
4 fillets of redfish, red snapper, or other
  firm fish, about 1-1/2 pounds raw
1 tablespoon olive oil or corn oil

Combine the spices on a flat plate. Press the fish fillets firmly into the spices, coating both sides. Heat the oil to almost smoking in a heavy skillet. Cook the fish about 2-1/2 minutes on each side, for fillets not more than 3/4 inch thick. Serve immediately.
Servings: 4 (4-1/2 ounces each cooked weight).

Entrees

Blackened Red Fish

3 teaspoons salt, optional
1/2 teaspoon red pepper
1/2 teaspoon white pepper
1/4 teaspoon black pepper
1/4 teaspoon dried thyme
1/4 teaspoon dried basil

1/4 teaspoon dried oregano
2 teaspoons paprika
8 skinless boneless fillets of fish,
   preferably redfish, pompano or tilefish
   about 1/4 pound each (See note.)*
1/2 cup melted butter

Combine salt, red pepper, white pepper, black pepper, thyme, basil, oregano and paprika in a small bowl. Dip the fish pieces on both sides in butter. Sprinkle on both sides with seasoned mixture. Heat a black iron skillet over high heat, about 5 minutes or longer (the skillet cannot get too hot) until it is beyond the smoking stages and starts to lighten in color on the bottom. Add two or more fish pieces, and pour about a teaspoon of butter on top of each piece. The butter may flame up. Cook over high heat about 1 minute and a half. Turn the fish, and pour another teaspoon of butter over each piece. Cook about a minute and a half. Serve immediately. Continue until all fillets are cooked.

NOTE:* Redfish and pompano are ideal for this dish. If tilefish is used, you may have to split the fillets in half. Place the fillet on flat surface, hold your knife parallel to the surface and split in half through the center from one end to the other. Any fillet must not be more than an inch and a half thick.
Servings: 8.

Entrees

Boneless Breast of Chicken and Lobster au Grand Marnier

4 chicken breasts (skinned, boned and gently flattened, must be double breasted), marinated overnight in 1 cup orange juice
4 African lobster tails (3 ounces), poached in water with 1 sliced lemon, cooled and removed whole from shell
2 teaspoons grand marnier

Salt and pepper to taste
Worcestershire sauce
1 stick butter (4 ounces)
Paprika
1 bunch parsley, chopped
3 ounces toasted sliced almonds for garnish
Orange sections for garnish

Sauce Grand Marnier:

2 cups chicken sauce*
Juice of 1 orange

4 tablespoons butter
4 tablespoons grand marnier

To cook chicken: Put marinated chicken breasts on flat surface, and brush with 2 tablespoons melted butter. Sprinkle with salt, pepper, worcestershire, chopped parsley and grand marnier. Place lobster tail in center of chicken breast, and fold chicken firmly over tail. Turn over, and place in baking pan. Brush top of each with 4 tablespoons of melted butter. Dash with paprika. Bake at 375 degrees for 25 minutes. Do not overcook.

*To drippings from baked chicken breasts, add enough chicken stock to measure 2 cups of chicken sauce.

Sauce Grand Marnier Prep:

Bring 2 cups of chicken stock to a boil. Stir in juice of 1 orange and 4 tablespoons butter (may be thickened with cornstarch mixed with a little stock); put aside. Place remaining grand marnier in small pan, and warm. Light carefully, and pour while flaming into chicken sauce. To serve, glaze chicken breast with sauce grand marnier, and sprinkle with sliced almonds. Garnish with orange sections. Serve remaining sauce on side.

Servings: 4.

Entrees

Breaded Oysters with Garlic Butter Sauce

1 pint shucked oysters, drained
2 large eggs beaten lightly
  with 2 tablespoons water

2 cups fresh bread crumbs
1/4 cup clarified butter

Sauce:

2 garlic cloves, minced
1 green onion, minced
1/2 cup dry white wine
1/2 teaspoon worcestershire sauce

3 tablespoons butter, cut into bits
  and softened
1 tablespoon fresh lemon juice
2 tablespoons fresh parsley leaves, minced

Pat the oysters dry, coat them with the egg mixture, letting excess drip off, and roll them in bread crumbs. In a skillet, heat 2 tablespoons of clarified butter over moderate high heat until hot, and in it, cook half of the oysters for 2 minutes on each side or until golden. Transfer oysters carefully to serving dishes, and keep warm in a slow oven. Cook the remaining oysters in remaining butter the same way, and keep warm. To make the sauce: To a skillet, add garlic and green onion, and cook over moderate heat, stirring for 30 seconds. Add wine, and reduce by half. Add worcestershire sauce, salt and pepper to taste, reduce the heat to low, and swirl in the butter. Remove the pan from the heat, stir in the lemon juice and parsley, and spoon the sauce over the oysters. Serve.
Servings: 4.

Entrees

Brioche and Oyster Pudding

6 tablespoons unsalted butter, softened
1/4 cup celery, chopped
4 ounces smoked ham,
  coarsely chopped
1 sprig fresh thyme or
  1/8 teaspoon dried
1 cup heavy cream
2 whole eggs
3 egg yolks
2 tablespoons fresh chives, minced
1/2 teaspoon salt

1 dozen oysters, shucked and coarsely
  chopped, liquid reserved
1 medium leek (white, tender green),
  chopped
12 parsley stems
1-1/2 cups milk
6 brioche rolls (10 ounces total),
  ends trimmed, sliced lengthwise
  3/8 inches thick
1-1/2 tablespoons fresh parsley, minced
4 to 5 drops hot pepper sauce

Preheat the oven to 350 degrees. In a large skillet, melt 1 tablespoon butter. Add leeks, celery, ham, parsley stems and thyme, and cook over moderate heat until leeks soften, about 5 minutes. Add milk, cream, and cook at bare simmer for 45 minutes. Meanwhile, lightly butter both sides of brioche slices using 4 tablespoons butter. Place on cookie sheet, and bake about 15 minutes, turning once, until lightly browned (leave oven on). Use remaining 1 tablespoon butter to grease a 9 inch springform pan. Arrange toasted brioche slices in the pan in 3 overlapping rows. Strain flavored milk and cream, pressing solids to extract as much liquid as possible. The recipe can be prepared at this point a day ahead. Cover, and refrigerate. Reheat milk before proceeding. In a medium bowl, beat together whole eggs and egg yolks. Slowly whisk in 1 cup of hot milk, then whisk in remainder. Add chives, parsley, salt, hot sauce and oysters with their liquid. Wrap the outside of the springform pan in a double sheet of aluminum foil. Pour oyster mixture into pan, distributing oysters evenly if necessary. Place the springform in a roasting pan, and set in oven. Pour in enough hot water to reach sides of springform pan. Bake for 35 to 40 minutes or until knife inserted 3 inches comes out clean from center. Transfer to a rack, uncover, and let rest 10 minutes. Run a knife around edge, and remove outer ring of pan. Using a large spatula, carefully slide pudding onto a large round platter. Serve warm or at room temperature.
Servings: 8.

Entrees

Cajun Shepherds Pie

1-1/2 pounds ground beef
2 eggs, beaten lightly
1/4 pound (1 stick) plus 3 tablespoons
  unsalted butter
1/2 cup green bell pepper,
  finely chopped
1/2 teaspoon hot sauce
3/4 cup evaporated milk
1 teaspoon salt
1-1/2 cups carrots, julienned*
1-1/2 cups zucchini, julienned*
1 cup yellow squash, julienned*

1/2 pound ground pork
1/2 cup very dry bread crumbs
3/4 cup onions, finely chopped
3/4 cup celery, chopped
1 tablespoon plus 1 teaspoon garlic,
  minced
1 tablespoon worcestershire sauce
2 pounds potatoes, peeled and quartered
1 teaspoon white pepper
1 cup onions, julienned*
Very hot cajun sauce for beef

Meat Seasoning Mix:
2 teaspoons cayenne
1-1/4 teaspoons black pepper
3/4 teaspoon ground cumin

1-1/2 teaspoons salt
1-1/4 teaspoons white pepper
3/4 teaspoon dried thyme leaves

Vegetable Seasoning Mix:
1/2 teaspoon salt
1/4 teaspoon onion powder
1/4 teaspoon cayenne

1/4 teaspoon white pepper
1/4 teaspoon garlic powder

*Julienne 1/8 inch thick and 2 inches long. Cut onion and carrot similarly.

In ungreased baking pan, combine beef and pork. Mix in egg and bread crumbs by hand until thoroughly mixed. Set aside. In saucepan, combine 3 tablespoons butter, chopped onions, celery, garlic, bell pepper, worcestershire, hot sauce and meat seasoning mix. Saute over high heat, about 5 minutes, stirring frequently and scraping pan bottom well. Remove from heat, and cool. Add sauteed veg-

etable mixture and 1/4 cup milk to meat, and mix well by hand. Form into 12x8 inch loaf, and center in the pan. Bake at 450 degrees until brown on top, about 30 minutes. Remove from pan, and pour off drippings, reserving 2-1/2 tablespoons. Set aside drippings and meat. Meanwhile, boil potatoes until tender. Drain, reserving about 1 cup of water. Place potatoes while still hot in large mixing bowl with remaining 1 stick butter, 1/2 cup milk, salt and white pepper. Stir with wooden spoon until broken up. Beat with metal whisk or electric mixer with paddle, until creamy and velvet smooth. NOTE: Mix in some of reserved potato water, if potatoes are not creamy enough. In large skillet, combine reserved drippings with carrots, onion and vegetable seasoning mix. Saute over high heat for 1-1/2 minutes, stirring frequently. Add zucchini and yellow squash, and continue sauteing until vegetables are noticeably brighter in color, about 3 to 4 minutes. Remove from heat. Mound undrained vegetables on top of meat loaf, away from edges. Layer the mashed potatoes evenly over top of vegetables, and to edges of meat, using all potatoes. Bake at 525 degrees until brown on top, about 8 to 10 minutes. Serve with very hot cajun sauce on side.
Servings: 6-8.

Entrees

Capaccio with Mustard Sauce

1 pound fillet of beef, well-trimmed
3 tablespoons olive oil
3 tablespoons madeira
1/4 cup sugar
1/4 cup salt

1 tablespoon pepper
*Mustard sauce
Gherkins
Pickled onions

Place beef in loaf pan or pie plate, just slightly larger than meat. Whisk madiera, sugar, salt and pepper in small bowl until mixed. Pour over beef. Turn beef to coat all sides. Cover beef with a pan or plate. Weight it down with 2 to 3 cans. Refrigerate, turning occasionally 2 days. Place beef with marinade in plastic bag, and seal. Refrigerate, turning bag occasionally for 24 hours. Make mustard sauce. Remove beef from marinade; pat dry. Cut beef across grain into paper thin slices. Serve with mustard sauce, gherkins and onions.
Servings: 6.

Mustard Sauce:
1/3 cup dijon mustard
1 clove garlic, crushed
1/4 cup vegetable oil
1 teaspoon fresh chives, finely chopped

2 teaspoons white vinegar
2 tablespoons sugar
1 teaspoon fresh parsley, finely chopped

Mix mustard, vinegar, garlic and sugar in small bowl. Gradually whisk in oil. Stir in parsley and chives. Serve.
Yield: 2/3 cup.

Entrees

Catfish Mousse with Crayfish Sauce

8 ounces skinned catfish fillets
1 egg yolk
1/2 cup heavy cream
Pinch of cayenne

1 egg
1/4 cup milk
1/2 teaspoon salt
2 cups crayfish sauce*

Grind catfish through finest blade of meat grinder, or blend until smooth in food processor. Press fish through fine sieve into medium mixing bowl. In another bowl, lightly beat egg, egg yolk, milk and cream. Whisk into fish. Beat in salt and cayenne pepper, and mix thoroughly. Divide mixture evenly into 4 buttered molds, filling each about 3/4 full. Put the molds in a large baking pan, and pour enough boiling water around to reach halfway up the sides. Bake in a preheated 325 degree oven until mousses have set and are firm to touch, about 20 minutes. Unmold onto individual plates, and top with crayfish sauce.

Crayfish Sauce:
3 tablespoons olive oil
2 pounds crayfish
1 leek, cleaned and chopped (white)
1 clove garlic, minced
2 sprigs fresh thyme
1 cup dry white wine
1 cup heavy cream

3 tablespoons vegetable oil
1 medium carrot, peeled and chopped
1 rib celery, chopped
3 tablesooons parsley, chopped
6 tablespoons bourbon
1-1/2 tablespoons tomato paste
Salt and pepper to taste

Heat oils over medium high heat in a frying pan. Add crayfish, cover frying pan, and cook 5 minutes, shaking often. Remove crayfish from the pan, setting aside 40 of most attractive for garnish. Separate tails from bodies, and remove meat from tails with finger. Set aside. Put bodies and tailshells in a food processor fitted with metal blade, and blend to crush. Reheat frying pan over medium heat, and add carrot, leek, celery, garlic, parsley, thyme and crushed crayfish shells. Cook gently for 5 minutes, stirring occasionally. Add bourbon, and cook over

155

Entrees

medium heat until reduced by half, 2-3 minutes. Add white wine, and stir in tomato paste. Return to boil, and reduce by 1/3, 4-5 minutes. Stir in cream, and reduce heat. Simmer slowly for 7 to 10 minutes. Add salt and pepper to taste. Strain into a bowl, pressing mixture with wooden spoon to extract as much liquid as possible. Reheat for 5 minutes, and serve with catfish mousse. Garnish mousse with crayfish tail meat and one whole crayfish per plate.
Servings: 8.

Catfish with Mustard Sauce

Mustard Sauce:

2 tablespoons unsalted butter
1 onion, chopped fine
1/2 cup dry white wine or vermouth
1 cup heavy cream

1/2 cup flat leaf parsley, chopped
2 tablespoons dijon mustard
Salt and black pepper to taste

Fish:

oil for deep frying
1/2 cup flour
1/2 cup white oatmeal

2 pounds catfish, cleaned and skinned
Salt and black pepper to taste

In a saucepan, melt butter. Add onion, and saute over low heat, stirring frequently until softened but not browned, 3 to 4 minutes. Add wine or vermouth, and cook uncovered, over medium heat until liquid is absorbed, about 5 minutes. Add cream, and reduce over medium heat by about 1/4, about 3 minutes. Remove from heat, and stir in parsley and mustard. Taste and season with salt and pepper. Set aside. Heat oil in deep fat fryer to 370 degrees. Combine flour and cornmeal. Dry fish well with paper towels, season with salt and pepper, and dredge in flour and cornmeal mixture. Carefully fry catfish until golden brown, about 4 minutes. Drain well on paper towel. Reheat sauce gently, and serve with catfish.
Servings: 4.

Entrees

Ceviche

1 pound fresh fish fillets,
  cut in 1 inch pieces
Juice of 6-8 limes
1/2 cup red onion, minced
2 cloves garlic, minced
2-3 jalapenos, canned or fresh,
  seeded and chopped

1 fresh tomato, peeled,
  seeded, and chopped
2 tablespoons olive oil
1/4 cup fresh coriander leaves,
  chopped
Salt and freshly ground black pepper
  to taste

Snapper, flounder or any white fish will do. Scallops also work well. Cover diced fish with lime juice, and refrigerate 4-6 hours. (Fish will be firm and white when done.) Drain fish. Add rest of ingredients, toss lightly and refrigerate 30 minutes. Season, and serve in scallop shells or on a lettuce leaf.
Servings: 4.

Chicken A L'Orange

2-1/2 pounds chicken pieces, skinned
1 cup orange juice
1/2 cup white wine
Paprika to taste

1 teaspoon peanut oil
1 medium onion, diced
1 large tomato, diced
4 ounces fresh mushrooms, diced

Preheat oven to 375 degrees. Place chicken pieces in a shallow baking pan. Combine the orange juice and white wine, and pour them over the chicken. Sprinkle seasonings over chicken. Bake at 375 degrees for 35 minutes. While chicken is baking, prepare the sauce by brushing a skillet with the peanut oil and heating over medium-high heat. Add the onions, tomato and mushrooms, and saute, stirring constantly. When onions are translucent, spoon the sauce over the chicken, and bake an additional 10 to 15 minutes.
Servings: 6 (3-1/2 ounces each cooked weight plus sauce).

Entrees

Chicken and Corned Beef Hash

1 whole chicken (2-1/2 pounds)
1 bunch fresh thyme or
  1-1/2 teaspoons dried
3/4 teaspoon fresh black pepper
1 cup clarified butter
2 medium red bell peppers,
  cut lengthwise 1/2 inch strips
6 poached eggs

1 head garlic, separated into cloves
1-1/2 teaspoons dried tarragon
1-1/2 teaspoons salt
1 pound red potatoes
1 large onion, sliced
3/4 pound corned beef, thinly sliced
1/2 cup parsley, chopped

Preheat oven to 400 degrees. Stuff chicken with garlic, thyme and tarragon. Sprinkle inside and out with 1/2 teaspoon salt and 1/4 teaspoon black pepper. Place chicken untrussed on rack, and roast until meat is just a bit underdone, 40 minutes. Let cool. Using fingers, remove chicken meat from bones in large 1 to 2 inch pieces. Meanwhile boil potatoes until tender but still firm, about 15 minutes. Let cool, cut into 1/4 inch thick slices. In a large heavy skillet, heat half clarified butter over high heat, about 1 minute. Arrange half potatoes and onion slices in even layer over bottom of pan, and place half peppers on top. Cook until potatoes begin to brown, about 20 minutes. Turn potatoes, and continue to cook until potatoes are browned and peppers are soft, 15 minutes. Sprinkle with 1/2 teaspoon salt and 1/4 teaspoon pepper. Transfer vegetables to a piece of aluminum foil, cover loosely and keep warm in oven. Repeat with remaining potatoes, onions and peppers. Combine the 2 batches of potatoes, onions and peppers, and toss with chicken and corned beef. Cook over moderate heat until meat is warmed through and chicken is fully cooked, 5 minutes. Add parsley, and toss. Divide hash among 6 warmed plates, and top with poached egg. Serve. Servings: 6.

Entrees

Chicken and Ham Jambalaya

Seasoning Mix:

2 whole bay leaves
1-1/2 teaspoons cayenne
1-1/4 teaspoons white pepper
3/4 teaspoon dried thyme leaves

1-1/2 teaspoons salt
1-1/2 teaspoons dried oregano leaves
1 teaspoon black pepper

2-1/2 tablespoons chicken fat or
  pork lard or beef fat
1-1/2 cups onions, chopped
1 cup celery, chopped
1/2 cup chicken, cut into
  bite size (3 ounces)
3/4 cup canned tomato sauce
2 cups seafood stock
2 cups uncooked rice, converted
1-1/2 dozen oysters in liquid
  (10 ounces)

2/3 cup tasso (about 3 ounces), chopped
1/2 cup andouille smoked sausage
  (3 ounces), chopped
3/4 cup green bell peppers, chopped
1-1/2 teaspoons garlic, minced
4 medium size tomatoes, peeled
  and chopped (1 pound)
1/2 cup green onions, chopped
1-1/2 dozen medium shrimp
  (1/2 pound), peeled

Combine seasoning mix ingredients in small bowl, and set aside. In a large saucepan, melt fat over medium heat. Add tasso and andouille, and saute until crisp, about 5 to 8 minutes, stirring frequently. Add onions, celery and bell pepper, stirring occasionally. Saute until tender but still firm, about 5 minutes, and scrape pan bottom well. Add chicken. Raise heat to high, and cook 1 minute, stirring constantly. Reduce heat to medium. Add seasoning mix and minced garlic. Cook about 3 minutes, stirring constantly 5 to 8 minutes. Add tomatoes and sauce; cook 7 minutes, and stir often. Stir in stock, and bring to boil. Next, stir in green onions, and cook about 2 minutes, stirring once or twice. Add rice, shrimp and oysters; stir well. Remove from heat. Transfer to ungreased 8x8 inch baking pan. Cover pan with aluminum foil, and bake at 350 degrees until rice is tender but still a bit crunchy, about 20 to 30 minutes. Remove bay leaves, and serve immediately.
Servings: 4 (main course).

Entrees

Chicken Big Mamou on Pasta

6 quarts hot water
3 tablespoons salt

1/4 cup vegetable oil
1-1/2 pounds fresh spaghetti
  or 1 pound dry

Seasoning Mix:
2 teaspoons dried thyme leaves
1 teaspoon white pepper
1/2 teaspoon dried basil leaves

1-1/4 teaspoons cayenne
3/4 teaspoon black pepper

1 pound plus 4 tablespoons
  unsalted butter
4 medium size garlic cloves,
  peeled
3-1/4 cups chicken stock
1 tablespoon plus 1 teaspoon hot sauce

2 tablespoons sugar
1 cup onions, finely chopped
2 teaspoons garlic, minced
2 tablespoons worcestershire sauce
2 cans (16 ounces) tomato sauce
2 cups green onions, finely chopped

Chicken Seasoning Mix:
1-1/2 tablespoons salt
1-1/2 teaspoons garlic powder
1 teaspoon black pepper
1/2 teaspoon dried basil leaves

1-1/2 teaspoon white pepper
1-1/2 teaspoons cayenne
1 teaspoon ground cumin

2 pounds boneless chicken, cut into 1/2 inch cubes

Place hot water, oil and salt in large pot over high heat. Cover, and bring to boil. When water reaches a rolling boil, add small amounts spaghetti at a time, breaking up oil patches as you drop spaghetti in. Return to boil, and cook to al dente stage (4 minutes fresh, 7 minutes dried). Do not overcook. During cooking time, use a wooden or spaghetti spoon to lift spaghetti out of water by spoonfuls,

and shake strands back into boiling water. When cooked, immediately drain spaghetti into colander. Run cold water over strands. If using dried spaghetti, first rinse with hot water to wash off starch. After pasta has cooled thoroughly, about 2 to 3 minutes, pour liberal amount of vegetable oil in hands, and toss spaghetti. Set aside in colander. Meanwhile, combine seasoning mix ingredients in small bowl, and set aside. In saucepan, combine 1-1/2 sticks butter with onions and garlic cloves. Saute over medium heat for 5 minutes, stirring occasionally. Add minced garlic and seasoning mix. Continue cooking over medium heat stirring often until onions are dark brown but not burned, about 8 to 10 minutes. Add 2-1/2 cups stock, worcestershire and hot sauce. Bring to fast simmer, and cook about 3 minutes stirring often. Stir in tomato sauce, and bring mixture to boil. Stir in sugar and 1 cup green onions. Gently simmer uncovered about 40 minutes, stirring occasionally. Combine ingredients of chicken seasoning mix in small bowl, and mix well. Sprinkle over chicken, rubbing with hands. In large skillet, melt 1-1/2 sticks butter over medium heat. Add remaining 1 cup green onions, and saute over high heat, about 3 minutes. Add chicken, and continue cooking for 10 minutes, stirring frequently. When tomato sauce has simmered about 40 minutes, stir in chicken mixture, and heat through. Melt 2 tablespoons butter in large skillet over medium heat. Add a bit less than 2 cups spaghetti, and beat 1 minute, stirring over medium heat. Add a bit less than 2 cups spaghetti, and beat 1 minute, stirring constantly. Add 1-1/4 cups chicken sauce and 2 tablespoons of remaining stock, and heat thoroughly, stirring frequently. Remove from heat.
Servings: 6.

Entrees

Chicken Breasts
with Mustard Persillade

2 whole chicken breasts, split,
  skin and rib bones left on

Persillade* (recipe follows)
1/4 cup dijon mustard

Rinse chicken breasts under cold running water; pat dry with paper towel. Heat oven to 425 degrees. Spread persillade in an even layer on a large sheet of waxed paper. Using a pastry brush, paint skin side of each chicken breast generously with dijon mustard. Dip mustard sides into persillade, and press firmly to make crumbs adhere. Place chicken breasts, crumb side up, in a baking dish. Bake until juices run clear when pierced with a skewer and topping is a deep golden brown, about 20 to 25 minutes. Serve.

*Persillade:
1/3 cup firmly packed parsley leaves
2 medium garlic cloves, peeled
4 tablespoons butter

1 cup fresh bread crumbs (2 slices)
Salt and pepper to taste

Insert metal blade in food processor container. Tear bread in pieces, and process to medium-fine crumbs; set aside. Process parsley until finely minced; set aside. With machine running, drop garlic cloves through food chute; process until minced. Place garlic and butter in a medium skillet. Cook on low heat until soft but not brown. Add bread crumbs to skillet, and stir over medium heat until lightly browned. Stir in parsley, salt and pepper to taste.
Servings: 4.

Entrees

Chicken in Red Pepper and Tomato Sauce

1 clove garlic
1/2 cup olive oil
3-1/2 pounds chicken, cut into
  serving pieces
1/2 pound smoked ham,
  cut into 1/4 inch strips

1 onion, minced
6 red bell peppers, roasted
6 tomatoes, peeled, seeded
  and chopped

In a large skillet, cook garlic in oil over moderate heat until golden brown, and discard. Pat chicken dry, and season with salt and pepper, and cook in oil over moderate heat for 10 minutes or until golden brown. Transfer to plate. Return chicken to skillet, and add ham and onion. Cook mixture over moderate low heat, stirring and shaking skillet for 5 minutes. Add peppers and tomatoes. Simmer for 10 to 15 minutes or until chicken is tender and sauce is thickened.
Servings: 4.   Nutritional Analysis: page 435.

Entrees

Chicken in Succotash

1 chicken (3-1/2 pounds), cut into
  serving pieces
2 tablespoons bacon fat or mixture of
  1 tablespoon butter and
  1 tablespoon oil
1 onion, chopped
3/4 cup canned chicken broth
10 ounce package frozen baby lima
  beans, thawed
1 sprig of thyme or 1/4 teaspoon dried,
  crumbled
1 sprig chervil or 1/4 teaspoon dried,
  crumbled
1-1/3 to 1-1/2 cups heavy cream
1-1/2 cups corn
Fresh lemon juice to taste
2 tablespoons fresh parsley leaves,
  minced
2 tablespoons snipped fresh chives

Pat chicken dry, and season with salt and pepper. In a large skillet, heat fat over moderate heat until hot but not smoking. Cook chicken in batches for 10 to 12 minutes or until golden on both sides. Transfer to paper towels to drain. Pour off all but 1 tablespoon fat from skillet, add onion, and cook over moderate heat, stirring for 2 minutes. Add broth, and deglaze the skillet over high heat, scraping up any brown bits. Place chicken in skillet, putting breast pieces on top. Simmer, covered over moderately low heat for 10 minutes. Add lima beans, thyme and chervil. Simmer mixture covered for 8 to 10 minutes or until chicken is tender. Transfer chicken with tongs to platter. Add 1-1/3 cups of cream to skillet, boil liquid until thickened slightly, skimming any fat that has accumulated around edges, and stir in corn. Simmer mixture for 1 to 2 minutes. Return chicken to pan. Simmer for 3 to 5 minutes or until chicken is reheated. Discard thyme and chervil, if fresh, or leave, if dried. Add enough of remaining cream to thin sauce, to desired consistency. Add lemon juice, salt and pepper to taste. Remove skillet from heat, and stir in parsley and chives.
Servings: 4.

Entrees

Chicken Porto

1/4 cup dried currants
1 cup chicken stock or
   canned chicken broth
1-1/4 pounds chicken breasts,
   skinless, boneless, cut lengthwise
   into 1/2 inch strips

1-1/4 cups ruby port
3/4 cup currant jelly
1-1/2 tablespoons cornstarch
1/2 cup flour
1/2 cup clarified butter
1/2 pound mushrooms, sliced thin

In small bowl, let currants soak in port, covered loosely for at least 12 hours. In large saucepan, whisk together port mixture, stock, jelly and cornstarch. Bring mixture to boil over moderate heat, whisking. Simmer, and stir occasionally for 10 minutes or until it is reduced to about 1-1/2 cups. Season the chicken with salt and pepper, and dredge it in flour, shaking off excess. In large skillet, heat clarified butter over high heat, until it is hot. Saute chicken for 2 minutes on each side or until golden. Add mushrooms, and cook mixture over moderate heat, stirring for 2 minutes or until mushrooms are browned lightly. Add port mixture, and bring it to boil. Cook mixture for 1 minute. Add salt and pepper to taste. Servings: 4.

Entrees

Chicken Stir Fry
with Summer Squash

4 skinless boneless chicken
  breast halves
1 egg white
1 tablespoon dry white wine
3/4 teaspoon salt
1 tablespoon cornstarch
3 tablespoons olive oil
1/2 medium onion, finely chopped

2-3 cloves garlic, finely chopped
1/2 pound zucchini (about 2)
  cut into julienne strips
1/2 pound yellow squash (about 2)
  cut into julienne strips
1/4 teaspoon finely ground pepper
1/4 cup basil leaves, coarsely chopped
Fresh spinach leaves for garnish

Trim fat and/or tendons from chicken. Cut into strips. Combine egg white, wine, 1/2 teaspoon salt and cornstarch in food processor, and mix until it becomes a very smooth emulsion, about 1 minute. Pour egg white mixture into a bowl, add chicken, and toss to coat. Let marinate in refrigerator overnight. When ready to assemble, bring a large pot of water to a boil, reduce to simmer, and add chicken, stirring gently to separate the pieces. Simmer until chicken is almost done, but still slightly pink in center, about 2 minutes. Do not let water boil. Drain into colander, and rinse under cold water to cool. Drain well. Dry with paper towels. In a large skillet or wok, heat oil, add onion, and saute over moderate heat for 1 minute. Add garlic, and cook for 30 seconds. Add zucchini and yellow squash, and stir fry until warmed through, about 3 minutes. Add chicken, and stir fry to warm through and finish cooking about 1 minute. Add pepper and basil, and toss well. Turn out onto platter. Serve warm or at room temperature.
Servings: 4.

Entrees

Chicken Tetrazzini

1/4 pound spaghetti
1/4 pound mushrooms, sliced thin
1/3 cup green bell pepper,
  coarsely chopped
3-1/2 tablespoons unsalted butter
2 tablespoons flour
3/4 cup milk

1/3 cup canned chicken broth
3 tablespoons heavy cream
1 large egg yolk
4 teaspoons medium dry sherry
1-1/4 cups cooked chicken or turkey
  meat, cut into 1/2 inch pieces
1/2 cup sharp cheddar, grated

In pot of boiling salted water cook the spaghetti for 10 to 12 minutes or until al dente, and drain. Rinse spaghetti, and drain well. In a skillet, cook mushrooms and bell pepper in 1-1/2 tablespoons butter over moderately low heat, stirring until softened; reserve. In heavy saucepan, melt remaining 2 tablespoons butter over moderately low heat; stir in flour. Cook roux, stirring for 3 minutes. Add milk and broth in stream. Whisking, bring mixture to boil, and remove pan from heat. In small bowl whisk together cream and egg yolk. Add 1/2 cup hot milk mixture in a steam, and whisk yolk mixture into milk mixture. Return pan to heat. Cook sauce over low heat, stirring until hot but not boiling. Stir in sherry and chicken. Transfer mixture to a large bowl. Add spaghetti, vegetable mixture, salt and pepper to taste. Toss mixture well. Transfer to a 3 cup gratin dish. Sprinkle with cheddar cheese. Bake mixture in preheated 375 degree oven for 25 minutes or until heated through and cheddar is bubbling.
Servings: 2.

Entrees

Chinese Lobster or Crabmeat Casserole

2 pounds lobster or crabmeat
1/4 cup butter or margarine
1 egg lightly beaten
3 tablespoons onion, minced
1 tablespoon soy sauce
1 tablespoon cornstarch
1/3 cup water

2 cups hot cooked rice
1 cup bean sprouts
1 tablespoon ginger, minced,
  candied or preserved
1 tablespoon orange rind, grated
Salt to taste

Heat the butter in a medium casserole in 300 degree oven. When it is melted, stir in the lobster or crab, picked over and broken into good sized lumps. Return to oven. Blend egg, onion, soy sauce and cornstarch mixed with water. Stir into the lobster, and continue to bake about 10 minutes, stirring 2 to 3 times. Remove casserole from oven, and push lobster mixture into the middle of casserole. Mix the rice and bean sprouts, and arrange them around the lobster. Top the rice with ginger and orange rind. Cover, and bake 20 minutes. Servings: 4.

Entrees

Clam-Hash Cakes

48 fresh clams or 1 cup canned, drained, minced

1/4 pound lean sliced bacon, chopped

1 small onion, minced

1 pound baking potatoes, peeled, chopped fine and reserved in a bowl of cold water

2 tablespoons fresh parsley leaves, minced

3 large eggs, beaten lightly

2 tablespoons butter or margarine

1 teaspoon drained bottled horseradish or to taste

1 teaspoon fresh lemon juice or to taste

In a skillet, cook bacon over moderate heat, stirring occasionally until crisp and golden brown. Transfer bacon with a slotted spoon to paper towels, and drain, reserving bacon fat in a bowl. In a skillet, cook onion in 1 tablespoon of reserved fat over moderate low heat until softened, and transfer to a large bowl. In a skillet, cook potatoes that have been drained and patted dry in 2 tablespoons of reserved fat. Cook over moderate high heat, stirring until tender, and transfer to the bowl with the onion. Stir into bowl the bacon, minced clams, 1 tablespoon of parsley, eggs, salt and pepper to taste. Combine mixture well. Heat large griddle or large skillet over moderate high heat, until hot. Brush griddle, with some of the reserved fat. Drop several scant 1/4 cups of clam mixture on griddle, and with fork, pat mixture into neat cakes about 1/4 inch thick. Cook for 1 minute on each side or until golden brown. In a saucepan, melt butter or margarine over moderately low heat. Stir in horseradish, the remaining 1 tablespoon parsley and lemon juice. Drizzle sauce over clam hash cakes. Garnish with lemon and parsley, and serve.

Servings: 4.

Entrees

Coconut Fried Shrimp

Shrimp
 (approximately 6 shrimp per serving)
1-1/4 cups flour
1/2 tablespoon double action
 baking powder

1/2 tablespoon salt
1 cup milk
1 whole egg
3 tablespoons butter, melted
Coconut, shredded long

Shell, and devein shrimp, leaving tail on. Split shrimp without separating. Sift flour with baking powder and salt, adding milk, egg and melted butter to make batter. Beat well. Dip each shrimp in batter, holding by tail, and let excess drain off. Roll in shredded coconut, and deep fry at 375 degrees until golden. Serve immediately.
Servings: 6-7.

Entrees

Cold Shrimp
with Four Herb Mayonnaise

2-1/4 teaspoons salt
1 egg yolk
1/4 teaspoon dijon mustard
1 tablespoon dry white wine
Pinch of sugar
3/4 cup safflower or vegetable oil
1 tablespoon warm water
2 tablespoons parsley, minced
2 tablespoons fresh basil, minced

3-1/2 pounds large shrimp, shelled
  with last section of tail intact
1-1/2 tablespoons lemon juice
5 to 6 drops hot pepper sauce
1 teaspoon anchovy paste
1/4 cup extra virgin olive oil
3 tablespoons chives, minced
3 tablespoons fresh tarragon, minced
  or 2 teaspoons dried

Bring a large pot of water to boil with 2 teaspoons salt. Add shrimp, and cook until shrimp are loosely curled and opaque, 2 minutes for medium shrimp, 2 to 3 minutes for large. Drain under cold running water, and pat dry with paper towels. Cover with damp towel, and refrigerate until serving time. (Shrimp can be peeled up to 5 hours ahead.) In a medium bowl, combine egg yolk, mustard, lemon juice, wine, hot sauce, sugar, anchovy paste and remaining 1/4 teaspoon salt. Whisk until thoroughly blended. Gradually whisk in safflower and olive oil, drop by drop at first, then in a thin stream. When all has been incorporated, whisk in 1 tablespoon warm water and fresh herbs. Serve immediately. To store, cover, and refrigerate up to 6 hours.
Servings: 5 dozen.

Entrees

Country Captain

1 chicken, cut in serving pieces
Salt, pepper, paprika
2 tablespoons butter
2 tablespoons olive oil
1 large onion, diced
1 green pepper, diced
4 cloves garlic, minced
1/2 pound mushrooms, sliced
1 can (14-1/2 ounces) tomatoes
1 cup parsley, finely minced

2 tablespoons dijon mustard
2 teaspoons worcestershire
2 tablespoons curry powder (or to taste)
1 teaspoon dry thyme or 1 tablespoon
  fresh
Salt to taste
Pinch of cayenne (or to taste)
1/3 cup currants
1/2 cup toasted almonds

Season chicken pieces well with salt, pepper and paprika. Brown chicken in butter and oil. Saute vegetables in oil. Add tomatoes and other ingredients, and simmer 5 minutes. Replace chicken in fry pan or baking dish, spoon sauce over, cover, and cook 25 to 30 minutes on medium heat, or until chicken is very tender. Add currants, and simmer 5 more minutes. Garnish with toasted almonds, and serve.
Servings: 4.

Country Ham with Redeyed Gravy

2 slices (1/4 inch thick) country ham,
  uncooked
1 tablespoons vegetable oil

1 cup strong black coffee
2 tablespoons all-purpose flour
1/2 teaspoon paprika

Cut gashes in fat to keep ham from curling. Saute ham in oil in a heavy skillet over low heat for 3 to 4 minutes each side. Remove ham from skillet, and keep warm. Combine coffee and flour. Add to pan drippings, stirring constantly, until thickened. Add paprika. Serve with ham.
Servings: 2.

Entrees

Crab/Artichoke/Mushroom Casserole

1 can (15 ounces) artichoke hearts
1/2 pound fresh mushrooms, sauteed
2-1/2 tablespoons flour
1/2 teaspoon salt
1/4 cup medium dry sherry
Red pepper to taste

1 pound crabmeat
4 tablespoons butter
1 cup cream
1 teaspoon worcestershire sauce
Paprika to taste
1/4 cup parmesan cheese

Place the artichoke hearts in the bottom of a baking dish, sprinkle with crabmeat, and top with sauteed mushrooms. Melt the butter in a saucepan, add remaining ingredients, except cheese, and cook, stirring well after each addition to form a smooth sauce. Pour the sauce over the artichoke crab layers, and sprinkle cheese on top. Bake for 20 minutes at 375 degrees.
Servings: 4.

Crabmeat Broccoli Casserole

12 slices bread
2-1/2 cups milk
1 cup mayonnalse
7 hard cooked eggs, finely chopped
1 pound fresh crabmeat

1 tablespoon plus 1 teaspoon fresh
  parsley, minced
2 packages (10 ounces) frozen broccoli
4 ounces sharp cheddar cheese,
  shredded

Remove crust from bread. Cut bread into 1/2 inch cubes. Combine bread cubes, milk and mayonnaise, and stir well. Cover, and refrigerate for 30 minutes. Remove mixture from refrigerator, and stir in eggs, crabmeat, onion and parsley. Cook broccoli according to package directions, and drain well. Arrange broccoli in lightly greased hotel pan. Spoon crabmeat mixture evenly over broccoli. Bake, uncovered, at 325 degrees for 40 minutes. Sprinkle with cheese, and bake an additional 5 minutes or until cheese melts.
Servings: 4.

Entrees

Crab Stuffed Shrimp

1 dozen large shrimp
1 medium onion, minced
1/2 medium size green pepper,
  finely minced
1/2 cup celery, finely minced
1/4 cup margarine, melted
1 pound crabmeat
2 teaspoons worcestershire sauce

1/8 teaspoon red pepper
1 tablespoon prepared mustard
1 egg, beaten
1/2 cup mayonnaise
3/4 cup cracker crumbs
Paprika
1/4 cup margarine, melted

Peel shrimp, leaving tails on, devein, and butterfly. Cook shrimp in boiling water for 1 minute. Drain, and place in shallow baking dish. Saute onion, green pepper and celery in 1/4 cup margarine in heavy skillet until tender; set aside. Combine crabmeat and next 6 ingredients. Mixing lightly, stir in sauteed vegetables. Top each shrimp with 3 tablespoons crabmeat mixture. Sprinkle with paprika, and drizzle 1/4 cup butter over shrimp. Bake at 350 degrees for 20 minutes. Broil 6 minutes, basting occasionally with margarine in bottom of pan. Servings: 4-6.

Entrees

Creole Gumbo

1 pound okra, sliced
3 tablespoons peanut oil
1/2 pound smoked ham, diced
2 quarts chicken broth
2 bay leaves
4 cloves garlic, minced

1 bunch green onions, chopped
3 teaspoons parsley, chopped
1/8 teaspoon cayenne pepper
1 tablespoon red wine vinegar
Salt, black pepper and hot sauce to taste
1-2 pounds shrimp, peeled and deveined

1-4 fresh tomatoes, peeled, seeded, chopped
Optional ingredients: diced cooked chicken, hot smoked sausage, crabmeat, oysters, fish

Brown okra in hot oil. Add the ham, and saute. Add chicken broth, vegetables and seasonings, and simmer 3 hours. Season the soup to taste. At this point, it may be refrigerated overnight. When ready to serve, bring soup to a simmer, stir in shrimp, bring it back to a simmer, turn off heat, and cover for 5 minutes. Serve immediately.
Servings: 8.

Entrees

Crustless Ham Quiche

1/2 pound fresh mushrooms, sliced
2 tablespoons margarine, melted
4 eggs
1 cup sour cream
1 cup small curd cottage cheese
1/2 cup parmesan cheese

1/4 cup all purpose flour
1 teaspoon onion powder
6 to 8 drops hot sauce
2 cups shredded monterey
  jack cheese
1/2 cup cooked ham, chopped

Saute mushrooms in butter in medium skillet until lightly browned. Drain well, and set aside. Combine next 7 ingredients in blender. Process until well blended. Combine egg mixture, mushrooms, cheese and ham. Pour into a greased 10 inch quiche pan or dish. Bake at 350 degrees for 45 minutes or until set. Quiche should be puffed and golden. Let stand 10 minutes before serving.
Yield: 1 10 inch pie.   Nutritional Analysis: page 436.

Crustless Spinach Quiche

1 large onion, chopped
1 tablespoon vegetable oil
1 package (10 ounces) frozen spinach,
  chopped, thawed and pressed dry

5 eggs, beaten
3 cups munster cheese, shredded
1/4 teaspoon salt and pepper

Saute onion in oil in large skillet until tender. Add spinach, and cook until excess moisture evaporates. Cool. Combine eggs, cheese, salt and pepper. Stir into spinach mixture. Pour into greased 9 inch pan. Bake at 350 degrees for 30 minutes or until set.
Yield: 1 9 inch pie.

Entrees

Deviled Seafood

2 cups cooked shrimp, crabmeat,
  lobster and fish in any
  combination, diced
5 tablespoons butter
2 tablespoons flour
2-1/2 cups milk scalded
Salt and white pepper to taste
1 teaspoon onion, grated

2 tablespoons parsley, minced
1/4 teaspoon dried oregano
1/2 teaspoon dry mustard
1 teaspoon worcestershire sauce
2 tablespoons cocktail sauce or ketchup
3 hard cooked eggs, chopped
1/3 cup bread crumbs

Preheat oven to 475 degrees. Melt 3 tablespoons butter over medium heat, and stir in flour and milk. Season to taste, and stir until smooth and thickened. Add onion, parsley, oregano, mustard, worcestershire sauce and cocktail sauce. Blend well. Gently fold in chopped eggs and seafood. Pour into greased baking pan, top with crumbs, dot with remaining butter, and bake 15 to 20 minutes.
Servings: 6.

Entrees

Dijon Pork Roast

1 pork roast,
  about 3 pounds with bone
2 cups beef stock
1/2 teaspoon garlic powder
1/2 teaspoon dry mustard
1 teaspoon thyme

1 medium carrot, sliced into
  1/4 inch rounds
1 medium zucchini, sliced into
  1/4 inch rounds
1/2 cup leeks, chopped
1 stalk celery, sliced
Dijon mustard

Trim all visible fat from the roast, and place the roast in a baking pan. Pour the stock over it. Combine the garlic powder, dry mustard and thyme, and rub the mixture over all sides of the roast. Arrange the chopped vegetables around the roast. Bake at 350 degrees for 1-1/2 hours, or until the roast is cooked through and tender, basting occasionally. Serve each slice of pork with a teaspoon or two of dijon mustard, plus vegetables.

Servings: 6 (4-1/2 ounces each cooked weight plus vegetables).

Egg-Sausage Casserole

1 pound lean sausage
6 eggs
1 teaspoon salt
1 teaspoon dry mustard

2 cups milk
2 slices bread, cubed
1 packed cup sharp cheddar cheese,
  grated

Brown sausage. Beat eggs. Add salt, dry mustard and milk to the eggs. Stir cubed bread, grated cheese and the browned sausage into the egg-milk mixture. Pour into a 7x11-1/2 dish, and cover. Refrigerate overnight. Bake 45 minutes, uncovered, at 350 degrees. Let stand 10 minutes before cutting.

Servings: 6-8.

Entrees

Fillet of Trout Provencale

4 tablespoons olive oil
1 small garlic clove, minced
1/4 cup seeded, peeled and
  chopped tomatoes
1 tablespoon dry white wine
1 teaspoon pernod, or to taste

3/4 pound trout, filleted,
  leaving skin intact
3 tablespoons unsalted butter
1 teaspoon fresh lemon juice or to taste
2 teaspoons snipped fresh chives

In a heavy saucepan, heat 2 tablespoons oil over moderately high heat until hot but not smoking. Add trout skin side down, and saute for 2 to 3 minutes or until skin is golden brown. Turn trout, and add remaining 2 tablespoons oil, garlic and tomato. Cook trout over moderate heat for 1 to 2 minutes or until it flakes when tested with a fork. Transfer the trout, skin side up, with a slotted spatula to heated plate, and keep warm. Add to the skillet the butter, lemon juice, wine and chives. Boil mixture until the butter is melted and sauce is emulsified. Stir in pernod, salt and pepper to taste, and pour sauce over trout.
Servings: 2.

Entrees

Flamed Mustard Steak

1 tablespoon butter
Salt and pepper, coarse ground
1/2 teaspoon sage leaves, crumbled

4 fillets of beef, 1-1/2 inches thick
1/4 teaspoon rosemary
1/4 cup cognac

In skillet, heat the butter, and in it, saute over high heat the fillets of beef for 4 minutes. Turn, and sprinkle with the salt, pepper, rosemary, sage and pepper. Cook to desired degree of doneness, 4 to 5 minutes per side for rare. Pour off excess fat from pan, and sprinkle fillets with cognac. Ignite cognac, and when flame burns out, transfer fillets to warm serving platter. Keep warm.

To skillet add:
4 teaspoons dijon mustard
1/4 teaspoon paprika

4 teaspoons mild brown or
  herb mustard

Combine:
2 tablespoons commercial sour cream   1/2 cup cream

Stir into mustard in skillet. Cook, stirring for 1 minute, and pour sauce over fillets. Serve.
Servings: 4.

Entrees

Flounder Nicole

1/4 pound fresh mushrooms, sliced
1 clove garlic, minced
1 tablespoon vegetable oil
3 tablespoons lemon juice
Salt and pepper to taste
Lemon slices, garnish

1 medium onion, chopped
1/4 teaspon dried whole basil
3/4 cup tomato, peeled and chopped
2 flounder fillets
1 pound fresh spinach

Saute mushrooms, onion, garlic and basil in oil until the onion is tender. Remove from heat. Stir in tomato and lemon juice; set aside. Sprinkle flounder with salt and pepper, and place in a greased baking dish. Top with vegetable mixture, cover, and bake at 350 degrees for 20 to 25 minutes or until fish flakes easlly when tested with a fork. Remove stems from spinach; then wash leaves in luke-warm water. Place spinach in dutch oven (Do not add water). Cover, and cook for 3 to 5 minutes or steam. Drain spinach well, chop, and arrange on a serving platter. Gently transfer fish and vegetables to platter. Garnish with lemon slices, and serve.
Servings: 2.   Nutritional Analysis: page 437.

Fried Softshell Crabs

8 live softshell blue-claw crabs
2 eggs, beaten
1/4 cup milk
2 teaspoons salt

1/2 cup flour
1/2 cup dry bread crumbs
Cooking oil

Dress crabs by cutting off the faces just back of the eyes, lift the top shells at both points, and remove the gills and digestive organs. Remove the aprons. Rinse crabs in cold water. Combine the eggs, milk and salt. Combine flour and crumbs. Dip crabs into egg mixture; then into flour mixture. Fry crabs in 1/8 inch hot (but not smoking) cooking oil in a heavy skillet for 8 to 10 minutes, or until brown on both sides. Or fry in deep fat heated to 375 degrees for 4 minutes.
Servings: 4.

Entrees

Gratin of Oysters and Mushrooms

1 bell pepper, shredded
4 tablespoons butter
1 quart oysters
4 tablespoons butter
1-1/2 cups heavy cream
2 tablespoons parmesan cheese, grated
Pinch of nutmeg
1 teaspoon pernod

3 shallots, chopped
1/2 pound small whole mushrooms
Salt and pepper to taste
4 tablespoons flour
1 cup breakfast cream
Pinch of paprika
Bread crumbs

Saute bell peppers and shallots in butter. After 2 to 3 minutes, add mushrooms and oysters, season to taste, and cook slowly about 4 minutes. In the top of a double boiler, melt the butter and blend in flour, stirring constantly. Slowly add cream grated cheese, nutmeg and paprika. Cook, stirring until thickened. Add sauteed bell pepper, onion, mushrooms and oysters; then add pernod. Pour into a baking dish, and sprinkle with bread crumbs. Brown under broiler, and serve. Servings: 8.

Entrees

Grillades and Grits

1-1/4 to 1-3/4 pounds round of veal or beef
2 teaspoons salt
1 teaspoon black pepper
1/8 teaspoon cayenne
1 tablespoon garlic, finely minced

2 tablespoons flour
1-1/2 teaspoons lard
1 cup onion, chopped
1 large ripe tomato, coarsely chopped
1 cup water, more, if necessary
2-1/2 to 3 cups cooked grits

Trim off all fat from meat, and remove any bones. Cut into pieces about 2 inches square, and pound out with mallet to about 4 inches square. Rub salt, black pepper, cayenne and garlic into pieces of meat on both sides. Rub in the flour. In large heavy skillet or saute pan, melt lard over medium heat, and brown grillades (meat) well on both sides. Lower heat, and add onion, tomato and water. Bring to simmer, cover loosely, and cook over low heat for 30 minutes, uncovering to turn meat over every 10 minutes. A rich brown gravy will form when meat is cooked. Remove it to heated platter, and place in preheated 200 degree oven to keep warm. Prepare grits, according to package. Serve meat. Gravy should be put on grits.
Servings: 4.

Entrees

Grilled Breast of Chicken with Tequila-Lime Butter

1 lime
8 boneless, skinless chicken breasts
  (10 ounces)
2 cups dry white wine
1/2 cup onion, sliced
1/4 cup carrot, sliced
1/4 cup celery, sliced

1 clove garlic, minced
1 cup olive oil
1 pound soft butter
1/4 cup tequila
1/4 teaspoon salt
1/4 teaspoon ground black pepper
4 cups chicken stock

Remove the zest from the lime. (Zest should be a very fine julienne). Blanch the zest in boiling water for 10 seconds. Cool under cold tap water. Squeeze the juice from the lime, reserving 1 tablespoon for the butter. Marinate the chicken breasts in the wine, vegetables, oil, lime pulp, and any excess juice over 1 tablespoon. Refrigerate for 12-24 hours. In a mixer, combine the butter, tequila, 1 tablespoon of lime juice, lime zest, salt and pepper to taste. Mix slowly until all ingredients are incorporated. Remove the chicken from the marinade, and grill over hot coals (about 5 minutes on each side or until firm and completely cooked). Brush with the tequila-lime butter 3 to 4 times during the cooking. In a saucepan, bring the stock to a boil over high heat. Reduce to 1 cup. Remove from heat, and whisk in the tequila-lime butter, 1 tablespoon at a time. Continue adding butter until the sauce is thickened enough to lightly coat a spoon. Adjust the seasoning with salt and pepper, as needed. Place the cooked chicken breasts on warm plates. Pour the sauce over, and serve with your choice of vegetables and starch.
Servings: 8.

Entrees

Grilled Chicken with Salsa

4 chicken breast halves (4 ounces),
  skinned and boned
1/4 teaspoon salt
1/4 teaspoon black pepper
1/3 cup fresh lime juice
2 teaspoons oil
1 cup tomatoes, diced
  (about 1 pound)
1/4 cup green onions, chopped

1-1/2 tablespoons fresh cilantro, minced
1-1/2 teaspoons fresh jalapeno pepper,
  minced, or to taste
1 yellow Holland pepper, diced
1 tablespoon red wine vinegar or
  lime juice to taste
Vegetable cooking spray
Thin green onion strips and yellow and
  red cherry tomatoes for garnish

Flatten each chicken breast half to 1/4 inch thickness using a meat mallet. Sprinkle both sides of chicken with salt and pepper. Place in a shallow baking dish. Combine lime juice and oil. Pour over chicken, turning to coat. Marinate in refrigerator for 15-30 minutes. Combine tomatoes and next 5 ingredients in a bowl. Stir well. Cover, and chill. Coat grill rack with cooking spray. Grill chicken 4 minutes on each side or until done. Brushing occasionally with reserved marinade. Serve with salsa. Garnish with green onion strips and cherry tomatoes, if desired.
Servings: 4 (186 calories each).

Entrees

Grilled Cornish Game Hens with Bacon Butter Stuffing

7 slices lean bacon
2 medium green onions, minced
1/4 cup parsley, minced
3 garlic cloves, minced
8 tablespoons cold butter (1 stick)

1/8 teaspoons cayenne
2 cornish game hens (1-1/2 pounds
 each), butterflied
Fresh black pepper

Light the grill or preheat the broiler. In a heavy skillet, cook bacon over moderately high heat, until fat is translucent, about 1 minute. Remove from heat, drain, and mince. In a food processor, combine bacon, shallots, parsley and 2 minced garlic cloves. Process until mixture is a very smooth paste. Add 4 tablespoons of butter, and process until blended. In a small saucepan, melt remaining 4 tablespoons butter with remaining minced garlic clove over low heat. Stir in cayenne pepper, and keep warm. Place hens breast side up on work surface. Use fingers to gently separate skin from meat without tearing skin. Stuff the bacon butter mixture under the skin of breast and thighs of each hen, spreading it into an even layer with your fingers. Lightly oil the hot grill or broiling rack. Brush the hens with garlic butter, and place skin side up on grill or rack. Cook for 10 minutes. Turn carefully, and cook 8 to 10 minutes more, basting once with garlic butter until crisp and brown. Season with salt and pepper to taste. Serve. Servings: 2 to 4.

Entrees

Grilled Salmon, Shrimp and Scallop Kabobs

2 (6 inch) pieces of salmon
 (2-3/4 pounds), skinned
12 sea scallops (3/4 pound), rinsed
 and patted dry
Dill sprigs for garnish

12 medium shrimp (1/2 pound), shelled
 leaving last joint and tail intact
1/2 cup firmly packed dark brown sugar
1/2 cup fresh lemon juice

In a shallow dish, let six wooden skewers soak in water, covered for 2 hours. Let drain on paper towels. Cut each salmon fillet crosswise into 6 (1 inch thick) slices; discard any small bones. Beginning with thick end of each slice, roll slice into coil. Thread 1 of the shrimp and 1 of the scallops onto skewer. Add 2 of the salmon coils, and add another scallop and shrimp. Make 5 more kabobs with remaining shrimp, scallops and salmon in same manner. This may be made a few hours in advance at this point and kept covered and chilled. In small bowl, stir together brown sugar and lemon juice until mixture is combined. Season kabobs with salt and pepper. Brush with brown sugar mixture, and grill over glowing coals, basting often. Grill 4 to 5 minutes on each side, or until salmon flakes and shrimp are pink and firm. Brush with remaining brown sugar mixture. Garnish with dill sprigs, and serve.
Servings: 6.

Entrees

Grilled Shrimp with Mustard Sauce

10 to 12 large uncooked shrimp,
  unshelled but slit and deveined
1-1/2 cups dry white wine
Juice of 1 lemon
10 black peppercorns, crushed
3 shallots, chopped

2 garlic cloves, crushed
1-1/2 tablespoons olive oil
8 to 10 lemon slices for garnish
2 tablespoons fresh parsley,
  chopped for garnish

Combine first 7 ingredients in medium bowl, and stir to coat shrimp thoroughly. Let marinate at room temperature for 2 to 3 hours. Remove shrimp, reserving marinade, and transfer to small broiler pan. Broil shrimp until they turn pink, about 8 to 10 minutes. Arrange on heated plates. Insert lemon slices between each. Spoon mustard sauce over shrimp, and sprinkle with parsley.

Mustard Sauce:
12 ounces light bodied red wine
1 large onion, sliced

Reserved marinade from shrimp
5 to 6 teaspoons dijon mustard to taste

Combine wine, onion and marinade in 2 quart saucepan. Bring to boil, and cook until liquid is reduced by 1/2. Strain. Return to saucepan over low heat, and whisk in mustard. Continue cooking, whisking constantly, until sauce is slightly thickened and coats whisk. Adjust seasoning.
Servings: 2.

Entrees

Lemon and Herb Stuffed Shrimp

1 pound medium or large shrimp, unpeeled
5 tablespoons olive oil
1/4 cup onion, finely chopped
1 teaspoon garlic, finely minced

1/4 cup fresh parsley, chopped
1/2 cup Italian bread crumbs
1 tablespoon lemon juice
1/2 cup dry white wine

Peel, and devein shrimp. Leaving tails on, cut along inner side, almost, but not quite through to the other side. Press open. Saute onion and garlic in oil, 3 minutes. Add next 3 ingredients. Saute 2 minutes. Press 1 tablespoon mixture into opening of each shrimp. Arrange on oiled plate. Pour wine around shrimp. Bake at 450 for 5 minutes. Place under hot broiler 30 seconds. Serve.
Servings: 4.

Lemon-Garlic Broiled Shrimp

2 cloves garlic, minced
1/4 cup lemon juice, fresh
1/4 teaspoon pepper
1 cup butter or margarine, melted

1/2 teaspoon salt
2 pounds large fresh shrimp, peeled and deveined

Saute garlic in butter until tender. Remove from heat, and stir in lemon juice, salt and pepper. Arrange shrimp in single layer in shallow baking pan. Pour butter sauce over shrimp. Broil 6 inches from heat 5 to 6 minutes or until shrimp are done, basting once with sauce. Serve.
Servings: 4-6.

Entrees

Lemon-Pepper Beef

1 pound lean top or bottom round
  steak, well-trimmed
1/4 cup dry red wine
2 to 3 tablespoons lemon juice
1/2 teaspoon salt

1 bay leaf
2 yellow or red sweet peppers,
  cut in eighths
Pepper to taste

Combine all ingredients in a large bowl or pan, and marinate overnight, or at least 6 hours in the refrigerator. Turn beef and peppers occasionally. Place beef on broiler pan about 4 inches from heat, and broil about 8 minutes. Turn, and add the pepper pieces to the pan. After six minutes or so, turn the peppers over; then broil about 4 minutes more over medium well done beef. Slice the beef thinly across the grain, and serve with the pepper.
Servings: 4 (3 ounces each cooked weight).

Lemon Stuffed Chicken Breasts

8 boneless chicken breast portions
2 tablespoons butter
1 tablespoon olive oil
2 tablespoons flour
1 cup white wine
1 cup chicken stock
2 shallots, minced

2 bay leaves
2 tomatoes, peeled, seeded,
  cut in strips
2 tablespoons parsley, chopped
1/4 cup heavy cream
Salt and pepper to taste

Remove skin from breasts, and flatten between 2 sheets of wax paper with the flat side of a meat mallet or a heavy fry pan. Breasts should be about 1/4 inch thick when pounded. Prepare stuffing. Place an egg shaped mound of stuffing on each breast, and roll up neatly. Dredge breasts in seasoned flour, and saute in butter and oil until lightly browned. Remove chicken, pour off excess fat, and add

Entrees

white wine to fry pan, scraping to release crusty bits. Add chicken stock, shallots and bay leaves. Replace chicken, and simmer 20 minutes. Add tomatoes, and simmer 5 minutes. Add cream, and season to taste. Garnish with parsley.

Stuffing:

2 tablespoons butter
1 tablespoon olive oil
3/4 cup onion, diced
1 cup fresh bread crumbs
Grated zest and juice of 2 lemons

1 tablespoon parsley
1 egg, beaten
Salt and pepper to taste
1/2 teaspoon dry basil,
   or 2 tablespoons fresh basil

Saute onion in butter and oil. Add bread crumbs, zest, lemon juice and seasonings. Mix in egg.
Servings: 8.

Lemon Veal Scaloppine

1 pound veal, sliced thin (8 slices)
Pepper to taste
1 tablespoon olive oil
1/4 cup dry white wine

1/4 cup chicken stock
Juice of 1 lemon (or 1 tablespoon
   of reconstituted lemon juice)
2 tablespoons fresh parsley, chopped

Pound the veal to about 1/2 its original thickness, or as thin as possible without tearing the meat. Sprinkle the meat with pepper. Heat the olive oil in a large nonstick frying pan and, when it is quite hot, brown the veal 1 minute per side. Add the wine, chicken stock, lemon juice and parsley, and continue to cook the veal, occasionally turning the slices, until the sauce has reduced to desired consistency (from 5 to 10 minutes).
Servings: 4 (3 ounces each cooked weight, plus sauce).

Entrees

Linguine and Shrimp with Basil Garlic Sauce

1/2 cup olive oil
2-1/2 cloves garlic, thinly sliced
1-1/2 tablespoons unsalted butter
1 onion, minced
1/2 cup fresh basil leaves,
  minced

1/2 cup fresh parsley leaves, minced
1 pound large shrimp,
  shelled and deveined
2 cups heavy cream
1 pound linguine
Parmesan cheese, grated (to taste)

In a jar with lid, combine oil and 1-1/2 garlic cloves. Store mixture, covered, in cool dry place (shaking occasionally) for 3 days. In large skillet, heat garlic oil and butter over moderate heat, until butter is melted. Cook onion and remaining garlic clove (minced), stirring for 3 minutes or until onion is softened. Add basil and parsley. Cook mixture over moderately low heat, stirring for 2 minutes. Add shrimp, and cook for 1 to 2 minutes on each side or until they are pink. Transfer shrimp with slotted spoon to plate, and keep warm., Add cream, to skillet, and boil mixture. Stir until it coats back of spoon. Add salt and pepper to taste. Keep sauce warm and covered. In pot of boiling salted water, cook linguine until al dente. Drain well, and transfer to heated serving bowl. Spoon sauce over linguine, and toss to coat well. Sprinkle dish with parmesan, and arrange shrimp on top.
Servings: 4-6.

Entrees

Macaroni Shells with Crab

You may substitute frozen crab for canned.

1 package (12 ounces) jumbo
  macaroni shells
2 cans (6-1.2 ounces each) crabmeat,
  drained
1-1/4 cups lowfat cottage or
  ricotta cheese

1/4 teaspoon dried marjoram
1/4 teaspoon dried rosemary
1/2 teaspoon garlic powder
1/4 cup fresh parsley, minced
3 cups tomato sauce

Cook the shells according to the package directions but without the salt. Drain, and spread the shells in a single layer on foil to prevent them from sticking together. In a medium bowl, combine the crab, cheese and seasoning, blending well. Then fill each shell with about 1 tablespoon of the crab-cheese mixture. Pour half the tomato sauce into the bottom of a 9x13 inch baking pan. Place the shells, open-side down, in a single layer on top of the sauce. Cover with the remaining sauce. Bake, covered, at 350 degrees for about 25 minutes. Remove the cover, and bake about 5 minutes longer, until bubbly.
Servings: 8 (1-1/2 cups).

Entrees

Marinated Shrimp with Shrimp Mousse

1/2 lemon, thinly sliced
1 small red onion, thinly sliced
1/2 cup calamate olives,
  quartered and pitted
1 tablespoon pimento, chopped
2 tablespoons vegetable oil
1 garlic clove, crushed or minced
1-1/2 teaspoons powdered mustard
1-1/2 teaspoons salt
1/4 cup plus 1 tablespoon
  fresh lemon juice
1-1/2 teaspoons red wine vinegar
2 bay leaves
2 to 3 drops hot pepper sauce

12 large shrimp in shell (about 1 pound)
  and 1/2 pound medium shrimp
  in shell also
2 tablespoons olive oil
1/4 cup dry white wine
1 large shallot, sliced
1/8 teaspoon ground coriander
1 tablespoon unflavored gelatin
1/2 cup mayonnaise
1/2 teaspoon paprika
1 cup heavy cream
Pinch of white pepper
1 tablespoon parsley, chopped

In a large bowl, make marinade. Combine lemon slices, red onion, olives, pimento, vegetable oil, garlic, mustard, 1 teaspoon salt, 1/4 cup lemon juice, vinegar, 1 bay leaf (crumbled) and hot pepper sauce. Shell large shrimp, leaving tails on. Reserve shells. Cook the shrimp in large sauce pan of boiling salted water, until translucent, about 1 minute. Drain, and add shrimp to marinade. Let cool in marinade; then refrigerate, tossing occasionally, for at least 2 hours, or overnight. Meanwhile peel medium shrimp, reserving the shells. In small skillet with a cover, warm the olive oil over moderate heat. Add reserved shrimp shells and saute, stirring occasionally, until pink and highly aromatic, 3 to 4 minutes. Add wine, 3/4 cup of water, shallot, remaining bay leaf and coriander. Bring to boil, cover, and simmer over low heat for 10 minutes. Add medium shrimp, and cook, uncovered until they just begin to lose their translucency, about 3 minutes. Strain through sieve into bowl. Remove shrimp, and set aside to cool. Discard solids. There will be about 1/2 cup liquid. If there is less, add water to equal 1/2 cup. If there is more, reduce to 1/2 cup. Sprinkle the gelatin into a food

Entrees

processor, and pour remaining 1 tablespoon lemon juice over it. Bring the reserved 1/2 cup of liquid to boil, and add to processor. Process until all gelatin is dissolved, about 2 minutes. Add mayonnaise, paprika and medium shrimp, and puree until smooth. With machine on, add cream. Pass the mixture through a sieve for finer texture, if desired. Taste, and season with remaining 1/4 teaspoon salt, the white pepper and more lemon juice, if desired.
Servings: 12.

Meatless Chili

1 can (40 ounces) kidney beans
1 can (15 ounces) chick peas
2 cloves garlic, minced
1 medium onion, chopped
1 tablespoon olive oil

1 can (8 ounces) tomato sauce
1 can (14-1/2 ounces) whole tomatoes
1 tablespoon oregano
1/2 teaspoon basil
3 tablespoons chili powder or to taste

Rinse kidney beans and chick peas. Set aside. Saute garlic and onion in olive oil. Add beans, chick peas and remaining ingredients, and bring to a boil. Simmer for 20 minutes or until thick.
Servings: 8 (1 cup - 115 calories each).   Nutritional Analysis: page 438.

Entrees

Monkfish Primavera

1/2 stick unsalted butter
1 clove garlic, minced
3/4 pound skinless monkfish fillet,
  trimmed and cut into 1 inch cubes
1-1/4 cups broccoli flowerets,
  blanched for 30 seconds
1 cup snow peas, trimmed and
  strings discarded

1/3 cup white part of leek,
  julienne strips
1/2 cup mushrooms, sliced
2 teaspoons gingerroot, peeled and minced
2 teaspoons orange rind, grated
2/3 cup bean sprouts
2 scallions, minced
1/4 cup parmesan cheese

In a large skillet, heat butter over moderately high heat until foamy, and in it, cook garlic and monkfish with salt and pepper to taste, stirring for 2 minutes, or until fish turns white. Add broccoli, snow peas, the carrot, leek, mushrooms, ginger root, orange rind and bean sprouts. Cook mixture, stirring for 4 to 5 minutes or until vegetables are cooked but still crisp. Transfer to a hotel pan, and sprinkle with scallions and parmesan cheese.
Servings: 2.

Moules Mariniere

5 pounds mussels, thoroughly
  cleaned and rinsed
1 cup fresh parsley, lightly
  packed, chopped
3/4 cup dry white wine
6 tablespoons unsalted butter

3 tablespoons green onions, minced
1-1/2 teaspoons salt
1-1/2 teaspoons freshly ground pepper
1/2 cup fish veloute
6 tablespoons whipping cream
Fresh parsley for garnish, chopped

Combine first 7 ingredients in a 5 to 6 quart dutch oven. Cover, and bring to boil; then simmer until mussels open, about 5 to 10 minutes, turning occasionally. Transfer mussels with slotted spoon to serving platter, and cool slightly. Discard top half of each shell. Cover mussels with foil, and keep warm. Cook pan juices over high heat until reduced by 3/4. Lower heat, and stirring constantly, add veloute and cream. When heated throughout, pour over mussels. Garnish lightly with parsley, and serve.
Servings: 4.

Entrees

Mushrooms and Eggs in Patty Shells

6 frozen patty shells
1/2 pound fresh mushrooms, sliced
2 tablespoons onion, chopped
2 tablespoons butter or margarine, melted
1/4 cup butter or margarine

3 tablespoons all purpose flour
1-1/2 cups milk
1/2 teaspoon salt
1/8 teaspoon red pepper
6 eggs, hard cooked
3 tablespoons dry white wine

Bake patty shells according to package directions. Set aside. Saute mushrooms and onion in 2 tablespoons melted butter until tender, and set aside. Melt 1/4 cup butter in heavy saucepan over low heat. Add flour, stirring until smooth. Cook 1 minute, stirring constantly. Gradually add milk. Cook over medium heat, stirring constantly until mixture is thickened and bubbly. Stir in salt and red pepper. Chop 5 eggs. Stir chopped eggs, mushroom mixture and wine into sauce. Cook until thoroughly heated. Spoon into patty shells. Cut remaining egg into 6 wedges. Place 1 wedge on each patty shell.
Servings: 6.

Entrees

Nordic Shrimp

1 pound medium shrimp,
  shelled and deveined
2 tablespoons parsley, chopped
1/4 cup margarine
1/2 teaspoon salt

1-1/2 cups mushrooms, sliced
1/2 cup green onions, sliced
1/4 teaspoon paprika
1/4 teaspoon pepper
1-1/2 cups jarlsberg cheese, shredded

Saute shrimp, mushrooms, green onions, parsley, salt, paprika and pepper in
butter until shrimp are tender. Spoon into individual shell shaped ramekins or
small baking dishes. Sprinkle generously with cheese. Place on a baking sheet,
and broil 4 inches from heat until cheese is golden. Serve immediately.
Servings: 6-8.

Orange French Toast

2 eggs beaten
1 cup orange juice
10 slices raisin bread
1-1/2 cups vanilla wafer crumbs
  (about 33 wafers)

2 to 3 tablespoons butter or margarine,
  divided
Additional butter (optional)
Maple syrup (optional)

Combine eggs and orange juice. Beat well with a whisk. Quickly dip each slice of
raisin bread into egg mixture, and coat bread on all sides with vanilla wafer
crumbs. Melt 1 tablespoon butter in a large skillet. Arrange 3 or 4 slices of bread
in a single layer in skillet. Cook over medium heat, 1 to 2 minutes on each side
or browned. Repeat with remaining bread slices, adding more butter as needed.
Serve with butter and warm maple syrup, if desired.
Servings: 5.

Entrees

Oven Fried Chicken

4 pieces chicken or turkey or veal etc.

1 egg, well beaten with
  1 tablespoon water

1/4 cup parmesan cheese (optional), grated

1 cup Italian style bread crumbs

1/2 stick butter or margarine, melted

Salt and pepper to taste

Pat dry chicken. Mix together dry ingredients. Dip chicken into egg wash mixture and roll in crumbs. Place in foil lined pan which has been coated with part of the butter. Dot chicken with remaining butter. Bake in 325 degree oven for one hour.

Servings: 4.   Nutritional Analysis: page 439.

Oysters Florentine

1 quart shelled oysters with liquid

6 tablespoons margarine

2 cups spinach, well drained and chopped

1/4 cup onion, chopped

1/8 teaspoon nutmeg

Salt and pepper to taste

2 tablespoons parsley, chopped

3 tablespoons flour

1 cup clam juice (canned or bottled)

1/4 cup cream

1/2 teaspoon garlic salt

1 tablespoon lemon juice

1/2 cup buttered bread crumbs

2 tablespoons parmesan cheese, grated

Melt 2 tablespoons of margarine in a skillet, and simmer in it the spinach and onion. Season to taste, and add nutmeg and parsley. In a saucepan, melt the remaining 4 tablespoons margarine, and make a cream sauce with the flour, clam juice, liquid drained from oysters and cream. Stir until smooth and thick. Season with garlic salt and lemon juice. Spread spinach on the bottom of a large flat-bottomed greased baking pan. Place oysters on top in one layer, and cover with sauce. Top with crumbs and cheese mixture. Bake in a hot oven, 400 degrees, for 15 to 20 minutes or until bubbly and golden.

Servings: 5-6.

Entrees

Oysters Gigi

12 strips bacon
2 teaspoons salt
1 teaspoon black pepper
3 eggs
2 cups flour
Oil for deep frying

2 dozen fresh shucked oysters, drained
1 teaspoon cayenne
1/2 teaspoon white pepper
12 ounces beer, not dark
2 cups seasoned Italian bread crumbs

Halve bacon slices, and fry until they become transparent and begin to render their fat, about 2 minutes. Wrap a half strip of bacon around each oyster and secure with a toothpick. In a small bowl, mix together salt and pepper; set aside. In a separate bowl, beat together eggs, beer and half of salt and pepper mixture. Mix together flour and remaining salt, pepper mixture, and place in a flat large pan. Place bread crumbs in another large flat pan. Pour oil in a heavy pot or deep fryer to 375 degrees. Roll bacon wrapped oysters in seasoned flour to coat well. Dip in beer batter, and stir to coat; then roll them in bread crumbs. Do not do all oysters at once. Deep fry oysters in hot oil until well browned, 2 to 3 minutes. Drain on a paper towel. Serve.
Servings: 6.

Entrees

Oyster Patties

3 teaspoons butter, melted
3 teaspoons flour
1/2 cup liquid from oysters
1-1/2 cups heavy cream
Salt and pepper to taste
2 egg yolks

1 pint oysters
2 tablespoons dry sherry
4 to 6 patty shells
1 small onion, grated
Parsley, chopped

Melt the butter and blend in flour. Add onion, and cook for a few minutes. Stir in the oyster liquid and 1 cup of cream, and continue stirring until sauce is thick and smooth. Season with salt and pepper. Gradually stir in remaining cream mixed with egg yolks. Continue stirring until thoroughly heated. Do not boil. Heat the oysters in the remaining liquid; then drain. Add sherry to sauce. Spoon sauce over heated oysters. Serve in patty shells, and sprinkle with parsley.
Servings: 4.

Oyster Pie

1 small onion, minced
1 pint oysters
1 tablespoon green pepper, minced
1/4 teaspoon black pepper
Cayenne to taste
Biscuit dough

1 large slice bacon, diced
1 tablespoon parsley, minced
2 teaspoons salt
1/2 teaspoon paprika
Juice of 1 lemon

Fry the onion and bacon until brown and crisp. In a shallow greased baking dish, put in a layer of oysters, about 1 pint. Sprinkle over them half of the onion and bacon, with half of the parsley, green pepper, salt, black pepper, paprika, cayenne and lemon juice. Put in the other half of the oysters, and cover with the remaining seasonings. Add 1 tablespoon butter. Cover with biscuit dough, and pierce the top with a knife to let out the steam. Bake until golden brown in 375 degree oven.
Servings: 4.

Entrees

Oyster, Spaghetti Mousse

1 cup short length spaghetti
4 tablespoons butter, melted
1 teaspoon parsley
Salt and pepper to taste
3 eggs, slightly beaten

1-1/2 cup hot milk
1 small onion, minced
1 cup American or cheddar cheese,
   grated
1 pint oysters, raw

Cook the spaghetti in boiling salted water until tender. Drain, and put into a greased baking dish. Add the hot milk, melted butter, onion, parsley, cheese and salt and pepper to taste. Add the pint of oysters and the three eggs. Set dish in a pan of water, and bake in a 375 degree oven until loaf is firm, about 1 hour. Servings: 4.

Paneed Veal with Czarino Sauce

Seasoning Mix:
2-1/4 teaspoons salt
3/4 teaspoons onion powder
1/4 teaspoon white pepper
1/4 teaspoon dry mustard

1-1/4 teaspoons paprika
1/2 teaspoon cayenne
1/4 teaspoon garlic powder

6 slices baby white veal (4 ounces),
   pounded until flat and even
3/4 cup all purpose flour
6 tablespoons unsalted butter
3/4 cup onions, julienned*
4 tablespoons vegetable oil
3/4 cup zucchini, julienned*

3/4 cup yellow squash, julienned*
1-1/2 teaspoons lemon juice
1 cup heavy cream
1/4 pound crawfish or small shrimp,
   peeled
1/4 cup parmesan cheese,
   finely grated

*julienne 1/8 inch thick and 2 inch long

Entrees

In a small bowl combine seasoning mix ingredients; mix well. Sprinkle each slice of veal with seasoning mix, using 1/4 teaspoon on each piece. In pan, mix thoroughly 1 tablespoon seasoning mix into flour. In large skillet, melt 2 tablespoons butter with 2 tablespoons oil over high heat. Meanwhile, dredge meat in seasoned flour, shaking off excess. Fry 3 pieces of veal in butter and oil until browned, about 1 minute per side, gently shaking pan in back and forth motion to keep butter from browning. Remove meat from skillet to a platter, and keep warm. Drain, and wipe skillet with paper towel; then add 2 tablespoons more each of butter and oil to skillet, and repeat with remaining veal. Place veal and serving platter in 200 degree oven to keep warm. Over high heat, saute onions, zucchini and yellow squash in butter oil mixture left in skillet, about 2 minutes. Stir frequently. Add lemon juice, remaining 2 tablespoons butter, remaining seasoning mix and cream. Bring to simmer, stirring occasionally. Add crawfish or shrimp, and cook 1 minute. Stir once or twice. Add parmesan, and continue cooking until cheese is melted and seafood is cooked through, about 1 to 2 minutes. If sauce starts to separate, add 1 to 2 tablespoons water, and stir until smooth. Remove from heat. To serve, place each piece of veal on serving plate, and top with portion of sauce.
Servings: 6.

Pan Fried Trout
with Chili Hollandaise

Chili Hollandaise:

1 small onion

1/4 cup sweet red pepper, minced

13 tablespoons butter

Salt and pepper to taste

1/4 teaspoon dried oregano

1 cup fish or chicken stock

1 teaspoon lemon juice

1 clove garlic

2 tablespoons sweet green pepper, minced

3 tablespoons chili powder

1/2 teaspoon cayenne pepper

1/4 cup dry white wine

3 egg yolks

Entrees

To prepare the hollandaise, mince onion, garlic and sweet peppers. In a small saucepan, heat 1 tablespoon butter; add onion, peppers and garlic. Cook over low heat until soft, about 1 to 2 minutes. Add chili powder, 1/4 teaspoon black pepper, cayenne and oregano, and continue sauteeing over low heat for 1 to 2 additional minutes. Add wine to the pan, and stir with a wooden spoon to deglaze. Add stock, and reduce gently over low heat to 1/3 cup, about 10 minutes. To finish hollandaise, melt remaining 12 tablespoons butter, put reduced mixture in the top of double boiler, and add egg yolks. Whisk together over low heat until mixture thickens, about 5 minutes, being careful not to overcook or it will curdle. Remove from heat, and whisk in melted butter in slow stream. Add a small amount of water, if mixture gets too thick. Add lemon juice, and season with salt. Keep warm.

Panfried Trout:

1 cup sour cream	1/2 cup buttermilk
1/2 teaspoon hot sauce	4 teaspoons spicy mustard
2 egg yolks	Salt and pepper to taste
1 cup flour	1/2 cup stone ground cornmeal
1/2 teaspoon cayenne pepper	4 trout fillets (6 ounces), skinned
1/2 cup peanut oil	

In a bowl, mix together sour cream, buttermilk, hot sauce, mustard, egg yolks, 1 teaspoon salt and 1/2 teaspoon black pepper. In another bowl, mix together flour, cornmeal, cayenne, 1 tablespoon salt, and 1 tablespoon black pepper. To cook, dip each of trout fillets in sour cream mixture, and coat evenly with flour mixture. Pan fry fillets, about 5 minutes total, turning once until golden brown. Drain. Serve fish with hollandaise on the side.
Servings: 4.

Entrees

Pasta with Garlic-and-Clam Sauce

1/2 cup onion, chopped
1/2 cup green peppers, chopped
4 cloves garlic, minced
2 tablespoons olive oil
1/2 pound mushrooms, sliced
2 cans (6 or 7 ounces each) minced
  clams, plus their liquid

1-1/2 teaspoons dried thyme leaves
Salt and pepper to taste
2 tablespoons fresh parsley, chopped
Dash of cayenne pepper
4 cups cooked spaghetti or
  linguine (about 8 ounces uncooked)
Parmesan cheese (optional)

Saute the onion, green peppers and garlic in the olive oil until onions are translucent. Add a little water, and cover, if necessary, to prevent sticking. Add the mushrooms, and continue heating in covered saucepan for about 3 minutes. Add the remaining ingredients except for the cheese, and heat until hot in the covered saucepan. Serve with pasta, and sprinkle with Parmesan cheese, if desired.
Servings: 4 (1 cup pasta, plus 1 cup sauce).

Entrees

Pasta with Smoked Trout

2 whole trout (1/2 pound each)
3 tablespoons olive oil
1/2 pound fresh tomatoes, peeled,
   seeded and chopped or 1 can
   (14 ounces) Italian tomato,
   drained, and pureed
1/4 cup brandy

Parmesan cheese, grated
1 pound penne, ziti or farfalle pasta
2 tablespoons shallots, finely chopped
1 cup half and half or light cream
1/4 teaspoon salt
1/2 teaspoon black pepper
Italian parsley, finely chopped

Skin, and fillet trout. Use tweezers to pull out any small bones. Cut the fish into 1/2 inch pieces. In a large pot of rapidly boiling water, cook pasta until cooked but firm. Meanwhile, heat oil in the skillet. Add shallot, and cook over low heat until soft and translucent, 5 minutes. Add tomatoes, cover, and simmer for 5 minutes. Add half and half, nutmeg, salt and pepper. Cook for 3 minutes. The sauce will still be thin at this point. Add brandy and pasta. Increase the heat to high, and cook. Toss frequently until pasta is tender but still firm and the sauce thickens, 2 to 3 minutes. Add trout and toss over heat until hot, about 30 seconds. Serve on a warm plate. Garnish with parsley and parmesan.
Servings: 4.

Entrees

Poached Chicken Breasts with Orange Mayonnaise

3 cups chicken stock or
  canned chicken broth
1 tablespoon orange rind, grated

1/4 teaspoon dried marjoram
2 whole boneless chicken breasts,
  halved

For Orange Mayonnaise:
2 large egg yolks
2 teaspoons fresh lemon juice
1 teaspoon dijon mustard
1/4 teaspoon salt
1-1/2 cups vegetable oil
1 tablespoon fresh orange juice

2 tablespoons orange rind, grated
1 tablespoon green onions
White pepper to taste
2 navel oranges, peeled, sectioned
  and pith and membranes discarded,
  for garnish

In skillet bring stock, orange rind and marjoram to boil. Add the chicken breasts in one layer, reducing heat to keep stock at bare simmer. Simmer, turning once for 7 minutes. Remove skillet from heat, and let chicken cook in stock for 20 minutes. To make orange mayonnaise, rinse a bowl with hot water, dry well and beat together the egg yolks, 1 teaspoon of lemon juice, mustard and salt. Add 1/2 cup of oil, drop by drop, beating constantly, and add remaining 1 teaspoon lemon juice. Add remaining 1 cup oil in stream. Beating constantly, add the orange juice, orange rind and green onions. Season mayonnaise with salt and white pepper. Thin the mayonnaise with water, if desired. Transfer chicken to cutting board, and pat dry. Slice chicken horizontally, and arrange on plate lined with lettuce. Coat the chicken with mayonnaise, garnish with orange sections, and serve remaining mayonnaise separately.
Servings: 4.

Entrees

Poached Eggs
on Potato and Bacon Pancakes

1/2 cup onion, chopped
1/2 teaspoon salt
1/4 teaspoon fresh ground pepper
4 large eggs, poached

1-1/2 cup russet baking potatoes,
  coarsely grated and peeled
2 slices lean bacon, chopped
1 cup watercress hollandaise*

In bowl, combine well the onion, potatoes, salt and pepper. Scatter bacon in 4 4-inch rounds, 2 inches apart on non stick griddle, and arrange 1/2 cup potato mixture on top of each round, patting out into 4-1/2 inch pancakes, covering the bacon completely. Cook the pancakes on griddle over moderately low heat, undisturbed for 20 minutes. Increasing heat to medium, cook pancakes 5 to 10 minutes more or until undersides are browned. The pancakes may be kept warm in preheated oven 250 degrees for 30 minutes. Remove hot poached eggs from water with slotted spoon, and pat dry carefully with paper towels. Arrange pancakes on heated breakfast plate. Top with poached egg. Spoon some of hollandaise over eggs. Garnish each serving with watercress sprig.
Servings: 4.

Watercress Hollandaise:

1 cup packed rinsed watercress
2 large egg yolks
2 teaspoons dijon style mustard
1/8 teaspoon white pepper or to taste

1 stick unsalted butter
4 teaspoons fresh lemon juice
1/4 teaspoon salt, or to taste

In small saucepan, cook watercress in 2 tablespoons water over high heat until just wilted, and drain in sieve. Refresh watercress under cold water, and squeeze out excess liquid. In another small saucepan, melt butter over moderate heat, and keep warm. In blender, blend egg yolks, lemon juice, mustard, watercress, salt and pepper for 5 seconds. Turn motor off, and scrape down sides of blender. With motor running, add butter in stream. Season hollandaise with salt and pepper. The sauce may be kept warm in bowl, covered with buttered round of wax paper in pan of warm water for up to 20 minutes.
Yield: 1 cup.

Entrees

Poached Grouper with Clams

1 medium onion, thinly sliced
1 clove garlic, minced
1 tablespoon butter or margarine
1-1/2 pounds grouper fillets
1 large tomato, thinly sliced
3 thin slices lemon

2 cans (6-1/2 ounces each) clams,
  minced, with juice
4 ounces dry white wine
1 teaspoon dried basil
Dash of salt and pepper

Lightly saute the onions and garlic in the butter in a large frying pan, until onions are translucent. Place fish fillets on top. Layer tomatoes, lemon slices, clams, clam juice and wine on top of the fish. Sprinkle with basil, salt and pepper. Cover the pan, and bring to a boil. Then turn down the heat, and simmer for about 20 minutes, or until fish flakes easily with a fork. Serve.
Servings: 4 (4-1/2 ounces each cooked weight).

Pork Loin Dubonnet

6 pork loin medallions (3 ounces)
Salt and black pepper
Olive oil, to saute
1 tablespoon sugar

1 cup veal or chicken stock
2 tablespoons cold butter,
  cut into 3 pieces
1 ounce red Dubonnet

Lightly season the pork, and saute in olive oil over high heat. Cook 3 to 4 minutes on each side. Remove from pan, and keep warm. Pour off excess oil. Add sugar and stock and boil over moderately high heat until reduced by half. Over very low heat, whisk in the butter one piece at a time. When all the butter is incorporated, remove from heat, and add the Dubonnet, then adjust the seasoning. Place pork medallions on warm plates, and strain the sauce over. Serve with your choice of vegetables and starch.
Servings: 2.

Entrees

Pork Loin Prosciutto

4-1/2 pounds very fresh boneless
   pork loin with fat trimmed
   to 1/4 inch and tied
5 to 6 thin sheets of fresh fatback
   (about 3/4 pound)
3/4 cup black peppercorns

5-1/4 cups plus 3 tablespoons
   coarse kosher salt
1/3 cup packed dark brown sugar
2 garlic cloves, cut in half
1-1/2 tablespoons cognac
2 teaspoons allspice berries *

Place thermometer in refrigerator (instant reader kind). Adjust thermostat until temperature reads 40-43 degrees. Place pork loin fat side down in ceramic or glass casserole to fit or in large plastic bag. Combine 5-1/4 cups salt with brown sugar. Rub mixture into meat, mounding and patting against sides and top of loin. Cover loosely with plastic wrap or twist bag so that it is loosely closed to allow for breathing. In separate dish or plastic bag, layer fatback with remaining 3 tablespoons salt; cover loosely. Refrigerate pork loin and fat separately to cure, turning meat over once a day for 5 days and patting curing mixture back up over meat each time. The salt will draw out liquid from meat to form brine. After 5 days, brush off any salt still clinging to meat with paper towel. Rub meat all over with cut sides of garlic. Sprinkle with cognac. Cover meaty side of loin with fatback slices, overlapping them as necessary and leaving 1 inch wide lengthwise strip of meat uncovered on each side. Tie with kitchen string at 2 inch intervals to secure fat. In spice mill, coarsely grind peppercorns and allspice berries. Pat and press seasoning mixture evenly over loin to coat meat completely. Cut rectangle of triple layered cheesecloth 10 inches longer than length of meat and 6 times its width. Spread cheesecloth on work surface with one of short sides nearest you. Place meat on cheesecloth parallel to edge so that 5 inches of cloth extend at each end of meat. Tightly roll loin in cheesecloth, and tie each end in knot as close to meat as possible. Tie 2 inch lengths of string from one end to hang meat. Adjust shelves of refrigerator to allow loin to hang freely. Tie loin to higher rack so it will hang with 4 inches of free space all around. Let hang this way for 5 weeks or more before cutting. To test if meat is cured, press it be-

Entrees

tween thumb and middle fingers. It should feel very firm yet still resilient. If it feels like rare steak, it should be allowed to hang longer. When prosciutto feels cured, cut about 1/2 inch off one end of meat. Let loin sit for 1 minute. Smell inside cut of meat. It should have fresh and sweet aroma. If it smells sour or moldy, test again by cutting further and give it another sniff. Do not eat cured meat if it does not smell appetizing. To serve, cut prosciutto into paper thin slices. To keep after cutting, cover cut side only with plastic wrap. Leave rest uncovered. It will keep refrigerated for at least 2 months.

*For more aromatic flavor, decrease peppercorns to 1/2 cup and substitute 1/2 cup dried sage leaves for allspice.

Yield: 3-3/4 pounds cured meat.

Pork Schnitzel

12 (1/4 inch thick) pork loin cutlets
  (about 1-1/2 pounds)
  flattened slightly
Flour for dredging
3 large eggs, beaten

1 cup fine white bread crumbs,
  combined with 1 tablespoon flour
1/4 cup clarified butter
2 tablespoons fresh lemon juice
12 thin lemon slices for garnish

Season pork cutlets with salt and pepper, and dredge in the flour, shaking off excess. Dip pork cutlets one at time into beaten eggs, coating completely, and letting excess drip off. Dredge in bread crumb mixture, coating them completely and transfer to plate. In a large heavy ovenproof skillet, heat clarified butter over moderately high heat until foam subsides. Brown cutlets, turning them. Sprinkle the cutlets with lemon juice, and bake covered in preheated 350 degree oven for 30 minutes. Invert cutlets onto heated platter, and garnish with lemon slices.
Servings: 4.

Entrees

Pork Tenderloin with Plums

5 pounds pork tenderloins

Trim. Place in 4 inch pan.

Marinade:

1-1/2 oranges

1-1/4 cups Spanish onions

1/4 bunch fresh dill, chopped

White pepper, freshly ground, to taste

1 bay leaf

1/2 cup bourbon

1 cup white wine

Remove orange zest, and reserve. Quarter or slice oranges, and place in bowl. Peel the onions, dice fine, and add to oranges along with the remaining ingredients. Blend well. Pour over pork tenderloins. Marinate overnight.

1 can purple plums

1 jar (12 ounces) plum preserves

1 quart chicken stock

1/4 cup cornstarch

1/2 cup water, cold

1/8 cup sugar

Salt, white pepper, to taste

Drain plums; reserve fruit. Place juice and preserves into saute pan. Drain marinade. Add to saute pan along with stock. Bring to boil. Dilute cornstarch in water with sugar. Stir into boiling liquid. Simmer 10 minutes. Strain. Season. Place in bain marie. Boil whole loins to order. Slice loins on bias. Place on a bed of wild rice. Garnish with plums, sauce and julienne of orange zest.
Servings: 10.

Entrees

Pork with Mole Sauce

2 pork tenderloins
2-3 tablespoons mole paste*
2 cloves garlic, minced
1/2 cup onion, diced
1 tart green apple, diced
2 tablespoons peanut oil

1-1/2 cups chicken stock
1 cup pineapple juice
1/4 cup raisins or currants
1 teaspoon comino
Salt and pepper to taste
1/4 cup sour cream

Rub tenderloins with mole paste* and sear in a hot, heavy fry pan. (An iron skillet works well.) Remove tenderloins, add peanut oil, and saute garlic, onion and apple. Remove, and set aside. Add chicken stock and juice, and stir to release bits clinging to the skillet. Replace tenderloins in pan, cover, and simmer for 20 minutes. Add raisins, comino, apples and onions, and simmer 10 minutes or until pork is tender. Remove pork, and keep warm. Whisk in sour cream, correct seasoning, and ladle onto warm serving platter.

*Mole paste is a blend of chilies and spices that can be found in the gourmet section of most supermarkets and specialty shops. A good mole should taste hot, spicy sweet and slightly bitter all at once.
Servings: 4-6.

Entrees

Pork with Mustard Seed Sauce

2 tablespoons vegetable oil
1/2 cup dry white wine
4 teaspoons mustard seed, crushed
   lightly in mortar with pestle
1-1/2 teaspoons dijon mustard

2 pounds piece of boneless pork loin,
   cut from loin end
2 teaspoons cornstarch,
   dissolved in 1 tablespoon water

In a flame proof heavy casserole, heat oil over moderately high heat until hot but not smoking. Brown pork, patted dry and seasoned with salt and pepper. Transfer pork to plate. Pour off all but 1 tablespoon oil in casserole. Add wine and mustard seeds. Return pork to casserole. Bring liquid to boil. Braise pork, covered in preheated oven at 325 for 55 minutes, or until meat thermometer registers 155 degrees. Transfer pork to cutting board, and let stand for 10 minutes. Skim fat from pan juices, stir cornstarch mixture, and stir into pan juices. Bring sauce to boil over moderately high heat. Stir, and season with salt and pepper. Remove casserole from heat. Whisk in mustard, and transfer sauce to heated sauceboat. Slice pork, arrange on heated platter, and serve with sauce. Servings: 4.

Entrees

Port Marinated Loin of Pork

1 boneless center cut pork loin
   (3 to 3-1/2 pounds) tied
6 cloves garlic
1/2 cup dark brown sugar
2 tablespoons dry mustard

2 cups tawny port
1/4 cup soy sauce
1 teaspoon hot chili oil or
   pinch of cayenne

With a skewer, make holes in pork loin on all sides, at 2 inch intervals. Put pork in nonreactive loaf pan. Crush garlic. Mix garlic with remaining ingredients, and pour over pork. Cover, and marinate in refrigerator for 48 hours. Heat oven to 425 degrees. Drain pork, and reserve marinade. Put pork in roasting pan, and roast in preheated oven 20 minutes, turning several times to brown all sides evenly. Lower heat to 375 degrees. Roast 30 minutes longer or until internal temperature registers 145 degrees. Remove from oven, and set aside to cool. If juices are not burned, add 1/3 cup cold water to pan, stirring with wooden spoon to deglaze. Add to reserved marinade. (If juices are burned, do not bother deglazing.) Simmer marinade in saucepan until mixture is reduced to approximately 2/3 cup, about 20 minutes. Strain. Cool pork, and serve. If serving later, refrigerate. Bring to room temperature before serving. Cut pork into slices. Ladle sauce onto plates, and arrange pork on sauce.

Servings: 8.

Entrees

Potato and Meat Fritters

Potato Mixture:

8 large potatoes, peeled

1 large egg

Filling:

1/2 pound ground beef chuck

1/2 pound ground pork

2 tablespoons vegetable oil

1 cup onion, chopped

2 garlic cloves, minced

1 tomato, chopped

1 teaspoon fresh parsley leaf, minced

1/4 cup dry white wine

1/2 cup raisins

6 brine cured olives,

1 hard boiled egg, chopped

pitted and chopped

Flour for dusting

Vegetable oil for frying

In a kettle, cover the potatoes with cold water, bring water to boil, and add pinch of salt. Simmer potatoes for 30 minutes or until tender, and drain. In bowl, mash potatoes with fork, and stir in egg, salt and pepper to taste. In a skillet, brown beef and pork in oil over moderate heat. Add onion and garlic, and cook mixture, stirring for 2 minutes. Stir in tomato, parsley and wine. Simmer the mixture, stirring for 10 minutes or until thickened, and add raisins, olives, hard-cooked egg, salt and pepper to taste. With floured hands, flatten 1/4 cup of potato mixture into 6 inch patty, and put 1 heaping tablespoon of filling in center. Fold patty around filling to form a football shape, and dust fritter with flour. Put on lightly-floured sheet of wax paper. Make fritters with remaining potato mixture and filling. In deep fryer, heat 3 inches of oil to 375 degrees. In it, fry fritters, two at a time for 2 minutes or until golden. Transfer to paper towel to drain. Keep warm on baking sheet in preheated 250 degree oven.
Servings: 16.

Entrees

Ragout of Salmon Al Portone

1 pound asparagus, trimmed, peeled and cut into 2 inch pieces
5 tablespoons unsalted butter
1 pound of center cut salmon fillets, skinned and cut crosswise into 6 serving pieces

2 tablespoons onion, minced
3 tablespoons tomato puree
1/2 cup dry white wine
3/4 cup heavy cream
1/4 cup hollandaise sauce
Fresh lemon juice to taste

In a saucepan of boiling salted water, simmer asparagus for 3 to 5 minutes or until tender. Drain asparagus in colander, refresh under cold water, and pat dry. In a large heavy skillet, heat 4 tablespoons butter over moderately high heat until foam subsides. In it, saute the salmon, patted dry and sprinkled with salt and pepper. Turn it once, for 4 to 5 minutes, or until it flakes. Transfer salmon with slotted spatula to a platter, and keep warm, covered loosely. Add onion to butter remaining in the skillet, and cook over moderately low heat, stirring until it is softened. Stir in tomato puree and the wine, and boil mixture until most of the liquid is evaporated. Add cream, boil the sauce, stirring occasionally until it has thickened slightly, and keep warm. In another skillet, saute asparagus in remaining 1 tablespoon butter over moderately high heat, stirring until it is heated through. Arrange decoratively around salmon. To the sauce, add hollandaise, lemon juice, salt and pepper to taste. Heat over moderately low heat, stirring until hot, but do not boil. Spoon over salmon and asparagus. Serve.
Servings: 6.

Entrees

Red Snapper with Basil and Rosemary

1 red snapper (7 pounds), head and tail attached but gills removed
Juice of 1 lemon
Salt to taste, if desired
Freshly ground pepper to taste
20 fresh basil leaves
6 fresh rosemary sprigs

3 whole garlic cloves, peeled
2 tablespoons olive oil
2 teaspoons paprika
1/4 cup dry sherry
8 shrimp, cooked and peeled for garnish
Parsley sprigs for garnish

Preheat oven to 400 degrees. Using a small boning or paring knife, make incisions lengthwise down the back of the fish, running the knife about 1 inch deep on each side of the backbone, holding the knife close to the bone. Sprinkle the fish inside the incisions, inside the cavity, and on the outside with lemon juice, salt and pepper. Distribute the basil leaves and rosemary sprigs evenly within the incisions and cavity of the fish. Insert garlic cloves inside the fish. Lay out a large rectangle of heavy-duty aluminum foil on a baking sheet, and rub the center with 1 tablespoon olive oil. Place the fish on the center of the foil, and brush the top with the remaining 1 tablespoon oil. Hold a small sieve over the fish, and dust evenly with paprika. Pour sherry over all. Bring up the edges of foil, tent style, folding and crimping the edges. Leave a small air pocket between the top of the fish and the foil. Seal ends of foil as neatly as possible. Place foil-wrapped fish in the oven, and bake 40 minutes. Open the foil, and carefully transfer the fish to a hot serving dish. Serve garnished with shrimp and parsley sprigs.
Servings: 6.

Entrees

Rib Roast with
Tarragon Butter Sauce

1 rib roast with bone (3 pounds)   Salt and pepper to taste

Tarragon Butter Sauce:
2 tablespoons white wine vinegar   2 teaspoons dry tarragon
3 tablespoons butter   Salt and pepper to taste

Heat oven and roasting pan to 500 degrees. Season the roast with salt and pepper. Put roast in pan, and sear at 500 degrees for 10 minutes. Lower heat to 350 degrees, and roast until internal temperature reaches 125 degrees. Let rest 20 minutes. To make sauce, degrease roasting pan. Over medium high heat, add wine vinegar to pan, and stir with wooden spoon to deglaze. Add tarragon. Scape juices into small nonreactive pot, and simmer until syrupy. Add butter, about 1/2 tablespoon at time, over low heat, whisking continuously. The butter should not melt completely, but soften to form creamy sauce. Do not allow sauce to boil. Season with salt and pepper to taste. Serve with roast.
Servings: 4.

Entrees

Risotto with Ham

2 tablespoons butter
2-1/2 tablespoons olive oil
1 medium onion, chopped
1 pound ham, chopped small
2 cloves garlic, minced
1 tablespoon fresh basil, chopped
  or 1-1/2 teaspoons dried
1 tablespoon parsley, chopped

3 cups risotto
2 quarts chicken stock, simmering
1 (14-1/2) can Italian plum tomatoes,
  seeded and chopped, juices reserved
3/4 cups parmesan cheese, grated
3 tablespoons butter,
  cut into 1 inch chunks
Salt and pepper to taste

In a heavy saucepan, combine butter and olive oil over medium heat. Add onion, ham, garlic, basil and parsley. Saute until onion is transparent, and ham is cooked, about 10 minutes. Add risotto, and cook an additional 4 to 5 minutes, stirring to coat all grains. Add one cup of stock, and stir to blend. When stock is absorbed, about 7 to 10 minutes, add tomatoes with their liquid, stirring until liquid is absorbed. Repeat, adding more simmering stock, cup by cup, stirring constantly and waiting between each addition until all liquid is absorbed. After all stock has been added and absorbed, test for doneness. Rice should be al dente. If grains are not yet tender, add more stock, and cook a little longer. Remove from heat, and stir in parmesan cheese and chunks of butter. Incorporate well, and season with salt and pepper. Risotto should have a thick, creamy consistency. Servings: 6.

Entrees

Roast Chicken with Pecan Stuffing

1 roasting chicken (3-1/2 pounds)
  with giblets
2 tablespoons butter
1/2 pound bulk sausage
1 cup onion, finely chopped
1 tablespoon loosely packed leaf sage
1/4 cup parsley, finely chopped
1 cup fine, fresh bread crumbs

1 egg, lightly beaten
Salt to taste, if desired
Freshly ground pepper to taste
1 cup toasted pecans
1 large onion, peeled
  and quartered
1/4 cup water

Preheat oven to 400 degrees. Remove gizzard, heart and liver from chicken. Cut away, and discard the tough outer membrane of the gizzard. Chop the soft, fleshy part of the gizzard, heart and liver. Heat the butter in a saucepan, and add sausage, breaking it up with the flat side of a metal spoon. Add the liver mixture and chopped onion. Cook, stirring about 3 minutes. Add sage. Cook about 3 minutes more or until sausage is cooked. Add parsley, pecans, bread crumbs, egg, salt and pepper to taste. Blend well, and let cool. Sprinkle chicken with salt and pepper, inside and out. Stuff chicken with pecan mixture, and truss. Place chicken on its side in a shallow baking dish, and scatter quartered onion around it. Roast chicken 20 minutes. Turn chicken to other side, and roast another 20 minutes, basting often. Turn chicken on its back, and continue roasting, basting often, another 20 minutes. Ten minutes before the chicken is done, add the water and continue baking. Remove from oven, and let stand 20 minutes before carving. Serve with pan juices.
Servings: 4 or more.

Entrees

Roasted Squab

4 squab
3 tablespoons olive oil
1 carrot, chopped
2 to 3 sprigs fresh thyme or
  1/2 teaspoon dried
Salt and pepper to taste

1 onion, chopped
4 cloves garlic, chopped
1/4 cup dry white wine
2-1/2 cups chicken and squab stock
  or veal stock

Heat oven to 425 degrees. Lightly oil roasting pan, and heat in preheated oven. Season birds with salt and pepper, inside and out, and rub with olive oil. Truss. Place trussed birds into roasting pan on their sides. Roast for 2 to 3 minutes, turn and roast an additional 2 to 3 minutes. Remove squab from pan, and add onion, carrot, garlic and thyme. Put squab on top of vegetables, breast sides up. Roast until squab are medium rare, 6 to 8 minutes. Transfer squab to platter, and put in warm place. Stir vegetables in pan, and continue to roast for 3 minutes. Pour off any excess oil, and add wine, stirring with wooden spoon to deglaze pan. Pour contents of pan into small saucepan, and add stock. Bring to boil, skimming any foam that forms on surface. Lower heat, and reduce by half. Strain through a fine sieve or cheesecloth. Untruss squab. They can be served either whole or with the breast meat removed from bone, and legs presented whole. Spoon sauce over the birds and serve.
Servings: 4.

Entrees

Roast Stuffed Rib of Veal

Veal Roast:
Have butcher prepare rib section of young veal. This should consist of 5 ribs on both sides of backbone. Crack, and remove short ends of ribs. The ready to roast ribs will weigh from 5 to 5-1/2 pounds. Preheat oven to very hot, 450 degrees. Place roast curved side up in shallow baking pan, and roast for 30 minutes. Reduce oven temperature to 325 degrees, and continue to cook for 1 hour. While roast is cooking, prepare stuffing. In a skillet, heat 2 tablespoons butter and cook:

2 tablespoons onion, finely chopped   2 cloves garlic, minced
2 shallots, minced

After 5 minutes, add:

1/2 cup smoked tongue, minced   1/2 cup cooked ham, minced
1 cup mushrooms, finely chopped   1/3 cup madeira

Cook for 5 minutes or until most of moisture has cooked away. Stir in:

1/4 teaspoon salt   Fresh ground pepper
1/2 cup dry bread crumbs

Increase oven temperature to 450 degrees. Remove roast from oven, and place curved side up on cutting board. Slice down to rib bones on both sides of backbone. Cut across rib bones following curve so that the fillet on each side is removed intact. Slice each fillet, lengthwise into 8 thin slices. Spread ribs with some of the stuffing. Replace slices of meat with a little of stuffing between slices. Cover roast with remaining stuffing, and sprinkle with 2 tablespoons grated parmesan cheese. Return roast to very hot oven, and cook for 15 to 20 minutes or until well browned.
Servings: 8.

Sauce:
Place roast on serving platter, and make gravy. Place roasting pan over direct heat, and add 1/2 cup boiling water. Cook, stirring in all brown crust from bottom of pan and sides. Add 2 tablespoons madeira or port, and swirl in 2 tablespoons butter. Strain gravy into saucepan, and serve separately.

Entrees

Room Temperature Rosemary Shrimp

2 cloves garlic, minced
2 tablespoons minced fresh rosemary
leaves or 1 tablespoon dried,
crumbled
1/4 cup dry white wine
2 tablespoons fresh lemon juice

1/3 cup olive oil
1 pound medium shrimp, unshelled
Lemon wedges
Toasted pie triangles or
french bread for accompaniment

In a small bowl, combine garlic, minced or crumbled rosemary, wine, lemon juice, salt and pepper to taste. In a large skillet, heat oil over high heat until hot, and saute shrimp, stirring for 3 minutes or until they have turned pink, and add rosemary mixture. Transfer mixture to a shallow baking dish large enough to hold shrimp in one layer, and let shrimp marinate, covered and chilled, stirring occasionally, for at least one hour or overnight. Arrange shrimp on platter, and garnish with lemon wedges. Serve.
Servings: 4.

Entrees

Scallops and Mushrooms in Port and Cognac Sauce

1/2 pound mushrooms, stems removed
  and reserved for another use
1 tablespoon fresh lemon juice
3 tablespoons unsalted butter

3/4 cup heavy cream
16 sea scallops, patted dry
1 tablespoon cognac
1 tablespoon tawny port

In a heavy skillet, combine mushrooms, lemon juice, 1 tablespoon butter, 1/4 cup water, salt and pepper to taste. Bring liquid to a boil, stirring occasionally, turning the mushroom caps for 5 minutes or until almost all liquid is evaporated. Add cream, and boil until it has thickened slightly. In a large heavy skillet, cook scallops in remaining 2 tablespoons butter, covered over moderately low heat, stirring occasionally for 3 to 5 minutes or until springy to touch. Transfer with slotted spoon to a bowl. Add cognac and port to large skillet, and deglaze skillet over moderately high heat, scraping brown bits. Stir in mushroom mixture, and bring sauce to boil Add scallops, salt and pepper to taste, and heat mixture over moderate heat, stirring, until scallops are heated throughout.
Servings: 4.

Entrees

Scallops Duxelles

2 pounds scallops
7 tablespoons butter
2 tablespoons onion, minced
3/4 pound mushrooms, minced
1 cup dry white wine
1 tablespoon lemon juice
2 tablespoons parsley, chopped
1/2 teaspoon salt and pepper
1/4 teaspoon nutmeg

1/2 cup water
1/4 teaspoon dried thyme
1 sprig parsley
1 small bay leaf
4 tablespoons flour
1 cup light cream
6 tablespoons parmesan cheese, grated
Pinch of cayenne

Melt 3 tablespoons of butter in a heavy skillet, and saute the onion until it is barely soft. Add mushrooms, and continue to cook until liquid evaporates. Stir in 1/2 cup wine, lemon juice, chopped parsley, salt, pepper and nutmeg. Cook until wine evaporates, and set aside. In a saucepan, heat rest of wine, water, thyme, sprig of parsley and bay leaf. Bring to a boil, and add scallops. Poach them gently 5 to 6 minutes or until white and tender. Strain them, reserving broth. In a skillet, melt remaining 4 tablespoons butter, blend in flour, and stir in cream and 1 cup scallop broth. Keep stirring until sauce is thick and smooth. Correct the seasoning. Combine 1/2 cup sauce with mushroom mixture, and spread on the bottom of a baking pan. Arrange scallops on top. Add rest of the sauce, 4 tablespoons cheese and cayenne, and pour over scallops. Sprinkle with remaining cheese, and bake 10 minutes in hot oven, 425 degrees, or brown under broiler. Servings: 4.

Entrees

Seafood Dirty Rice

2 cups white rice
1/2 cup red bell pepper, diced
1/2 cup green bell pepper, diced
1/2 cup onion, diced

4 cups stock (crawfish)*
1 tablespoon seasoning mix*
2 tablespoons butter

Melt butter, and add peppers and onion. Cook over low heat, 3 to 4 minutes. Do not brown. Add stock, and boil. Add seasoning mix and rice, and cook tightly covered until all liquid is absorbed.

*Seasoning Mix:
1-1/2 teaspoon salt
1 teaspoon cayenne pepper
1/2 teaspoon white pepper
1/2 teaspoon black pepper

1/2 teaspoon thyme
1 teaspoon paprika (sweet)
1 teaspoon basil

Crush leaves of thyme and basil, and mix all seasonings thoroughly.

*Crawfish Stock:
Crawfish shells & heads
Carrots
Celery
Onion

Bayleaf
Thyme
Parsley stems
(Quantity as desired)

Rinse heads, and place in pot with 1/2 the volume of carrot, celery and onion mixture. Add seasonings, and simmer 1 hour. Skim off any impurities. Strain. Servings: 4.

Entrees

Sea Scallops with
Sauvignon Blanc Cream Sauce

4 tablespoons clarified butter
1-1/2 pounds medium scallops
1/4 teaspoon salt
1/8 teaspoon white pepper
1/4 cup brandy

1/4 cup sauvignon blanc
  or dry white wine
1 cup heavy cream
1 tablespoon fresh tarragon leaves
  or 1/2 teaspoon dried

In a large skillet, warm butter over moderately high heat. When it begins to simmer, add scallops. Season with salt and pepper, and saute, tossing occasionally until opaque, about 1 minute. Add brandy, swirl to warm, and ignite with match. When flames subside, add wine, cream and tarragon, and bring to boil. Using a slotted spoon, remove cooked scallops, and place in a warm dish. Cover, and set aside. Boil sauce until thick enough to coat back of spoon, about 5 minutes. Return scallops and any accumulated juices to pan. Stir briefly to warm, and serve.

Servings: 4.

Entrees

Sesame Chicken

3/4 cup sesame paste
1/4 cup dark soy sauce
3 medium garlic cloves, crushed
  thru garlic press
2 tablespoons red wine vinegar
2 pounds chicken breasts, trimmed
  of excess fat, boneless, skinless

1/3 cup brewed black Chinese tea
1-1/2 tablespoons Chinese hot oil
2 tablespoons oriental sesame oil
2 tablespoons sugar
1/2 cup scallions, sliced
1 bunch watercress for garnish

In a small bowl, combine sesame paste, tea, soy sauce, hot oil, garlic, sesame oil, sugar and vinegar. Whisk until well blended. Stir in scallions. Next, place chicken in large glass baking dish. Pour marinade over chicken. Turn to coat well. Cover, and refrigerate for 24 hours. Let chicken return to room temperature before proceeding. Preheat broiler. Place chicken on rack over broiler pan. Broil chicken about 3 inches from heat, turning carefully, so as not to break crust. Broil for 5 minutes on each side, until outside is slightly charred and chicken is still juicy but no longer pink. Let rest for 10 minutes. Garnish with sprigs of watercress. Servings: 6.

Entrees

Sesame Sauteed Catfish with Lemon Butter

1/2 cup plus 1 tablespoon
  parsley, minced
1 cup dry bread crumbs
1/2 cup sesame seeds
Salt and pepper to taste
1/4 cup all purpose flour
2 eggs

1 teaspoon water
4 catfish fillets,
  each weighing 6 to 8 ounces
3 tablespoons unsalted butter
1 tablespoon lemon juice
4 lemon wedges
3 tablespoons peanut oil

In a shallow bowl, combine 1/2 cup of parsley with bread crumbs, sesame seeds, salt and pepper. Put flour into another bowl. In a third shallow bowl, beat eggs with water. Dredge each fillet in flour, and dip in beaten eggs. Coat with bread crumbs mixture on both sides. Melt butter, and stir in lemon juice. Dip edges of the lemon wedge in remaining tablespoon of parsley. Heat oil in frying pan over medium heat. Saute coated fillets, turning once, until each side is well browned, 3 to 5 minutes per side. Put fillets on a warm plate. Garnish with lemon and lemon butter.
Servings: 4.

Entrees

Seviche

1 pound skinless, boneless fillets
 of fish, such as bluefish, red snapper,
 mackerel, or seafood,
 such as bay scallops
1 tablespoon olive oil
1/2 teaspoon crumbled dried oregano
7 tablespoons lime juice
1 cup ripe tomatoes, peeled, seeded,
 cubed and drained
4 or more canned serrano chilies,
 drained and chopped

1/2 cup red onion, finely chopped
1/2 cup avocado, diced
2 teaspoons fresh coriander,
 finely chopped
Salt to taste, if desired
Freshly ground pepper to taste
1/4 cup heart of celery,
 finely diced
Grated rind of 1 lime

Cut the fish into 1/2 inch cubes. If bay scallops are used, cut them into quarters. Put the pieces in a bowl, and add the lime juice. Cover, and refrigerate, stirring occasionally, 12 hours or longer. Add the remaining ingredients, and chill until ready to serve.
Servings: 6.

Entrees

Shark or Swordfish Picata

2 lemons
3 eggs
1/4 cup milk
Salt and pepper to taste
6 tablespoons clarified butter
   or 3 tablespoons butter

3 tablespoons oil
1/2 cup parmesan cheese, grated
3/4 cup flour
1-1/2 pounds swordfish or shark,
   cut into 3/4 inch thick slices
2 to 3 tablespoons capers

Cut the ends off one of the lemons, and pare away rind and white pitch down to the flesh. Cut the lemon into paper thin rounds, removing any seeds. Grate cheese. Whisk eggs, cheese, 3 tablespoons of flour and enough milk to make batter the consistency of a heavy cream. Cut fish across the grain into 1/4 inch slices. Sprinkle with salt and pepper. Heat the butter and oil in a large frying pan over medium heat, dust fish pieces with flour, and dip in batter. Pan fry them, turning once, until coating is golden brown, and fish tests done, about 3 minutes total. Transfer fish to warm plates. Squeeze juice from second lemon into frying pan used for fish, stirring with a wooden spoon to deglaze the pan. Add salt and pepper to taste. Top each piece of fish with a few capers and lemon slices. Pour lemon butter over all.
Servings: 6.

Entrees

Shrimp Alfredo

1 pound large shrimp, shelled
  and deveined
1 teaspoon shallot, minced
1/4 teaspoon garlic, minced
1/2 stick unsalted butter (1/4 cup)
1/2 pound fettuccini,
  cooked al dente and drained

4 large egg yolks
1 cup half and half
1/2 cup fresh parmesan, grated
2 teaspoons fresh parsley leaves,
  minced

In a large skillet, cook shrimp, shallot and garlic in butter over moderate heat. Stir for 3 to 4 minutes, or until shrimp are firm and opaque. Reduce heat to moderately low heat, and stir in fettuccini. In bowl, lightly beat together egg yolks, half and half and parmesan. Add the egg mixture to shrimp mixture, and cook, stirring for 3 to 4 minutes or until sauce is thickened. (Do not let boil.) Stir in parsley, salt and pepper to taste.
Servings: 4.

Entrees

Shrimp and Rice Almondine

2-1/2 pounds shrimp, cooked,
  shelled and deveined
3/4 cup rice, cooked
1 tablespoon lemon juice
3 tablespoons salad oil
2 tablespoons margarine
1/4 cup green pepper, minced
1/4 cup onion, minced

1/8 teaspoon pepper
Dash of cayenne
1 can condensed tomato soup
1 cup heavy cream
1/2 cup dry sherry
3/4 cup almonds,
  slivered and blanched

Spread cooked rice in large baking pan. Arrange shrimp on top, and sprinkle
with lemon juice and salad oil. Heat butter in saucepan, and cook green pepper
and onion over low heat, about 5 minutes or until soft. Stir in salt, pepper,
cayenne, soup, cream, sherry and half of almonds. Pour over the shrimp in
casserole, and stir gently to mix. Bake 35 minutes, uncovered in moderate 350
oven. Sprinkle the remaining almonds on top. Continue to bake 20 minutes
longer or until bubbly and brown.
Servings: 6-8.

Entrees

Shrimp Chinois

3 cups small broccoli flowerets
3 cups small cauliflower flowerets
2 zucchini, cut into 1 inch pieces
3/4 stick (6 tablespoons)
  unsalted butter
16 large shrimp, shelled, deveined
  and butterflied

1 cup snow peas, strings removed
1 cup mushrooms, thinly sliced
1/4 cup scallions, thinly sliced
1 large tomato, peeled,
  seeded and chopped
2 cups hollandaise

In large saucepan of boiling salted water, cook broccoli and cauliflower for 3 to 5 minutes or steam until just tender. Remove vegetables, and refresh in cold water. Drain. Add zucchini, and cook for a few minutes or until tender. Drain. Refresh in large bowl of cold water, and drain. In large heavy skillet, heat butter over moderately high heat until hot. Cook shrimp and snow peas, stirring for 2 minutes, or until snow peas are tender. Stir in tomato, broccoli, cauliflower and zucchini. Cook mixture over moderate heat for 2 minutes or until heated thoroughly. Season with salt and pepper. Transfer the mixture with a slotted spoon to heated bowl. Toss gently with hollandaise. Divide mixture on heated plates, and serve with parsley.
Servings: 4.

Entrees

Shrimp Cypremont Point

2 pounds large shrimp, deheaded
1/2 teaspoon cayenne
1/4 teaspoon white pepper
1/4 cup dry vermouth
1/4 cup worcestershire sauce
1/2 cup parsley, chopped

2 teaspoons salt
1/4 teaspoon black pepper
1 cup (1/2 pound) butter
1/2 cup lemon juice or
 2 fresh lemons
1/2 cup green onions, chopped

Peel, and devein shrimp, leaving tails on. Sprinkle shrimp generously with salt and pepper. Arrange in single layer on baking pan. Melt butter over medium heat, and add vermouth, lemon juice, worcestershire, green onions and parsley. Simmer for 3 minutes; then pour over shrimp. Bake shrimp in preheated 375 degree oven just until pink, 10 to 15 minutes.
Servings: 6-8 (4 entree).

Shrimp Marinara

26 to 30 shrimp
Egg noodles (quantity desired), cooked
1 onion, chopped
1/4 cup olive oil
1 green pepper, chopped
1 carrot, chopped
1 mushroom, sliced
2 teaspoons garlic
1/3 cup English peas

1/2 cup red wine
1 can (6 ounces) tomato paste
1-1/2 tablespoons whole basil
1 tablespoon oregano
1 pinch of sugar
1 pinch of pepper
1/2 cup water
1/2 cup romano cheese, grated

Place all ingredients, except noodles, in a saucepan and cook for 10 minutes. Put noodles in plates; add sauce to top. Sprinkle with cheese. Serve.
Servings: 6.

Entrees

Shrimp Rockefeller

1/2 onion, diced
6 cups spinach, chopped
1/2 teaspoon pernod
3/4 pound shrimp, peeled
2 tablespoons unsalted, fat free
  chicken stock
1-1/2 teaspoons minced fresh herbs
  or 1/2 teaspoon dried

1/4 cup low fat milk
1-1/2 teaspoons arrowroot,
  dissolved in 2 tablespoons chablis
Salt, optional
1/2 ounce jarlsberg cheese, shredded

Lightly coat frying pan with vegetable oil spray. Saute the onion over medium heat until soft, about 3 minutes. Stir in spinach and pernod. Simmer, tossing until spinach wilts, about 5 minutes. Remove from heat, and set aside. In a covered steamer, steam shrimp for 3 minutes. Remove from heat, and set aside. For sauce, bring chicken stock and herbs to simmer in a saucepan. Whisk in milk, arrowroot and wine mixture. Cook until sauce is thickened. Do not boil. Season to taste. Put spinach in an ovenproof dish. Arrange shrimp on spinach, top with sauce, and sprinkle with cheese. Put under preheated broiler until cheese melts. Serve.
Servings: 4.

Entrees

Shrimp with Marinara Sauce

1 medium onion, chopped
1/4 cup olive oil
1 medium size green pepper, chopped
1 carrot, scraped and finely chopped
1 cup fresh mushrooms, sliced
2 cloves garlic, crushed or minced
1/3 cup frozen English peas
1/2 cup red wine
1 (6 ounces) can tomato paste

1-1/2 teaspoons dried whole basil
1 teaspoon dried oregano
Pinch of sugar
1/4 to 1/2 teaspoons pepper
1/2 to 1 cup water
1 pound large shrimp, peeled and deveined
Hot cooked linguine
Romano cheese (optional), grated

In a large skillet, saute onion in hot oil for 1 to 2 minutes. Add next 4 ingredients, and saute until vegetables are tender. Add peas, wine, tomato paste and seasonings, stirring well. Thin mixture with 1/2 to 1 cup of water to reach desired consistency. Bring sauce to boil, reduce heat, and simmer 5 minutes. Add shrimp, cook 3 to 5 minutes or until shrimp are done. Serve over linguine. Sprinkle with cheese, if desired.
Servings: 4-6.

Entrees

Smoked Bluefish with Pasta

2 cups heavy cream
1 teaspoon dried thyme
1/2 teaspoon cayenne
1/4 teaspoon white pepper
4 cups smoked bluefish, cut into
  small pieces
1 pound angel hair pasta,
  fresh, if possible

1 teaspoon dried basil
1 teaspoon salt
1/2 teaspoon black pepper
1/2 teaspoon fresh garlic, minced
1/4 cup green onions, chopped
1/4 cup parsley, chopped
1/2 cup olive oil

Pour the cream in a large heavy skillet, and place over high heat. Bring to a simmer. Stir often. Add herbs and seasonings, and let it reduce until thick, 10 to 15 minutes. Add smoked fish, green onions and parsley, and continue to cook 2 to 3 minutes more. In salted water, cook pasta until al dente. Drain, and mix with olive oil. Let stand a few minutes. Divide pasta in bowls, or put in hotel pan, and spoon sauce equally over pasta.
Servings: 4.

Entrees

Smoked Salmon Crepe Spirals

1/2 pound smoked salmon, thinly sliced
2 tablespoons unsalted butter, cut into
  pieces, at room temperature
4 crepes*

2 tablespoons cream cheese
  at room temperature
2 teaspoons fresh lemon juice
2 teaspoons snipped fresh dill

In a food processor, puree half smoked salmon. Add cream cheese, butter and lemon juice. Blend mixture until smooth. Transfer puree to a bowl, and stir in dill. On the paler side of each crepe, spread thin 1/4 of salmon puree. Top each crepe with 1/4 of salmon slices, and roll crepes tightly to enclose filling. Chill crepes, seam side down, covered for at least 1 hour or until firm enough to slice, and then slice diagonally into 1/4 inch thick spirals.

*Crepe Batter:
1 cup all purpose flour
3 large eggs
1/2 teaspoon salt

1/2 cup milk
2 tablespoons unsalted butter,
  melted and cool

In a processor, blend flour, 1/2 cup plus 2 tablespoons water, milk, eggs, butter and salt for 5 seconds. Turn off motor, and with a rubber spatula, scrape down sides of container. Blend batter for 20 seconds more. Transfer the batter to a bowl, and let stand, covered for 1 hour. The batter may be made up to one day in advance and kept covered and chilled. To make the crepes, heat oil in a crepe pan. Pour just enough batter into hot pan to cover the bottom. Return pan to heat, constantly moving the pan so the crepe will not stick. Turn crepe on other side after 1 minute. Cook side until firm. Place on parchment paper, and store. Servings: 4.

Entrees

Sole Fricassee with Green Olives

1/4 cup unsalted butter
4 slices lean bacon, cut in 1/2 inch
  pieces, cooked crisp and drained
1/4 cup pitted green olives, drained
1/3 cup dry white wine
2 flat anchovy fillets, mashed
1 tablespoon fresh parsley leaf, minced

1/4 pound mushroom, sliced
4 small white onions, peeled, cooked in
  boiling water until tender and drained
2-1/2 pounds sole fillets
1/2 cup fish stock, white
Fresh lemon juice to taste

In a heavy skillet, heat 2 tablespoons of butter over medium high heat, until foam subsides. Saute the mushrooms with bacon, stirring for 2 to 3 minutes or until liquid the mushrooms give off is evaporated. Add onions and olives. Saute mixture, stirring for 1 minute, and keep warm. Arrange sole in a buttered skillet or flameproof baking dish just large enough to hold in one layer. Add wine and enough of the stock to just cover the sole. Cover the mixture with a buttered piece of wax paper. Bring the liquid to a boil, remove the skillet from heat, and let mixture stand for 5 to 8 minutes or until sole flakes when tested with fork. Transfer sole with slotted spatula to a platter, and keep warm, covered loosely with foil. Add anchovies to cooking liquid, and bring to a boil. Boil mixture until reduced to about 1/3 cup. Remove skillet from heat. Swirl in remaining 2 tablespoons of butter cut in bits, until incorporated. Season sauce with lemon juice, salt and pepper to taste. Spoon sauce over sole, top with olive mixture, and sprinkle with parsley.
Servings: 6.

Entrees

Sole with Broccoli Cream Sauce

1-1/2 cups broccoli, trimmed,
 peeled and chopped, plus 1/4 cup
 small flowerets
1 red bell pepper, minced
2 tablespoons unsalted butter

4 pieces sole fillet (6 ounces)
1/2 cup onion, minced
1 cup dry white wine
1/4 cup heavy cream

In a saucepan of boiling salted water, cook the chopped broccoli until tender and drain, reserving 3 cups of boiling liquid. Refresh the broccoli in bowl of ice, and drain it. In a saucepan, cook bell pepper in 1 tablespoon butter, covered over moderately low heat, stirring until softened. Keep warm and covered. In a skillet large enough to hold sole in one layer, combine onion, wine and reserved cooking liquid. Bring the liquid to a boil, and simmer the mixture for 10 minutes. Add the sole, poach it, covered at bare simmer, turning once for 10 to 12 minutes or until it just flakes,. Transfer sole with spatula to plate, and keep warm, covered. Strain 1/2 cooking liquid into blender, and puree it with the cooked broccoli, cream, salt and pepper to taste. Transfer the sauce to saucepan, and cook over moderately low heat, stirring until it is heated through. In a small saucepan of boiling salted water, blanch the broccoli flowerets for 1 minutes; drain. In small bowl, toss with remaining 1 tablespoon butter, salt and pepper to taste. Cover the bottom of a heated platter with a layer of the sauce. Arrange the sole on top, and garnish platter with broccoli flowerets and 2 tablespoons of bell pepper. Add remaining bell pepper to remaining sauce, and serve with sole.
Servings: 4.   Nutritional Analysis: page 440.

Entrees

Spaghetti Squash Parmesan

1 whole spaghetti squash,
  about 8 inches long
2 tablespoons butter or margarine

4 tablespoons grated Parmesan cheese
1 teaspoon garlic powder

Boil the whole squash in a large pot of water for about 1 hour to 1-1/4 hours or until tender, turning it every 15 minutes. Cut the squash in half, and remove the seeds. Scoop out the squash, and toss with the remaining ingredients.
Servings: 8 (1/2 cup).

Stir-Fry Vegetables

2 cups fresh vegetables, finely chopped
1 tablespoon peanut oil
1 clove garlic, minced
1/4 teaspoon ginger

2 tablespoons grated hard cheese
Tamari sauce or
  soy sauce to taste

In a large skillet or wok, heat the oil. Add the garlic and ginger; then add the vegetables requiring the most cooking such as carrots, broccoli, green pepper and so on. Stir constantly, adding the vegetables that require less cooking as you go along. If necessary, add a tablespoon or two of water to prevent sticking. Cook until tender-crisp. Spoon over cooked grain, sprinkle with cheese and tamari sauce, if desired, and serve.
Servings: 1 as main course, 4 as side dish.

Entrees

Swordfish or Halibut Italiano

4 swordfish or halibut fillets
1/8 teaspoon pepper
2 tablespoons butter, melted
1/4 pound fresh mushrooms, sliced
1/2 cup whipping cream
1 tablespoon dijon mustard
1 tablespoon dry fine bread crumbs

1/8 teaspoon salt
1/2 cup fresh parsley, chopped
2 tablespoon lemon juice
1 tablespoon all purpose flour
1/4 cup milk
2 tablespoons parmesan cheese, grated
1/4 teaspoon paprika

Arrange fillets in lightly greased baking dish. Sprinkle with salt, pepper and parsley; set aside. Combine butter and lemon juice in a skillet. Add mushrooms, and saute 2 to 3 minutes. Add flour, stirring until smooth. Gradually add whipping cream and milk. Cook over medium heat, stirring constantly until mixture is thick and bubbly. Stir in mustard. Spread sauce over fillets. Sprinkle with cheese, bread crumbs and paprika. Bake at 350 degrees for 25 to 30 minutes or until fish flakes easily when tested with a fork.
Servings: 4.

Tamale Pie

1 cup cornmeal
1 tablespoon lard
1/2 pound chopped steak,
   rolled in flour
1 cup stoned olives, cut in halves

3 cups boiling water
1 onion, minced
1 cup tomato sauce
1 pimento, minced
Monterey jack and cheddar cheese,
   grated, quantity desired

Sprinkle 1 cup of meal into the boiling water, stirring to keep from lumping. Add salt to taste. When thick enough, approximately 25 minutes, set mush aside. Heat 1 tablespoon fat in saucepan. Add onion and steak, and saute for 2 minutes. Add tomato sauce, pimento and olives. Put half the mush into greased baking dish. Spread meat over this. Cover with the rest of the mush. Sprinkle grated cheese on top. Bake in 400 degree oven until cheese is bubbling. Serve with tomato sauce.
Servings: 4.

Entrees

Tartare of Tuna

1-1/2 tablespoons olive oil
1 large egg yolk
3 tablespoons fresh lemon juice
1 teaspoon snipped fresh dill
1 teaspoon fresh chives
1 teaspoon dijon mustard
1 anchovy fillet, mashed to paste

1 tablespoon red onion, minced
1 tablespoon small capers,
  drained and minced
6 ounces very fresh skinless
  boneless tuna steak, cut into
  1/4 inch dice, chilled

Garnish:
Radicchio leaves
American caviar
Belgian endive, trimmed and
  separated into leaves

Red bell pepper, julienned
Toast points or pumpernickel

In a bowl, whisk together the oil, egg yolk, lemon juice, dill, chives, mustard, anchovy paste, onion and capers. Add salt and pepper to taste, and gently stir in tuna into the dressing. Arrange radicchio in center of two plates. Spoon tartare onto it. Spoon caviar on top of tartare. Arrange endive around edge of plates, and top with bell peppers. Serve with toast points or pumpernickel.
Servings: 4.

Entrees

Tomato Pasta with Goat Cheese and Garlic Sauce

1 to 1-1/2 cups heavy cream
8 cloves garlic, crushed lightly
2 ounces goat cheese, cut into bits

1/2 pound fresh tomato pasta
 or 6 ounces dried
2 tablespoons fresh parsley leaves, minced

In a small saucepan, bring 1 cup cream to boil. Add garlic, and simmer for 10 to 12 minutes or until garlic is softened. Transfer garlic with slotted spoon to blender or food processor. Add goat cheese and 1/2 cup hot cream. Puree mixture until very smooth. Return sauce to pan, and if it is too thin, add some of the remaining 1/4 cup cream. Sauce may be made up to 4 hours in advance. Keep covered and chilled. Reheat on low. If sauce needs to be thinned, add 1 to 2 tablespoons of heavy cream. In pot of boiling salted water, cook pasta, stirring occasionally for 3 minutes for fresh pasta or 7 to 9 minutes for dried, until al dente, and drain well. Toss pasta with sauce, parsley, salt and pepper to taste. Serve immediately.
Servings: 2 (main), 4 (side).

Entrees

Trout Almandine Arnaud

2 small to medium speckled trout,
  tenderloined
Cold milk for soaking
1 cup flour

1-1/2 teaspoons salt and pepper
1/8 teaspoon cayenne
Vegetable oil for deep frying

Almandine Sauce:
1-1/2 sticks unsalted butter
1-1/3 cups blanched slivered almonds

2 tablespoons fresh lemon juice
1 teaspoon fresh ground black pepper

Rinse the fillets, and dry thoroughly with paper towels. Place in a pie dish or bowl, and add cold milk just to cover. Combine flour and seasonings in bowl. Meanwhile, preheat oil in deep fryer to 375 degrees. Coat fillets by lifting them one at time out of milk, letting excess drain off over bowl for 30 seconds. Drop them in seasoned flour to cover evenly. Fry, and keep warm in oven while preparing almandine sauce. In a heavy saucepan, melt butter over low heat; then add almonds, and cook over low heat, until butter begins to turn brown. Remove pan from heat immediately, and add lemon juice and black pepper. Mix well; then return pan to low heat for 1 minute. Remove from heat again, and mix sauce thoroughly with a spoon. To serve, place fried fillets on heated plates, and spoon about 1/2 cup sauce over each. Place half of the almonds on each portion on top of fish; the other half should surround fish.
Servings: 2.

Entrees

Trout Baked on Orange Wild Rice

2 cups wild rice, rinsed well
  and drained
1-1/2 teaspoons salt
3/4 stick (6 tablespoons) butter
1 large bunch of green onions,
  chopped, reserving 1/4 cup
  green part for garnish

6 trout (3/4 pound), cleaned and
  boned or fillets
1/2 lemon, cut into 6 wedges
1 cup fresh orange juice
2 teaspoons orange rind, grated
6 thin slices of orange and
  parsley sprigs for garnish

In a saucepan, combine wild rice with the salt and 6 cups of cold water. Bring the water to a boil, and simmer mixture for 35 to 40 minutes or until wild rice is just tender. Drain wild rice if all the water has not been absorbed. Toss rice with 3 tablespoons of butter and green onions. Spread wild rice evenly in buttered baking pan. Cut the remaining 3 tablespoons of butter in equal parts to put on fish fillets. Season fillets with salt, pepper and lemon. Arrange the fillets on top of the rice. Pour the orange juice over mixture, and bake, covered with buttered wax paper and foil in preheated 400 degree oven for 30 minutes, or until trout flakes. Sprinkle wild rice with reserved green onions and orange rind, and garnish with parsley sprigs.
Servings: 6.

Entrees

Turkey-Apple Stir-Fry

1 tablespoon peanut or
  vegetable oil
1 medium apple, chopped
1 small onion, chopped
1 clove garlic, minced or crushed
1/2 cup green pepper, diced
2 stalks celery, chopped
1 tablespoon butter or margarine

1 tablespoon whole-wheat flour
1 cup chicken stock
1/4 teaspoon curry powder
1/2 teaspoon lime juice
1/4 teaspoon fresh gingerroot, minced
2 cups cooked turkey, diced
1/2 teaspoon salt

Heat the oil in a wok or medium-sized skillet over medium heat. Add the apple, onion and garlic, and cook, stirring often, until tender. Add the green pepper and celery, and stir-fry 2 minutes more. Remove from the heat, and set aside. In another large skillet, melt the butter or margarine, and stir in the flour. Cook, stirring for a minute or two, until the flour is golden brown. Slowly stir in the chicken stock, curry powder, lime juice and ginger. Then, add the apple mixture and the turkey, and simmer until heated through. Stir in the salt, and serve. Servings: 4 (1-1/2 cups).

Entrees

Turkey Pompadour

Breast of baked turkey
3 shallots, chopped
1 cup champagne
Salt and white pepper to taste
1/2 cup cream
Dash of lemon juice

8 small sausages
3 truffles (or mushrooms), sliced
1/2 cup chicken or turkey broth
3 egg yolks
Butter

Slice the breast of baked turkey, and put aside. In a saucepan, place eight small sausages, three chopped shallots and truffles. Cover with champagne, chicken or turkey broth, salt and white pepper. Simmer until sausages are tender. Thicken with yolks of three eggs and cream. Add pat of butter during the thickening process. Pour sauce over slices of turkey. Add dash of lemon. Serve sauce on toast, noodles, rice or vegetables.
Servings: 4.

Entrees

Veal Chops Stuffed with Morels

2 (1 inch thick) veal chops
  (1/2 pound each)
2 tablespoons unsalted butter
1/2 cup dry white wine
1 teaspoon fresh parsley leaves, minced

1/2 ounce fresh morels, washed
  well, patted dry or 1/4 ounce dried,
  soaked in hot water for 30 minutes,
  rinsed well and patted dry

Pat chops dry, and season with salt and pepper. Make an incision about 1 inch long with sharp paring knife, along fat side of chops. Cut pocket in each chop by moving knife back and forth carefully through incision. Stuff chops with morels, chopped coarse. In a heavy skillet, heat butter over moderate heat until foam subsides. Cook chops for 4 minutes on each side. Add wine and chops for 5 minutes. Transfer chops with a slotted spatula to plates, and sprinkle with parsley. If desired, reduce pan juice over high heat for 3 minutes, and serve with chops.
Servings: 2.

Veal Cordon Bleu

20 slices veal (3 ounces),
  top round cutlets
10 slices ham (1 ounce each)
10 slices Swiss cheese (1/2 ounce each)
Flour, as needed

3 eggs
1 pound bread crumbs, fresh
1/2 cup oil
1/2 cup butter

Pound veal until desired thickness. Place cheese and bread crumbs on veal. Place on ham, and cover with second slice of veal. Dust veal with flour. Dip veal in egg, and saute in oil and butter. Saute veal to golden brown; finish by baking in 350 degree oven for 5 to 7 minutes.
Servings: 10.

Entrees

Veal with Oysters and Artichoke over Pasta

1-1/4 cups cold water
 (9 quarts water in all)
3-1/2 tablespoons salt
2 lemons, halved
1/2 pound fresh spaghetti or
 1/3 pound dry
1/2 pound (2 sticks) unsalted butter
1/2 cup green onion, finely chopped

3/4 cup heavy cream
9 oysters in liquid, about 7 ounces
5 tablespoons olive or vegetable oil
2-1/2 teaspoons garlic powder
1 large artichoke
1/2 pound boneless white veal
 cut 1-1/2x1-1/4 inch
 julienned strips

Seasoned Flour Mix:
1/4 cup all purpose flour
1-1/4 teaspoons white pepper
1 teaspoon ground cayenne

1-1/2 teaspoons salt
1 teaspoon onion powder
1/2 teaspon paprika

Combine the 1-1/4 cups cold water with oysters. Refrigerate at least one hour. Strain, and reserve oysters and liquid in refrigerator until ready to use. In a large soup pot, combine 6 quarts of water, 3 tablespoons oil, 2 tablespoons salt, garlic powder and lemons. Cover, and bring to boil over high heat. Meanwhile, cut stem off artichoke. Trim artichoke top down by about 1/2 inch. Add artichoke and stem to boiling water. Cover pan, and boil until leaves can be pulled off easily, about 25 minutes. Stir occasionally, and drain. Cool artichoke slightly; then remove each leaf, and scrape off edible parts from bottom of each with spoon. Remove the innermost leaves covering fuzzy choke. With teaspoon, scoop out choke from center and discard, leaving artichoke heart intact at bottom. Cut artichoke heart into thin slices. Chop edible parts off, and discard stringy leaves. Trim end of stem. Cut off, and discard stringy skin. Slice at the tender center of stem. The total of slices and trimmings should be about 2/3 cup. Set aside. Place remaining 3 quarts water, 2 tablespoons oil and 1-1/2 tablespoons salt in large

Entrees

pot over high heat. Cover, and bring to boil. When water reaches rolling boil, add small amounts of spaghetti at time to pot, breaking up oil patches as spaghetti is dropped in. Return to boiling, and cook, uncovered, until al dente, 4 minutes fresh and 7 minutes dry. Do not overcook. During cooking time, use wooden spoon to lift by spoonful out of water, shaking strands back in to separate. When done, place in colander, and drain. After spaghetti has cooled thoroughly, about 2 to 3 minutes, pour liberal amount of vegetable oil in hands, and toss spaghetti. Set aside, still in colander. Combine seasoned flour ingredients in medium size bowl, and mix well. Add veal, and toss until all pieces are well coated and as much flour as possible is absorbed. In a large skillet, melt 1 stick butter over high heat. Add veal pieces in single layer, and saute until golden brown and crispy on all sides, about 4 minutes. Add reserved artichoke, green onions and 4 tablespoons more butter. Cook for 2 minutes while shaking pan fairly vigorously in back and forth motion. Stir in 1/4 cup oyster water, cook, and shake the pan 1 minute. Add remaining 4 tablespoons butter, remaining 1 cup oyster water and cream. Continue cooking and shaking pan 1 minute more. Add oysters, and shake pan until butter is completely melted, 2 minutes. Add pasta, and toss until pasta is coated and heated through, about 2 minutes. Serve immediately.
Servings: 3.

Warm Chicken Liver Salad

1/2 pound chicken livers
1/2 cup flour
Salt and pepper to taste

Mixed greens
1 cup salad dressing of your choice
4 tablespoons vegetable oil

Toss chicken livers in flour, and shake dry. Heat in cast iron skillet over medium heat until hot. Add 4 tablespoons of vegetable oil and chicken livers. Season with salt and pepper. Cook until golden on both sides but still pink. Pour off oil, and add one tablespoon of the same kind of vinegar used in the dressing. Remove livers to a plate. Toss greens with dressing. Top with chicken livers, and garnish with sliced scallions, if desired. Serve.
Servings: 4.

Entrees

Wild Turkey
with Cornbread Dressing

1 young wild turkey (9 pounds)
1-1/2 teaspoons salt
1 teaspoon lemon pepper seasoning
12 cups cornbread crumbs
12 slices bread, cubed
4 cups onions, chopped
4 cups celery, chopped
4 teaspoons rubbed sage
2 teaspoons salt

1 teaspoon pepper
1/4 cup bacon drippings, melted
6 eggs, beaten
1-1/2 cups water
Vegetable oil
1 cup chicken broth
Apple wedges
Fresh sage sprigs
Fresh rosemary sprigs

Rinse turkey thoroughly with cold water, and pat dry. Combine 1-1/2 teaspoons of salt and lemon pepper seasoning. Sprinkle over surface and in cavity of turkey. Combine cornbread crumbs and bread cubes in a large mixing bowl. Add onion, celery, sage, 2 teaspoons of salt, pepper, bacon drippings and eggs. Mix well. Stir in water until desired consistency is reached. Stuff dressing lightly into cavity of turkey. Set remaining dressing aside. Close cavity of turkey with skewers. Tie ends of legs together with string. Lift wingtips up and over back, tucking under bird securely. Brush entire bird with vegetable oil. Place breast side up on a rack in a roasting pan. Bake at 325 degrees for 1-1/2 hours. Cut cord holding drumstick ends together. Bake an additional 1 hour, basting frequently with chicken broth. Turkey is done when drumsticks are easy to move. Spoon reserved dressing into a lightly greased 13x9x2 inch baking dish. Bake at 350 degrees for 45 minutes. Transfer turkey to serving platter, and spoon baked dressing around turkey on platter. Garnish with apple wedges and sprigs of fresh herbs. Servings: about 12.

Entrees

Zesty Chicken and Rice

4 chicken breast halves
  (skinned, if desired)
1/2 cup bottled Italian salad dressing
2/3 cup uncooked regular white rice
1 bag (16 ounces) frozen vegetable combination (broccoli, red peppers, bamboo shoots, and straw mushrooms)

1 can (2.8 ounces) french fried onions
1-3/4 cups chicken broth
1/2 teaspoon Italian seasoning

Preheat oven to 400 degrees. Place chicken in a 9x13 inch baking dish. Pour salad dressing over chicken. Bake uncovered 20 minutes. Place rice, vegetables, and 1/2 can french fried onions around and under chicken. Combine broth and Italian seasoning. Pour over chicken and vegetables. Bake uncovered for 25 minutes. Top with remaining onions, and bake 2 to 3 minutes longer. Let stand 5 minutes before serving.
Servings: 4.

ACCOMPANIMENTS

Accompaniments

Contents

Accompaniments

Accompaniments

Accompaniments

Culinary Commentary

Chef Marcel Massenet is a certified executive pastry chef with over 25 years of experience in bakeries, hotels and restaurants. With a formal French baking and pastry education, he worked in Europe, the Caribbean, and Australia before coming to the United States. Massenet owns a French pastry shop, Normandy Farm, in Charleston, South Carolina.

A FEW SLICES OF HISTORY

As we bite into a loaf of crispy bread or a favorite sandwich, we enjoy an experience shared by others for many centuries in almost every part of the world. To think about the beginning of bread making, we must look back several thousand years.

About 6,000 to 8,000 years ago, nuts and grains were soaked to make doughs, but soon man realized that grinding them would make a more palatable product. The earliest record of milling grains by stone dates to 4,000 B.C. By 2,000 B.C., mills were powered by slaves or cattle.

Around 450 B.C., Greeks mastered the single wheel mill to finally produce a fine product. The Romans refined this system to get something close to today's whole grain flour.

From that time, bread became more tasty, and bakers never stopped improving their art. The early breads were all unleavened. According to legend, an Egyptian baker mistakenly let a batch of dough sit overnight. The next morning it was double the size, so the man baked only part of it. Because the Egyptian Pharoah had proclaimed strict laws against waste, the baker, fearful for his life, mixed the rest of the dough with a new batch. When the dough doubled again on the third day, the man realized that he had created a much lighter and flavorful product. Hence, leavened bread was discovered.

The Egyptians became real masters in the art of bread baking. Bread ovens were built next to temples, and bakers were equal to priests. At the same time, Persia and China were trying to make a light bread by the process of fermentation. Later, both Greece and Rome had many kinds of bread made with wheat, barley and rice. Around 100 B.C., there were more than 250 commercial bakeries in Rome and two hundred years later, the first school for bakers was founded there.

In the Middle Ages, bakers guilds were created, and laws were written to protect bakers from unfair practices and competition.

Until about 200 years ago only the rich had the privilege of eating white bread.

On this side of the Atlantic Ocean, Indians, then Pilgrims, used stone mortars. White flour became more accessible as settlers moved west, and wheat was successfully grown.

Baking powder was introduced in 1856 and, from breweries, in 1868, came a by product which is commonly known as "yeast."

Today, many bakers are highly mechanized, but next time you walk by a bakery, remember this beautiful smell was not created overnight.

Culinary Commentary

Chef Susan Wigley is a certified culinary educator and certified working chef. In addition to teaching at the University, she is a menu design consultant.

FLOWER COOKERY

No table setting is ever complete without fresh flowers. But recently the roses have begun dropping their petals on our plates. The use of flowers as garnish is becoming a New Age standard. We are discovering that many old favorites are more than just a pretty face. Actually what seems new to us is merely the revival of an old custom. As it turns out, many flowers have interesting flavors and textures and were once considered an essential part of the culinary repertoire.

Rose petals, perfumed jellies, and scented geranium leaves once lent their fragrances to teas and dessert syrups. Nasturtiums were a common salad ingredient, along with squash blossoms and gardenia petals. Violets were candied and used on celebratory desserts. These old ideas are now being given new interpretation by our most talented young chefs. Sinclair Phillip of Sooke Harbor House, British Columbia, uses black pansy syrup with his dessert custards. Other young chefs serve rose sorbet, add marjoram blossoms to fresh tomato soups, and cast Johnny-Jump-Ups across their salads.

The list of edible flowers is long and colorful and offers endless possibilities. It includes all species of chrysanthemums, daylilies, nasturtiums with their spicy watercress flavor, garden pinks (dianthus) which add a delicate hint of cloves, and violas (pansies and Johnny-Jump-Ups). Roses exude excellent flavor and fragrance, calendula is good in soups and vegetable dishes, and geraniums come in many exotic scents: lemon, apple, rose, peppermint, nutmeg. Beebalm (Monarda), hollyhocks, impatiens, lilacs, English daisies, lavender, chicory and portulaca are others that appear commonly in dishes around the country. Of course, nearly all culinary herbs have lovely and edible flowers. Some outstanding ones are chives, sage, rosemary, basil (especially cinnamon basil), pineapple sage (vivid red), mint, marjoram, fennel, and thyme.

Before you go grazing in the flower beds, however, there are a few things to keep in mind. First of all, flower names are confusing, and it is important to identify them correctly before using them as food. For example, daylilies are edible, but Belladonna lilies (actually amaryllis) are poisonous. Plants that you are not sure of should be identified by their Latin names. Books listing plants only by their common names should not be relied upon. Consider any plant inedible unless you find evidence of its safety in a reference book on edible plants. Secondly, different varieties of the same flower taste differently. Only taste testing will tell you which geranium has the best flavor.

The following is a list of poisonous plants commonly found in the

Culinary Commentary

Southeast. No part of these plants should be used either in cooking or for garnish.

Poisonous Plants

Amaryllis (Hippeastrum puniceum)

Azalea (Rhododendron spp.)

Buttercup (Ranunculus spp.)

Caladium (Caladium bicolor)

Daffodil (Narcissus Pseudonarcissus)

Hydrangea (Hydrangea spp.)

Iris (Iris spp.)

Yellow Jessamine (Gelsemium Sempervirens)

Lantana (Lantana spp.)

Narcissus (Narcissus spp.)

Oleander (Nerium Oleander)

Poinsettia (Euphorbia pulcherrima)

Wisteria (Wisteria floribunda and Wisteria sinensis)

The texts listed below are recommended for determining possible toxicity or edibility of a plant or flower. You may also call your local agricultural extension office for information.

Sturtevant's Edible Plants of the World, U.P. Hedrick, editor, Dover Publications, 1972.

Poisonous Plants of the United States and Canada, John M. Kingsbury, Prentice-Hall Inc., 1964.

The Oxford Book of Food Plants, G.B. Masefield, et. al., Oxford University Press, 1975.

For more inspiration on the uses of edible flowers, look up the delightful book by Leona Woodring Smith called The Forgotten Art of Flower Cookery. Another source of information is Organic Gardening magazine which frequently features recipes for blossom cookery. Bon Appetit!

Accompaniments

Acorn Squash
with Raisins and Walnuts

1 3/4 to 1 pound acorn squash,
  halved crosswise and seeds and
  strings discarded
1 tablespoon unsalted butter, softened

2 tablespoons walnuts, coarsely chopped
2 tablespoons raisins
2 teaspoons dark brown sugar,
  firmly packed

Sprinkle squash cavities with salt and pepper to taste. Slice off ends of squash to form flat bottoms, and arrange squash cut side down in well-buttered shallow baking pan. Prick squash skin lightly with sharp knife, and bake squash in preheated 425 oven for 25 to 30 minutes, or until tender. While squash is baking, combine in small bowl the walnuts, raisins, brown sugar, butter and salt to taste. Invert squash halves in pan, and fill cavities with the raisin mixture. Bake squash for 10 minutes more.
Servings: 2.

Accompaniments

Apple-Cinnamon And Raisin Muffins

2 cups all purpose flour
1 tablespoon baking powder
1 egg
2/3 cup unsweetened apple juice
1 teaspoon cinnamon
1/2 cup nuts, chopped

2/3 cup dark brown sugar, packed
1/2 teaspoon fresh nutmeg, grated
1/3 cup safflower oil
1 tart cooking apple,
  unpeeled and finely diced (1 cup)
1/2 cup raisins

Preheat oven to 400 degrees. Generously butter 12 muffin cups, each 2-1/2 inches in diameter. In a large bowl, sift together flour, brown sugar, baking powder and nutmeg. In medium bowl, combine egg, oil and apple juice. Whisk until blended. In medium bowl, toss together the apple and cinnamon until evenly coated. Stir in raisins and nuts. Pour egg mixture over sifted dry ingredients, and fold lightly 3-4 times with a rubber spatula to partially combine. Add apple mixture and distribute evenly, using as few strokes as possible. Do not over mix. Quickly divide batter amount into prepared muffin cups. Bake in middle of the oven for 25 minutes or until golden and spring back to touch. Let cool in the pan for 2 minutes. Cool on wire rack for 20 minutes.
Servings: 12.

Apple Pecan Squash

2 medium acorn squash
1/2 cup butter or margarine
1/2 teaspoon salt
1 cup pecans, chopped

2 cups apples, finely chopped
1 teaspoon cinnamon
2 teaspoons lemon juice
Generous dash nutmeg

Cut squash in half crosswise, and remove seeds. Bake, cut side down, in shallow pan at 350 for 45 minutes. Remove cooked squash from shells, and mix with butter or margarine, apples, cinnamon, salt, lemon juice and pecans, reserving 1/4 cup pecans for topping. Spoon mixture into shells, and top with nutmeg and remaining pecans. Bake at 350 for 10 minutes.
Servings: 4.

Accompaniments

Apple Pull-Apart Bread

3 to 3-1/2 cups all-purpose flour,
  divided
2 tablespoons sugar
1 package dry yeast
1 teaspoon salt
1 cup milk
1/2 cup butter or margarine,
  melted and divided
1 egg, beaten

1 large cooking apple,
  peeled and chopped
2/3 cup sugar
1/2 cup pecans, finely chopped
1/2 teaspoon ground cinnamon
1 cup powdered sugar, sifted
1 to 1-1/2 tablespoons hot water
1/2 teaspoon vanilla extract

Combine 1 cup flour, 2 tablespoons sugar, yeast and salt in a large bowl. Blend well. Heat milk and 2 tablespoons butter to 120 degrees. Add egg. Blend well. Add milk mixture to flour mixture. Beat at medium speed of an electric mixer until smooth. Stir in enough remaining flour to make a stiff dough. Turn dough out onto a lightly floured surface, and knead 4 or 5 times or until smooth and elastic. Cover, and let rest 20 minutes. Combine apple, 2/3 cup sugar, pecans and cinnamon. Set aside. Divide dough in half. Cut each half into 16 equal pieces. Shape each piece into a ball, and roll out on a lightly floured surface to a 2-1/2 inch circle. Place 1 teaspoon apple mixture in center of circle. Pinch edges together to seal, and form a ball. Dip each ball into remaining melted butter. Place 16 balls in a greased 10 inch tube pan. Sprinkle with 1/4 cup apple mixture. Repeat procedure with remaining dough, apple mixture and butter. Place remaining 16 balls over first layer of balls, and sprinkle evenly with remaining apple mixture. Bake at 350 degrees on lowest rack in oven for 40 minutes or until golden. Let cool 10 minutes. Invert onto a serving platter. Combine 1 cup powdered sugar, water and vanilla, stirring until smooth. Drizzle over bread. Yield: one 10 inch coffee cake.

Accompaniments

Apple-Ricot Rice Souffle

3-1/2 cups half and half
1-1/4 cups short grain rice
2 egg yolks
6 tablespoons powdered sugar
2 tablespoons butter
6 tablespoons apricot jam

4 tablespoons applesauce
3 egg whites
1/4 teaspoon cream of tartar
1/2 teaspoon almond extract
2 tablespoons applesauce
1 tablespoon light rum

In a sauce pot, bring half and half to a boil, and stir in rice. Turn heat down, and cover, stirring frequently. When rice is tender, remove from heat. Beat egg yolks with sugar, and stir into rice being careful not to curdle eggs. Butter souffle dishes, and spread a layer of rice on the bottom of each. Next spread a thin layer of jam, and repeat the process making sure to end with a layer of jam. Finish with a thin layer of applesauce on each. Beat egg whites until frothy. Add cream of tartar, and continue until peaks can be formed. Next, fold in the remainder of the ingredients, and spread over applesauce. Place in oven preheated to 350 degrees for approximately 20 minutes. Spoon rum over top, and ignite. Allow rum to burn off. Serve.
Servings: 4.

Accompaniments

Applesauce Bran Muffins

1-1/2 cups 100% bran cereal
1 cup skim milk
1 egg, slightly beaten
1/2 cup unsweetened applesauce
2-1/2 tablespoons butter, melted

1 cup all purpose flour
2-1/2 teaspoons baking powder
1/4 cup brown sugar
Non-stick vegetable spray

In a large bowl, combine the cereal and milk. While letting the milk absorb into the cereal, melt butter. In a small bowl, add melted butter to egg and applesauce. Stir into the large bowl. Add dry ingredients. Stir until blended. Spray muffin pan with vegetable spray or line with baking cups. Fill 3/4 full. Bake at 400 degrees for 15 minutes or until golden brown.
Servings: 12.

Artichoke Balls

2 tablespoons olive oil
1/2 teaspoon onion, chopped
3 cloves garlic, minced
1 can (14 ounces) artichoke hearts, drained and mashed

1-1/3 cups seasoned breadcrumbs
3 eggs, lightly beaten until fluffy
1 cup parmesan cheese, grated

Heat oil in skillet, saute onion and garlic, and mix artichoke hearts and 1 cup bread crumbs. Add eggs, onions, garlic and 1/3 cup of cheese. Mix, and refrigerate for 1 hour. Form 1 inch balls. Refrigerate until ready to serve.
Yield: 3 dozen.

Accompaniments

Artichoke Dressing Casserole

2 cans (14 ounces) artichoke hearts,
  reserve liquid
1 box (1 pound 8 ounces) Italian
  bread crumbs
1/2 cup olive oil

2 cloves garlic, minced
1 cup romano cheese or parmesan
  cheese, fresh grated
Salt and pepper to taste
Juice of 2 lemons

Mix artichoke juice, crumbs, olive oil and lemon juice. Mash artichoke thoroughly, and add to above mixture. Add cheese and garlic. Blend well. Bake in 350 degree oven for 20 minutes. This fills 2-1/2 quart casserole.
Servings: 6-8.

Asparagus with Chopped Egg and Butter Sauce

3/4 pound asparagus (white if
  available) trimmed and peeled
1 small onion
2 hard cooked large eggs, chopped fine

1 tablespoon fresh parsley
  leaves, chopped
Pinch nutmeg
1 stick butter or margarine, melted

In saucepan, cover asparagus and onion with salted water, and bring to boil. Remove pan from heat, let asparagus and onion stand in water uncovered for 5 minutes or until asparagus is tender, and drain vegetables. Transfer asparagus to heated platter, and discard onion. In bowl, combine egg, parsley, nutmeg and salt and pepper to taste, and add butter in stream, whisking until sauce is emulsified. Serve sauce with asparagus.
Servings: 4.   Nutritional Analysis: page 434.

Accompaniments

Asparagus with Orange Butter Sauce

1/3 cup butter
2 tablespoons orange rind, grated
1/4 cup orange juice

1-1/2 pounds asparagus
Orange slices, peeled

Combine butter, orange rind, and juice in a saucepan. Bring to boil. Reduce heat, and simmer until mixture is reduced by half and slightly thickened, stirring occasionally. Set aside, and keep warm. Snap off ends of asparagus, and remove scales from stalks with knife or peeler. Cook asparagus, for 6 to 8 minutes until al dente. Arrange asparagus in serving dish. Pour sauce over asparagus and garnish with orange slices. Serve.
Servings: 6.

Baby Carrots Bourbonnaise

3/4 pound baby carrots, scraped
2/3 cup orange juice
2 tablespoons butter
2 tablespoons brown sugar

2 tablespoons bourbon
1/8 teaspoon salt
1 teaspoon fresh dill, chopped

Place carrots in saucepan with orange juice. Cook, covered for 12 to 15 minutes or until tender, and drain, reserving juice. Combine reserved juice, butter, sugar, bourbon and salt, and cook over low heat until butter melts, stirring occasionally. Do not boil. Pour over carrots, and sprinkle with dill.
Servings: 4.

Accompaniments

Bacon, Corn and Tomato Melange

3 slices lean bacon, chopped
1 small onion, minced
1 cup corn (fresh, if possible)

1 tomato peeled, seeded and chopped
1 tablespoon fresh basil leaves, minced

In skillet, cook bacon over medium heat, stirring until crisp. Transfer with slotted spoon to paper towels to drain. In fat remaining in skillet, cook onion and corn over moderate low heat, stirring for 5 minutes. Stir in salt and pepper, tomato and pinch of sugar. Cook mixture, covered stirring occasionally for 10 to 15 minutes, or until corn is tender. Stir bacon and basil in, and serve. Servings: 2.

Baked Apples Stuffed with Sausage and Cranberries

1 pound bulk sausage meat
1 teaspoon dried sage, crumbled
1 cup cranberries, picked over
3 ribs celery, chopped fine
8 apples

1 onion, chopped
1/2 teaspoon dried thyme, crumbled
1/2 cup fresh bread crumbs
1/2 cup fresh parsley leaves, minced

In a large skillet, cook crumbled sausage, over moderate heat, until no longer pink. Stir in onion, dried sage, thyme, cranberries, salt and pepper to taste, and cook mixture, stirring occasionally until cranberries begin to pop. Stir in bread crumbs, celery and parsley. Remove skillet from heat. (This may be done one day in advance. Keep covered and chilled.) Cut top 1/2 inch of apple, core with melon ball cutter, and scoop out flesh, reserving it and leaving 3/4 inch shell. Chop flesh coarse, and stir into stuffing. Divide stuffing among apples, mounding it, and arrange apples in baking pan. Pour 1 inch hot water into the pan, and bake, covered tightly with foil, in preheated oven 375 degrees for 1-1/2 hours, or until crisp tender. Arrange on heated serving tray. Garnish, and serve. Servings: 8.

Accompaniments

Baked Tomato Florentine

4 strips bacon, diced
1 package (10 ounces) frozen spinach
1/3 cup Italian bread crumbs

4 medium size tomatoes
3/4 cup Swiss cheese, shredded
1/4 teaspoon ground nutmeg

Cook bacon until crisp, and drain. Cut 1/2 inch slices from top of each tomato, and scoop out pulp. Combine remaining ingredients with bacon. Spoon into tomato, and bake uncovered at 350 for 15 minutes.
Servings: 4.

Baked Tomatoes
Stuffed with Mushrooms

8 medium tomatoes, ripe
  but still very firm
1/2 pound mushrooms,
  coarsely chopped
Boiling water
2 tablespoons butter or margarine
4 tablespoons flour
1/4 teaspoon dried basil
1/4 teaspoon dried oregano

1-1/3 cup milk
1/4 teaspoon worcestershire sauce
1 cup soft bread crumbs
2 tablespoons parmesan cheese grated
1 tablespoon parsley, minced
2 tablespoons butter, melted
Anchovy fillets
Salt and pepper to taste

Cover tomatoes with boiling water, let stand 2 minutes, drain and skin. Scoop out insides carefully, leaving shells. Saute mushrooms in butter, and stir in flour, salt and pepper to taste, basil and oregano. Slowly stir in milk, continuing to stir until sauce is thick and smooth. Add worcestershire sauce. Lay tomato shells in shallow buttered casserole, and fill with mushroom sauce. Mix together crumbs, cheese, parsley and butter, and top tomatoes with mixture. Bake 15 to 20 minutes in moderate oven (350). Cross 2 anchovy fillets on each tomato before serving.
Servings: 8.

Accompaniments

Broccoli and Ham Gratin

3/4 stick unsalted butter
  (6 tablespoons)
1/4 cup all purpose flour
2 cups milk
1/2 cup fresh parmesan, grated
1/2 cup Swiss cheese, grated

1 pound broccoli trimmed, cooked in
  boiling salted water until just tender
  and chopped coarse (4-1/2 cups) or
  steamed until al dente
1/4 pound cooked ham, chopped
1 cup coarse dry bread crumbs

In saucepan, melt 4 tablespoons of butter over moderately low heat, add the flour and cook roux, stirring for 3 minutes. Add milk. Whisking, bring mixture to boil, and simmer, stirring for 5 minutes. Stir in parmesan cheese, Swiss cheese and salt and pepper to taste, and cook mixture, stirring until cheese is melted. In well buttered 14 inch gratin dish, combine broccoli and ham. Pour sauce over mixture. Sprinkle the bread crumbs over top, dot with remaining 2 tablespoons butter, and bake gratin in preheated 375 degree oven for 30 minutes or until it is bubbling.
Servings: 6-8.

Broccoli and Rice Casserole

1 stick (4 ounces) butter
1 medium onion, chopped
20 ounces broccoli, chopped
1 cup rice

1 can cream of chicken soup
10 ounces milk
8 ounces of processed cheese

Saute butter and onion. Mix in casserole baking dish with all ingredients until well blended. Bake at 350 degrees for 40 minutes.
Servings: 4.
Nutritional Analysis: page 435.

Accompaniments

Broccoli Carrot Supreme

1/4 cup butter
10 ounces broccoli, cooked and drained
1 teaspoon salt
1 teaspoon thyme
1/2 cup medium dry white wine
1/2 cup pecans, chopped

4-6 carrots, sliced
8 ounces small white onions, drained
Dash pepper
1 bay leaf
1/4 cup heavy cream

Melt butter in skillet, add carrots and onions, and cook for 4 minutes, stirring to coat vegetables. Add seasonings and wine. Cover, reduce heat to low, and cook for 20 minutes or until carrots are tender. Discard bay leaf, and stir in cream, broccoli and pecans. Heat for a few minutes before serving.
Servings: 4-6.   Nutritional Analysis: page 435.

Browned Brussel Sprouts

1/4 pound brussel sprouts
1 tablespoon olive oil
3 tablespoons butter

2 tablespoons fresh tarragon, chopped
  or other fresh herbs
Salt and pepper to taste

In a saucepan of boiling salted water, cook sprouts until tender, approximately 4 minutes, or steam al dente. Drain, and chill in ice water. Slice sprouts in halves, and pat dry. Just before serving, heat olive oil in large frying pan. Add butter, and when it foams and turns nut brown, add sprouts, and toss. Cook over high heat, stirring occasionally, until sprouts are browned and tender, 3 to 4 minutes. Toss in tarragon. Season with salt and pepper.
Servings: 4.

Accompaniments

Brussel Sprouts de Luxe

1 quart brussel sprouts or
  3 packages frozen, al dente
1/2 cup carrots, chopped
1/4 cup onion, chopped
1/4 cup celery, chopped

1/2 cup cooked chestnuts, broken up
1-1/2 cups condensed consomme
3 tablespoons butter or margarine
Salt and pepper
2 thin slices lemon, quartered

Arrange sprouts in greased casserole. In a saucepan, add carrots, onion, celery, chestnuts and consomme. Bring to boil, reduce heat, and simmer for 10 minutes. Add butter, seasoning to taste and lemon pieces. Pour over sprouts, and bake in moderate oven, 350 degrees for 30 minutes. Cover for the first 20 minutes. Servings: 6.

Brussel Sprouts
in Light Bechamel Sauce

4 cups fresh brussel sprouts
1/4 cup water
1 teaspoon basil
1 tablespoon butter
  or margarine

1 tablespoon all-purpose flour
1 cup lowfat milk
2 to 4 cloves garlic, minced
  or crushed
Pinch of chervil (optional)

Wash the brussel sprouts, and pull off any yellowing leaves. Trim the ends, and make a small gash in the bottom of each one to help them cook to tenderness. Place them in a saucepan with the water and the basil, and bring to a boil. Reduce heat, and simmer for about 10 minutes. Melt the butter or margarine in a large skillet over medium low heat. Add the flour and brown, stirring constantly to form a roux. Stir in the milk and garlic, and cook until the sauce has thickened slightly. Serve over the cooked brussels sprouts. (This makes about 1 cup sauce). Servings: 8 (1/2 cup sprouts, with 2 tablespoons of sauce).

Accompaniments

Brussel Sprouts with Hazelnuts

2-1/2 to 3 pounds fresh brussel
  sprouts, trimmed (about 6 cups)
1/4 cup plus 3 tablespoons butter

1-1/2 cups skinned toasted hazelnuts
  (about 7-1/2 ounces), coarsely chopped
Fresh white pepper and salt to taste

In a large saucepan, bring lightly salted water to a boil. Add brussel sprouts, and cover saucepan, heat to boiling. Boil uncovered until tender. Drain. Melt butter in large skillet over medium high heat, shaking pan constantly, until butter is slightly brown. Add brussel sprouts. Saute over high heat, stirring constantly, approximately 2 minutes. Add hazelnuts, and season with salt and pepper. Saute 1 minute. Serve.
Servings: 12.

Buttered Egg Noodles

3 quarts water
1 tablespoon salt
1 pound egg noodles, medium

1/2 cup butter
Salt and pepper to taste

Bring water to boil in marmite. Add noodles to boiling water. Cook al dente. When done, remove from heat. Cool noodles under running cold water. Strain in colander. Melt butter in sautoir, and toss noodles. Season.
Servings: 10.   Nutritional Analysis: page 435.

Accompaniments

Buttered Noodles
with Crisp Browned Shallots

Vegetable oil for frying shallots
1/2 pound medium egg noodles
2 tablespoons unsalted butter, softened

1/2 pound large shallots, peeled
and sliced thin, crosswise
Salt and pepper to taste

In a large skillet, heat 1/2 inch of oil over moderately high heat until hot but not smoking. Fry shallots, stirring occasionally for 2 to 3 minutes or until golden. Transfer with slotted spoon to paper towel to drain. In pot of boiling salted water, cook noodles 7 to 9 minutes or until tender, drain well, and return to kettle. Toss noodles with butter, salt and pepper to taste. Transfer to heated serving dish. Sprinkle with shallots. Serve.
Servings: 4.

Butternut Squash Puff

3 cups butternut squash,
  cooked, mashed
2 eggs, beaten
1/4 cup half and half
2 tablespoons butter or margarine,
  melted
1 tablespoon orange rind, grated

1/2 teaspoon lemon rind, grated
2 tablespoons all purpose flour
1 tablespoon sugar
1/4 teaspoon salt
1/8 teaspoon pepper
Pecan halves (optional)

Combine all ingredients except pecans, and mix well. Spoon into greased 1-1/2 quart casserole. Place casserole in 13x9x2 inch baking pan. Pour hot water into pan 1/2 inch deep. Bake at 350 degrees for 50 minutes or until set. Garnish with pecan halves.
Servings: 6.

Accompaniments

Carrots and Celery with Pecans

2-1/2 cups water
1/4 teaspoon salt
4 medium carrots, sliced diagonally
6 ribs celery, sliced diagonally

1 cup pecans, chopped
1/2 teaspoon dried whole dill weed
1/4 cup margarine, melted

Combine water and salt, and bring to boil. Add carrots, cover, and reduce heat. Simmer for 10 minutes. Add celery, cover, and simmer an additional 5 minutes or until celery is crisp and tender. Drain well. Saute pecans and dill weed in butter until pecans are golden. Toss with carrots and celery.
Servings: 6.   Nutritional Analysis: page 435.

Carrot Fettuccini

1 pound carrots
3 tablespoons unsalted butter
1/2 cup onion, minced
1/4 pound sliced cooked ham,
  cut into thin strips
2 cloves garlic, minced

1/2 cup dry white wine
1 cup heavy cream
1 cup frozen peas, thawed
1 tablespoon dijon style mustard
Salt and pepper to taste

With swivel bladed vegetable peeler, shred carrots into fettuccini like strands. In large skillet, heat butter over moderately high heat until foam begins to subside, and in it cook the onion and ham, stirring for 3 minutes. Add carrot strands, garlic and wine. Cook mixture, covered, over moderate low heat, stirring occasionally for 10 minutes or until almost all liquids are evaporated and carrots are almost tender. Add cream and peas, bring to boil, and simmer covered for 5 minutes or until liquid is reduced by half. Stir in the mustard and salt and pepper to taste. Serve.
Servings: 4.

274

Accompaniments

Carrots with Cognac

4 cups carrots, sliced diagonally,
very thin or julienned
2 tablespoons butter
4 tablespoons cognac

4 tablespoons water
Salt and pepper to taste
1 tablespoon parsley, minced

Melt butter in medium casserole. Stir in remaining ingredients, except parsley, keeping salt and pepper on light side. Cover tightly, and bake in oven at 300 degrees for 20 minutes or until carrots are tender, and liquid is absorbed. Sprinkle with parsley, and serve.
Servings: 5-6.

Cauliflower Pea Casserole

1 large cauliflower
1 package (10 ounces) frozen
English peas, thawed
1/2 cup almonds, slivered
1/2 teaspoon curry powder
3 tablespoons butter or margarine, melted and divided

2 tablespoons all purpose flour
1-1/4 cups commercial sour cream
1-1/2 teaspoons onion salt
1/8 teaspoon white pepper

Separate cauliflower into flowerets. Cook in small amount of unsalted boiling water, 6 to 8 minutes or until crisp tender or steamed al dente. Drain well. Place cauliflower and peas in greased 2 quart casserole. Set aside. Saute almond and curry powder in 1 tablespoon butter in skillet. Cook, stirring constantly, until almonds are browned. Remove from heat, and set aside. Combine remaining 2 tablespoons butter and flour in heavy saucepan, and stir until smooth. Cook 1 minute, stirring constantly. Gradually stir in sour cream. Cook over low heat, stirring until thoroughly heated. Stir in salt and pepper. Pour over cauliflower mixture, and sprinkle almonds over top. Cover, and refrigerate. Remove, and let stand 30 minutes. Bake uncovered for 25 to 30 minutes at 350 degrees. Serve.
Servings: 6-8.

Accompaniments

Cavatelli with Broccoli

1 pound cavatelli (short curled pasta)
2-1/2 cups broccoli flowerets
6 anchovy fillets, rinsed,
  patted dry and chopped
1/4 cup olive oil

2 pimentos, sliced thin
1 tablespoons butter, melted
1/4 cup parmesan cheese, grated
1 cup romano cheese, grated

Cook cavatelli in boiling salted water for 7 minutes or until al dente. Drain. In a steamer, set over boiling water, and steam broccoli for 4 minutes or until crisp and tender. In a large skillet, cook anchovies in oil over moderate heat, stirring for 30 seconds. Stir in pimento, cavatelli, broccoli, butter and pepper to taste. Sprinkle mixture with parmesan and romano cheese, and toss until combined well and heated through.
Servings: 4-6.

Cheddar Biscuits

1-1/2 cups unbleached flour sifted with:
  1-1/2 teaspoons double action baking powder and
  1/2 teaspoon salt
1/4 cup cold lard
1/2 cup milk plus additional milk for brushing the biscuits
1/4 cup sharp cheddar cheese, finely grated

In a bowl, blend the flour mixture and the lard until the mixture resembles meal. Make a well in the center, add the milk, and stir the mixture until it just forms a dough. Roll out the dough 1/2 inch thick on a floured surface, cut into rounds, with a 2 inch cutter, and transfer to a buttered baking sheet. Gather the scraps, and prepare more rounds in same manner. Brush biscuits with additional milk, sprinkle with cheddar, and bake in preheated oven 425 degrees for 20-25 minutes, until golden. Transfer biscuits to serving dish.
Servings: 12.

276

Accompaniments

Cheesy Puff Top Tomatoes

1 onion flavored bouillon cube,
  crushed
2 egg whites
1/2 cup cottage cheese

2 tablespoons plus 1 teaspoon
  parmesan, grated
3 medium tomatoes

Combine bouillon and cottage cheese ingredients. Let stand 5 minutes, and stir in parmesan cheese. Beat egg whites until soft peaks form, fold into cottage cheese mixture and set aside. Cut tomatoes in half. Place cut side up on baking pan. Cover, and bake at 350 for 5 minutes. Spoon cottage cheese mixture over cut surface of tomato. Broil tomatoes 5 inches from heat, 3 to 5 minutes.
Servings: 6.

Cherry Tomato Bake

1 pint ripe cherry tomatoes
3 tablespoons scallions, diced
1/4 cup fresh parsley, minced
1 medium clove garlic, crushed

1/4 teaspoon thyme
1/2 teaspoon salt
1/8 teaspoon black pepper
2 tablespoons parmesan cheese, grated

Remove any stems from the tomatoes, and place the tomatoes in a baking dish. Sprinkle the scallions on top. In a small bowl, combine the remaining ingredients. Sprinkle this mixture over the tomatoes. Bake at 375 degrees for 3 minutes. Stir, turning the tomatoes, and bake an additional 3 minutes. Mix, and serve.
Servings: 4 (1/2 cup).

Accompaniments

Chestnut and Oyster Gratin

2 pounds fresh raw chestnuts
2 dozen large oysters, drained,
  reserve liquid
1 cup heavy cream
1-3/4 pounds small red potatoes,
  pared, cut into 1/8 inch thick
  slices (5 cups)

1 large onion, chopped
7 tablespoons butter
1/4 teaspoon white pepper
1/8 teaspoon cayenne
1/4 teaspoon nutmeg
Salt to taste
1 cup parmesan cheese

Cut an X in round end of each chestnut with sharp knife. Boil chestnuts in large saucepan of water until cuts open, 20 to 25 minutes. Drain, and let cool briefly. Shell, and peel chestnuts while still warm (approximately 4 cups). Combine oyster liquid, cream and potatoes in large saucepan. Heat to boiling over high heat. Reduce heat to low, and simmer until potatoes are tender, about 15 minutes. Stir occasionally. Transfer potatoes and about 1-1/4 cups of liquid to medium bowl. Saute onion in 2 tablespoons of the butter in small skillet over medium high heat until the pieces are wilted, about 5 minutes. Add onion to potatoes, and add white pepper, cayenne and nutmeg. Toss gently. Season to taste with salt. Heat oven to 450 degrees, and butter pan. Spread half the potato mixture in bottom of dish. Arrange chestnuts over potatoes, and oysters over chestnuts. Add remaining potato mixture in even layer. Sprinkle with cheese, and dot with remaining butter. Bake until top is golden brown, about 15 minutes. Let stand 3 minutes before serving.
Servings: 12.

Accompaniments

Corn and Grits Timbales

1-3/4 cups heavy cream
1-1/2 teaspoons kosher salt
1/4 cup yellow grits (not instant)
1/8 teaspoon grated nutmeg
1/2 cup corn kernels

1 garlic clove, minced
1/2 teaspoon white pepper
2 large eggs, beaten lightly
1/4 cup parmesan cheese

In small saucepan, combine 1 cup of cream, garlic, 1/2 teaspoon salt, 1/4 teaspoon pepper and grits. Bring liquid to boil over moderate heat, and simmer mixture, stirring for 20 minutes. In bowl, stir together remaining 3/4 cup cream, 3 eggs, remaining 1 teaspoon salt, remaining 1/4 teaspoon pepper and nutmeg until custard is combined well. Divide grits mixture among 4 buttered 3/4 cup timbale molds or ramekins, and sprinkle with parmesan and corn. Spoon custard into molds, and stir the mixture together gently. Bake timbales in baking pan of hot water in preheated 300 degree oven for 20 to 25 minutes or until tester comes out clean. Remove molds from pan, and let timbales cool for 5 minutes. Run a thin knife around edges of molds, and invert timbales onto heated serving plates.
Servings: 4.

Accompaniments

Cornbread, Bacon and Pecan Stuffing

2 cups cornbread, crumbled*
1/3 cup pecans, chopped coarsely
1/4 pound bacon, diced
2 tablespoons butter
1 rib celery, chopped
1 onion, chopped
1 capon liver, minced (optional)

1/2 teaspoon dried thyme
1/2 teaspoon dried sage
Salt and pepper
1/4 cup heavy cream
1/3 cup chicken stock
2 tablespoons dry sherry

Heat oven to 325 degrees. On baking sheet, toast cornbread and pecans in preheated oven until golden, about 10 minutes. In heavy frying pan, cook bacon over medium low heat until crisp, about 5 minutes. Transfer bacon with slotted spoon to mixing bowl, and discard all but 2 tablespoons of bacon drippings. Add cornbread and pecans to bacon. Melt butter in frying pan with bacon drippings. Add celery and onion, and cook over medium heat, stirring frequently until vegetables are tender, about 2 minutes. Stir in liver (optional), thyme, sage, salt and pepper. Add to bowl. Add cream, stock and sherry to frying pan, stirring with wooden spoon to deglaze. Toss with stuffing, and season to taste. Cool until ready to stuff and roast turkey.

*Cornbread:
1 cup white cornmeal
1 cup milk
3 tablespoons butter, melted
1/2 teaspoon salt

1/2 cup flour
1 egg beaten
1 tablespoon baking powder

Heat oven to 400 degrees. Put an 8 inch frying pan or baking pan in oven. In large mixing bowl, combine cornmeal, flour, milk, egg, 1 tablespoon melted butter, baking powder and salt. Beat until smooth. Brush heated pan with remaining 2 tablespoons butter, and pour in batter. Bake on center rack in preheated oven until set and lightly browned, 25 to 30 minutes. Turn cornbread out onto rack.
Yield: 1 loaf.

Accompaniments

Corn Fritters

2 pounds corn kernels, frozen
1-1/2 cups flour or as needed
8 eggs
Oil, as needed

2 teaspoons salt
1/2 teaspoon nutmeg, ground
1/4 teaspoon white pepper

Mix all ingredients together. Using 2 ounce scoop, place batter into sautoir with shallow, heated fat. Shape into pancakes; fry both sides to golden brown. Servings: 20.

Cornmeal Yeast Rolls

3/4 cup milk
1 cup water, boiling
1/2 cup water, warm
  (105 to 115 degrees)
1/3 cup sugar
2 teaspoons salt

1-1/4 cup regular cornmeal
1 package dry yeast
1/2 cup butter or margarine, melted
2 egg yolks, slightly beaten
4-5 cups all purpose flour

Scald the milk, then cool to 105-115 degrees. Combine cornmeal and boiling water in a large bowl. Let stand 10 minutes. Dissolve yeast in warm water in medium size bowl. Let stand for 5 minutes. Add scalded milk, butter, sugar, egg yolks and salt to yeast mixture. Blend well. Gradually add to cornmeal, stirring well. Gradually stir in enough flour to make soft dough. Turn dough out onto lightly floured surface, and knead about 5 minutes until smooth and elastic. Place dough in a greased bowl, turning to grease top. Cover, and let rise in a warm place, 85 degrees, free from draft, for one hour or until doubled in bulk. Punch dough down, cover, and let rise again in warm place, 85 degrees, free from draft, for 1 hour or until doubled in bulk. Bake 400 for 18 to 20 minutes or until golden brown.
Servings: 8.

Accompaniments

Crabmeat Lusianne

1 pounds lump crabmeat, picked
1 pound lightly salted butter
1 cup converted rice
1/2 teaspoon cayenne pepper
1/2 teaspoon salt
2 teaspoons black pepper

2 teaspoons white pepper
4 teaspoons garlic powder
1 bunch green onions, sliced
1 cup slivered almonds, toasted
A pinch of saffron

Cook rice with saffron; set aside. Combine cayenne pepper, black pepper, white pepper, garlic powder and salt in skillet. Add butter, crabmeat, green onion and almonds. Heat until butter is melted, and all ingredients are combined. Add saffron rice, and toss together. Serve on a 9 inch round plate.

For garnish: 2 oranges, 1 lemon, 1 lime, 3 strawberries, 6 sprigs of parsley.
Servings: 6.

Accompaniments

Cranberry Hazelnut Cornbread Dressing

3/4 cup hazelnuts, toasted
 and skinned
1 teaspoon salt
1 large egg
1 cup onion, thinly sliced
1 cup canned chicken broth
1 additional cup of chicken broth
 if baking separately
1 cup yellow cornmeal

1/2 cup all purpose flour
2-1/4 teaspoons double action
 baking powder
3/4 cup milk
3/4 cup green bell pepper, chopped
3/4 cup fresh cranberries,
 chopped coarse
1/3 cup fresh parsley leaves, minced

In spice grinder or food processor, grind fine 1/2 cup hazelnuts. In bowl, whisk together ground hazelnuts, cornmeal, flour, salt and baking powder. In another bowl, whisk together egg and milk. Add mixture to cornmeal mixture. Whisk batter until combined. Heat an oiled baking pan 8x8x2 inch, in preheated 425 degree oven for 10 minutes or until it is very hot. Add batter, spreading evenly, and bake cornbread in middle of oven for 8 to 10 minutes, or until tester comes out clean. Loosen edges of corn bread with knife, invert cornbread onto rack, and let cool until it can be handled. In skillet, combine onion, bell pepper and 1 cup of broth. Bring broth to boil, and simmer mixture, covered for 5 minutes or until vegetables are just tender. In large bowl, combine corn bread, crumbled coarse, cranberries, parsley, onion mixture, remaining 1/4 cup hazelnuts, salt and pepper to taste. Stir stuffing until it is combined well, and let cool completely before stuffing turkey, or bake separately. Spoon stuffing into shallow baking dish, moisten it with additional 1 cup broth, and bake covered in preheated 325 degree oven for 1 hour and 30 minutes or until top is browned lightly.
Yield: 8 cups or fills 14 pound turkey.

Accompaniments

Cream Fruit Mold

1 can (15 ounces) mandarin oranges
1/2 cup orange juice
1 envelope unflavored gelatin
1 cup sour cream
2 bananas, sliced

1/2 cup sugar
1/4 cup lemon juice
2 eggs beaten
1 package (3 ounces) cream cheese
1/2 cup pecans, chopped

Drain oranges, reserving syrup, and add water to syrup to equal 3/4 cup liquid. Combine liquids, sugar, juices and gelatin. Stir over medium heat until dissolved. Stir half of hot mixture into eggs, and return all to saucepan. Cook 2 minutes, stirring often, and remove from heat. Add sour cream and softened cream cheese, and beat with electric beater until smooth. Place in refrigerator, and when slightly thickened, fold in oranges, bananas and pecans; then pour into 5-1/2 cup ring mold. Chill until firm, and serve.
Servings: 6-8.

Accompaniments

Creamy Lemon Chive Pasta
with Asparagus

1/2 pound fettuccine
2 tablespoons unsalted butter, softened
1/4 cup heavy cream
1/2 cup parmesan cheese, grated
1 teaspoon lemon rind, grated
1 thin lemon slice, quartered for garnish

1/2 pound asparagus, trimmed,
  stems peeled and cut
  diagonally 1/2 inch pieces
2 large egg yolks
1 tablespoon snipped fresh chives
  plus additional for garnish

In a pot of boiling, salted water, cook fettuccine for 3 to 4 minutes for fresh pasta or 8 to 10 minutes for dried pasta, until al dente. Drain pasta, and put immediately in a large bowl of cold water. In a saucepan of boiling water, cook the asparagus for 3 to 4 minutes or until tender. Drain, and add to pasta. In a large skillet, cook pasta and asparagus in butter over moderately low heat. Stir until mixture is heated through. Remove the skillet from heat. In a small bowl, whisk together cream and egg yolks. Add mixture and parmesan to skillet, stirring to coat the pasta with sauce. Cook mixture over low heat, stirring until parmesan is melted. Stir in 1 tablespoon chives, lemon rind, salt and pepper to taste. Mound pasta on heated plates, and garnish each dish with additional chives and lemon quarter.
Servings: 4.

Accompaniments

Crunchy Vegetable Medley

1 small onion, sliced and
  separated into rings
3 cloves garlic, minced
2 tablespoons margarine, melted
1 cup water
1 teaspoon beef flavored bouillon
  granules
2 cups broccoli flowerets
1 cup cauliflower flowerets
1 cup brussel sprouts, halved

3/4 cup carrots, sliced
1/2 cup fresh mushrooms, sliced
1/4 cup green pepper, chopped
1/2 cup slivered almonds, toasted
1/4 cup walnuts, chopped
3 tablespoons sesame seeds, toasted
1 teaspoon poppy seeds
1/2 teaspoon soy sauce
1/8 teaspoon dried whole basil

Saute onion and garlic in margarine in large skillet until tender. Add water and bouillon granules, stirring until bouillon is dissolved. Add next 6 ingredients and bring to boil. Cover, reduce heat to low and cook 5 minutes. Drain well. Combine vegetables and next 6 ingredients, tossing gently. Garnish, and serve.
Servings: 6-8.

Dah's Biscuits

3 cups all-purpose flour
1-1/1 tablespoons baking powder
3/4 teaspoons baking soda

1/4 teaspoon salt
1/2 cup butter or margarine
1-1/2 cups buttermilk

Combine flour, baking powder, soda and salt. Cut in butter with a blender until mixture resembles coarse meal. Add buttermilk, stirring just until dry ingredients are moistened. Turn dough out onto a lightly floured surface, and knead lightly 4 or 5 times. Roll dough to a 1/2 inch thickness. Cut with a 2 inch cutter. Place biscuits on a lightly greased baking sheet. Bake at 450 degrees for 10-12 minutes or until golden. Brush with melted butter. These are delicious served with country ham and mustard spread.
Yield: about 2-1/2 dozen.

Accompaniments

Deep Fried Corn and Cheddar Filled Crepes

1 cup cooked corn
2 teaspoons jalapeno chilies,
  seeded, pickled
2 large eggs, beaten lightly
Flour for dredging crepes

1/4 pound sharp cheddar cheese, grated
2 tablespoons scallions, minced
8 crepes*
1 tablespoon vegetable oil
2 cups fresh bread crumbs

In a bowl, toss together corn, cheddar, chilies and scallion. Working with 1 crepe at a time, mound 2 heaping tablespoons of corn mixture in center of each crepe, and fold bottom third of crepe up over filling. Fold in 1 inch of each side, and fold down top third of crepe to enclose filling completely, forming a rectangle. In bowl, stir together eggs and oil. Dredge crepes carefully in flour, dip in egg mixture, and coat them with bread crumbs. In deep fryer, heat enough oil to cook at 380 degrees for 30 seconds on each side. Transfer as fried to paper towels to drain.
Servings: 4 (luncheon) or 8 (first course).

*Crepe Batter:
1 cup all purpose flour
3 large eggs
1/2 teaspoon salt

1/2 cup milk
2 tablespoons unsalted butter,
  melted and cool

In blender or processor, blend flour, 1/2 cup plus 2 tablespoons water, milk, eggs, butter and salt for 5 seconds. Turn off motor, and with rubber spatula, scrape down sides of container. Blend batter for 20 seconds more. Transfer batter to bowl, and let stand, covered for 1 hour. The batter may be made up to one day in advance and kept covered and chilled. To make the crepes, heat oil in a crepe pan. Pour just enough batter into hot pan to cover the bottom. Return pan to heat, constantly moving the pan so the crepe will not stick. Turn crepe on other side after 1 minute. Cook side until firm. Place on parchment paper, and store.
Yield: 20 crepes.

Accompaniments

Dill Potatoes

4 medium potatoes, cut into chunks
3/4 cup vegetable or
  meat stock

1 teaspoon dried dill weed
1/4 teaspoon salt (optional)
Black pepper to taste

Place all ingredients except salt and pepper in a saucepan, and bring to a boil. Then lower the heat to simmer, and cook until the potatoes are tender and the broth has reduced somewhat. Mash potatoes just a little with a fork, add the salt (if desired) and the pepper, and serve.
Servings: 4 (1 cup, plus broth).

Accompaniments

Double Fried Hush Puppies

1 cup cornmeal
2 teaspoons sugar
3/4 teaspoons salt
1/2 cup milk
6 scallions, chopped
5 egg whites
3/4 cup cake flour

2 teaspoons baking powder
1-1/4 cups corn, cooked fresh
  or frozen
2 egg yolks, at room temperature
Oil for deep frying
2 teaspoons ground cumin, mixed
  with 2 teaspoons salt (optional)

In medium bowl, sift together 1/4 cup of cornmeal, cake flour, sugar, baking powder and salt. In food processor or blender, puree 1 cup of corn with milk. Mix in the egg yolks. Form a well in dry ingredients. Pour in corn puree, and stir to combine. Stir in remaining 1/4 cup corn kernels and scallions. In deep fryer or large heavy saucepan, heat 4 inches oil to 385 degrees. Beat 2 of egg whites until soft peaks form, and fold into batter. Working in batches, drop batter by teaspoon into hot oil without crowding. Fry, turning occasionally until well-browned all over, about 5 minutes. Remove with slotted spoon, and drain on paper towels. Remove any bits of fried batter from oil to keep clean as you work. Place remaining 3/4 cup cornmeal in large paper bag. In large bowl, beat remaining 3 egg whites lightly with fork until frothy. Again, working in batches, coat drained, fried hushpuppies in egg white, and place in paper bag. Close, and shake to coat with cornmeal. Shake off any excess, and return to hot oil. Fry for about 3 minutes, turning until when tapped with spoon, they sound as if hard shell has been formed. Drain on paper towels. Sprinkle with salt or cumin salt, if desired. Serve hot, warm or room temperature.
Yield: 4 dozen.

Accompaniments

Eggplant and Oyster Rice Stuffing

1-1/2 teaspoons salt
6 tablespoons vegetable oil
1 cup onion, chopped
1 cup green bell pepper, chopped
24 oysters shucked,
　reserving liquid
1 cup scallion greens, thinly sliced

Cayenne to taste
1-1/2 cups medium grain rice
　or short grain, cooked
1-1/4 pounds eggplant, trimmed
　and cut in 1/2 inch thick slices
1 teaspoon garlic, minced

In a large saucepan, bring 3 cups salted water to boil. Stir in rice, and cook it covered over low heat for 20 minutes or until water is absorbed and the rice is tender. In a large heavy skillet, preferably cast iron, heat 2 tablespoons oil over moderately high heat until hot but not smoking, and brown eggplant in batches, (adding 3 tablespoons of remaining oil, as necessary) for 4 to 6 minutes or until tender. Transfer to paper towels to drain. Let eggplant cool until it can be handled, and cut into 1/2 inch pieces. Add the remaining 1 tablespoon oil to skillet, and in it, saute the onion and bell pepper. Stir until they are browned and softened. Add garlic, oysters and eggplant, and cook mixture over moderately high heat stirring occasionally for 1 minute. In large bowl, combine rice, eggplant mixture, half the reserved oyster liquid, scallion greens, cayenne and salt to taste. Stir stuffing until it is combined well, and let cool completely before stuffing turkey. The stuffing can also be baked separately. Spoon stuffing in shallow baking dish. Moisten it with remaining oyster liquid. Bake covered in preheated 325 degree oven for 1 hour and 30 minutes.
Yield: 8 cups or fills 14 pound turkey.

Accompaniments

Eggplant Shrimp St. Bernard

1/2 cup vegetable oil
3 cups eggplant, peeled and diced
1-1/2 cups onion, diced small
1/4 pound unsalted butter
2 whole eggs
3/4 cup cream or milk

3/4 tablespoon baking powder
1 cup corn flour
1/2 cup cornmeal
1/2 cup water
12 shrimp

In a large skillet, heat oil until very hot. Add eggplant and onion, and cook on high heat until brown. Add butter, and simmer until very soft. Cool; then puree eggplant, eggs and onion in food processor or blender. Add milk or cream. Blend. Add baking powder and corn flour, and blend. Put cornmeal in small bowl. Heat water to a boil, and add to cornmeal. Stir, and add to ingredients in blender. When thoroughly blended, remove to bowl. Dip pieces of shrimp in batter, and fry in deep fat until golden brown at 350 degrees. Plan on 8 to 12 pieces of shrimp per person. The shrimp have wonderful crisp covering. Servings: 4-6.

Accompaniments

Fettucini with Smoked Salmon and Whiskey

1 cup heavy cream
1/4 cup Irish whiskey
1/2 pound fettuccini, preferably fresh
1/2 pound smoked salmon, shredded
  or cut into julienne strips

3 tablespoons unsalted butter
  at room temperature
2 ounces red caviar or golden caviar
1/4 teaspoon pepper, salt to taste

In a large saucepan, boil cream over moderately high heat until reduced by half, 8 to 10 minutes. Add whiskey, and continue boiling for 15 seconds longer. Remove from heat. In a large pot of boiling lightly salted water, cook fettucini until tender but still firm, 2 to 3 minutes for fresh or 8 to 10 minutes for dried. Drain well. Add salmon and butter to whiskey cream mixture. Stir over moderately low heat until salmon is heated through and butter is melted. Add half of the caviar. Pour sauce into warmed serving dish or dishes. Add pepper and salt to taste. Add fettuccini, and toss to coat. To serve, divide fettucini among 4 warmed shallow bowls, top each serving with 1/4 of the remaining caviar. Serve with additional fresh pepper.
Servings: 4.

Fondant Potatoes

4 pounds potatoes
1/2 cup butter

Chicken stock, seasoned, as needed
Salt and white pepper to taste

Select uniform medium potatoes. Wash, and peel; wash again. Tourne into egg shape and size. Place in roasting pan. Melt butter, and brush potatoes. Pour stock into plaque with potatoes to cover half the height of potatoes. Season potatoes. Bake potatoes in 420 degree oven; brush with butter frequently. Potatoes will be ready when stock is absorbed and upper part of potatoes is golden brown.
Servings: 10.

Accompaniments

Fourteen Karat Ring Mold

1 envelope unflavored gelatin
1/3 cup sugar
1/4 teaspoon cinnamon
1/4 cup cold water
3/4 cup boiling water

1 (8 ounces) carton plain yogurt
1 cup carrots, finely grated
1/2 cup pineapple, drained and crushed
1/2 cup pecans, finely chopped

Mix together gelatin, sugar and cinnamon. Add 1/4 cup cold water, and let stand 5 minutes. Add 3/4 cup boiling water, and stir until gelatin is dissolved. To this, add yogurt, stirring until smooth. Chill until slightly thickened, and add carrots, pineapple and pecans. Pour into oiled 9 inch mold, and chill until firm. Serve. Servings: 4-5.

Fried Okra in Curry Batter

1 large egg
1-1/4 tablespoons fresh lemon juice
1 clove garlic, minced
1 teaspoon turmeric
1 teaspoon curry powder
1/2 teaspoon salt

1/8 teaspoon cayenne or to taste
1/4 pound okra, halved lengthwise
Flour for dredging
1 cup fresh bread crumbs
Vegetable oil for deep frying

In a bowl, whisk together egg, lemon juice, garlic, turmeric, curry powder, salt and cayenne. Dredge okra in flour, shaking off excess. Dip in egg mixture, letting excess drip off, and roll in breadcrumbs. In large deep skillet, heat 1 inch of oil to 360 degrees, and in it, fry okra in batches, turning for 2 minutes or until golden, transferring with slotted spoon as it is fried to paper towels to drain. Keep okra warm on baking sheet lined with paper towels in preheated 200 degree oven.
Servings: 4.

Accompaniments

Fried Tomatoes with Gravy

4 large ripe tomatoes
1/4 cup plus 2 tablespoons butter or
  margarine, divided
1 tablespoon brown sugar
1 cup milk

1/4 cup plus 2 tablespoons all purpose
  flour, divided
1/4 teaspoon salt
1/8 teaspoon pepper

Cut tomatoes into 1/2 inch slices. Dredge in 1/4 cup flour. Melt 1/4 cup butter in large skillet over medium heat, add tomatoes, and cook until golden brown, turning once. Arrange tomatoes in serving platter. Sprinkle with salt, pepper and brown sugar, and keep warm. Melt remaining 2 tablespoons butter in pan drippings, and add remaining 2 tablespoons flour, stirring until smooth. Cook 1 minute, stirring constantly. Gradually add milk, and cook over medium heat, stirring constantly, until thickened. Spoon over tomatoes. Serve immediately. Servings: 8.

Fried Zucchini Sticks with Sesame-Chive Dressing

1 pound zucchini
Salt to taste
1-1/2 cups cold water

1-1/2 cups all purpose flour
3 cups vegetable oil
*Sesame chive dressing

Soak zucchini in large bowl of cold water for 10 minutes. Rinse under cold running water. Trim zucchini, and cut lengthwise into 1/4 inch thick slices. Cut into 3x1/4 inch sticks. Place in bowl of heavily salted ice water; set aside. Pour 1-1/2 cups cold water into shallow bowl. Gradually sift flour over water, stirring to mix. Heat oil at 350 degrees. Shake excess water from a handful of zucchini

Accompaniments

sticks, drop into batter, lift, and shake off excess batter. Carefully slip zucchini into oil. Do not crowd. Cook until golden brown, 2 to 3 minutes. Remove with slotted spoon to paper towel to drain. Keep sticks warm on baking sheet in oven set at lowest setting. Serve hot with dressing.
Servings: 6.

*Sesame Chive Dressing:

2 egg yolks at room temperature
1 tablespoon lemon juice
1 tablespoon tarragon vinegar
1-1/2 teaspoons dijon mustard
1/2 teaspoon garlic, finely chopped
1/8 teaspoon salt
1/8 teaspoon white pepper

Hot red pepper sauce
1/2 cup vegetable oil
1/2 cup olive oil
3 tablespoons sour cream
1/2 teaspoon sesame oil
2 tablespoon fresh chives, chopped
1 tablespoon fresh parsley, chopped

Place egg yolks, lemon juice, vinegar, mustard, garlic, salt, pepper and red pepper sauce to taste in blender or food processor. Process until smooth with motor running. Add oils in thin steady stream. Blend until smooth. Remove to small bowl, and fold in remaining ingredients. Refrigerate covered until chilled. Dressing can be stored covered in refrigerator for several days.
Yield: 1-1/2 cups.

Accompaniments

Fruited Cous Cous Dressing

2 cups chicken stock or 1 cup canned
  broth, diluted with 1 cup water
1 cup pitted prunes, chopped
1/2 cup fresh parsley, chopped
1 teaspoon lemon zest, grated
1/2 teaspoon cinnamon
1/2 teaspoon ground cumin
1/2 teaspoon fresh pepper

1-2/3 cups instant cous cous
1/2 cup pine nuts
1/2 pound slab bacon,
  cut into 1/4 inch dice
6 tablespoons unsalted butter
2 medium onions, chopped
2 medium tart green apples,
  peeled, cored and chopped (1-1/2 cup)

In medium saucepan, combine stock, prunes, parsley and lemon zest. Slowly bring to a boil over low heat. Simmer, covered for 5 minutes. Add cinnamon, cumin and pepper, and stir in cous cous. Remove from heat, and let stand until cous cous absorbs all the liquid, about 15 minutes. Meanwhile in a large heavy skillet, cook pine nuts over moderately high heat, tossing pine nuts until lightly toasted, about 3 minutes. Place nuts in a large bowl. Preheat oven to 350 degrees. Add bacon to skillet, and saute over moderately high heat stirring until golden brown, about 3 minutes. With slotted spoon, add bacon to nuts, discard fat in pan. Add butter to skillet, and melt over high heat. Add onions and apples, and cook until softened but not browned, about 5 minutes. Scrape mixture into bowl. Fluff up the cous cous with fork, and add to bowl. Toss well to combine. Turn mixture into buttered large shallow baking dish. Bake the dressing covered until heated through, about 20 minutes. Fluff with fork before serving. Servings: 6.

Accompaniments

Garlic Rosemary Tuiles

2 large garlic cloves, unpeeled
2 teaspoons sugar
1/2 teaspoon salt
2 tablespoons fresh parmesan cheese, grated

1/2 stick unsalted butter, softened
1 large egg white, room temperature
4 tablespoons all purpose flour
2 tablespoons rosemary leaves, fresh or dried

In a small saucepan of boiling water, boil garlic, covered for 20 minutes, drain, and let cool. Pat garlic dry, peel, and mash into a paste with a fork. In a bowl with an electric mixer, cream the butter, add sugar, and beat mixture until light and fluffy. Beat in 2 teaspoons of garlic paste. Discard any remaining garlic paste, add egg white and salt, and beat mixture at low speed for 5 seconds, or until just combined. It will appear lumpy and separated. Add flour and parmesan and stir mixture until just combined. Transfer mixture to small bowl, and chill covered for 4 hours, or overnight. Arrange rounded teaspoon of mixture 3 inches apart on buttered baking sheets. With back of fork dipped in cold water, flatten carefully to form 1-1/2 inch rounds. Sprinkle the rosemary over rounds. Bake in batches in the middle of a preheated oven, 425 degrees, for 6 to 8 minutes or until edges are golden. Immediately transfer tuiles with spatula to rolling pin, pressing them gently against rolling pin to help them curve. Let cool, and remove carefully from rolling pin.
Servings: 4.

Accompaniments

Ginger Carrots

5 medium carrots, scraped
  and cut into 1/4 inch slices
1/4 cup butter or margarine, melted
1 tablespoon honey

1 pinch salt
1 pinch ground cinnamon
1 pinch ground ginger

Cook carrots in a small amount of boiling water, 20 minutes or until crisp-tender. Drain. Combine carrots, butter, honey, salt, cinnamon and ginger in a medium saucepan. Cook over medium heat, stirring gently, until carrots are well-coated and heated.
Servings: 10.

Gratin of Scallops and Grapefruit

1 pound fresh sea scallops,
  halved and tendons removed
1 cup dry white wine
3 whole peppercorns
2 whole cloves

1 pink grapefruit*
Salt and black pepper to taste
5 tablespoons unsalted butter
1/3 cup fresh bread crumbs
2 tablespoons parmesan cheese, grated

Put scallops, wine, peppercorns and cloves in saucepan, and bring to boil. Lower heat, and simmer until just cooked, 1 to 2 minutes. Strain liquid into another saucepan, discard peppercorns and cloves, and put scallops into mixing bowl. Toss scallops with grapefruit and salt and pepper. Heat broiler. Bring reserved liquid to boil, and reduce to about 1/3 cup, about 5 minutes. Divide scallops and grapefruit among individual ramekins (4). Add any juices to the reduced sauce. Over very low heat, whisk 4 tablespoons butter into reduced liquid, bit by bit. Pour over scallops. Combine breadcrumbs and cheese, and sprinkle over each portion. Dot evenly with remaining butter. Place ramekins under broiler until crumbs are browned, about 1 minute.
*Grapefruit: To prepare, remove skin and pith. Cut sections away from membrane. Halve and seed sections.
Servings: 4.

Accompaniments

Green Beans and Lima Beans with Herb Butter

1-1/2 pounds green beans, trimmed,
  boiled in unsalted water for 5 minutes
  and refreshed under cold water
2 packages (10 ounces) frozen small
  lima beans boiled in salted water
  for 5 minutes or until tender
  and refreshed under cold water

1 stick unsalted butter
3 tablespoons fresh parsley leaves, minced
4 scallions, minced
2 tablespoons fresh dill, snipped
2 ribs celery, including green leaves,
  minced
1 garlic clove, minced

Pat dry the green beans and lima beans. Divide butter between 2 large sauce-pans, heat over moderate heat until melted, and cook beans separately in 2 pans, stirring to coat with butter, until heated through. In bowl, combine the parsley, scallions, dill, celery and garlic. Divide the mixture between the pans, cook beans, stirring for 2 minutes, season with salt and pepper, mix, and serve.
Servings: 8.

Green Beans and Tomatoes with Basil

1 pound green beans, trimmed
3 tablespoons unsalted butter
4 small tomatoes, quartered

1 garlic clove, forced through press
5 tablespoons fresh basil leaves, minced
  or 5 teaspoons dried crumbled

In saucepan of boiling salted water, cook green beans for 4 to 5 minutes or until tender. Drain, and refresh under cold water. In a large skillet, cook garlic in butter over moderately low heat, stirring for 2 minutes. Add green beans and 2/3 of basil, and cook mixture, stirring, until beans are heated through. Add tomatoes, remaining basil, salt and pepper to taste, and cook mixture, tossing together gently until tomatoes are just heated through.
Servings: 4 to 6.

Accompaniments

Green Bean Saute

3 pounds green beans
1/2 cup butter, clarified

3 cloves garlic, peeled
Salt and white pepper to taste

Clean, and wash green beans. Blanch in boiling, salted water. Cool under running cold water. Place quantity needed in sautoir. Saute. Crush garlic, and add to beans. Season when sauteing.

Servings: 10.   Nutritional Analysis: page 437.

Green Beans Italienne

1 cup onion, chopped
2 tablespoons butter or margarine
1 can (14-1/2 ounces) whole tomatoes,
  undrained and quartered

1 can (16 ounces) green beans
1 teaspoon salt
3/4 teaspoon ground oregano
3/4 teaspoon pepper

Saute onion in butter in a large saucepan over low heat until tender. Add remaining ingredients. Simmer 15 minutes or until thoroughly heated.

Servings: 10.

Grilled Marinated Eggplant

4-6 eggplants
2 cloves garlic
Olive oil

Balsamic vinegar
Black pepper
Salt

Split eggplants lengthwise, and cut 2 or 3 slits through the flesh along each cut side. Do not cut through the skin. Rub cut sides with garlic, and sprinkle with fresh ground black pepper and salt. Drizzle olive oil and vinegar over eggplant, and let stand thirty minutes or until ready to grill. Place cut side down on hot grill, and grill until tender (4 minutes).

Servings: 10.

Accompaniments

Gustonian Rice Medley

1st Section

3 ounces butter

2 cloves of garlic, chopped

4 ounces onion, chopped

8 ounces rice

16 ounces chicken stock

1/2 teaspoon salt

2 teaspoons soy sauce

2nd Section

1 pound strip boneless chicken

4 cloves of garlic, chopped

2 teaspoons of fish sauce

4 ounces onion, chopped

8 teaspoons of all purpose flour

1/4 teaspoon black pepper

1/2 pound broccoli

1/2 pound cauliflower

1 cup water

Melt butter in a pan. Saute garlic and onion. Place rice in pan, and saute until rice is lightly white. Put rice in casserole dish. Add chicken stock, salt and soy sauce. Put lid over casserole, and put in oven. Bake at 400 degrees for 30 minutes; then turn heat down to 300 for 20 more minutes. Mix chicken with garlic (2 cloves), fish sauce, onion, black pepper and 3 teaspoons of flour. Mix well, and let marinate. About 10 minutes before the rice is done, start cooking the chicken. First heat oil and saute the rest of the garlic; then put in chicken, and let cool. Then add vegetables, and cook for about five minutes. Add flour and water mixture, and cook for two more minutes. Serve over rice.

Servings: 6.

Accompaniments

Herbed Cheddar Bread

1 package baking yeast
1/4 cup warm water
1/2 cup skim milk
2 tablespoons reduced-calorie margarine
1 tablespon sugar
1 egg
2 egg whites
1 teaspoon oregano, crushed*

1 teaspoon marjoram*
1 teaspoon thyme*
2 to 2-1/2 cups whole wheat flour
1-1/2 cups cheddar cheese, grated
Vegetable coating spray
*Use 2 teaspoons, minced,
  if using fresh herbs

Dissolve yeast in warm water. Heat milk and margarine until margarine is melted. Add sugar, and allow to cool slightly. Add eggs and herbs, and beat until smooth. Add half of the flour and the cheese, and mix well. Mix in remaining flour with wooden spoon. Add a little more flour, if dough is sticky. Turn out on a lightly floured board, and knead four minutes until smooth. Place in a 1-1/2 quart glass baking dish that has been coated with vegetable coating spray. Let rise until doubled. (About 30 minutes.) Bake at 350 degrees for 30 minutes. Spray top with vegetable coating spray, and bake five minutes more to brown. Let cool slightly. Serve warm.
Yields: 16 slices (1 slice per serving).

Accompaniments

Holiday Mincemeat Mold

1 envelope unflavored gelatin
1/4 cup cold water
1 package (6 ounces) cherry
  flavored gelatin
3-1/2 cups boiling water
1 jar (20-1/2 ounces) brandy
  flavored mincemeat

1 can (8 ounces) crushed pineapple,
  drained
1 small apple, unpeeled and
  finely chopped
1 cup pecans or walnuts,
  chopped

Soften unflavored gelatin in cold water, and set aside. Dissolve cherry flavored gelatin in boiling water, and add unflavored gelatin mixture, stirring until gelatin dissolves. Chill until consistency of unbeaten egg whites. Stir in mincemeat, pineapple, apple and pecans. Pour into lightly oiled 8 cup mold. Chill until firm, and serve.
Servings: 12-14.

Honey-Nut Glazed Carrots

2 cups carrots, sliced into rounds
  1/4 inch thick
Water
2 teaspoons sliced almonds

1 teaspoon butter
2 teaspoons honey
Dash nutmeg

Steam the carrots over a small amount of water until just tender. Heat a small skillet over medium heat. Measure the almonds into the skillet and toast, stirring constantly, until golden brown. Remove the pan from the heat, and remove the almonds, setting aside. When the carrots are done, melt the butter in the same skillet you used for the almonds. Add 2 to 3 teaspoons of liquid from the steaming carrots, and add the carrots. Stir in the honey and toasted almonds until the carrots are well-coated. Sprinkle with nutmeg, and serve.
Servings: 4 (1/2 cup).   Nutritional Analysis: page 437.

Accompaniments

Lemon Rice with Toasted Almonds

3 tablespoons olive oil

1/4 cup onion, chopped

1-1/2 cups chicken broth

2 ounces green onion, chopped

1 tablespoons lemon basil concentrate

1 cup long grain rice

1 clove garlic, chopped

3 tablespoons lemon juice

2 ounces almonds, toasted

Combine olive oil and rice. Saute for 5 minutes. Add onion and garlic. Saute for an additional 3 minutes. Add chicken broth and lemon juice. Bring to a boil, and simmer, covered, for 15 minutes. Add green onion, almonds and lemon basil concentrate, mixing well. Cover, and let stand 10 minutes prior to serving.

Servings: 6.

Nutritional Analysis: page 437.

Accompaniments

Lettuce, Apples, Walnuts and Stilton Cheese

1/4 cup walnut pieces
1 medium head romaine lettuce,
  torn into 1 inch pieces
1/2 bunch watercress stems, trimmed
6 tablespoons olive oil or 4 tablespoons
  olive oil and 2 tablespoons walnut oil
3 tablespoons raspberry or red wine
  vinegar
1/4 teaspoon salt

Pepper to taste
1/2 large red delicious apple,
  cored
1/2 large granny smith or golden
  delicious apple, cored
1/2 tablespoon fresh lemon juice
4 ounces stilton cheese,
  crumbled (1/2 cup)

Heat oven to 350 degrees. Bake walnuts in small baking dish until lightly toasted, about 8 minutes. Cool to room temperature. Combine romaine and watercress in large bowl. Whisk oil, vinegar, salt and pepper to taste in small bowl until blended. Slice each apple half into 12 thin wedges. Brush lightly with lemon juice to prevent discoloration. When ready to serve, toss salad greens with salad dressing to coat. Arrange greens on 4 salad plates. Arrange 6 apples wedges, alternating red and green skins, around the rim of each plate. Sprinkle cheese over salad, and place walnuts in center of each salad. Serve immediately. Servings: 4.

Accompaniments

Louisiana Grits Bread

2 cups grits, well cooked
1 heaping tablespoon butter
1 cup flour, sifted
Pinch of salt

1 teaspoon baking powder
2 cups milk
3 eggs, separated and beaten

Put hot grits in a bowl. Add butter, salt and beaten yolks of eggs; then add the milk. Put baking powder with flour into mixture, and fold in whites of eggs. Pour this into a baking pan, and bake in hot oven until brown, 15 minutes.
Servings: 4.

Maque Choux

2 dozen ears fresh corn
2 medium onions, chopped fine
6 large ripe tomatoes, peeled
  seeded and chopped

1 cup (1/4 pound) butter
2 large bell peppers, chopped fine
2 teaspoons salt
2 teaspoons black pepper

Shuck corn. Work with one cob at a time. Hold over bowl, and cut away the kernels in layers. Do not end up with whole kernels. Scrape knife down cob to milk. Heat butter in dutch oven over medium high heat. Add onion, bell pepper and tomatoes, and saute until onions are transparent, about 15 minutes. Stir in salt and pepper. Add corn and milk from cob, and stir well. Reduce heat to medium, and cook until corn is tender, 20 to 30 minutes. If mixture begins to dry before corn is tender, add a little milk and little more butter.
Servings: 6-8.

Accompaniments

Mexican Black Eye Peas

1 package (16 ounces) dried
  black eyed peas
2 pounds bulk pork sausage
1 medium onion, finely chopped
1 can (28 ounces) whole tomatoes,
  undrained

1/2 cup water
2 tablespoons sugar
2-1/2 tablespoons chili powder
2 tablespoons garlic salt
1/4 teaspoon pepper
2-1/2 tablespoons celery, finely chopped

Sort and wash peas. Place in large dutch oven. Cover with water 2 inches above peas, and let soak overnight. Brown sausage in heavy skillet, stirring to crumble. Add onion, and cook until tender. Drain. Drain peas well, and stir in sausage and remaining ingredients. Bring to boil. Cover, reduce heat, and simmer 1-1/2 hours. Add water, if necessary. Add more seasonings, if necessary.
Servings: 10.

Moist Gingerbread

1 cup butter or margarine, softened
1 cup of sugar
3/4 cup molasses
3 cups all purpose flour
1 teaspoon ground cinnamon
1/4 teaspoon salt

3/4 cup boiling water
2 eggs, beaten
1/2 cup buttermilk
2 teaspoons ground ginger
1/2 teaspoon ground cloves
2 teaspoons baking soda

Cream butter. Gradually add sugar, beating at the medium speed of an electric mixer until light and fluffy. Beat in eggs, molasses and buttermilk. Combine flour, spices and salt. Dissolve soda in boiling water. Add flour mixture to creamed mixture alternately with soda water, beginning and ending with flour mixture. Beat well. Pour batter in greased and floured 13x9x2 inch baking pan. Bake for 40 minutes or until wooden pick comes out clean. Cut into squares. Serve warm or at room temperature.
Yield: 1 loaf.

Accompaniments

Mushrooms Supreme

1-1/2 pounds fresh mushrooms, quartered
1 tablespoon butter or margarine, melted
1 beef flavored bouillon cube
1/2 cup hot water
1/4 cup margarine
2 tablespoons all purpose flour
Dash of pepper
1/2 cup whipping cream
1/4 cup fine dry bread crumbs
1/4 cup parmesan cheese

Saute mushrooms in 1 tablespoon butter in large skillet over medium heat, 8 to 10 minutes. Drain well. Dissolve bouillon cube in hot water, and set aside. Melt 1/4 cup butter in small saucepan. Add flour, and stir until smooth. Blend in pepper, whipping cream and bouillon. Stir into mushrooms. Pour mixture into greased pan. Top with bread crumbs and cheese. Bake uncovered at 350 degrees for 30 minutes. Serve.
Servings: 6.   Nutritional Analysis: page 438.

Mustard Batter Onion Rings

1 large onion, cut 3/8 inch slices, (1/2 pound)
1/2 teaspoon fresh pepper
1/2 cup plus 1 tablespoon seltzer or club soda
1/2 cup all purpose flour
1 teaspoon salt
2 tablespoons spicy brown mustard
Vegetable shortening for deep frying

Separate onion slices into rings, and in bowl, let rings soak in ice and cold water for 15 minutes. While onion rings are soaking in small bowl, whisk together flour, salt, pepper, mustard and seltzer until batter is smooth. Drain onions, and pat dry. Dip onion rings into batter, coating them well and letting excess drip off. In a deep fryer, fry in batches in 375 degree fryer, turning for 3 minutes or until golden brown. Transfer to paper towel, and drain. Season with salt, and serve.
Servings: 2.

Accompaniments

New Potatoes with Canadian Bacon and Chives

2 pounds small red potatoes,
  quartered
1 tablespoon white wine vinegar
1/2 pounds Canadian bacon,
  chopped fine

1/2 stick unsalted butter,
  cut in bits, softened
1/2 cup canned chicken broth
1/4 cup snipped fresh chives

In saucepan, combine potatoes, with enough salted water to cover them by 2 inches. Bring water to boil, and simmer potatoes for 8 to 10 minutes, or until just tender. Drain, and in a bowl, toss gently with butter, broth and vinegar. Add chives, Canadian bacon, salt and pepper to taste, and toss mixture gently until combined well. Serve.
Servings: 6.

Okra Bacon Casserole

1-1/2 pounds small young fresh okra
3 fresh tomatoes, chopped
1 medium onion, chopped
1/2 bell pepper, chopped

5 strips bacon
Salt and pepper to taste
Hot sauce to taste

Slice okra into thin rounds. Grease casserole. Place layers of okra, tomato, onion and bell pepper. Season each layer with salt, pepper and hot sauce to taste. Lay bacon overlapping on top. Bake for 1-1/2 hours at 350 degrees.
Servings: 6-8.   Nutritional Analysis: page 438.

Accompaniments

Orange-Glazed Pea Pods

To remove the ends and strings from the pea pods, simply snap off the tip of the pod with your finger, and pull the string down the length of the pod.

1 cup fresh pea pods
1 tablespoon sugar
1 teaspoon cornstarch

1/2 teaspoon orange peel, finely shredded
1/4 cup orange juice
2 tablespoons sliced almonds, toasted

Rinse pea pods. Remove ends, and string. Cut pea pods in half diagonally. In a small saucepan, cook pea pods, covered, in a small amount of boiling water for 3 minutes. Drain. Cover, and set aside. In a small saucepan, combine sugar and cornstarch. Stir in orange peel and juice. Cook, and stir until thickened and bubbly. Cook, and stir 5 minutes more. Pour over hot pea pods, stirring to coat. Transfer to a serving dish. Sprinkle sliced almonds on top. Serve immediately. Servings: 4.

Orange-Glazed Sweet Potatoes

4 medium sweet potatoes
Boiling water to cover
1/4 cup orange juice

1/4 teaspoon cinnamon
1/8 teaspoon salt

Wash the sweet potatoes, and drop them in enough boiling water to cover them. Cover the pan. When the water comes to a boil again, reduce the heat to low, and cook until tender. Drain the potatoes, let cool for a few minutes, and peel. (Rinsing in tepid water will help make them cool enough to hold.) In a medium saucepan, combine the orange juice, cinnamon, salt and cooked sweet potatoes. Cook over low heat, stirring occasionally, until most of the juice is gone, about 6 to 7 minutes.
Servings: 4 (1 potato each).   Nutritional Analysis: page 438.

Accompaniments

Orange Stuffing for Ducks

3 cups bread cubes, toasted
2 cups celery, finely diced
1 tablespoon orange peel, grated
2/3 cup orange sections, diced
3/4 teaspoon salt

1/2 teaspoon poultry seasoning
Dash of pepper
1 beaten egg
1/4 cup butter or margarine, melted

Toss together bread, celery, orange peel, diced orange sections and seasonings. Combine egg and butter. Add to bread mixture, tossing lightly. Makes enough stuffing for a 5-pound duckling.

Oven Fried Zucchini

2 medium zucchini
2 tablespoons parmesan cheese, grated
1/4 cup plus 1 tablespoon commercial
  Italian salad dressing

1/4 cup Italian style bread crumbs
2 tablespoons romano cheese, grated

Cut zucchini in half lengthwise, and cut each half into 8 strips. Combine bread crumbs and cheeses. Dip zucchini in Italian salad dressing, and roll in bread crumb mixture. Place zucchini in single layer on lightly greased baking sheet. Bake at 475 degrees for 5 minutes. Turn, and bake an additional 3 to 4 minutes or until golden brown. Serve.
Servings: 4.

Accompaniments

Parmesan Rounds

3/4 cup parmesan cheese, grated
1/2 cup all purpose flour
1/8 teaspoon red pepper
1/4 cup butter or margarine, softened

2 tablespoons water, cold
2 tablespoons walnuts, finely chopped
1 tablespoon parsley flakes

Combine first 3 ingredients; then cut in butter with a blender, until mixture resembles coarse meal. Sprinkle with cold water, 1 tablespoon at a time, evenly over surface. Stir with fork until dry ingredients are moistened. Shape the dough into 1-1/2 inch thick log, and set aside. Combine walnuts and parsley in a shallow pan, and roll log in mixture to coat evenly. Cut log with a serrated knife into 1/4 inch slices. Space on ungreased baking sheet. Bake at 375 degrees for 12 minutes or until lightly browned. Cool on a wire rack.
Servings: 6.   Nutritional Analysis: page 439.

Pasta with Garlic and Clam Sauce

1/2 cup onion, chopped
1/2 cup green peppers, chopped
4 cloves garlic, minced
2 tablespoons olive oil
1/2 pound mushrooms, sliced
2 cans (6 or 7 ounces each)
   clams, plus their liquid, minced
1-1/2 teaspoons dried thyme leaves

Salt and fresh ground black pepper
   to taste
2 tablespoons fresh parsley, chopped
Dash of cayenne pepper
4 cups cooked spaghetti
   or linguine (about 8 ounces uncooked)
Parmesan cheese (optional), grated

Saute the onion, green peppers and garlic in the olive oil until onions are transluscent. Add a little water, and cover, if necessary, to prevent sticking. Add the mushrooms, and continue heating in the covered saucepan for about 3 minutes. Add the remaining ingredients except for the cheese, and heat until hot in the covered saucepan. Serve with pasta, and sprinkle with parmesan cheese if desired.
Servings: 4 (1 cup pasta, plus 1 cup sauce, 326 calories).

Accompaniments

Pear Fritters with
Pear Custard Sauce

Pear Custard Sauce:

3 ripe pears
1 teaspoon lemon juice
3/4 cup half and half
1 teaspoon cornstarch

1/2 cup granulated sugar
3/4 cup heavy cream
6 egg yolks

Pear Fritters:

1/2 cup cheddar cheese, grated
   (2 ounces)
1/2 cup granulated sugar
2 tablespoons cornstarch
1 teaspoon cinnamon
1/2 cup heavy cream
2 eggs
2 tablespoons lemon juice

Confectioners sugar
1-1/2 cups flour
1/4 cup baking powder
1 teaspoon salt
1 cup beer
1 teaspoon lemon juice
9 ripe pears
Oil for frying

For sauce, peel, core and mince pears. In heavy saucepan, bring 1 cup water and 5 tablespoons sugar to simmer. Add pears and lemon juice, and continue simmering until liquid thickens to a syrup, about 10 minutes. Remove pan from heat, and cool. In another saucepan, bring heavy cream and half and half to simmer. Meanwhile, whisk egg yolks with cornstarch and remaining 3 tablespoons sugar until lemon colored. Gradually whisk hot cream into egg yolk mixture. Return this mixture to pot, and cook, stirring constantly over low heat until thick, about 10 minutes. Do not boil mixture. Remove pan from heat, and cool to room temperature. Combine with cooled pear mixture. Chill.

For fritters, grate cheese, and mix with all dry ingredients together. Whisk liquid ingredients except 1 teaspoon of lemon juice together, and stir into dry mixture.

Accompaniments

Ser Let batter rest for 15 to 20 minutes before using. Peel, and core pears. Cut into 1/4 inch slices. Combine 2 tablespoons lemon juice, 1 quart water and pear slices. Let sit for 3 to 4 minutes. Remove from water, and drain. Heat oil to 375 degrees in deep fat fryer. Pat pear slices dry, and dip slices into batter. Drop battered slices in hot cooking oil. Be careful not to splatter or overcrowd, and fry until golden brown. Turn once, about 1 minute total. Remove fritters from cooking oil. Drain, and repeat with remaining slices. Put confectioners sugar on top, and serve with sauce.
Servings: 12.

Peppered Pickled Eggs

12 eggs
1-3/4 pints white vinegar
20 peppercorns

Pinch cayenne pepper
Coriander seeds to taste

Hard boil eggs. Place eggs in pickle jar. Boil vinegar for 10 minutes, and pour over eggs. Add peppercorns, cayenne pepper and coriander seed to mixture. Leave uncovered 48 hours. Then cover.

Pork Stuffing

1 medium onion, finely chopped
1 teaspoon thyme, finely chopped
1 tablespoon parsley, finely chopped
1 teaspoon sage, finely chopped
1/8 cup chestnut puree

1/4 cup pork fat
1/4 cup pork, chopped
1/3 cup butter
1/2 cup fresh ground pepper

Cook onion in butter with the herbs. Season with salt and pepper. Add bread crumbs and chestnut puree. Mix in pork and pork fat, and cook on medium heat until done. Allow to cool before inserting into turkey neck. Bread sauce may also be served as an accompaniment.
Servings: 4.

314

Accompaniments

Prune Apple Dressing

1 cup onion, chopped
1/2 cup celery, chopped
1/2 cup butter
2-1/2 cups tart apples, peeled,
  cored and chopped
1 cup pitted prunes, chopped

5 cups dry bread, crumbled
Salt and black pepper to taste
1/2 teaspoon dried thyme
1/2 teaspoon dried sage
1/2 teaspoon ground coriander
1/4-1/3 cup chicken stock or water

In large heavy skillet, saute onion and celery in butter until they begin to color. Add apples, and saute 2 to 3 minutes more. Add prunes, bread and seasoning. Continue to cook, stirring several minutes longer. Adjust seasoning. Add liquid, enough to moisten bread. The mixture should be on the dry side because apples will give off more moisture. Spoon dressing in bowl, and keep warm or put into cavity of bird.
Yield: 6 cups.

Pumpkin Bread

6 cups sifted flour
5-1/4 cups sugar
3-1/2 teaspoon baking soda
2-1/2 teaspoon salt
1-3/4 teaspoon nutmeg
1 teaspoon ginger
3-1/2 teaspoons cinnamon

1-1/8 teaspoon allspice
1 teaspoon cloves
1-3/4 cups salad oil
7 eggs
5/8 cup water or other liquid
1 large can pumpkin
1-3/4 cups walnuts

Mix dry ingredients, and make a well in the center. Add the eggs, water, oil and pumpkin, and mix well. Stir in nuts, and place in buttered and floured tins. Bake at 350 degrees until done.
Yield: 1 loaf.

Accompaniments

Rice and Cheese Croquettes

3 tablespoons butter
1 cup milk
2 teaspoons onion, finely chopped
1/2 teaspoon dry mustard
Dash of cayenne
2 cups sifted bread crumbs
Oil for deep frying
3 tablespoons flour

1 cup sharp cheddar cheese.
  shredded
1/2 teaspoon salt, approximately
1/8 teaspoon pepper
2 cups cooked rice
1 egg beaten with 2 tablespoons water
Cheese pimento sauce

Melt butter in saucepan, add flour, and stir with wire whisk until blended. Bring milk to boil, and add to the butter flour mixture, stirring vigorously with whisk. Add cheese, onion and seasonings, and mix well. Add rice, and fold into sauce. Chill. Shape mixture into 12 croquettes. Roll in crumbs and in beaten egg and again in crumbs. Let croquettes dry. Heat oil to 385 degrees. Fry until golden brown. Drain, and serve with sauce.
Servings: 6.

Rice-Spice Mold

4 cups cooked rice
1 teaspoon lemon juice
2 teaspoons curry powder
2/3 cup sour cream

1 tablespoon vinegar
1 tablespoon vegetable oil
1/2 cup raisins
2/3 cup mayonnaise

Combine vinegar, lemon juice and oil, and stir in hot cooked rice. Add curry, and mix. Add raisins, pecans, sour cream and mayonnaise, and mix thoroughly. Place in 6 cup mold. Chill for several hours, and serve.
Servings: 4-6.

Accompaniments

Rice with Mushrooms

1-1/2 cups rice
3-1/4 cups chicken broth
1-1/2 cups mushrooms, sliced
2 ounces pimentos, diced
2 ounces green onion, chopped

1 teaspoon garlic salt
2 tablespoons dill weed
1 tablespoon butter
Salt to taste
Pepper to taste

Bring chicken broth to a boil. Stir in rice, cover, and simmer for 20 minutes. While the rice is simmering, saute the rest of the ingredients until they are lightly browned. Add to cooked rice. Remove from heat, and let stand for 5 minutes. Servings: 6.

Accompaniments

Sausage and Bell Pepper Hush Puppies with Mustard Sauce

1/4 cup sour cream
Fresh lemon juice to taste
1/2 cup red bell pepper, chopped
1/2 teaspoon vegetable oil
1 large egg
1/2 cup yellow cornmeal
1-1/4 teaspoons double action
   baking powder
1/8 teaspoon cayenne pepper

1/4 cup scallions, thinly sliced
1 tablespoon dijon mustard
1/4 pound kielbasa or cooked smoke
   sausage quartered lengthwise and
   cut crosswise into 1/4 inch pieces
1/4 cup milk
1/4 cup all purpose flour
1/4 teaspoon salt

In small bowl, whisk together sour cream, mustard, lemon juice and salt to taste. In skillet cook the kielbasa and bell pepper in 1/2 teaspoon oil over moderate heat, stirring occasionally for 5 minutes or until bell pepper is tender. In bowl, whisk together egg and milk. Sift together the cornmeal, flour, baking powder, cayenne and salt. Whisk the mixture until well combined. Transfer kielbasa mixture with slotted spoon to bowl, add scallions, and stir the batter until combined. In deep skillet or deep fryer, heat 1-1/2 inches of additional oil to 320 degrees. Add tablespoon of batter and fry, turning once for 1-1/2 to 2 minutes or until golden. Transfer with slotted spoon to paper towels to drain. Serve with mustard sauce.
Servings: 20.

Accompaniments

Sausage Hazelnut Stuffing

1 pound fresh pork sausage meat
1/2 stick (1/4 cup) unsalted butter
1 pound onions, chopped
2 tablespoons fresh sage leaves,
  chopped or 1 tablespoon dried
  crumbled
1 cup hazelnuts, toasted,
  skinned and chopped
1-1/2 teaspoons pepper

Fillets reserved from boned turkey or
  1/2 pound chicken breast,
  skinless and boneless
2 cups celery, chopped
1/4 pound cooked ham,
  cut into 1/4 inch cubes
3 cups dry 1/4 inch bread cubes
1 cup fresh parsley leaves, minced
2 teaspoons salt

In a large skillet, cook sausage meat over moderate heat. Stir, and break up lumps until no longer pink. Transfer with slotted spoon to a large bowl. Let cool. Remove, and discard white tendons from turkey fillets (or chicken) with a sharp knife. With food processor, grind fillets coarse. Add sausage, grind mixture until blended, and transfer to the large bowl. Pour off fat from skillet, and add butter. Cook the onion, celery and sage covered over moderately low heat. Stir occasionally until vegetables are softened. Let mixture cool in skillet, and add to large bowl with ham, 2 cups bread cubes, crushed fine in plastic bag, remaining 1 cup bread cubes left whole, the hazelnuts, parsley, eggs, salt and pepper. Combine mixture well. The stuffing may be made up to one day in advance, if kept covered and chilled. If stuffing, bring back to room temperature.
Servings: 8.

Accompaniments

Sauteed Broccoli Provencale

2 garlic cloves, chopped
4 anchovy fillets
1 tablespoon drained capers
  plus 1 tablespoon caper juice
1/4 cup vegetable oil

8 cups broccoli flowerets, steamed
  al dente and patted dry
1/2 cup red onion, minced
1 teaspoon red wine vinegar

Mince together the garlic, anchovy fillets and capers. In a large skillet, heat oil over moderately high heat until just smoking. Saute the broccoli and onion, stirring for 3 minutes. Add garlic mixture, and saute for 1 minute. Stir in caper juice, vinegar, salt and pepper to taste. Serve.
Servings: 4.   Nutritional Analysis: page 440.

Sauteed Butternut Squash and Ham with Fennel

1-1/2 pounds butternut squash
1-1/2 teaspoons fennel seeds
2 tablespoons unsalted butter

1-1/2 cups 2x1/4 inch pieces
  cooked ham strips
Fresh lemon juice to taste

Halve squash lengthwise. Seed and peel squash. Cut squash into 2x1/4 inch matchsticks, and in large skillet, saute with ham and fennel seeds in butter over moderately high heat. Stir occasionally for 6 to 8 minutes or until tender. Season squash mixture with lemon juice, salt and pepper.
Servings: 4 to 6.

Accompaniments

Sauteed Tomatoes with Sage

1 large tomato, cut into
  1/2 inch slices
2 tablespoons unsalted butter, melted
1 teaspoon sage, crumbled

1/2 teaspoon salt
1/4 teaspoon yellow cornmeal
1 tablespoon vegetable oil

One at a time, dip tomato slices on both sides in melted butter. Sprinkle with sage and salt; then coat well with cornmeal. In large skillet, heat oil. Add tomato slices, and cook over moderately low heat, turning once, until lightly browned on both sides, 6 to 8 minutes.
Servings: 4.

Sauteed Yams
with Prunes and Bacon

2 pounds yams
6 slices bacon
2 tablespoons butter

3 tablespoons medium dry sherry
  or to taste
6 pitted prunes, chopped fine

Peel yams, and cut into 3/4 inch cubes. In saucepan of boiling, salted water, cook yams for 8 minutes, drain and pat dry. In a large heavy skillet, cook bacon over moderate heat until crisp, and transfer to paper towel to drain. Reserve 3 tablespoons fat in skillet. Add butter to fat, and heat until foaming. Add the yams, and saute over moderately high heat, stirring for 3 minutes or until barely tender. Stir in sherry, 1/2 cup water and prunes. Bring liquid to boil, and simmer mixture, stirring for 5 minutes or until liquid is evaporated. Stir in bacon, crumbled with salt and pepper to taste. Serve.
Servings: 6.

Accompaniments

Scallion Duchesse Potatoes

3 pounds large boiling potatoes
1 cup milk
1/2 cup plain yogurt
1/2 stick unsalted butter, soft

1-1/2 cups scallions, minced
  including the greens
2 large egg yolks
White pepper to taste

In a pot, combine potatoes and enough cold water to cover by 1 inch. Bring water to boil, and simmer potatoes for 25 to 30 minutes or until tender. While potatoes are cooking, combine in a small saucepan 1/2 cup scallions and milk. Bring milk to simmer 15 minutes. Drain potatoes, return to kettle, and cook covered over moderate heat, shaking kettle, for 5 minutes to evaporate any excess water. Peel potatoes, and mash coarsely. In a heated bowl with electric mixer, beat while still hot with milk mixture, yogurt, yolks, butter, remaining 1 cup scallions, white pepper and salt (to taste) until smooth. With large pastry bag fitted with 1/2 inch star tip, pipe potatoes decoratively into buttered 2 quart gratin dish, 10 inches long, and bake in preheated oven, 400 degrees for 20 minutes.
Servings: 8.

Accompaniments

Seafood Sausage

1-1/2 pound skinless sole fillets
5 large whole eggs
1 large egg white
3/4 teaspoon salt
1/2 teaspoon white pepper
3/4 cup heavy cream

1/4 cup scallops
1/4 pound shrimp, shelled,
  deveined and chopped
1/4 pound cooked lobster, chopped
1/4 pound salmon, chopped

Grind fish through fine disk of food processor. Puree by pulsing motor, and transfer to bowl. Chill fish, covered for 30 minutes. In food processor, blend fish, whole eggs, egg white, salt and pepper until mixture is combined. With motor running, add cream in stream, and blend mixture until combined. Transfer mixture to bowl, and chill it covered for 1 hour. Fold in scallops, shrimp, lobster and salmon, and divide mixture among 6, 11-inch square sheets of foil lined with buttered parchment paper of same size. Form mixture into 6 logs, using the foil and parchment to roll the mixture up, and crimp the ends together securely. Each log should be 2 inches in diameter. In kettle of boiling water, poach the sausages at a simmer for 7 to 9 minutes or until metal skewer inserted comes out hot. Transfer sausage to cutting board. Carefully remove foil and parchment. With serrated knife, slice sausage crosswise into 3/4 inch slices.
Servings: 6.

Accompaniments

Simple Pickled Eggs

16 hard boiled eggs
1/2 ounce black peppercorns
1/2 ounce whole ginger

1/2 ounce allspice
1 quart vinegar

Boil peppercorns, ginger, allspice and vinegar together 10 minutes. Pour over eggs, and seal jars.
Servings: 16.

Smothered Okra

3 tablespoons lard
2 cups onion, thinly sliced
2 pounds fresh okra, stems and
  tips removed, sliced 1/2 inch thick
1-1/2 teaspoon salt
1/2 teaspoon black pepper
1/8 teaspoon cayenne

1/2 teaspoon mace
1/4 teaspoon sugar
1/4 teaspoon chili powder
1 can (1 pound) whole peeled
  tomatoes, drained
1/4 teaspoon thyme
2 teaspoons creole mustard

In heavy saute pan, melt lard over medium heat. Saute onion until light brown, about 15 to 20 minutes, stirring frequently. Add sliced okra, and saute for 15 minutes more, gradually adding salt, pepper, cayenne, mace, sugar and chili powder. Add drained tomatoes and thyme, and continue to saute. Break up tomatoes with stirring spoon as mixture cooks. Add mustard. Cover pot, and cook over low heat for 30 minutes longer, uncovering to stir from time to time. Serve hot or chilled as salad.
Servings: 8.

Accompaniments

Southern Potato Rolls

2 packages dry yeast
1-1/2 cups warm water
  (105 degrees to 115 degrees)
1/3 cup sugar
1 tablespoon salt
2 eggs

1/2 cup butter or margarine, softened
1/2 cup potatoes, cooked and mashed
5-1/2 to 6 cups bread flour, divided
1 egg, beaten
1 tablespoon water
Sesame seeds or poppy seeds

Dissolve yeast in 1-1/2 cups warm water in a large bowl. Stir in sugar and salt. Let stand 5 minutes. Add 2 eggs, butter, mashed potatoes and 3 cups flour. Beat with electric mixer on medium speed for 2 minutes or until smooth. Stir in enough remaining flour to make a stiff dough. Turn dough out onto a floured surface, and knead until smooth and elastic (about 4 to 5 minutes). Place in a well-greased bowl, turning to grease the top. Cover, and chill 2 hours or until doubled in bulk. Punch dough down, and separate into thirds. Work with one third of dough at a time. Leave remaining dough in refrigerator. Divide each third into 12 portions. Roll each portion into a 12 inch rope. Moisten ends with water, and press together to make a circle. Twist each circle forming a figure eight, or coil the rope starting at one end, and wrap around forming a wider circle each time. Tuck loose ends under. Repeat procedure with remaining dough. Place on greased baking sheet. Combine 1 egg and 1 tablespoon water. Brush each roll with egg mixture. Sprinkle with seeds. Bake at 400 degrees for 10 to 12 minutes or until golden.
Yield: 3 dozen.

*To freeze, prepare, and bake rolls as directed. Let cool. Place in an airtight container, and freeze. To serve, let thaw. Wrap in aluminum, and reheat at 350 degrees.

Accompaniments

Southern Rice

Vegetable cooking spray
1 cup celery, sliced
3/4 cup green onions, sliced
3/4 cup green pepper, sliced
2-3/4 cups chicken broth

1 teaspoon poultry seasoning
1/2 teaspoon salt
1/8 teaspoon pepper
1-1/2 cups long-grain rice, uncooked
1/4 cup pecans, chopped and toasted

Coat a large, non-stick skillet with cooking spray. Place over medium high heat until hot. Add celery, green onions and green pepper. Saute until tender. Stir in broth and next 3 ingredients. Bring to a boil. Spoon rice into a shallow 2 quart baking dish. Add hot broth mixture. Cover, and bake at 350 degrees for 30 minutes or until rice is tender and liquid is absorbed. Sprinkle with pecans. Servings: 6 to 8.

Spanish Rice

1 tablespoon olive oil
1/2 cup brown rice, uncooked
1/2 cup onions, chopped
1-1/4 cups canned tomatoes
1 medium green bell pepper, chopped fine

1 clove garlic, minced
  or crushed
1/4 teaspoon salt
1 teaspoon paprika

Heat oil in a large skillet on medium heat. Add the rice, and cook until browned, stirring constantly. Add the onions, and cook until golden, still stirring constantly. Add a little water, if necessary, to prevent sticking. Place the rice and onions in the top part of a double boiler, and set it over boiling water. Add the remaining ingredients to the rice, cover, and steam for about 1 hour. Servings: 4 (3/4 cup).

Accompaniments

Special Oriental Rice

1 tablespoon vegetable oil
1 pound ground chuck
1/4 teaspoon garlic salt
1/4 cup soy sauce
1 cup cabbage, shredded
1 cup celery, chopped
3/4 cup green pepper, chopped

1 medium onion, chopped
1-1/2 cups carrots, sliced
1/2 pound fresh mushrooms, sliced
1 can (5 ounces) water chestnuts,
  drained and sliced
2 cups cooked rice
1 package (6 ounces) frozen or fresh
  Chinese pea pods

Heat oil in large dutch oven. Add ground chuck and garlic salt, and cook, stirring to crumble until meat is browned. Drain, and stir in next 8 ingredients. Cover, and simmer 20 minutes, stirring occasionally. Stir in rice and pea pods. Simmer 5 minutes.
Servings: 6.

Spinach Mushroom Casserole

2 pounds fresh spinach
1/2 cup onion, chopped
2 tablespoons butter or margarine,
  melted
1/2 teaspoon salt

1 cup (4 ounces) cheddar cheese,
  shredded and divided
1/4 pound small fresh mushrooms
2 tablespoons margarine, melted

Remove stems from spinach, wash leaves thoroughly, and pat dry. Place in dutch oven (do not add water). Cover, and cook at high heat, 3 to 5 minutes. Drain spinach well, chop, and set aside. Saute onions in 2 tablespoons butter until tender, and add spinach and salt, tossing gently. Spoon into lightly greased hotel pan, and sprinkle with 1/2 cup cheddar cheese. Saute mushrooms in 2 tablespoons butter, and place over cheese layer. Sprinkle with remaining cheese (1/2 cup). Bake at 350 degrees for 20 minutes. Serve.
Servings: 6.

Accompaniments

Steamed Buttermilk Brown Bread

1/2 cup cornmeal
1/2 cup whole wheat flour
3/4 teaspoon baking soda
1/2 cup raisins
1/4 cup molasses

1/2 cup all purpose flour
2 tablespoons sugar
Dash of salt
1 cup buttermilk

Combine cornmeal, both flours, sugar, baking soda and salt in medium bowl. Stir in raisins. Combine buttermilk and molasses, and add to dry ingredients, stirring well. Spoon mixture into well greased 4-cup mold, and cover tightly with aluminum foil. Place mold in a shallow rack in a deep kettle with enough water to come halfway up the sides of the mold. Steam bread 2 hours in continuously boiling water, adding water, if needed. Unmold bread onto wire rack to cool. Yield: 1 loaf.

Accompaniments

Steamed Vegetable Medley with Sour Cream and Bacon

1 red bell pepper
6 small red potatoes, skinned
1 head of cauliflower,
  separated into flowerets
1 bunch broccoli,
  separated in flowerets
1-1/2 pounds asparagus, trimmed

1/2 stick unsalted butter
  (1/4 cup melted)
2 tablespoons fresh lemon juice
2 cups sour cream
6 green onions, minced
8 slices bacon,
  cooked and crumbled

Broil bell pepper on rack of broiler pan under preheated broiler about 6 inches from heat, turning frequently for 15 to 20 minutes, or until skin is charred and blistered. Enclose pepper in bag, and let stand until cool enough to handle. Discard stem, skin and seeds, and slice pepper thin. In steamer, cook potatoes for 15 to 20 minutes or until tender, transfer to platter, and keep warm, covered. In steamer, steam cauliflower and broccoli, 4 to 5 minutes, until al dente. Transfer to platter. Steam asparagus 4 to 5 minutes or until tender but al dente. In bowl, combine butter and lemon juice. Season the vegetables with salt and pepper, and spoon mixture over them. In another bowl, combine sour cream and scallions, and top vegetables with mixture. Arrange pepper strips on asparagus to resemble ribbons, and sprinkle bacon over vegetables.
Servings: 6-8.

Accompaniments

Stir-Fry Vegetables

2 cups fresh vegetables, finely chopped
1 tablespoon peanut oil
1 clove garlic, minced
1/4 teaspoon ginger
2 tablespoons hard cheese, grated
Tamari or soy sauce to taste

Have your vegetables ready; use any combination you like. In a large skillet or wok, heat the oil. Add the garlic and ginger; then add the vegetables requiring the most cooking, such as carrots, broccoli, green pepper, and so on. Stir constantly, adding the vegetables that require less cooking as you go along. If necessary, add a tablespoon or two of water to prevent sticking. Cook until tender-crisp. Spoon over cooked grain. Sprinkle with cheese and tamari sauce, if desired, and serve.
Servings: 1 (main course) or 4 (side dish).

Stuffed Baked Sweet Potatoes

6 medium sized sweet potatoes
1 teaspoon salt
1 can (6 ounces) frozen orange juice,
 thawed
1/2 cup pecans, chopped
Vegetable oil
3 tablespoons butter, softened
1 cup crushed pineapple, drained
12 large marshmallows

Wash potatoes, and rub with vegetable oil. Bake at 400 degrees for 1 hour or until done. Split potatoes in half, lengthwise. Carefully scoop out pulp, leaving shell intact, and mash pulp. Add salt, butter, orange juice concentrate and pineapple to mashed pulp, and mix well. Stuff potato shells with pulp mixture, and sprinkle with pecans. Cut each marshmallow in half. Place 2 halves cut side down on each potato shell. Place potatoes in baking pan, and bake at 400 degrees until lightly browned on top. Serve.
Servings: 6.

Accompaniments

Sweet Potato Pecan Bread

2 cups flour
2/3 cup firmly-packed light brown sugar
1-1/2 teaspoons baking powder
1 teaspoon ground cinnamon
1/2 teaspoon baking soda
3/4 cup ripe banana, mashed

1/3 cup safflower oil
3 egg whites
1 teaspoon vanilla
2-1/2 cups raw sweet potato, shredded
3/4 cup pecans, chopped

Heat oven to 350 degrees. Oil an 8x4x2-1/2 inch loaf pan. Set aside. Combine flour, brown sugar, baking powder, cinnamon and baking soda. Set aside. In a large bowl, mix banana, oil, egg whites and vanilla. Add reserved flour mixture, and mix until combined. Stir in sweet potato and pecans. Place into prepared pans. Bake at 350 degrees until a cake tester inserted into the center comes out clean, 55 to 60 minutes. Let stand in pan for 10 minutes. Loosen with a metal spatula. Turn out onto a wire rack to cool. Wrap tightly, and refrigerate until ready to serve. Serve warm or at room temperature.
Yield: 1 loaf.

Sweet Potato Rum Casserole

3 large sweet potatoes,
  cooked and mashed
1/2 cup firmly packed dark brown sugar
1/2 cup pecans, coarsely chopped
1-1/2 teaspoons vanilla extract
Pecan halves

1/4 cup plus 2 tablespoons margarine,
  melted
1/2 cup flaked coconut
1/4 cup dark rum
6 large marshmallows

Combine all ingredients except marshmallows and pecans. Spoon into lightly greased pan. Bake uncovered at 325 degrees for 45 minutes. Arrange marshmallows and pecan halves on top. Continue baking until marshmallows are lightly browned.
Servings: 6.

Accompaniments

Sweet Spiced Beets

1 pound small fresh beets,
  washed and trimmed
Water to cover
3 whole cloves
1/4 cup raisins
Dash of allspice
2 teaspoons butter or margarine

1 slice fresh ginger root,
  1/4 inch thick, minced
1 teaspoon orange
  or lemon rind, grated
1 teaspoon red wine vinegar
2 teaspoons honey

Place the beets in water to cover in a saucepan. Bring to a boil, add the cloves, and reduce the heat to simmer. Let cook, uncovered, for 20 minutes. Add the raisins and allspice, and cook 5 minutes more. Drain, and rinse with cold water until the beets are cool enough to handle. Peel, and cut them into bite-size chunks. Heat a large saucepan over medium heat. Add the butter. When the butter is melted, add the ginger, orange or lemon rind and vinegar, and cook, covered, about 5 minutes. Add the beets, raisins and the honey. Stir, and cook until heated through.
Servings: 4 (1/2 cup).

Tomato and Artichoke Heart Bake

1 can (14 ounces) artichoke hearts,
  drained
1 can (28 ounces) whole tomatoes,
  drained
1/2 cup green onions with tops,
  chopped

2 tablespoons butter or margarine,
  melted
1 tablespoon sugar
1/2 teaspoon dried whole basil
Salt and pepper to taste

Rinse artichokes with water, drain, and cut artichokes and tomatoes into quarters. Saute green onions in butter until tender. Stir in artichoke hearts, tomatoes and remaining ingredients. Pour mixture into lightly greased baking dish. Bake at 325 degrees for 10 to 15 minutes or until heated through.
Servings 4-6.

332

Accompaniments

Tomato Bread

1-1/3 cup low-sodium tomato juice
1 tablespoon vegetable margarine
1 tablespoon sugar
1/2 teaspoon basil, dried
  or 1 teaspoon fresh, minced
1/2 teaspoon oregano, dried
  or 1 teaspoon fresh, minced

1/3 cup parmesan cheese, grated
1 package active dry yeast
1/4 cup warm water
2-3/4 to 3 cups whole wheat flour
Vegetable coating spray

Heat juice and margarine until margarine melts. Add sugar, herbs and cheese. Stir yeast and water together. Add to tomato mixture. Stir in half the flour using a large, wooden spoon for about two minutes. Gradually mix in remaining flour to make a soft dough that clings together in a ball and leaves sides of bowl. Knead on a lightly floured board until smooth and elastic, 5-8 minutes. Spray a 4x8 loaf pan with vegetable coating spray. Place dough in pan, and spray top of dough. Let rise in a warm place until doubled in size (about 30 minutes). Bake at 375 degrees about 25 minutes. Spray top again with vegetable coating spray, and bake another 5 minutes to brown loaf.
Yield: 1 loaf - 18 slices (1 slice per serving).

Tomatoes with Mustard and Brown Sugar Dressing

1/4 cup vegetable oil
2 teaspoons dark brown sugar
Salt and pepper to taste
4 scallions, chopped

1 tablespoon cider vinegar
1-1/2 teaspoons dijon style mustard
3 medium tomatoes, sliced

In small bowl, whisk together oil, vinegar, brown sugar and mustard. Season dressing with salt and pepper to taste. Arrange tomato slices on serving platter, and drizzle on dressing. Sprinkle scallions on top.
Servings: 4.

Accompaniments

Turnip Casserole

7 medium turnips, peeled
and cut into 2x3/8 inch strips
2 large carrots, scraped
and cut into 2x3/8 strips
1 small onion, chopped
1/2 teaspoon salt
1 cup frozen peas, thawed

1 jar (4 ounces) pimento,
drained and chopped
1 can (10 ounces) cream of chicken
soup, undiluted
1 carton (8 ounces) sour cream
1/4 teaspoon dried basil
1-3/4 cups herb seasoned stuffing mix
1/4 cup margarine, melted

Place first 4 ingredients in dutch oven, cover vegetables with water, and bring to boil. Cover, and cook 5 to 10 minutes or until vegetables are tender. Drain. Add peas and pimento, and set aside. Combine soup, sour cream and basil. Stir into vegetable mixture. Spoon into greased pan. Combine stuffing mix and butter, and spread mixture over casserole. Bake at 350 degrees for 25 to 30 minutes. Serve. Servings: 8.

Accompaniments

Vegetable Gratin

3 tablespoons unsalted butter
1/2 onion, chopped
1 small clove garlic, smashed
2 thin slices ginger
2 small potatoes, peeled and
  sliced thin
2 small carrots, sliced thin
2 small turnips, sliced thin
2 parsnips, sliced thin

Salt and pepper to taste
2 tablespoons fresh bread crumbs
3 tablespoons heavy cream
2 medium eggs
1 egg yolk
1/4 cup carrots, cut into
  1/4 inch dice
1/4 cup turnips, cut into
  1/4 inch dice

In a saucepan, heat 2 tablespoons butter. Add onion, garlic and ginger. Cover, and cook over low heat until vegetables are soft, about 10 minutes. Add remaining tablespoon butter and the potatoes, stirring to coat. Add sliced carrots, turnips, parsnips and 3/4 teaspoon salt, stirring to coat. Cover, and cook over very low heat, stirring occasionally for 20 minutes. Add 1/3 cup water, cover, and cook until vegetables are tender enough to mash with back of wooden spoon (about 20 minutes). Remove from heat. Heat oven to 375 degrees. Butter 4 5-ounce ramekins. Coat with bread crumbs. Place a piece of brown paper or towel on bottom of baking pan large enough to hold ramekins. Puree cooked vegetables by pushing through food mill into large mixing bowl. Cool. When puree is cool, stir in cream, eggs and egg yolk. Fold in carrots and turnips. Season to taste with salt and pepper. Divide mixture evenly in prepared ramekins. Pour boiling water into paper lined baking pan, 1/2 way up sides of ramekins. Bake in preheated oven until mixture is set and feels firm to touch, 35 to 40 minutes. Allow to rest 5 minutes in warm place. Invert molds onto serving dishes. Serve immediately.
Servings: 4.

Accompaniments

Whole-Grain Buttermilk Bread

1 cup warm water
  (105 to 115 degrees)
1 package active dry yeast
1 tablespoon honey
4 cups unsifted all-purpose flour
  (approximately)
2 cups buttermilk

1 tablespoon salt
1 cup wheat germ
2-1/2 cups rye flour
1 egg white, slightly beaten
  with 1 teaspoon water
3 tablespoons rolled oats

Place warm water in large bowl. Stir in yeast and honey; then 1 cup all-purpose flour. Let stand in warm place until bubbly, 20 to 25 minutes. Mix in buttermilk and salt. Add 2-1/2 cups more of all-purpose flour. Mix to blend. Beat until smooth. Stir in wheat germ and rye flour to make a stiff dough. Turn out on a floured surface, and knead until dough is springy, kneading in more all-purpose flour, if necessary. Place dough in greased bowl. Cover, and let rise in warm place until doubled, about 1-1/2 hours. Punch dough down, and let rest 5 minutes. Divide in half. Shape each half into a loaf, and place in a greased 9x5 inch loaf pan. Let rise until doubled, about 45 minutes. Brush lightly with egg white mixture. Sprinkle each loaf with 1-1/2 tablespoons of rolled oats. Bake at 350 degrees until loaves are well-browned and sound hollow when tapped, 40 to 45 minutes.
Yield: 2 loaves.

Loaves will have a better shape if you bake them in pans slightly smaller than standard - about 8-1/2x4-1/2 inches.

336

Accompaniments

Whole Wheat Mushroom Dressing

2 tablespoons butter or margarine
1/3 cup dry white wine
1 pound small mushrooms, halved
1/3 cup green onions, chopped
2-1/4 cups whole wheat bread cubes,
  toasted

1/2 cup slivered almonds, toasted
1/4 to 1/2 teaspoon salt
1/2 teaspoon dried whole thyme
1/4 teaspoon dried whole marjoram
1/4 to 1/4 cup chicken broth
  (optional)

Combine butter, wine, mushrooms and green onions in medium saucepan. Cook over low heat 10 minutes or until mushrooms are tender. Add next 5 ingredients to mushroom mixture, stirring well. Add chicken broth, if desired, for a moister consistency. If not using as a stuffing, spoon dressing into lightly greased casserole. Bake at 325 degrees for 25 to 30 minutes.
Servings: 4-6.

Wild Rice with Mushrooms

3/4 cup butter, clarified
3/4 cup onions
3/4 cup wild rice, blanched
1-1/4 cup white rice, long grain
1 quart chicken stock, boiling

1 bay leaf
1-1/4 cup mushrooms, fresh
1/3 cup butter, clarified
1/2 bunch parsley, chopped

Heat butter in sautoir. Peel onion, and dice fine. Saute diced onion in butter. Add rice to onions. Saute until hot. Add chicken stock and bay leaf. Bring to boil, and cover with tight fitting lid. Bake in 350 degree oven, 15 to 20 minutes. Wash mushrooms, and slice. Heat butter in russe. Add sliced mushrooms. Saute until tender. Add to mushrooms. Stir mushroom mixture into rice.
Servings: 10.

Accompaniments

Yellow Rice

1 medium onion, diced
1 clove garlic, crushed
4 large mushrooms, diced
1/4 teaspon salt
1/4 teaspoon pepper
1/4 teaspoon turmeric

1 tablespoon fresh parsley, minced
1 tablespoon oil
2 cups cooked brown rice
1/3 cup golden raisins
1/4 cup unsalted dry-roasted nuts,
    chopped

Saute the onions, garlic, mushrooms and seasonings in the oil in a large skillet until onions are translucent. Stir in the rice, raisins and nuts. Heat throughly, and serve.
Servings: 6 (1 cup).

Yellow Squash
with Basil and Parmesan

1/2 pound summer squash, trimmed
    and cut crosswise 1/4 inch slices
1 tablespoon parmesan cheese, grated

1 tablespoon olive oil
2 tablespoons fresh basil leaves,
    shredded

In steamer, cook squash for 2 minutes or until al dente. Transfer to bowl. Drizzle squash with oil, sprinkle with basil, and season with salt and pepper. Let squash cool to room temperature, and serve sprinkled with parmesan cheese.
Servings: 4.

Accompaniments

Zucchini and Corn

1/2 cup onion, chopped
1/4 cup butter or margarine,
  melted
1/2 teaspoon salt
1/4 teaspoon dried whole basil

1/3 cup green pepper chopped
4 cups zucchini, sliced
1-1/2 cups fresh corn
1/4 teaspoon dried whole oregano

Saute onion and green pepper in butter until tender. Stir in remaining ingredients, cover, and simmer 8 to 10 minutes or until zucchini is crisp and tender. Servings: 6.

Zucchini Bread

3 eggs
2 cups sugar
1 cup vegetable oil
2 cups zucchini, peeled and grated
3 teaspoons vanilla
3 cups flour

1 teaspoon salt
1 teaspoon baking soda
1/4 teaspoon baking powder
3 teaspoons cinnamon
1 cup of walnuts or pecans

Beat the eggs until light and foamy. Add the oil, the sugar, the vanilla and the zucchini. Slowly add the mixed, dry ingredients, and when combined, stir in the nuts. Pour into greased, floured pans, and bake at 350 degrees until done. Yield: 1 loaf.

Accompaniments

Zucchini Stuffed with Veal and Prosciutto

4 zucchini
1/2 pound lean ground veal
1/2 cup (3 ounces) prosciutto,
  minced
2 raw chicken livers,
  (2 ounces) minced
1/2 cup parmesan cheese, grated

1 whole large egg,
  beaten lightly
1 large egg white,
  beaten lightly
3 tablespoons butter, softened
2 tablespoons canned tomato puree
Pinch of nutmeg

Half the zucchini lengthwise, and scoop out flesh, leaving shells. Let shells drain, salted and inverted on paper towels for 15 minutes. Chop flesh, and let drain, salted in colander for 15 minutes. Squeeze any remaining liquid, and put flesh in bowl. Arrange shells cut side up in shallow glass baking dish large enough to hold in one layer. In skillet, cook veal over moderate high heat, stirring and breaking up meat, until no longer pink. Transfer the veal to bowl of zucchini, and stir in prosciutto, chicken livers, parmesan, whole egg, egg white, butter, tomato puree, nutmeg, salt and pepper to taste. Mound mixture in zucchini shells, and bake in preheated 375 degree oven for 35 to 40 minutes, or until stuffing is golden.
Servings: 40.

Accompaniments

Zucchini with Olives

This is a recipe that can be served hot or cold.

2 medium zucchini
1 tablespoon olive oil
1 large clove garlic, crushed
6 black olives, diced

1 teaspoon dried parsley
1/4 teaspoon salt
1/4 teaspoon black pepper
1/2 teaspoon marjoram

Wash, and dice the zucchini. Heat the oil in a saucepan. Stir in all ingredients, and reduce the heat to low. Cook, covered, for about 10 minutes.
Servings: 4 (2/3 cup).

DESSERTS

Desserts

Contents

Desserts

Desserts

Culinary Commentary

Chef Armin Gronert, a German certified master pastry chef, has experience as an educator, administrator, and executive chef. He currently teaches baking & pastry arts at the University. Early in his career, Gronert owned a sugar design school in Bad Ems, Germany, where courses in sugar artistry and chocolate and marzipan modeling were taught. Upon leaving Germany, Gronert worked as an executive chef at the prestigious Coccoloba Hotel in Anguilla, British West Indies. Prior to joining the University, he served as a chef instructor at the Culinary Institute of America.

HISTORY OF CHOCOLATE
FROM XOCOATL TO CHOCOLATE BARS

In 1519, Emperor Montezuma II made a fatal error. He mistook Spanish conqueror Hernan Cortes for Quetzalcoatl, a bearded, white-skinned god scheduled by Aztec legend to reappear on earth that year. Cortes rewarded Montezuma's opulent welcome by taking his gold, his empire, and eventually his life. Cortes sent his king, Carlos V, a supply of cacao beans. The Aztecs used the beans to brew xocoatl, a cold, rather bitter drink so prized that it was reserved for the society upper classes. Xocoatl held a prominent place in Central America as a beverage associated with divinity and power (Montezuma drank as many as 50 golden cups of it a day). It was also thought of as an aphrodisiac. Cortes made a delicate reference to that possibility in a letter that accompanied the samples he sent back home to King Carlos.

Spanish courtiers didn't much care for the stuff until they tried making it with hot water and a bit of sugar. Spain and the rest of Europe thereupon went mad for it. Chocolate houses became the rage all over the continent.

Chocolate didn't make the transition from a drink to a candy until the 19th Century. An English company, called Fry & Sons in 1847, combined plant fat and chocolate liquor from fermented cacao beans with sugar to form chocolate bars. In 1876, the Swiss added dried milk to make milk chocolate. The innovations proved popular, and national variations soon developed. By the turn of the century, Milton Hershey in the US had launched the Hershey bar with stunning success.

Hershey and other modern chocolate makers have tried to produce synthetic chocolate with no success. No one can apparently reproduce the flavor of the cacao bean, but the experimenting goes on.

Like coffee beans, cacao beans come in a number of quality levels. The best beans are called Criollo in the trade; those have a mild, nutlike flavor. Forastero beans are of the bulk or ordinary grade with a strong, harsh character. Trinitario beans are of an intermediate grade; those from the West Indies have a full, fruity flavor while Trinitarios from Venezuela have an outstanding aroma.

Individual chocolate formulas are trade secrets. How a given bar will taste depends on factors like the blend and quality of the beans, the style of processing, and the amount of cocoa butter mixed in. Recipes have also evolved that cater to regional or national tastes.

Culinary Commentary

European-style chocolate, for instance, has a sour, cheeselike milk character, combined with distinct cooked and caramelized milk notes. The Droste milk bars are examples of the style.

American chocolate tends to have a low milk flavor; some, sour cheesy flavor; and others, a stronger cocoa flavor and coarser texture. The Hershey bars are good examples. The American style seems to derive, in some respects, from European chocolate.

British-style chocolate, exemplified by Cadbury's (now also made in America), has a dominant cooked-milk character that suppresses the chocolate. The milk makes the texture soft and creamy.

No matter how chocolate is made and what the effects on the waistline, the world can't seem to get enough of it. Americans alone eat an average of 10 pounds of chocolate a year.

Culinary Commentary

Gladys Fulton of Summerville, South Carolina, was the grand prize winner in the 35th Pillsbury Bake-Off® Contest. She is a special friend to the University.

I developed my love of cooking way back in the 1930's, while helping my mother prepare family meals.

Over the years, I have combined many foods (using leftovers), often coming up with a one time food combination to serve my family. (Some were exceptionally good).

In developing my prize winning Pennsylvania Dutch Cake and Custard Pie, I combined ingredients I thought would blend well. When they did, it was a matter of getting the right amount of each ingredient to work together. Tasting, testing and improving until I finally felt it was right was important.

From the very first phone call informing me I was a finalist in the Pillsbury Bake-Off, I've had the most exciting experience anyone could hope for in a lifetime. To have won the grand prize in the Pillsbury Bake-Off is "The Impossible Dream Come True" and my feet haven't touched ground since.

Everyone involved with putting the 35th Pillsbury Bake-Off together made sure that the 100 Finalists felt special. I'm sure each of the finalists will agree, everything was first class.

So-o-o, if a 66 year old grandma can do it - you all go for it, too.

Culinary Commentary

Serve warm with cinnamon ice cream.

Pennsylvania Dutch Cake and Custard Pie

1 package (15 ounces) Pillsbury All Ready Pie Crusts

Filling:

1/3 cup sugar	2/3 cup dairy sour cream
2 tablespoons flour	1/3 cup molasses
1 teaspoon apple pie spice*	1 egg, beaten
1 cup applesauce	

Cake:

1/2 cup sugar	1-1/4 cups Pillsbury BEST®
1/4 cup margarine or butter, softened	All Purpose or Unbleached Flour***
1/2 cup sour milk**	1 teaspoon baking powder
1 egg	1/2 teaspoon salt
1 teaspoon vanilla	1/4 teaspoon baking soda

Glaze:

1/2 cup powdered sugar	2 tablespoons coffee

Prepare pie crust according to package directions for filled one-crust pie using 9 inch pie pan or 9 inch deep dish pie pan. (Refrigerate remaining crust for a later use.) Heat oven to 350 degrees. In medium bowl, combine 1/3 cup sugar, 2 tablespoons flour and apple pie spice; mix well. Stir in remaining filling ingredients; blend well. Set aside. In small bowl, combine 1/2 cup sugar and margarine; beat until well blended. Add sour milk, 1 egg and vanilla; beat until smooth. Lightly spoon flour into measuring cup; level off. Add flour, baking powder, salt and baking soda; mix well. Spoon into crust-lined pan. Carefully pour filling

Culinary Commentary

mixture over batter. Bake at 350 degrees for 45 to 60 minutes or until center springs back when touched lightly and top is deep golden brown. Meanwhile, in small bowl, combine glaze ingredients; blend well. Drizzle over hot pie. Serve slightly warm with cinnamon ice cream.
Servings: 8-10.

Tips:
*One-half teaspoon cinnamon, 1/4 teaspoon ginger, 1/8 teaspoon nutmeg and 1/8 teaspoon allspice can be substituted.
**To make sour milk, add 1 teaspoon lemon juice to 1/2 cup milk; let stand 5 minutes.
***If using self-rising flour, omit baking powder, salt and baking soda.

High Altitude:
Above 3500 Feet: Increase flour in cake to 1-1/3 cups. Bake as directed.

Nutrition Information Per Serving:
Serving Size: 1/10 of recipe

		Percent U.S. RDA Per Serving	
Calories	390	Protein	6%
Protein	5 g	Vitamin A	8%
Carbohydrate	59 g	Vitamin C	*
Fat	15 g	Thiamine	10%
Cholesterol	56 mg	Riboflavin	10%
Sodium	330 mg	Niacin	6%
Potassium	220 mg	Calcium	10%
		Iron	10%

*Contains less t han 2% of the U.S. RDA of this nutrient.

Desserts

Amaretto-Hot Fruit Compote

1 can (16 ounces) peach halves
1 can (16 ounces) pear halves
1 can (15-1/2 ounces) pineapple chunks
1 can (17 ounces) apricot halves
1 can (16-1/2 ounces) pitted
  dark sweet cherries
2 bananas, sliced

1 teaspoon lemon juice
1 package (2-1/4 ounces) sliced
  almonds, toasted and divided
1/4 cup butter or margarine
1/3 cup amaretto or
  other almond-flavored liqueur

Drain fruits, reserving syrup for other uses. Combine canned fruits in a large bowl. Set aside. Combine bananas and lemon juice, and toss gently. Add to fruit mixture. Layer half each of fruit mixture and macaroon crumbs in a 2-1/2 quart baking dish. Sprinkle with 3 tablespoons sliced almonds, and dot with 2 table-spoons butter. Repeat procedure. Pour amaretto evenly over fruit mixture. Bake at 350 degrees for 30 minutes. Sprinkle with remaining almonds. Stir before serving.
Servings: 12 to 14.

Ambrosia

2 medium-size yellow grapefruit
2 medium oranges
2 small dessert apples

1/2 cup orange juice
1/4 cup shredded coconut

Peel grapefruit with sharp knife, cutting deeply enough to remove white pith. Cut grapefruit crosswise into 1/4 inch slices. Peel oranges in the same way, and cut into 1/4 inch slices. Using apple corer or sharp knife, remove center core from apples. Cut crosswise into 1/4 inch slices. Arrange fruit slices in overlapping circles in large shallow dessert bowl. Pour orange juice over all. Chill until serving time. Sprinkle with coconut.
Servings: 4 (125 calories each).   Nutritional Analysis: page 434.

Desserts

Apple and Cheddar Gratin

2 pounds green apples, peeled
  and cut into 1/4 inch slices
1/2 cup raisins
1/2 teaspoon cinnamon
1/4 cup lemon juice
3/4 cup dark brown sugar,
  firmly packed

1/2 cup all purpose flour
1/8 teaspoon salt
1/2 stick (1/4 cup) butter, unsalted
  cut into bits
1 cup extra sharp cheddar,
  finely grated

In a well-buttered shallow baking dish, arrange apple slices, and sprinkle with raisins, cinnamon and lemon juice. In a small bowl combine sugar, flour and salt. Blend in butter until mixture resembles coarse meal, and toss mixture with cheddar. Sprinkle the cheddar mixture over apple mixture, and bake in upper third of preheated 350 degree oven for 30 minutes or until apples are tender. Servings: 4.

Apple Fritters

2 cups flour
2 cups beer, room temperature
4 to 5 tart apples, peeled, cored, and
  sliced in rings
1 cup sugar

1 tablespoon cinnamon
1 teaspoon ginger
Oil for deep frying
Confectioner's sugar

Mix beer and flour, cover, and let stand 2 hours. Mix sugar and spices, and turn apple rings in the mixture. At serving time, drop apple rings into beer batter to coat, and then into hot (375 degrees) oil. Dust with confectioner's sugar to serve. Servings: 8. Nutritional Analysis: page 434.

Desserts

Apple-Prune and Apricot Compote

1/3 cup raisins
1 cup prunes, pitted
16 ounces frozen apple juice
  concentrate
1 cup dried apricots

2 whole cloves
1 cinnamon stick
1 tablespoon lemon juice, fresh
3 green apples, tart
1 cup creme fraiche or sour cream

Place raisins and prunes in a small saucepan, cover with water, and bring to a boil. Reduce heat, cover, and simmer until prunes are soft and plumped (about 20 minutes). Drain, and place in bowl. Place apple juice concentrate in a medium saucepan with 2 cups water, add apricots, cloves and cinnamon, and bring to a boil. Reduce the heat, cover, and simmer, until apricots are plumped and tender (about 20 minutes). Remove from the heat, and with a slotted spoon, transfer apricots to the bowl of prunes. Add lemon juice to the pan of apple juice. Peel, core, and slice each apple into 8 wedges, and drop the pieces into the saucepan to prevent discoloration. Cover and simmer, stirring once or twice until tender, 5 to 7 minutes. Add apples and liquid to bowl of fruit. Serve at room temperature, or chilled and topped with creme fraiche or sour cream.
Servings: 6.

Desserts

Apricot Cake

1 cup dried apricots (unsulphured)
1 cup water
2 cups sugar (preferably "raw" sugar)
1/4 pound plus 2 tablespoons butter
1 teaspoon vanilla extract
1-1/2 teaspoons lemon peel, grated
  (organic undyed lemon, if possible)

2 eggs
2 cups whole wheat pastry flour
1/2 teaspoon salt
2-1/4 teaspoons baking powder
1 cup milk

Soak apricots in water for about 2 hours. Add 1/2 cup sugar and 2 tablespoons butter, and simmer gently until sugar and butter dissolve. Put mixture through blender or food mill. Set aside. Cream remaining butter and sugar. Add vanilla, lemon peel and eggs one at a time, stirring well. Add sifted flour, salt and baking powder alternately with milk, and beat until smooth, but do not overbeat. Pour batter into an 8 inch springform pan. Spread apricot puree gently over top of batter, slightly thinner toward the middle. Bake at 350 degrees for about 1 hour, until cake pulls away from sides of pan. During baking, the apricot puree will penetrate the cake and end up in a layer at the bottom. Top each piece with a dollop of whipped cream, or leave as is - delicious either way.
Servings: 6-8.

Desserts

Baked Apple Sliced with Pecan Sauce

1 yellow apple, peeled,
  cored and cut into 1/2 inch slices
1 teaspoon fresh lemon juice
1 tablespoon dark rum
1/8 teaspoon cinnamon
1/3 cup heavy cream

1-1/2 tablespoons dark brown sugar,
  firmly packed
1 teaspoon butter, unsalted
2 tablespoons pecans, chopped and
  toasted lightly
1/4 cup water

In a baking pan large enough to hold apple slices on one layer, whisk together lemon juice, 2 teaspoons rum, cinnamon and water. Add apple slices, and turn to coat with mixture. Arrange apple slices in one layer, and bake in preheated 375 degree oven for 18 to 20 minutes or until tender. In a heavy saucepan combine cream and brown sugar. Cook mixture over moderate heat, stirring for 6 to 8 minutes or until thickened. Stir in butter, remaining 1 teaspoon rum and pecans. When butter is melted, pour sauce over apple slices.
Servings: 2.

Desserts

Baked Yams
with Amaretto Crumble Topping

5 pounds yams or sweet potatoes
12 tablespoons unsalted butter
1/4 to 1/2 cup brown sugar to taste
1/4 cup amaretto liqueur or dark rum
1/4 cup orange marmalade

2 teaspoons powdered ginger
   (omit if using gingersnaps, below)
1/2 teaspoon salt
24 Italian almond macaroons
   or 20 gingersnaps

Preheat oven to 375 degrees. Bake yams for 1-1/2 hours until very tender. Let stand until cool enough to handle. Peel yams. Mash well with 4 tablespoons butter, brown sugar, liqueur, marmalade, ginger and salt. Pulverize cookies in food processor or blender. Add remaining 8 tablespoons butter, and process until well mixed. The recipe can be made a day in advance at this point. Refrigerate yams and amaretto topping separately. Preheat oven to 400 degrees. Generously butter large shallow baking dish. Spread mashed yams evenly in dish. Pinch or cut cookie topping into small pieces, and scatter evenly over yams. Bake for about 30 minutes, until yams are heated through and topping is melted. Transfer to broiler, and cook for 12 minutes to crisp and brown topping.
Servings: 8.

Desserts

Banana Cake

1/2 cup shortening
1 cup and 2 tablespoons sugar
2 tablespoons honey
2 eggs
1-1/4 teaspoons vanilla
2-1/2 cups sifted flour

2-1/2 teaspoons baking powder
1/2 teaspoon soda
1/2 teaspoon salt
1-1/4 teaspoons cinnamon
1 cup mashed bananas, mixed
    with 2-1/2 tablespoons milk

Cream shortening and sugar thoroughly. Add honey, and beat thoroughly. Add eggs, beat, and add vanilla. Sift dry ingredients together, and add to creamed mixture alternately with banana-milk ingredients, stirring only enough after each addition to blend thoroughly. Pour into 2 greased 9 inch layer pans, and bake at 375 degrees for 25 minutes. Frost with desired icing, adding sliced bananas as decorations.
Servings: 6-8.

Benne Seed Wafers

3/4 cup butter or margarine, softened
2 cups brown sugar, firmly packed
1 egg, beaten
1 cup all-purpose flour

1/2 teaspoon baking powder
1/4 teaspoon salt
1 can (1.87 ounces) sesame seeds
1 teaspoon vanilla extract

Cream butter. Gradually add sugar, beating well. Add egg. Beat well. Sift together flour, baking powder and salt. Add to creamed mixture, beating well. Stir in sesame seeds and vanilla, and mix well. Drop dough by teaspoonfuls onto waxed paper-lined baking sheets. Bake at 325 degrees for 10 minutes or until edges are lightly browned. Cool 5 minutes. Carefully remove to wire racks to cool completely.
Yield: about 8 dozen.

Desserts

Berry Parfait

2 cups raspberries, blackberries, strawberries, or blueberries
1/2 cup plain yogurt

1 (3 ounces) package cream cheese, softened
1 tablespoon honey

Spoon the berries into a blender or food processor, and run it at low speed for a few seconds. Set aside. Combine the yogurt, cream cheese and honey in the blender or food processor, and blend until you have a smooth mixture. Spoon the berries and the yogurt mixture, alternately, into chilled parfait glasses, and serve cold.

Servings: 4.   Nutritional Analysis: page 434.

Variations:
Peach Parfait. Substitute 2 cups sliced fresh peaches for the berries.
Cherry Parfait. Substitute 2 cups chopped sweet ripe cherries for the berries.

Desserts

Berry Tapioca

1/3 cup quick-cooking tapioca
2-1/2 cups water
2 tablespoons lemon juice
1/4 cup honey

2 cups fresh berries
   (blackberries, strawberries,
   raspberries, blueberries)
2 cups heavy cream

Put the tapioca in the top of a double boiler, add the water, and cook over medium heat for 15 minutes. Stir in the lemon juice and honey. Mash the berries a little, and stir them into the pudding. Let cool. Whip the cream until stiff, and fold it into the pudding. Chill in goblets.

Variations:
Peach Tapioca. Substitute 2 or 3 fresh peaches, peeled and cut in small chunks, for the berries.
Orange Tapioca. Substitute 2 or 3 fresh oranges, peeled, seeded, and cut into small chunks, for the berries
Servings: 6.

Desserts

Black Bottom Parfait

1/2 cup plus 2 tablespoons sugar, divided
2 tablespoons cornstarch
2 cups skim milk
2 eggs, separated
1/2 teaspoon unflavored gelatin

1/4 cup processed cocoa, sifted
1 tablespoon dark rum
1/4 teaspoon cream of tartar
1/2 teaspoon vanilla extract
Grated chocolate (optional)
Fresh cherries (optional)

Combine 1/2 cup sugar and cornstarch in a medium saucepan. Gradually stir in milk. Cook over medium heat, stirring constantly, until mixture comes to a boil. Cook 1 minute, stirring constantly. Remove from heat. Beat egg yolks at medium speed of an electirc mixer until thick and lemon colored. Gradually stir about one-fourth of hot mixture into yolks. Add to remaining hot mixture, stirring constantly. Bring mixture to a boil over low heat, and cook 1 minute, stirring constantly. Remove from heat, and transfer 1 cup mixture to a small mixing bowl. Add gelatin to hot custard in small mixing bowl. Beat with a wire whisk until gelatin dissolves. Set aside gelatin mixture to cool completely. Add cocoa and dark rum to remaining custard in saucepan. Beat with a wire whisk until cocoa thoroughly dissolves. Spoon chocolate custard equally into 6 parfait glasses, and set aside to cool completely. Beat egg whites (at room temperature) in a medium mixing bowl at high speed of an electric mixer until foamy. Add cream of tartar, and continue to beat until soft peaks form. Gradually add remaining sugar, one tablespoon at a time, beating until stiff peaks form, and sugar dissolves. Fold in vanilla. Beat reserved cooled custard in mixing bowl with a wire whisk until smooth. Fold in beaten egg white mixture. Spoon meringue mixture evenly over chocolate layer in parfait glasses. Cover, and chill thoroughly. If desired, garnish with grated chocolate and fresh cherries.
Servings: 6 (161 calories each).

Desserts

Bourbon Pecan Cake

1 pounds pecans
1/2 cup raisins
2 teaspoons nutmeg
1/2 cup bourbon
1-1/2 cups flour

1 teaspoon baking powder
1/2 cup butter
2 cups plus 2 tablespoons sugar
3 eggs, separated
Cherries and pecan halves for garnish

Break pecans coarsely, and cut raisins in half. Soak nutmeg in bourbon 10 minutes. Sift flour, and set 1/2 cup aside. Cream butter and sugar, slowly while adding egg yolks. Add bourbon and flour to mixture; then beat until blended, and fold in raisins. Beat egg whites until stiff, and fold into sugar-egg mixture. Grease and line large tube pan. Fill with batter, and let set. Put cherries and nuts on settled batter. Bake at 325 degrees for 1-1/2 hours or until done. Remove, cool, and turn over so cherries are on top.

Servings: 6-8.   Nutritional Analysis: page 434.

Desserts

Caramel Peanut Pie

2 cups sugar, divided
2 tablespoons all purpose flour
2 cups milk
1 teaspoon vanilla extract
1/4 cup sugar

1 cup water, boiling
5 eggs, separated
1 cup peanuts, chopped
2 9-inch pastry shells, baked

Place 1 cup of sugar in a heavy skillet, and cook over medium high heat, stirring constantly until sugar melts and forms light brown syrup. Reduce heat to low, and gradually add boiling water, stirring constantly with wire whisk. Remove from heat. Combine 1 cup sugar and flour in heavy saucepan, and stir well. Add egg yolks, milk and caramelized sugar mixture; stir well. Cook over low heat, stirring constantly until mixture thickens. Stir in chopped peanuts and vanilla. Pour into pastry shells. Beat egg whites at room temperature until foamy. Gradually add 1/4 cup sugar, 1 tablespoon at a time, beating until stiff peaks form. Spread meringue over hot filling, sealing to edge of pastry. Bake pie at 350 degrees for 12 to 15 minutes or until golden brown. Cool to room temperature.
Servings: 12.

Desserts

Carrot Cake

2 cups whole wheat pastry flour
2 teaspoons baking soda
1 teaspoon salt
2 teaspoons cinnamon

1/4 cup vegetable oil
1-1/2 cups honey
4 eggs, well-beaten
3-1/2 cups carrots, grated

Sift together the flour, soda, salt and cinnamon. Stir in oil and honey, and then the well-beaten eggs. Mix in the grated carrots. Oil and flour two 8 inch layer pans or one 8 inch spring pan. Pour in batter, and bake in a 350 degree oven for 35 minutes. Remove from pans, and cool on a cake rack while you prepare the cream cheese frosting below - also delicious unfrosted.

Cream Cheese Frosting:

8 ounces cream cheese
1/4 pound butter

3 cups powdered sugar

Have cream cheese and butter at room temperature. Cream together, using a spoon or fingers. Add powdered sugar until desired consistency is reached. Makes enough frosting for a two-layer cake.
Servings: 6-8.

Desserts

Cheese Cake

Crust:

1 cup fine graham cracker crumbs   1/4 teaspoon melted margarine
2 tablespoons sugar

Mix together, and press into bottom of springform pan. Bake 5 minutes in 300 degree oven.

Filling:

2 packages (8 ounces) cream cheese   1 teaspoon grated lemon rind
1/2 cup sugar   1 teaspoon vanilla
1 tablespoon lemon juice   2 eggs, separated

Beat egg whites until stiff. Add sugar and set aside. In large mixing bowl, mix cheese with lemon juice, rind and vanilla. Add yolks, one at a time, beating well after each addition. Fold egg whites into mixture. Pour over crumb crust. Bake 45 minutes at 300 degrees. While filling bakes, make topping.

Topping:

1 cup commercial sour cream   1 teaspoon vanilla
1 tablespoon sugar

While cake is still hot, spread topping, and return to oven. Bake at 300 degrees 10 to 20 minutes (time varies with different types of ovens). Cool; then carefully remove side. Top with your choice of pie fruit fillings or a chocolate sauce topping.
Servings: 6-8.

Desserts

Chess Pie

6 ounces butter
1 cup sugar
2 tablespoons flour
1 tablespoon cornmeal
3 eggs

1 teaspoon vanilla
1/2 cup milk
1/4 teaspoon salt
2 tablespoons lemon juice
1 pie shell

Mix dry ingredients. Cream with butter. Add rest of ingredients. Pour into pie shell, and bake at 350 degrees for 15 minutes; then at 250 degrees for 45 minutes.
Servings: 6-8.

Desserts

Chocolate Banana Cake

2 ounces unsweetened chocolate
3 eggs
2 teaspoons baking powder
1/4 teaspoon salt
2/3 cup buttermilk
1 cup pecans, chopped
1 cup butter or margarine, softened

2-3/4 cups sugar
3 cups all purpose flour
1/4 teaspoon baking soda
1 cup mashed banana
1 tablespoon vanilla extract
*Chocolate frosting

Place chocolate in top of double boiler, and bring water to a boil. Reduce heat to low, and cook until chocolate melts. Set aside to cool. Cream butter, and gradually add sugar, beating well with an electric mixer. Combine flour, baking powder, soda and salt, and add to cream mixture, alternately with banana, buttermilk and melted chocolate, beginning and ending with flour mixture. Mix well after each addition, and stir in vanilla and pecans. Spoon batter into 3 greased and floured 9 inch round cake pans. Bake at 350 degrees for 30 minutes or until pick inserted comes out clean. Cool in pans for 10 minutes. Remove from pans, and cool completely. Spread chocolate frosting between layers including the top and sides of the cake.

*Chocolate Frosting:
1/3 cup butter or margarine, softened
5 cups sifted powdered sugar
1/3 cup cocoa

1/4 teaspoon salt
1/2 cup to 1/2 plus 1 tablespoon
  evaporated milk

Combine the first 4 ingredients in mixing bowl, and beat at low speed setting of an electric mixer. Gradually add milk until frosting reaches desired spreading consistency. Beat until smooth.
Servings: 6-8.

Desserts

Chocolate Bread Pudding

2/3 cup plus 1 tablespoon sugar
1 cup heavy cream
8 ounces semisweet chocolate,
  coarsely chopped
5 eggs separated
1/4 pound butter, unsalted and
  cut into pieces

1 tablespoon vanilla extract
2 cups fresh bread crumbs,
  made from 5 slices firm white bread
*Custard sauce
Strawberries, sprigs of mint, seedless
  raspberry jam for garnish

Preheat oven to 350 degrees. Butter 8 inch square baking pan or 8x13 inch souffle dish or cake pan, and dust with 1 tablespoon sugar. In a medium saucepan, bring cream to a simmer. Meanwhile, place chocolate in food processor, and chop finely, 15-20 seconds. With machine on, pour in hot cream. As soon as mixture is smooth, add 1/3 cup sugar and egg yolks, 1 at a time. Add butter and vanilla. Process just until smooth. In a large bowl, combine whites until soft peaks form. Gradually beat in remaining 1/3 cup sugar, and continue to beat until whites are glossy and stand in stiff peaks. Stir 1/3 egg whites into chocolate mixture to lighten it. Fold in remaining whites until white streaks remain. Turn into prepared baking pan. Place baking pan in roasting pan, and add enough warm water to reach half way up sides of baking pan. Bake in center of oven 45-50 minutes or until pudding is set and cake tester comes out clean with just a few crumbs. Remove, and cool on rack for 10 minutes. Then invert onto serving platter, and serve warm with custard sauce.

*Custard Sauce:
6 egg yolks
2-1/2 cups milk
1 teaspoon vanilla extract

2/3 cup sugar
1-1/2 tablespoons brandy

In a large bowl, combine egg yolks and 1/3 cup sugar. Beat until sugar dissolves and mixture is light colored, about 3 minutes. In a heavy medium saucepan,

Desserts

combine remaining 1/3 cup sugar and milk. Bring to a boil. Gradually whisk milk into egg yolk mixture in a thin stream. Return custard to sauce pan. Cook over moderately low heat, stirring constantly until custard is thick enough to coat back of a wooden spoon, about 10 minutes. It should register 180 degrees on instant reading thermometer. Do not let custard boil or the eggs will curdle. Remove from heat, and strain into a bowl. Stir in brandy and vanilla. Serve warm at room temperature, or chilled.
Servings: 6-8.

Chocolate Cheese Dream Pie

Crust:
Graham cracker crust

Filling:
2 envelopes unflavored gelatin
1-1/2 cups water
2/3 cup nonfat dry milk
1/2 cup part-skim ricotta cheese
2/3 cup lowfat cottage cheese
Sweetener equivalent
  to 14 teaspoons sugar

2 tablespoons plus 2 teaspoons cocoa
  (unsweetened)
2 teaspoons each vanilla extract and
  vanilla butternut flavor
1 teaspoon chocolate extract
12 ice cubes

Preheat oven to 350 degrees. Prepare crust. Cool completely. Sprinkle gelatin over water in a small saucepan. Let soften a few minutes. Heat over low heat, stirring frequently, until gelatin is completely dissolved. In a blender, combine gelatin mixture with remaining ingredients, except ice cubes. Blend until smooth. While continuing to blend, add ice cubes, 2 at a time. Blend until mixture thickens, about 1 minute. Spoon into cooled crust, discarding any remaining bits of ice. Chill.
Servings: 8.

Desserts

Coconut Pudding Cocado

2-1/2 cups shredded coconut
2-1/2 cups sugar
2-1/2 cups water
Pinch of salt
10 cups milk

5 sticks cinnamon
7-1/2 egg yolks, beaten to mix
1-1/4 cups heavy cream, whipped until
  it holds a stiff peak
2/3 cup browned, slivered almonds

Butter glass bowl. Put sugar and water in a saucepan, and boil steadily until syrup spins a thread when a little is lifted on spoon (230-245 candy thermometer). Add coconut and salt, and cook, stirring constantly until coconut absorbs sugar syrup and looks dry. Scald 7-1/2 cups milk and cinnamon. Cover, and let stand 15 minutes to infuse. Strain, and add coconut mixture; then stir constantly over low heat until thoroughly mixed. Stir remaining milk into egg yolks. Stir in a little coconut mixture; then add it gradually to remaining coconut mixture in pan. Cook over low heat. Stir constantly until mixture thickens. Do not let boil. Cool slightly. Pour into butter bowls, and refrigerate. When cocado is cold, cover with whipped cream piped through star shape in a pastry bag. Decorate with slivered almonds, and serve.

Servings: 6.

Nutritional Analysis: page 436.

Desserts

Coconut Upside Down Cake

In a flat-bottomed 8 inch iron skillet melt:

6 tablespoons butter   1/2 cup "raw" or brown sugar

Add:

1-1/2 cup fresh shredded coconut

Batter:

1-1/2 cup whole wheat pastry flour   3/4 cup sugar (preferably "raw" sugar)

2-1/2 teaspoon baking powder   1 egg plus 1 egg yolk, well beaten

1/2 teaspoon salt   1/2 teaspoon vanilla extract

1/2 cup butter   1/2 cup coconut (or dairy) milk

Sift flour, baking powder and salt three times. Cream butter, sugar, eggs and vanilla. Mix half of creamed mixture into dry ingredients; then half of the liquid; then the other half of creamed mixturer; then the last half of liquid. Do not overmix. Pour into skillet on top of coconut. Bake at 350 degrees about 35 minutes. Remove from the oven, and loosen the sides with a knife. Immediately flip over onto a cake platter. Serve warm or cool.

Servings: 6-8.

Desserts

Coffee Chocolate Cheesecake

3/4 cup graham cracker crumbs (about 9 squares)
1 teaspoon brown sugar
1-1/2 tablespoons butter or margarine, melted
1/2 cup semisweet chocolate chips
1/4 cup firmly packed brown sugar
1/4 cup granulated white sugar

1 container (15 ounces) part-skim ricotta cheese
3/4 cup plain lowfat yogurt
2 eggs or substitute
4 egg whites
1/3 cup coffee liqueur
1 tablespoon cornstarch
Fresh strawberries (optional)

Preheat the oven to 350 degrees. Combine the crumbs, the 1 teaspoon of brown sugar and the melted butter or margarine in a small bowl. Press firmly into the bottom of a 10 inch springform pan. Bake for 10 minutes; then set aside, and let cool. Leave oven on. Melt the chocolate chips in a double boiler. Mix the ricotta cheese and yogurt in a blender or food processor, adding small amounts at a time. Blend until smooth. Add the eggs, and blend briefly. Combine the cheese mixture and melted chocolate in a large bowl. Stir in the coffee liqueur, sugars and cornstarch, and pour over the baked crust. Bake for 1 hour and 15 minutes, or until cake is set in the middle. Turn off oven, leave cake inside with oven door open, and let cool for 2 hours. Chill for at least 4 hours. Release sides of pan, and garnish the cake with fresh sliced strawberries, if desired.
Servings: 12.

Desserts

Coffee Ice Cream

2 cups heavy cream
1 cup sugar

1 cup fresh brewed espresso
1 piece vanilla bean

Scald cream in heavy sauce pan with vanilla. Meanwhile, beat yolks with sugar until pale. Add hot espresso and vanilla bean, and whisk into scalded cream. Cook until thick over low heat, but do not boil. Discard vanilla bean, and cool. Freeze according to ice cream maker's instructions.
Servings: 6-8.

Cranberry Cobbler

3 cups cranberries
3/4 cup sugar, divided
1/2 cup all purpose flour

3/4 cup walnuts, chopped
1 egg
1/3 cup butter or margarine, melted

Place cranberries in lightly greased 8 inch square baking dish. Sprinkle with walnuts and 1/2 cup sugar, and set aside. Combine egg and remaining 1/4 cup sugar, and beat at the high speed of an electric mixer until smooth and slightly thickened. Add flour and butter. Beat at low speed of an electric mixer until smooth. Spoon batter over berry mixture, and bake at 325 degrees for 45 to 50 minutes or until lightly browned. Serve warm with ice cream.
Servings: 6-8.

Desserts

Creamy Raspberry Swirl Cheesecake

1/2 cup graham cracker crumbs
16 ounces cream cheese, softened
2 eggs, room temperature
1-1/2 teaspoons vanilla extract
3 cups sour cream
1/3 cup seedless raspberry jam

1 cup sugar
1 tablespoon cornstarch
2 tablespoons fresh lemon juice
1/4 teaspoon salt
Fresh raspberries for garnish

Preheat oven to 350 degrees. Wrap outside of 8x2-1/2 inch springform pan in double layer of aluminum foil to prevent seepage. Grease the pan or spray with vegetable shortening. Sprinkle the graham cracker crumbs over the bottom of the pan, and tap to distribute evenly. Heat the raspberry jam over moderately low heat, stirring until melted and smooth, and set aside. In a large mixer bowl at medium speed, beat together cream cheese and sugar until very smooth, about 3 minutes. Beat in cornstarch. Add eggs, 1 at a time, beating well for 30 seconds after each addition. Add lemon juice, vanilla and salt, and beat until well-blended. Beat in sour cream. Pour about 1/3 of cheese filling into prepared cake pan. Drizzle half of the raspberry jam over the filling. Add another third of the filling, and repeat with remaining jam. Top with remaining filling. Using a small spatula or knife, cut down through batter, and swirl to marble jam throughout filling without cutting into the crumb crust. Set the springform pan in larger roasting pan, and surround with 1 inch of hot water. Bake for 45 minutes. Turn off the oven, and let the cake continue to cook in hot oven without opening door for 1 hour longer. Remove pan to rack, and let cool to room temperature about 1 hour. Cover with plastic wrap being careful not to touch surface of cheesecake, and refrigerate at least 4 hours, or overnight, until completely chilled. Run a thin metal spatula around edge of cake, and remove sides of springform. Use a spatula to smooth sides of the cake, if necessary. Refrigerate until serving time. Garnish with raspberries, if desired.
Servings: 6-8.

Desserts

Date Bran Bars

1 cup all-purpose flour
1-1/2 teaspoons baking powder
3/4 cup dates, chopped
1/2 cup boiling water
1/4 cup margarine, softened

1 teaspoon vanilla extract
1 egg, slightly beaten
1/3 cup orange juice
1-1/2 cups fiber cereal
1/4 cup nuts, chopped

In a small mixing bowl, stir together the flour and baking powder. Set aside. Stir together the dates and the boiling water. Set aside. In a large mixing bowl, combine the margarine, vanilla and egg. Beat well. Add the flour mixture and the orange juice. Mix well. Fold in the dates, cereal and nuts. Spread the mixture evenly in a lightly greased 8x8x2 inch baking pan. Bake at 350 degrees for about 30 minutes or until a wooden toothpick inserted in the center comes out clean. Cool in the pan. Cut into 24 bars.
Servings: 24 (1-1/3x2 inches).

Desserts

Delicious Fruitcake

2-1/4 pounds candied fruits
1/2 pound dates
1 cup raisins
1-3/4 cups flour
1 cup pecans
1-1/2 cups walnuts
1 cup shortening
1/2 cup sugar
1/2 cup honey

5 eggs, beaten
1 teaspoon baking powder
1 teaspoon salt
1-1/4 teaspoons cinnamon
1/2 teaspoon allspice
1/2 teaspoon mace
3/4 teaspoon cloves
6 tablespoons unsweetened pineapple
   juice

Dredge fruits in 1/4 cup of the flour. Add nuts. Cream shortening with sugar, add honey, and beat thoroughly. Add eggs, and beat until smooth. Sift dry ingredients, and add alternately with fruit juice; beat smooth. Pour batter over floured fruits, and mix well. Line greased baking pans with heavy waxed paper, allowing 1/2 inch to extend above all sides of pan. Spoon batter into pans without packing. Bake at 250 degrees 3 hours. Place pan of water on bottom shelf while baking to keep cake moist. Makes 5 pound cake.

Desserts

Double Strawberry Custard

Custard:

1 cup sugar

1/2 cup sweet red wine

1 tablespoon lemon juice

Sauce:

1 pint fresh strawberries

1/4 cup sugar

1 quart fresh strawberries, crushed

8 eggs

3 tablespoons amaretto

In a saucepan, combine the sugar, wine, lemon juice and 1 quart of strawberries. Boil the mixture for 5 minutes; then put it through a fine strainer. Beat the eggs thoroughly, and put them through a fine strainer, adding them to the strawberry mixture. Pour into a buttered flan mold or deep baking dish. Cover, and place the dish in a pan of hot water. Bake in a preheated 350 degree oven for 45 minutes; then cool the flan 3 to 4 hours, or until firmly set. Prepare the sauce by blending the remaining strawberries, the sugar, and liqueur to puree. Unmold the chilled flan onto a chilled platter, and spoon the sauce over as you serve.

Servings: 4 to 5

English Toffee Bars

2 sticks butter, softened

2 cups flour

1 teaspoon vanilla

1 egg yolk

1/4 teaspoon salt

1-1/2 cups sugar

1-1/2 cups pecans

Separate egg, and reserve white. Mix all ingredients except pecans until a smooth dough has formed. Stir in pecans. Press dough into 2 greased cookie sheets. (Dough will be very thin). Brush the dough with the reserved egg white, and sprinkle pecans over the pans evenly. Bake at 325 degrees, 25-30 minutes. While hot, cut into 1x2-1/2 inch bars.

Servings: 8.   Nutritional Analysis: page 437.

Desserts

Feather Orange Cake

3/4 cup shortening
1-1/4 cups sugar
1/4 cup honey
3 eggs
2-1/4 cups sifted flour
3-1/2 teaspoons baking powder

1/2 teaspoon salt
3/4 cup water
1/4 cup nuts, chopped
1/4 cup orange juice
1-1/2 tablespoons grated orange rind

Cream shortening, sugar, honey and eggs for 5 minutes on low speed in mixer. Sift together dry ingredients, and add alternately with water, nuts, juice and rind. Bake in 2 wax paper-lined layer cake pans in 350 degree oven for 30 to 35 minutes, or until done. Cool and remove from pans. Ice with boiled or confectioners' sugar icing to which orange juice and peel have been added.
Servings: 6-8.

Fudge Pecan Pie

1/3 cup butter
3 squares unsweetened chocolate
  (3 ounces)
4 eggs
2 tablespoons flour

3 tablespoons light corn syrup
2 cups sugar
1/4 teaspoon salt
1 teaspoon vanilla
1/2 cup pecans, chopped

Melt butter and chocolate in double boiler. Beat eggs until light. Add flour, syrup, sugar, salt and vanilla, and beat well. Stir in pecans. Pour into unbaked pie shell. Bake 35 minutes at 350 degrees. Let cool. Serve with vanilla ice cream.
Servings: 6-8.

Desserts

Grand Gingerbread Men

1/3 cup butter
1 cup molasses
1/2 cup yogurt
1/4 cup sugar (preferably "raw" sugar)
3-1/4 cups unbleached white flour

1-1/2 teaspoon baking soda
1/2 teaspoon cloves, ground
2 teaspoons cinnamon, ground
2 teaspoons ginger, ground
1/2 teaspoon salt

Cream butter and molasses together. Add yogurt and sugar. Sift in flour, soda, spices and salt. Mix well. (The dough will be fairly stiff.) Roll out dough on a floured board, and cut into gingerbread-men shapes, or form shapes with your hands without rolling out. Place on a lightly oiled cookie sheet, and bake at 350 degrees for 12 to 15 minutes.
Yield: about 2 dozen.

Grapefruit Sorbet

2 cups fresh squeezed grapefruit juice   2 cups simple syrup
(See recipe this section.)

Mix all ingredients in an ice cream maker. Freeze according to ice cream maker's directions.
Servings: 6-8.

Desserts

Grape Strudel

2 pounds grapes, seedless
1/2 cup hazelnuts or almonds, ground
3 tablespoons lemon juice
1 tablespoon cinnamon
1/2 cup wildflower honey

1/4-1/2 box filo dough
1 egg
1/4 cup oil for baking
1/2 teaspoon vanilla extract
1/2 teaspoon rum extract

Cut all grapes in half, and place in bowl. Add all other ingredients except egg and oil. Mix together. Carefully place filo leaves (about 6-10) on table, and evenly spread grape mixture on top of filo leaves. Roll the whole mixture like a roulage. Make sure ends are tucked in. Place on oiled baking sheet. Cover with egg wash, and bake at 350 to 375 degrees for 40 minutes. Serve with whipped cream. Servings: 6-8.

Desserts

Heavenly Almond Cake

1/2 pound almonds, blanched and
chopped coarse
10 large eggs, separated, the whites
at room temperature
1/4 teaspoon cream of tartar
1/2 cup cake flour (not self rising)

1 teaspoon double action baking powder
1-1/4 cup granualated sugar
1 teaspoon vanilla
Confectioner's sugar for
sifting on cake

Line bottom of a 10 inch springform pan with lightly oiled round of wax paper.
Do not line sides. In an electric spice grinder, grind almonds in small batches to
fine powder, and sift ground almonds into a bowl. Sift flour and baking powder
into a bowl, and combine mixture well. In another bowl, beat egg yolks with an
electric mixer until pale. Add granulated sugar, a little at a time, beating mixture
for 5 to 10 minutes or until thick and pale. Beat in vanilla. In another bowl, beat
egg whites with a pinch of salt until frothy. Add cream of tartar, and beat whites
until they just hold stiff peaks. Sprinkle the flour mixture over the yolk mixture.
Add whites, and fold mixture together gently but thoroughly. Pour the mixture
into springform pan, and bake cake in middle of a preheated oven, 375 degrees
for 50 minutes or until tester comes out clean. If top of cake browns too quickly,
tent loosely with foil. Leave cake in pan, and invert onto rack. Let cool completely. Run a thin-bladed knife around edge of the pan to loosen sides of cake.
Remove the cake from pan, and discard wax paper. Transfer cake to serving
plate, and dust lightly with confectioner's sugar.
Servings: 6-8.

Desserts

Honey Spice Cake

1/3 cup shortening
1 cup brown sugar
1/2 cup honey
2 eggs, beaten
2-1/2 cups sifted flour
1-1/2 teaspoons baking powder

1/2 teaspoon soda
1/2 teaspoon salt
1/2 teaspoon cinnamon
1/4 teaspoon nutmeg
1/2 teaspoon clove
1 cup sour milk or buttermilk

In mixer, thoroughly cream shortening, sugar, honey and eggs for 5 minutes on slow speed. Sift dry ingredients, and add, alternately with sour milk, to creamed mixture. Pour into 2 wax paper-lined 9 inch layer cake pans, and bake at 350 degrees 25 to 30 minutes. Cool 15 to 20 minutes before removing from pans. Frost with icing below.

Icing:

1 cup heavy cream
1/4 cup honey
Dash of salt

1/4 teaspoon vanilla
1/2 cup confectioner's sugar

Whip cream, and add honey, salt and vanilla. Mix gently. Add confectioner's sugar and blend. Best when used at once.

1-1/2 cups pecans, finely chopped
2 medium apples
3 eggs
1 cup sugar

1/2 cup flour
2 teaspoons baking powder
1/2 teaspoon salt
1 teaspoon vanilla

Beat eggs. Add sugar, and heat. Sift, and add flour, baking powder and salt. Add vanilla, pecans and apple. Bake at 325 degrees for 35 minutes.
Servings: 6-8.

Desserts

Jam Tart

7 ounces butter
1/2 cup sugar
2 tablespoons dry marsala,
  more, if necessary
2 cups not too sweet strawberry,
  raspberry or other jam (low sugar type)

1 egg
1 small lemon
1 egg yolk
2 cups flour

For pastry, cut butter into 1/3 inch cubes. If using a food processor, pare zest from lemon in strips. Process lemon zest with sugar until well minced. Process in butter. Mix egg yolk and marsala, and blend into butter mixture. Add flour, and blend until dough begins to clump. Add 1 teaspoon more marsala, if needed. If dough is too soft, wrap in plastic, and refrigerate until firm, about 1 hour. Butter and flour 9 inch fluted tart pan with removeable bottom. On a generously floured work surface, roll 2/3 of the dough to 13 inch circle. Line tart pan, and trim edges even with top of pan. Reserve scraps. Fill tart crust with jam. Roll remaining 1/3 dough to 10 inch long rectangle, and cut dough, lengthwise into 10 even strips. Put 5 strips over top of tart at even intervals. Place remaining 5 strips across those on tart to form lattice. Pinch the ends of the strips to the bottom of the crust. Brush lattice strips with lightly beaten egg. Heat oven to 375 degrees. Bake on lowest rack until crust is golden, 25 to 30 minutes. Cool.
Servings: 6-8.

Desserts

Jiffy Fruitcake

(Starts with a mix.)

1 package date bar mix and filling
1/2 cup hot water
1/4 cup honey
3 eggs
1/4 cup flour
1/2 teaspoon baking powder
1 teaspoon cinnamon

1/4 teaspoon nutmeg
1/4 teaspoon allspice
1 cup golden raisins
1 cup candied cherries, halved
1/2 cup candied pineapple
1 cup pecans, chopped
1/4 cup cranberry juice or brandy

In a large bowl, blend date filling from package of date bar mix with hot water. Add honey. Beat in eggs one at a time. Combine dry date bar mix with flour, baking powder, spices, prepared fruits and nuts. Add, alternately to mix with cranberry juice. Spoon into greased and lined, long (3-1/2x12x4 inch) or tube (10 inch) angel food cake pan. Bake at 325 degrees 60 to 70 minutes or until cake tests done in center. Let stand in pan 10 minutes before removing. Cool on cake rack. Cake must be thoroughly cold before storing. Freeze, if desired. Servings: 6-8.

Desserts

Lemon Wafers

1/2 cup butter or margarine, softened
3/4 cup sugar
2 eggs

1 cup plus 2 tablespoons
  all-purpose flour
1-1/2 teaspoons lemon extract

Cream butter. Gradually add sugar, beating until light and fluffy. Add eggs, beating well. Add flour, and stir in lemon extract. Drop batter by level teaspoonfuls onto greased baking sheets. Bake at 350 degrees for 8 minutes or until edges are lightly browned. Remove to wire racks to cool.
Yield: about 5 dozen.   Nutritional Analysis: page 438.

Lime Sorbet

1 cup lime juice
1 cup water

2 cups simple syrup
  (See recipe this section.)
1 egg white

Mix all ingredients, and freeze in an ice cream maker according to instructions.
Servings: 6-8.

Desserts

Low-Fat Cheesecake

Crust:

1-1/2 cups oatmeal, uncooked
1/2 cup brown sugar

1/4 cup margarine, melted
  (soft tub type)

Filling:

2 cups nonfat cottage cheese
1/2 cup granulated sugar
1 tablespoon lemon juice

4 egg whites
1 cup nonfat sour cream alternative
2 teaspoons vanilla

Topping:

1 cup nonfat sour cream alternative
1 to 2 teaspoons vanilla

2 tablespoons granulated sugar

For crust, combine all ingredients. Mix well. Firmly press onto bottom and sides of ungreased 12-inch springform pan, about 1-1/2 inches high. Bake in preheated moderate oven (350 degrees) about 18 minutes or until golden brown. Cool. For filling, drain cottage cheese overnight in coffee filter. Place in blender on high for 30 seconds or until smooth. Combine cottage cheese, sugar and lemon juice, mixing at medium speed on electric mixer until well-blended. Add egg whites, one at a time, beating well after each addition. Blend in sour cream alternative. Pour into prepared crust. Bake in preheated moderate oven (350 degrees) about 50 minutes. For topping, combine all ingredients. Mix well. Spread over baked cheesecake. Continue baking in moderate oven (350 degrees) about 10 minutes. Loosen cake from rim of pan. Cool before removing rim. Chill several hours before serving. Garnish with mandarin orange slices.
Servings: 6-8.

Desserts

Melon Sorbet

2 cups pureed flesh of any type of
   melon, i.e. honeydew or cantaloupe

2 cups of simple syrup
(See recipe this section.)
Juice of one lemon

Mix all ingredients in an ice cream maker, and freeze according to ice cream maker's directions.
Servings: 6-8.

Desserts

Mousse Glacees

Orange:

5 eggs
8 ounces sugar
20 ounces heavy cream
1 ounce grand marnier

Juice of 1/2 lemon
Juice of 1 orange (3 ounces)
Grated orange rind

Whip eggs and sugar over steam until it ribbons. Whip over bowl of ice until it cools. Whip heavy cream half way, and fold into base. Add flavorings.

Coffee:

8 eggs
8 ounces sugar
1 ounce coffee liqueur
3 packages instant coffee (Dilute in liqueur and heat until dissolves)

1/2 teaspoon vanilla essence
1 quart heavy cream

Whip eggs and sugar over steam until it ribbons. Whip over bowl of ice until it cools. Whip heavy cream half way, and fold into base. Add flavorings.

Chocolate:

8 eggs
8 ounces sugar
1 ounce creme de cacoa liqueur

5 teaspoons cocoa powder
  (make paste with liqueur)
1 quart heavy cream

Whip eggs and sugar over steam until it ribbons. Whip over bowl of ice until it cools. Whip heavy cream half way, and fold into base. Add flavorings.
Servings: 6-8.

Desserts

Oatmeal Cake

1-1/4 cups hot water	1 teaspoon soda
1 cup oatmeal	1/4 teaspoon salt
2 eggs	1 cup brown sugar (firm)
1/2 cup margarine	1 cup white sugar
1-1/2 cups sifted flour	1 teaspoon vanilla

Combine eggs, sugars and margarine. Add flour, vanilla, soda and salt. Combine oatmeal and hot water; let stand 20 minutes. Add to the first ingredients, and blend well. Bake 350 degrees in a 13 x 9 pan for 35 minutes.

Icing:

1 cup brown sugar	1 cup coconut
1/4 cup margarine	1/2 cup evaporated milk

Combine all ingredients for icings in a pan, and cook on top of stove until margarine is melted and sugar is dissolved. Pour over hot cake, and return to oven for additional 15 to 20 minutes.
Servings: 6-8.

Orange Fruit Compote with Cognac

4 nectarines, cut in 1/2 inch pieces	2 papayas or mangos, peeled, seeded
1/3 cup orange juice, fresh	and cut into 1/2 inch pieces
1 tablesooon orange rind, fresh, grated	1/2 cup sugar
2 tablespoons cognac	1 ounce bittersweet chocolate, chopped

In a bowl, combine nectarines and papayas. Add orange juice, orange rind, sugar and cognac. Toss compote gently. Serve sprinkled with chocolate.
Servings: 6-8.

Desserts

Pan Cookies

2-1/4 cups all purpose flour
1 teaspoon baking soda
1 teaspoon salt
1 cup butter, softened
3/4 cup sugar
3/4 cup firmly packed brown sugar

1 teaspoon vanilla extract
2 eggs
1 (12 ounces) package (2 cups)
  semi-sweet chocolate chips
1 cup walnut pieces

Preheat oven to 375 degrees. Grease and flour a 10x15 inch teflon baking pan. In small bowl, combine flour, baking soda, and salt; set aside. In large bowl, combine butter, sugar, brown sugar and vanilla extract; beat until creamy. Beat in eggs. Gradually add flour mixture; mix well. Stir in chocolate chips and nuts. Spread evenly into baking pan. Bake for about 18 minutes or until cake tester comes out dry. Cool; cut into 2 inch square.
Servings: 6-8.

Peach Cobbler

4 cups sliced peaches, fresh or canned,
  unsweetened, drained
2 tablespoons lemon juice
1/2 cup whole-wheat flour
1/3 cup brown sugar

1 teaspoon cinnamon
2 tablespoons butter or margarine
6 tablespoons plain lowfat yogurt
  (optional)
Dash cinnamon (optional)

Preheat oven to 375 degrees. Place the peaches in a 9 inch pie pan or shallow casserole dish, and sprinkle with lemon juice. In a bowl, blend the dry ingredients. Cut in the butter with two knives, or a pastry blender, to make a coarse, crumbly texture. Spread over the peaches. Bake about 30 minutes. If desired, top each serving with a tablespoon of yogurt and a dash of cinnamon.
Servings: 6 (3/4 cup).   Nutritional Analysis: page 439.

Desserts

Peach Compote with Sparkling Wine

1 cup sugar
1 teaspoon vanilla
1 bottle sparkling wine or champagne, well chilled

2 cups water
4 inch cinnamon stick
2 pounds peaches, peeled and pitted

In a small saucepan, combine sugar, cinnamon stick and water. Bring mixture to boil, stir until sugar is dissolved, and simmer syrup for 10 minutes. Transfer syrup to bowl. Discard cinnamon stick, and stir in vanilla. Let syrup cool, and chill covered for 1 to 2 hours or until cold. Puree 1-1/2 pounds peaches with 6 tablespoons chilled syrup. Cut remaining peaches into 1/2 inch pieces. Divide peaches among 6 stemmed glasses, divide peaches among glasses, and pour 3 to 4 ounces of sparking wine in each glass.

Peach Crisp

3-4 cups fresh peaches, sliced
1/2 cup light brown sugar
1 teaspoon ginger
1/4 teaspoon nutmeg
1 cup all-purpose flour

1 cup sugar
1/4 teaspoon salt
1 egg, beaten
1 stick butter, melted

Toss sliced, peeled peaches with brown sugar and spices, and let stand 15 minutes. Pour into a shallow baking dish. Mix flour, sugar, salt and egg together. Crumble mixture over peaches. Pour melted butter over the top. Bake at 400 degrees until bubbly and brown (about 45 minutes). Serve with vanilla ice cream.
Servings: 6-8.   Nutritional Analysis: page 439.

Desserts

Peanut Butter Cookies

1 cup vegetable oil
1 cup peanut butter, unhomogenized
1 cup honey
1 teaspoon salt

1 teaspoon baking soda
2 eggs
1 teaspoon vanilla
2 cups whole wheat flour

Mix oil and peanut butter. Add honey, salt and soda; stir well. Add eggs and vanilla; then flour. When well blended, spoon onto a lightly oiled cookie sheet by the teaspoonful. Press down with a floured fork, if desired. Bake in a 350 degree oven for 10-11 minutes. Let cool on pan several minutes or cookies will crumble. Yield: approximately 50 cookies.

Pears in Caramel Sauce

29 ounces pear halves in heavy syrup
1/4 cup almonds, toasted and sliced

1/2 cup sugar
1/4 cup heavy cream

Drain pears, reserve 1/4 cup syrup, pat them dry and arrange in one layer on platter. In small heavy skillet, melt sugar over moderately high heat. Stir with fork and cook, swirling skillet gently until amber colored. Remove skillet from heat, and put in sink. Pour reserve pear syrup down side of skillet, being careful not to splatter. Add cream in same manner, and stir mixture until caramel is dissolved, and sauce is smooth. Let cool for 5 minutes. Pour over pears, and sprinkle with almonds.
Servings: 6-8.

Desserts

Pear Mincemeat

2 firm pears (1 pound)
1/4 orange including rind
  and pith, cut in 1 inch pieces
1/3 cup light brown sugar,
  firmly packed
1/8 teaspoon mace or nutmeg
2 tablespoons brandy or to taste

1 tablespoon fresh lemon juice
1/4 cup golden raisins
3 tablespoons dried currants
1/4 teaspoon cinnamon
1/4 teaspoon allspice
1/2 cup walnuts, toasted lightly
  and chopped fine

Peel, quarter and core pears. Toss them with lemon juice, and in a food processor, chop them coarse with orange. In a heavy saucepan, combine pear mixture with raisins, currants, brown sugar, cinnamon, allspice, mace and 1 cup water. Bring mixture to boil, stir, and simmer it, stirring occasionally for 40 to 50 minutes or until thickened. Stir in walnuts and brandy, and transfer mixture to bowl. Let cool. Let stand covered, and chilled for 2 days before using.
Servings: 6-8.

Desserts

Pear Spice Cake

Graham crackers or ginger snaps, crumbled

1 tablespoon butter

Preheat oven to 350 degrees. Butter a 10-inch cake pan, and coat with graham cracker or gingersnap crumbs.

2 eggs, beaten
1 cup sugar
1/2 teaspoon salt
1-1/2 cups flour
1/2 teaspoon baking powder
1/2 teaspoon baking soda

1 teaspoon cinnamon
3/4 teaspoon ginger
1/4 teaspoon nutmeg
1/4 teaspoon cloves
4-5 firm, ripe pears, peeled
   and thinly sliced

Beat eggs and sugar until light. Sift, and add dry ingredients, and gently fold in pears. Pour into pan, and bake 45 minutes or until the top springs back when lightly pressed. Let cool 5 minutes, remove from pan, and put on a cake plate. Serve warm, dusted with powdered sugar, and topped with a dollop of whipped cream.
Servings: 6-8.

Pineapple, Papaya and Honeydew with Tequila

2 cups fresh pineapple chunks
2 cups honeydew melon chunks
4 tablespoons fresh lime juice
2 tablespoons triple sec

2 cups papaya chunks
2 tablespoons sugar, or to taste
3 tablespoons tequila

In a bowl, combine pineapple, papaya and melon. Sprinkle fruit with sugar and lime juice, and toss mixture gently until combined well. Add tequila and triple sec, and toss gently.
Servings: 6-8.

390

Desserts

Pineapple Parfait

1 can (8 ounces) crushed pineapple
  in natural juices, drained
1 cup lowfat, small curd cottage cheese

1/2 cup evaporated skim milk
1/4 teaspoon rum extract
1 cup sliced fresh strawberries

In small bowl, blend together drained pineapple and cottage cheese. Using electric mixer at high speed, beat evaporated milk in another small bowl until it is consistency of whipped topping. Fold into pineapple mixture along with rum extract. Layer 2 tablespoons pineapple mixture and 2 tablespoons berries in each of 4 large parfait glasses. Repeat layering; top each portion with 1/4 cup pineapple mixture.
Servings: 4 (88 calories each).

Pineapple Upside Down Cake

1 stick butter
Sliced pinepples or pineapple rings
  on bottom of pan
1 cup sugar
2 eggs

5 tablespoons pineapple juice
1 cup brown sugar
1 cup flour
1 teaspoon baking powder

Melt butter and brown sugar slowly in frying pan, or cake pan. Beat sugar and yolks until light; then alternate juice and flour into this. Add baking powder, and fold in beaten whites. Pour this into the pan over the first mixture, and bake in a medium oven for 35 minutes. Turn out bottom upward, and serve with whipped cream.
Servings: 6-8.   Nutritional Analysis: page 439.

391

Desserts

Praline Fruit Compote

16 ounces peach slices, undrained
16 ounces pear slices, undrained
1 tablespoon cornstarch
17 ounces apricot halves, drained
1/3 cup pecans, coarsley chopped, toasted

1/4 cup golden raisins
1/4 cup orange marmalade
1/4 cup praline liqueur
3 tablespoons butter or margarine

Drain peaches and pears, reserving 3/4 cup syrup. Add cornstarch to syrup, mixing well, and set aside. Combine peaches, pears, apricots, pecans and raisins in lightly greased 2 quart casserole. Combine marmalade and liqueur; pour over fruit; pour cornstarch mixture over fruit, and stir to blend. Dot with butter, cover, and refrigerate. Remove from refrigerator, and let stand 30 minutes. Bake, uncovered, at 350 for 30 minutes or until thoroughly heated. Serve warm. Servings: 6.

Pumpkin Walnut Ring

1 cup plus 2 tablespoons cake flour
1 teaspoon cinnamon
1/2 teaspoon ground cloves
1/2 cup walnuts, coarsely chopped
3/4 cup plus 2 tablespoons
   brown sugar, packed light
1 cup solid pack pumpkin,
   unsweetened, canned puree

1 teaspoon baking soda
1/2 teaspoon nutmeg
1/4 teaspoon salt
2 eggs, room temperature
6 tablespoons safflower or corn oil
2 tablespoons walnut oil
*Chocolate walnut glaze

Preheat oven to 350 degrees. Spray inside of 6-cup bundt pan or savarin ring with non-stick spray or grease and flour pan. In medium bowl, combine flour, baking soda, cinnamon, nutmeg, cloves, salt and walnuts. Whisk together to

Desserts

blend. In a mixer on medium speed, beat together eggs, brown sugar, safflower oil and walnut oil until very smooth, 2 to 3 minutes. Beat in pumpkin until combined. Add all of the rest of the dry ingredients, and beat just until incorporated. Scrape batter into prepared pan, and bake in middle of oven for 30 minutes or until cake tester emerges clean from thickest part of the cake. Let cool in pan on rack for 10 minutes. Unmold onto rack, and let cool completely.

*Chocolate Walnut Glaze:
1 ounce semisweet chocolate   1 tablespoon walnut oil
1 ounce milk chocolate

In a small saucepan, melt the semisweet and milk chocolate with walnut oil over hot, not simmering, water. Stir constantly.
Servings: 6-8.

Raspberry Ice Cream

1-1/2 pints fresh raspberries   4 egg yolks
2 cups heavy cream   3/4 cup sugar

Puree raspberries in food processor. Scald cream in a sauce pan, and in the meantime, beat yolks with sugar until pale. Add a few tablespoons of cream to the yolk mixture, and then add the yolk mixture to the saucepan with the remaining scalded cream. Cook the custard over a low heat until thick, but do not boil. Chill the mixture, and freeze according to the packaging directions on your ice cream maker.
Servings: 6-8.   Nutritional Analysis: page 440.

Desserts

Rhubarb Delight

4 cups water
2 cups sugar
gelatin
1/4 cup quick-cooking tapioca

6 cups 1-inch rhubarb pieces
2 envelopes (6 ounces) strawberry

Put the water in a saucepan; add the sugar and tapioca. Over medium heat, stir this mixture until it thickens a little. Add the rhubarb, and continue cooking for about 15 minutes. Remove the saucepan from the heat; stir in the gelatin until it dissolves. Pour the mixture into a glass dessert dish, and chill in the refrigerator for 2 hours, or until it is set. Serve cold.
Servings: 6 to 8.   Nutritional Analysis: page 440.

Rhubarb Strawberry Bavarian

3 cups rhubarb, coarsely chopped
1 cup orange juice
3 ounce package strawberry
  flavored gelatin

1/2 cup whipping cream
3 tablespoons sugar
Orange peel (optional)

Combine rhubarb and orange juice in saucepan. Cover, and cook over medium heat, 8 to 10 minutes or until tender. Remove from heat, and add gelatin, stirring until gelatin dissolves. Set aside to cool. Beat whipping cream until foamy, gradually add sugar, beating until soft peaks form. Fold into gelatin mixture, and spoon into dessert dishes. Chill until firm. Garnish with orange peel, if desired.
Servings: 6-8.

Desserts

Ruby Pears with Devonshire Cream

Ruby Pears:

2 cans (29 ounces) pear halves, drained
2 cups ginger ale
Juice of 1 orange
Juice of 1/2 lemon
2 tablespoons butter, melted

1 4-inch cinnamon stick
3 whole cloves
1-1/2 cups red currant jelly
*Devonshire Cream

Arrange pears, cut side up, in a 13 x 9 x 2 inch baking dish. Combine next 6 ingredients, and pour over pears. Cover dish, and refrigerate overnight. Remove from refrigerator, and allow to sit at room temperature for 30 minutes. Cover, and bake at 350 degrees for 30 minutes. Melt jelly in a small saucepan over low heat. Beat in 3 tablespoons of pan juices. Remove pears from liquid. Place pears in a serving dish; pour jelly mixture over pears. Serve with Devonshire Cream.
Servings: 8 to 10

*Devonshire Cream:

1 cup whipping cream
1/3 cup commercial sour cream
2 tablespoons powdered sugar

1 teaspoon vanilla extract
Ground cinnamon (optional)

Whip cream until soft peaks form. Fold in next 3 ingredients. Garnish with cinnamon, if desired.
Yield: 2-1/2 cups.

Note: Pears may be served cold. Prepare as directed except omit butter. Chill before serving.

Desserts

Russian Cake

5 to 6 cups broken mixed cake,
  leave icing on
1 cup sweet juice (pineapple,
  fruit cocktail syrup, etc.)

3/4 cup red wine
Ice cream or whipped cream for
  topping

Mix the broken pieces of cake together in large mixing bowl with a wooden spoon. Put the mixture into a deep 8 inch square cake pan or round baking dish. Pack it down very lightly with the back of a spoon. Pour the sweet juice evenly over the top of the cake, and let it soak in for about 4 minutes; then pour the red wine evenly over the cake. Pack it down firmly this time. To serve, cut the cake into rectangles or wedges if you use a round pan. Lift onto plates with spatula or pie server. Top with whipped cream for serving.
Servings: 6-8.

Sand Tarts

2 cups flour
4 teaspoons sugar
1 cup butter
Confectioner's sugar

1/2 teaspoon salt
1 teaspoon vanilla
1 cup nuts, chopped, any kind

Sift flour, sugar and salt. Cut in butter. Add nuts and vanilla, and mix well. Form crescents, and bake at 200 degrees for 40 minutes. Cool. Dust with confectioner's sugar.
Servings: 6-8.   Nutritional Analysis: page 440.

Desserts

Sauteed Bananas
with Maple Praline Sauce

1/2 cup maple syrup
1/4 cup heavy cream
1/4 cup pecans, chopped
Ice cream, if desired

2 bananas, peeled and halved lengthwise
  and then crosswise
2 tablespoons unsalted butter

In a saucepan combine maple syrup, cream and pecans, and bring to a gentle boil over moderate heat. Cook mixture, stirring occasionally, for 18 to 20 minutes or until thickened. In a skillet, saute bananas in butter over moderately high heat for 1 to 2 minutes on each side or until they are lightly browned. Transfer bananas to a heated platter, and spoon sauce over them or use them to top vanilla ice cream.
Servings: 4.

Sherried Bananas Dunbar

3 ripe bananas
1 cup sugar
3 cloves
1/4 cup butter

Shortening
2 cups water
1/2 lemon, sliced
2 tablespoons sherry

Cut bananas in half, lengthwise. Fry in shortening until golden brown, and remove from skillet. Brown sugar in skillet. Add water, and cook until it forms a thick syrup. Add cloves, lemon, butter and sherry, and simmer for 10 minutes. Add bananas, and simmer for 5 minutes. Can be served as vegetable or dessert.
Servings: 6.

Desserts

Simple Syrup Dessert Sauce

2 cups sugar
2 cups water

Zest of half a lemon

Mix sugar, water and zest in a saucepan, and bring to a boil. Simmer for two minutes, and strain through a sieve. Cool, and refrigerate. Will last up to a month in an airtight container.

Sour Cream Apple Pie

Pie Dough:
1 cup pastry flour
All-purpose shortening

1 cup ice water
1/2 ounce salt

Rub shortening into flour, dissolve salt in water, combine, and retard.

Walnut Streusel:
1 cup walnuts, chopped or pieces
1 cup bread flour
2/3 cup brown sugar
2/3 cup granulated sugar

2 tablespoons cinnamon
1/8 teaspoon salt
1/2 pound butter

Combine sugars, seasonings, and butter. Add flour and nuts.

Filling:
1/2 pound apples
  (peel, core, slice 1/8 inch)
1-1/2 cups sour cream
1-3/4 cups granulated sugar

1/3 cup bread flour
2 whole eggs
4 teaspoons vanilla
1-1/2 teaspoons salt

Combine these ingredients, and mix with apples. Scale 9 ounce pieces in tins, and flute edge. Fill shells, mounding in center, keeping fluted eges clean. Bake 450 degrees, 10 minutes, and finish at 375 degrees until apples are cooked. Remove. Divide streusel, and cover each pie carefully to enclose filling and highlight fluted edge. Return to oven 375 degrees, 10 minutes.
Yield: 5 (9-1/4x1-1/4").

Desserts

Sour Cream Spice Cake

1/2 cup margarine or other shortening	1 teaspoon cinnamon
1/2 cup sugar	1/2 teaspoon cloves
1/2 cup honey	1/4 teaspoon ginger
1 egg	1/2 teaspoon allspice
2 cups sifted flour	1/2 cup water
1/4 teaspoon soda	2/3 cup pecans or walnuts, chopped
1 teaspoon baking powder	1-1/2 cups sour cream
1/4 teaspoon salt	1/4 cup honey

Cream shortening, sugar and honey until thoroughly blended. Add egg, and beat. Sift dry ingredients, and add alternately with the water, beating after each addition. Spoon into 8-inch layer cake pans that have been greased and lined on the bottom with wax paper. Bake at 350 degrees for 25 to 30 minutes. Cool briefly, remove from pans, and finish cooling. Spread remaining ingredients together, and smooth between and on top of cake. Or put on an icing made with confectioner's sugar, 1/4 cup margarine, 3 tablespoons hot milk, a dash of salt and 2 teaspoons lemon juice.
Servings: 6-8.

Spiced Pecans

1 pounds pecan halves	1/2 cup sugar
1 egg white	1/2 teaspoon salt
1 teaspoon cold water	3/4 teaspoon cinnamon

Beat egg white and water until frothy. Combine seasoning ingredients in a large bowl. Toss nuts with egg white mixture; then with sugar mixture. Bake on a buttered baking sheet for 1 hour at 225 degrees, stirring every 15 minutes. When done, nuts should be completely dry.
Servings: 6.   Nutritional Analysis: page 441.

Desserts

Spiced Sweet Potatoes with Apples and Raisins

1/2 cup raisins
1 pound sweet potatoes, peeled
   and cut crosswise in 1/3 inch slices
1/4 teaspoon cinnamon

1 tablespoon orange liqueur
1 green apple
4 tablespoons unsalted butter
1/4 cup fresh orange juice

In a small bowl, let raisins soak in 1/4 cup water combined with orange liqueur for 20 minutes. In a steamer, set over simmering water, steam sweet potatoes, covered, for 15 to 20 minutes or until just tender. In a large skillet, cook apple, cored, quartered, and cut into 1/4 inch slices in 2 tablespoons of butter over moderate heat, stirring for 2 minutes. Stir in cinnamon and orange juice, and cook apples, covered, for additional 5 minutes. Stir in sweet potatoes, raisin mixture and salt to taste. Simmer the mixture, uncovered, for 3 minutes, and swirl in remaining 2 tablespoons butter.
Servings: 6.

Strawberry Compote in Wine Sauce

2 pints strawberries,
   hulled and halved
3 tablespoons cointreau

1 teaspoon fresh orange rind, grated
1/4 cup sugar, or to taste
2 tablespoons sweet vermouth

In a bowl, combine strawberries, orange rind and sugar. Stir mixture gently until combined, and let stand 30 minutes. Add cointreau and vermouth. Toss compote gently, and serve immediately.
Servings: 6.

Desserts

Strawberry-Yogurt Pie

4 egg whites
1/4 teaspoon cream of tartar
1/4 teaspoon salt

1/2 teaspoon vanilla extract
2 cups fresh strawberries
1 cup lowfat unflavored yogurt

Preheat oven to 250 degrees. Using electric mixer at high speed, beat egg whites, cream of tartar and salt in large bowl until soft peaks form. Add sugar, 1 tablespoon at a time; beat after each addition until stiff peaks form. With mixer at low speed, stir in vanilla extract. Spread meringue in 8 inch pie plate to form a shell. Bake for 1 to 1-1/2 hours or until firm and light brown. Set on wire rack to cool completely. Hull, wash and dry strawberries; slice thickly. Fold into yogurt, and chill until serving time. To serve, spoon strawberry-yogurt mixture into meringue shell. Serve immediately. This dessert does not keep well.
Servings: 8 (59 calories each).

Super Carob Nut Cookies

2 cups corn oil
1-1/2 cups brown sugar
2 eggs
1 teaspoon vanilla
3/4 cup whole wheat flour
3/4 cup unbleached flour

2 tablespoons wheat germ
2 teaspoons baking soda
1/2 teaspoon salt (optional)
1 cup carob chips
1 cup nuts

Mix oil, sugar, eggs and vanilla. Add dry ingredients, and mix well. Add chips and nuts, and mix well. Spoon onto cookie sheet, and flatten slightly. Bake at 350 degrees for 12-14 minutes.
Yield: about 4 dozen cookies.

Desserts

Tender White Cake

1 cup sugar
6 tablespoons light-colored honey
1/2 cup shortening
1 teaspoon salt
1/2 cup egg whites

2-1/2 cups sifted cake flour
4-1/2 teaspoons baking powder
1/3 teaspoon cream of tartar
3/4 cup milk
1 teaspoon almond flavor

Beat together sugar, honey, shortening, salt and 1/4 cup egg whites at low speed for 5 minutes in electric mixer. Sift dry ingredients together, and add to mixture. Combine milk, almond flavor and remaining 1/4 cup egg whites, and add over 3-minute period. Continue beating 2 minutes at low speed. Bake in two layer pans lined on the bottom with waxed paper. Bake at 325 degrees for 30 minutes. Cool, and frost with favorite icing.
Servings: 6-8.

Tropical Fruit Macedoine

1 cup fresh papaya, cubed
1 cup fresh pineapple, cubed
1 cup fresh mango, cubed

2 ripe bananas, sliced
1/4 cup rum
1/4 cup shredded coconut

Toss the fruit lightly in a bowl with the rum. Chill in the refrigerator for at least 2 hours. Spoon the fruit into chilled goblets, and garnish with the coconut before serving.
Servings: 6.

Desserts

$250.00 Cookies

2 cups butter
2 cups sugar
2 cups brown sugar
4 eggs
2 teaspoons vanilla
4 cups flour
5 cups oatmeal, blended into a powder

1 teaspoon salt
2 teaspoons baking powder
2 teaspoons baking soda
24 ounce bag of chocolate chips
1 (8 ounce) plain chocolate bar, finely grated
3 cups chopped nuts, any kind

Cream together butter, sugar and brown sugar. Add eggs and vanilla to this mixture. Mix together flour, oatmeal, salt, baking powder and baking soda. Mix the sugar/butter mixture together with the flour/oatmeal mixture while adding the chocolate chips, chocolate bar and nuts. Place golf-ball sized cookies 2 inches apart on ungreased cookie sheet. Bake 375 degrees for 6 minutes (no more than 8) - cookies harden as they cool.

Servings: 16.   Nutritional Analysis: page 441.

Vanilla Ice Cream

3 cups half and half
5 egg yolks

1 cup sugar
1 piece of split vanilla bean

Scald the half and half in a heavy saucepan with the vanilla bean. Beat yolks and sugar until pale. Add a few tablespoons of the scalded half and half to the yolks, and then put the yolk mixture into the saucepan with the remaining scalded cream. Cook custard over low heat until thick. Do not allow mixture to boil. Cool mixture, and freeze according to your ice cream maker's instructions.

Servings: 6-8.   Nutritional Analysis: page 441.

Desserts

Vanilla Ice Cream

3 cups whipping cream
1 vanilla bean, split
10 egg yolks

1-3/4 cups sugar
Pinch of salt

Heat cream with vanilla bean until nearly boiling. Add hot cream a little at a time to the beaten egg yolks and sugar mixture. Cook this mixture over a pot of simmering water, stirring constantly, until it coats the back of a spoon. (Do not overcook!) Cool quickly over ice water to prevent curdling. Mix can be refrigerated for a couple of days at this point or put into the ice cream freezer immediately and churned.
Servings: 6-8.

Yammy Custard

6 baked yams
4 tablespoons butter
1/2 teaspoon nutmeg
1/2 cup cane syrup
Pecans for garnish

1 cup cinnamon sugar
1 teaspoon ground ginger
2 beaten egg yolks
Enough hot cream to moisten

Mix the yams with cinnamon sugar, butter, ground ginger, nutmeg and egg yolks. Add the cane syrup and hot cream to moisten. Top with pecans, and bake in a moderate oven (350 degree) for 20 minutes. Serve with whipped cream or fresh cream, clotted.
Servings: 6-8.

RESTAURANT
FAVORITES

Lowcountry Restaurant Favorites

Contents

Culinary Commentary

An instructor and Johnson & Wales' alumna, Chef Donna Leventhal has worked in various fine restaurants across the United States. In addition to her teaching, she is a food writer and nutrition consultant.

A GLIMPSE OF LOWCOUNTRY CUISINE

As "The Hospitality College of the South," Johnson & Wales University at Charleston is honored to have been welcomed so warmly by the Lowcountry and its residents. Over the years we have been charmed by the famous Charleston hospitality and intrigued by the indigenous Lowcountry cuisine.

Admittedly, Lowcountry cuisine is unique in that it utilizes the native foods of the region and reflects cultural influences which have been assimilated over the years. As in any other regional American cuisine, European cooking methods were carried on during colonization and expanded upon to accommodate the accessibility of local ingredients. The most profound factors for determining the local food supply include the climate and components of the soil. Obviously, these elements determine the kinds of plants and animals that thrive in this region. Trading opportunities with this port city also encourage the incorporation of "exotic" food imports into the "native" cuisine.

The Carolina coastal plain area has moist and temperate climatic conditions and a preponderance of rivers, lakes, swamps, and marshlands - at or below sea level! The Charleston area residents look to the Atlantic as a funnel for currents, humidity and frequent hurricanes. Inundated with water, we harvest an abundance of crabs, shrimp and oysters. Waterfowl, alligators, deer, snakes and a myriad of birds thrive in the intense heat and humidity of our summers, while wild ducks feed off our marshlands in Fall and Winter months.

Peaches, pomegranates, and figs - even if these were gifts of the Spanish settlers - are popular in Charleston. Rice, hominy grits, okra, tomatoes, eggplant, corn and sweet potatoes are also prominent foods. In the Lowcountry, cornbread and greens are cooked in well-seasoned cast iron skillets and hot pepper vinegars are frequently used for flavor enhancement.

There are many distinctive features of the Lowcountry which truly set it apart from any other area of the country. Only the Carolina coastal region can boast of Geechees who speak Gullah and weave the beautiful sweetgrass baskets. But in culinary terms the Lowcountry is also known for its oyster roasts, crabcakes and especially the famous she-crab soup. Lowcountry frogmore stews, rice breads and corn oysters are unparalleled elsewhere. As for red rice and benne seed wafers, one must migrate to South Carolina to savor these authentic treats. Finally Hoppin' John (a rice and bean dish) is uniquely and proudly Carolinian!

Newcomers to the Lowcountry can savor the comfort of satisfying foods, friendly people and a pleasing environment. Further delights

Culinary Commentary

await as one truly explores the ambience and unique cuisine of the Charleston area.

A few of the recipes in our recipe book reflect the spirit of the Lowcountry, such as Smothered Alligator, Crab Cakes and Benne Seed Wafers. Our chilled Corn and Crab Flan with Spicy Tomato Vinaigrette even sounds like it belongs in South Carolina! For the most part, however, we humbly offer our collection of recipes in the spirit of sharing and hope that we will learn to practice the culinary artistry of Lowcountry cuisine as we strive for excellence in the field of hospitality education.

For a broader understanding of Lowcountry cuisine, Hoppin' John's Lowcountry Cooking, by John Taylor, is an excellent reference.

Taylor, J.M. (1992). Hoppin' johns lowcountry cooking
   New York: Bantam Books.

406

Lowcountry Restaurant Favorites

Gator Jambalaya

2 pounds sliced, tenderized alligator
  tail meat, cut into 1 ounce medallion
1 pound smoked sausage, cut into
  1/4 inch slices
1 green bell pepper, julienne
1 red bell pepper, julienne

1 ounce butter
Salt and pepper
1 quart jambalaya sauce
7 cups rice pilaf
3 cups Carolina greens

Sprinkle gator meat with salt and pepper. In a heavy iron skillet, melt butter over high heat. Add gator meat, and braise on one side for about 90 seconds. With a metal spatula, flip gator medallions so that they do not stick to pan. Add sausage and peppers as other side of gator browns. Saute for 3 minutes. Add jambalaya sauce. Allow to simmer for about 3 minutes. Spoon rice pilaf into deep dishes. Top with Carolina greens and gator jambalaya.
Servings: 6.

Mesquite Grilled Pulled Mallard with Apple Cider Glaze

4 small Mallard ducks (2 to 3 pounds)
  or other "mild" flavored duck
1 stalk celery
2 large onions

Salt
Pepper
2 apples

Apple Cider Glaze:

1 gallon apple cider
1 stick cinnamon
1/2 orange

4 tablespoons cornstarch
2 tablespoons water

Preheat oven to 350 degrees. Clean and dress birds for roasting. Rub birds inside and out with salt and pepper. Coarsely chop onion and celery. Quarter apples. Mix celery and apples, and fill body cavity of birds with this mixture. Roast 2 to 3 hours until brown and leg disjoints easily. Remove birds from roasting pan, and cool for 30 minutes at room temperature. Remove and discard stuffing. Finish cooling birds in refrigerator. Pull meat from bones, discarding bones, skin and excess fat.

This operation may be done a day in advance provided that the ducks are cooked, but not overcooked and the meat is completely cooled and then covered tightly to prevent drying, and refrigerated.

If the grill you intend to use has large openings in the grate, leave the duck meat in larger pieces to prevent it from falling through.

Apple Cider Glaze:

Place apple cider and cinnamon in a heavy non-corrosive sauce pan. Boil over moderate heat until reduced to 1 pint (45 to 75 minutes). During last 5 minutes of reduction add sliced orange. Strain through fine sieve to remove orange and cinnamon from pot. Mix cornstarch with cold water and blend until smooth. Return cider to boil. Wisk in cornstarch in a slow steady stream. Stop adding cornstarch when a thick syrup consistency is reached. Keep warm until service (if sauce becomes too thick, more cider may be added). Grill pulled duck over hot coals flavored with hickory or mesquite until hot. Place on bed of washed and diced lettuce. Garnish with wedged apple and top with 1 to 2 ounces of the glaze. Servings: 8.

Carolina Greens

6 strips of bacon, diced
1 large bunch of kale

1 medium onion, diced

Saute bacon in a large skillet. Add onions and kale. Once bacon is browned, reduce heat to low. Stir contents as kale cooks down, leaving covered when not stirring. Cook until kale is soft, about 20 minutes.
Servings: 6.

Lowcountry Restaurant Favorites

 ## Death by Chocolate

Crust:

7 tablespoons margarine, melted
1/2 cup graham cracker crumbs

1 cup pecans, chopped
1 teaspoon cinnamon

Mix well and press in the bottom of a 9 inch springform pan. Bake 8 minutes at 325. Cool.

Filling:

2 sticks of butter
1 tablespoons cornstarch
1 tablespoon vanilla
18 ounces semi sweet chocolate chips, melted

1/2 box powdered sugar
6 large eggs
1/4 cup whipping cream

Soften butter slightly in large bowl in microwave (about 1/3 to 1/2 way melted) for 3 to 3-1/2 minutes on low. Mix butter (with electric mixer) with powdered sugar, vanilla and cornstarch. Melt chocolate chips in microwave in separate bowl until it stirs smooth. Pour into butter mixture and mix together well. Then add eggs 3 at a time and mix well. Scrape sides and mix well again. Add whipping cream and mix until blended in. Pour into crust. Bake 10 minutes at 350. Cool in refrigerator about 6 hours before cutting from pan.
Servings: 6.

Lowcountry Restaurant Favorites

Carolina Crabcake

1 pound lump crabmeat
1 pound special white crabmeat
1/4 cup fresh bread crumbs

2 lemons, juice only
1 cup mayonnaise (preferably homemade)
6 scallions, diced

Combine all of the above ingredients in large bowl. Mix very gently, not to destroy texture of crabmeat. Scale into 4 ounce portions, then dip in egg and roll in fresh bread crumbs to form patties. Store on sheet pan with waxed paper. Let cool at least 2 hours prior to use. Saute crabcakes in clarified butter until golden brown.
Yield: 10 cakes.

Grilled Sea Scallops
Over Sweet Pepper and Cilantro Coulis
with Shoestring Vegetables

Scallops:
30 sea scallops, 20 to 30 count, lightly poached

Marinade for Sea Scallops:

2 tablespoons olive oil
2 ounces balsamic vinegar
1 tablespoon brown sugar
1/2 teaspoon white pepper
1/2 teaspoon cayenne pepper

1 teaspoon cumin
1 teaspoon chili powder
1/2 teaspoon garlic, chopped fine
1/4 cup water

Add all marinade ingredients into a medium size bowl and mix well using a whisk. Add lightly poached scallops and let sit for a minimum of one half hour.

Sweet Pepper and Cilantro Coulis:

4 large sweet peppers (red preferred)
3 teaspoons cilantro, chopped
1/2 teaspoon white pepper
1 teaspoon apple cider vinegar

3 teaspoons honey
3 large shallots
1 tablespoon olive oil
1/2 cup water

Seed and dice red peppers (medium dice). Peel and chop shallots. Saute peppers and shallots together in olive oil and 1/2 cup water. Simmer for 20 minutes or until peppers are soft completely through. Using a high speed blender, place peppers and shallots and all remaining ingredients (except cilantro) in a bowl, blending until smooth, and then run through a medium strainer. Add cilantro and set aside at room temperature. Grill scallops on hot gas or charcoal grill (only one minute per side) and arrange on a bed of coulis. Preferred garnish: Shoestring Vegetables and Low Calorie Sourcream Hearts.
Servings: 5.

Lowcountry Restaurant Favorites

 **BBQ Shrimp & Grits**

Lowcountry Grits:

1 cup heavy cream

1/2 pound butter

1 quart water

2 cups instant grits

Salt and white pepper to taste

Heat cream and water to boil. Add butter, salt and pepper. Slowly add grits, and reduce heat. Cook 20 minutes. Be careful not to scorch mixture.

Southern Comfort BBQ Sauce:

1/4 pound bacon, diced

1/2 cup red onion, diced fine

1/2 cup red bell pepper, chopped

1/2 cup green bell pepper, chopped

2 bottles (14 ounces) ketchup

1/2 cup brown sugar

1 (1.7 ounces) bottle bourbon

Salt and pepper to taste

Cook bacon until 3/4 done. Add onions and peppers, and saute until done. Flame with bourbon. Add remaining ingredients, and season. Simmer 10 minutes; then cool. The sauce will last under refrigeration for several weeks.

Shrimp:

Saute or poach shrimp in 1 tablespoon of butter. Place in bourbon BBQ Sauce, and simmer for 1 minute.

Servings: 8.

Praline Creme Brulee

1/4 cup sugar
4 yolks
1 teaspoon cornstarch

1-3/4 cups heavy cream
1 tablespoon vanilla extract
1 tablespoon brandy

Praline:

1/4 cup toasted slivered almonds
1/4 cup granulated sugar

2 tablespoons water

Beat sugar and yolks with whip or in a mixer to ribbon stage. Bring heavy cream to a boil, remove from heat, and slowly pour (while continuously beating) into egg yolk and sugar mixture. Return mixture into saucepan, and set over medium heat. Continue to stir, until mixture is thick enough to coat a spoon. Do not let mixture come to a boil. Maximum temperature should not exceed 170 degrees. Remove from heat, and strain through a fine sieve; then add vanilla extract and brandy. Pour in individual ramekins. Chill. Top with approximately 1/8 inch of praline mixture, and serve.

Praline:

Boil the sugar and water mixture until the sugar caramelizes. Stir in the almonds. Bring to a boil. Pour onto a marble slab or small sheet pan. Let stand for approximately 10 minutes. Break into pieces, and pulverize in a food processor into a coarse powder.

Servings: 6.

Lowcountry Restaurant Favorites

Carolina Blue Crab and Scallop Cakes

1 pound backfin crabmeat, cleaned
6 ounces cooked and chopped scallops, any size will do
1 tablespoon celery, chopped
1 tablespoon bell pepper, chopped
1 tablespoon parsley, chopped
1 tablespoon basil, chopped
1 teaspoon dijon mustard

Approximately 2 tablespoons mayonnaise and 1 beaten egg
1/2 cup ground saltines
1 few healthy shots of tabasco
1 tablespoon worcestershire
Juice from 1/2 lemon
1 teaspoon old bay seasoning

Combine all ingredients in a large bowl. Shape into cakes, and saute in butter until brown on both sides.
Servings: 6.

A.W. SHUCK'S®
Seafood Restaurant & Oyster Bar
On Shem Creek

Harbor Fish Chowder

This rather spicy tomato-based stew has been a favorite of Shuck's regulars for years. While our recipe calls for whiting as the fish ingredient, any firm textured mild fish will do nicely.

2 pounds whiting fillet, skin on
1 can crushed tomatoes
1 can fancy tomato sauce
Small can chopped clams with juice,
   Note: If available, shuck your own.
   Reserve the liquor, and chop the
   clams fine. About a dozen medium
   top necks would be perfect!!

2 pounds green pepper & onions mix,
   rough cut
Salt and pepper to taste
2 ounces old bay seasoning
1 tablespoon hot sauce
1 teaspoon sugar

Using either a stock pot or dutch oven over medium high heat, begin by pouring in crushed tomatoes, tomato sauce and pepper/onion mix. Bring to boil. Reduce heat to medium, and add remaining ingredients. Reduce to low heat, and let simmer untill vegetables are tender.
Servings: 6.

Lowcountry Restaurant Favorites

THE MILLS HOUSE
HOTEL

Shrimp & Grits Cakes

Grits Cakes:

1 cup cooked grits
1/2 cup cornmeal
1 whole egg

2 tablespoons bacon grease or cooking
 oil
Salt and white pepper, as needed

Mix all ingredients (except grease) together in a mixing bowl. Heat grease or oil in a 12-inch saute pan until very hot. Spoon in grits batter in approximately 2 ounce portions to form small cakes. Brown cakes on both sides. Remove cakes to a plate on the side while preparing shrimp sauce. You can use the same pan without washing for the shrimp.

Shrimp Sauce:

1/4 pound whole butter, melted
1-1/2 pounds small shrimp, peeled,
 deveined, tails removed
1 rounded teaspoon garlic, minced
1 cup mushrooms, sliced

1 bunch scallions, thinly sliced
1/2 cup flour
1 cup half and half
Salt and white pepper, as needed

Heat butter in a 12-inch saute pan over medium high heat until it sizzles. Add shrimp, mushrooms and garlic; saute until shrimp become firm. With a slotted spoon, remove the shrimp and mushroom mixture to a small bowl. Set aside. Stir scallions into the remaining liquid in the pan. Sprinkle flour over the liquid, and whisk until all lumps are dissolved. Whisk in half and half, and simmer for a few minutes until proper consistency is reached. Add shrimp mixture into the sauce, and mix well. Ladle over grits cakes, and serve immediately. Serve with crisp bacon slices and fresh sliced tomatoes.
Servings: 6.

Lowcountry Restaurant Favorites

The Colony House

Shrimp with Smoked Sausage and Roasted Peppers

1 cup onion, diced
1/2 pound smoked sausage, cut
 same size as shrimp
1 pound shrimp, peeled and deveined

1 cup red bell pepper, roasted, peeled
 and seeded cut into strips
2 ears fresh corn, cut off cob
Seasoning*

*Seasoning:

1/8 teaspoon cayenne
1/8 teaspoon black pepper
1/8 teaspoon white pepper
Pinch of thyme

Pinch of oregano
Pinch of garlic powder
1/2 teaspoon salt
4 tablespoons butter

Saute top ingredients, and add seasoning. When shrimp are barely done, remove with other ingredients to hot plates. Reduce pan juices by 1/2 to form a sauce.

This dish echoes two Southern favorites, shrimp and smoked pork. It is a seasonal preparation featuring freshly harvested corn and late summer red bell peppers sweet from so much sun.
Servings: 4.

Lowcountry Restaurant Favorites

Crab Dip

4 pounds special crabmeat
2-1/2 pounds machine picked crabmeat
2 large buffalo onions, chopped
2 large buffalo bell peppers, chopped
1 small bottle ketchup
1/2 cup mayonnaise

1/2 cup sour cream
1 tablespoon white pepper
1 tablespoon old bay
1 tablespoon horseradish
2 cups shredded cheddar cheese

Combine crabmeat, onions, bell peppers and all other ingredients in mixing bowl, and blend together.
Servings: 6.

Lowcountry Restaurant Favorites

Breast of Duckling Oriental

This dish is very popular at Robert's. Its taste claims kinship to Peking Duckling. This course can be served as a quick luncheon dish if extra sauce is left.

Cooking the Duckling:

3 whole duck breasts
  (12 to 14 ounces each)
3 tablespoons salad oil
1 tablespoon of Robert's Seasoning
1/2 teaspoon thyme
1-1/2 tablespoons red wine vinegar
1 tablespoon honey
2 tablespoons shallots, chopped
2 teaspoons garlic, chopped
1 can (10 ounces) chicken broth
1 cup raspberry preserves (seedless)

2 tablespoons Japanese bean paste
  (Miso Paste)
1 tablespoon soy sauce
1 tablespoon lemon juice
2 tablespoons Chinese hoisin sauce
1/2 teaspoon chopped garlic
1/2 teaspoon of Chinese five spice
  seasoning (optional)
1-1/2 tablespoons cornstarch
  diluted with wine
1/2 cup dry red wine

Heat the oil in a large, heavy-bottomed skillet over high heat. Saute the breasts skin side down for five minutes. Turn them over, sprinkle with Robert's Seasoning, and reduce the heat to medium. Continue cooking until the meat feels firm but springy to the touch - about 3 minutes. Remove the breasts from the skillet, and keep them warm in a 140 degree oven. Drain the fat from the skillet, and add the shallots, thyme, vinegar, broth, honey and garlic. Cook, stirring frequently, one to two minutes. Lower the heat, and simmer the sauce until it is reduced by half - about 10 minutes. Add remaining ingredients except cornstarch mixture, and bring to a slow boil. Add diluted cornstarch mixture and stir with a wire whip until a boil starts again. Reduce heat, and simmer three minutes. Place cooked duck breasts on cutting board, and try to remove as much skin as possible. Slice each half breast in 3 to 4 slices.
Servings: 6 (3 whole breasts).

Lowcountry Restaurant Favorites

Chef's Tips: Most supermarkets sell just the elegant breast from the duckling. If it is not obtainable to buy whole breasts, bone the meat from the whole duck carcass yourself. Start at the top of the breast bone with a small sharp knife, and slowly scrape the meat from the rib cage until the breasts fall off. Roast the remaining carcass and hind quarters in a 350 degree oven for 1 hour and 20 minutes. Cool and shred meat from the bones. Use in salads or soups. You can also pull whole legs and thighs from the carcass, and serve as a main course the next day with the same sauce. The duck breast can be served with rice pilaf, wild rice or a simple prepared vegetable.

Lowcountry Restaurant Favorites

Louis's Charleston Grill
Crab Cakes

1 pound fresh cooked lump crabmeat
1 cup homemade or good quality
   mayonnaise
3 tablespoons extra-fine cracker meal
Large pinch of cayenne pepper
1/8 teaspoon ground celery seed

1/8 teaspoon dry mustard
1/4 teaspoon lemon juice
1 egg white
1-1/4 cups fresh bread crumbs
   made from 5 slices fresh white bread
   with crust removed

Mix mayonnaise, cracker meal, pepper, celery seed, mustard, lemon juice and egg white. Set aside. Carefully pick crabmeat free of shells without breaking up the nice large pieces. Gently fold crabmeat into mayonnaise mixture. Divide, and form the mixture into six equal patties, rolling carefully in the fresh bread crumbs. Refrigerate one hour before cooking. Just before cooking, reroll in bread crumbs. Heat a 10 inch skillet or sautepan with 6 tablespoons clarified butter. When hot, add crab cakes, and saute gently for 2 minutes. Carefully turn, and continue sauteing for 2 additional minutes. Remove with spatula, and place cakes on absorbent paper towels for a few seconds to drain. Place crab cakes on a warm serving platter. Serve with plenty of lemon wedges, melted butter and tartar sauce.
Yield: 6 crab cakes.

Variation: Replace the crabmeat with cooked and peeled crawfish tails. Add a few drops each of hot sauce and worcestershire sauce. This will transform the dish into spicy Pawleys Island Inn Crawfish Cakes.

422

Lowcountry Restaurant Favorites

Ettoufee

1 cup green peppers, sliced
1 cup onions, diced
1 cup celery, diced
1/2 tablespoon salt
1/2 tablespoon basil
1/2 tablespoon thyme
1/2 tablespoon oregano
1 cup oleo
1/2 tablespoon flour

1/2 tablespoon minced garlic
1/2 tablespoon black pepper
2 tablespoons cayenne pepper
2 tablespoons white pepper
1 bay leaf
1 tablespoon worcestershire
28 ounces of shrimp
Hot pepper to taste

Roux:
Combine 1 cup melted oleo and 1/2 tablespoon flour. Cook until dark brown, stirring constantly. Do not simmer, as the roux will burn. Add vegetables to roux, and cook until soft. Next, add spices and base; then add one can of clam juice and 1/2 can of water. Bring mixture to a boil stirring constantly, taking care not to burn.

Note: To avoid burning roux, place in oven at 350 degrees until brown. Adjust hot pepper to taste. After sauce is made, saute 7 ounces of shrimp per person. Add sauce, and thin, if necessary, with water. Garnish with green onions.

HEALTHFUL
HINTS
&
NUTRITIONAL
ANALYSES

Healthful Hints

In 1807, a French diplomat named Constantin Francois de Chassebeouf decried the amount of lard, butter, salt pork, greasy puddings, coffee and tea Americans consumed. Another, Francois Jean Marquis de Chastellux, in his book Travels in North America said, "The days pass in heaping indigestions upon one another. American's consumption of spirits completes the ruin of the nervous system." Today, we Americans are hopefully more enlightened with regards to nutrition. Eating "lighter" is eating better.

Eating is, however, an emotional act. So much of what we like is tied with our feelings of home, our family, and our culture. These foods to which we feel so fondly may not be "light." They may be full of fat, sodium, sugar, or cholesterol, as well as feeling. Should we denounce our favorites? Giving up these foods is almost like abandoning a part of our heritage. What can we do to eat healthier and still retain this nostalgic part of ourselves?

The answer is to modify our favorite recipes. There may be some recipes which are difficult to adjust without losing the original identity of the dish. If this occurs, remember: moderation in all things. If you plan to eat a food that is higher in calories, fat, sodium, or sugar than you normally would eat, consider the portion size and the frequency with which you eat that type of food. Eating a piece of cheesecake during the holidays shouldn't affect your health, but to binge on such foods could. Use good judgement, and remember that you can lie to your head, but your body will know the truth.

The US Department of Agriculture and US Department of Health and Human Services has published the third edition of the Dietary Guidelines for Americans. Seven guidelines have been established for the general healthy population to prevent such conditions as obesity, heart disease, hypertension, adult onset diabetes, and cancer. These guidelines are also good for feeding a family. Children need to be taught healthy habits at an early age, in part because many of the aforementioned conditions are hereditary and can be prevented or their onset delayed by following a healthy lifestyle.

The first guideline is to eat a variety of foods. This is our assurance that we are taking in all the nutrients our bodies require. No single food gives us everything we need. Remember that the total diet over several days is more important than a single meal. One way to insure variety is to choose different foods from the five food groups everyday.

FOOD GROUP	SERVINGS PER DAY
Vegetables (1/2 cup cooked or 1 cup raw)	3-5
Fruits (1/2 cup juice or 1 piece fruit)	2-4
Grains (1/2 cup cereal, pasta, rice or 1 slice bread)	6-11
Dairy (1 cup non-fat milk, yogurt or 1 ounce low-fat cheese)	2
Protein (3 ounces meat, fish, poultry, 2 tablespoons peanut butter, 1 egg or 2 egg whites, 1/2 cup dried beans or peas)	2

Healthful Hints

The second guideline is to maintain a healthy weight. Whether your weight is healthy or not depends on how much of your weight is fat, where in your body the fat is located and whether or not you have weight-related medical problems, such as high blood pressure, adult onset diabetes or a family history of such problems. The following table is derived from the National Research Council, 1989.

Height*	Weight in pounds*	
	19-34 years	35 years+
5'0"	97-128	108-138
5'1"	101-132	111-143
5'2"	104-137	115-148
5'3"	107-141	119-152
5'4"	111-146	122-157
5'5"	114-150	126-162
5'6"	118-155	130-167
5'7"	121-160	134-172
5'8"	125-164	138-178
5'9"	129-169	142-183
5'10"	132-174	146-188
5'11"	136-179	151-194
6'0"	140-184	155-199
6'1"	144-189	159-205
6'2"	148-195	164-210
6'3"	152-200	168-216
6'4"	156-205	173-222
6'5"	160-211	177-228
6'6"	164-216	182-234

*Height and weight are without shoes and clothes, respectively

The ranges are given to account for those who have more muscle and bone, which weighs more than fat, though it takes up less space. For example, an athlete could weigh in the upper range while appearing to be very slim. Excess fat in the abdomen is associated with greater health risk than fat stored in the hips and thighs. If you find you are outside the ranges of weight for your health, see your doctor.

The third dietary guideline is to choose a diet that is low in fat, saturated fat and cholesterol. Choose an amount that provides less than 30% of the day's total calories. To determine this amount, multiply the total calories you consume by .30 and divide by 9. (Each gram of fat contains 9 Calories.) For example, if you consume 1800 calories per day, your equation would look like this: 1800 x .3 = 540 ÷ 9 = 60 grams of fat per day (maximum). In general, most

Healthful Hints

people should aim for 40-67 grams per day. If you are trying to lose weight, aim for the lower range.

Less than one third of the fat that you eat should be from saturated fat. Using the guideline, this would mean that you should not exceed 12-22 grams of saturated fat per day. All fats contain both saturated and unsaturated fat. The fat in animal products is the main source of saturated fat. The tropical oils (coconut, palm, palm kernel oil and cocoa butter) and hydrogenated fats also supply saturated fats. Hydrogenated or processed fats are found in shortening, margarine, and most peanut butters. When you can see oil floating on top in a jar of peanut butter you know it has not been hydrogenated. (Stir this back in, and refrigerate to keep it in solution).

Animal products are the source of all cholesterol. The National Cholesterol Education Program recommends no more than 300 mg of cholesterol per day. Eating less fat from animal sources helps you to stay within that amount.

These goals regarding fat are for all adults and children over the age of two. The following tips are found in the 1990 edition of the <u>Dietary Guidelines for Americans</u>:

<u>Fats and Oils</u>

*Use fats and oils sparingly in cooking.
*Use only small amounts of salad dressings and spreads, such as butter, margarine, and mayonnaise. One tablespoon of most of these spreads provide 10-11 grams of fat.
*Choose liquid vegetable oils over shortening, butter, lard, salt pork, or bacon grease.
*Check labels on foods to see the amount of fat and saturated fat the product contains.

<u>Meat, Poultry, fish, dry beans, and eggs</u>

*Have two or three servings, with a daily total of about six ounces. Three ounces of cooked lean beef or chicken without skin is about the size of a deck of cards and provides about 6-9 grams of fat.
*Trim fat from meat and take the skin off poultry before cooking.
*Have cooked dry beans and peas instead of meat occasionally.
*Moderate the use of egg yolks and organ meats.

<u>Milk and milk products</u>

*Have two or three servings daily. (Count as one serving: 1 cup milk or yogurt or about 1-1/2 ounces of cheese.)

Healthful Hints

*Choose skim or low fat milk and fat-free or low-fat yogurt and cheese most of the time. One cup of skim milk has only a trace of fat, 1 cup of 2% milk has 5 grams of fat, and 1 cup of whole milk has 8 grams of fat.

The fourth guideline is to choose a diet with plenty of vegetables, fruits, and whole grains. Generally, these foods are low in fat and calories and rich in fiber, complex carbohydrates (energy) and vitamins A, C, E, and B vitamins. In order to insure that you consume all of those nutrients, be sure that your choices include plenty of dark green and deep yellow vegetables, citrus fruits or juices, and melons or berries. Choose fruits as desserts. Choose whole grains when choosing starches.

The fifth guideline is to use sugar only in moderation. There are many forms of sugar. Table sugar, brown sugar, raw sugar, fructose, dextrose, maltose, lactose, honey, syrup, corn sweetener, high fructose corn syrup, molasses and fruit juice concentrate are all forms of sugar. Most of these provide concentrated calories and few, if any, vitamins. They can contribute to being overweight and to dental cavities.

The sixth guideline is to use salt and sodium only in moderation. The American Heart Association suggests 12000 mg of sodium for every 1000 Calories consumed. A modest amount would be 2000-3000 per day. Using salt sparingly, if at all, and limiting use of processed and salted foods is helpful in adhering to this goal.

The final guideline is to consume alcoholic beverages in moderation, if at all. A moderate amount for men is no more than two drinks per day and for women, no more than one drink per day. There are some groups that should never consume alcohol. They are: women who are pregnant or trying to conceive, those who plan to drive or engage in other activities requiring attention or skill, those using any medications, those with a history of alcohol-related problems, and children or adolescents. About 85% of the alcohol used in cooking remains in the dish. This is significant, especially to those with alcohol-related problems.

The Dietary Guidelines should give you an idea of what you need to watch the foods you eat. Knowing what to modify in cooking is the first step towards making your recipes more healthful. There are basically four ways to modify a recipe to be more in line with the Dietary Guidelines.

1. Substitute an ingredient.
2. Reduce an ingredient.
3. Eliminate an ingredient.
4. Change preparation method.

428

Healthful Hints

The first step in recipe modification is to examine your recipe. The following tips are from Eating Well magazine, 1991.

1. Does the fat content appear too high? (More than two tablespoons of oil, butter, or margarine in a recipe for four people is too much.)
2. Could the fat be halved? If a recipe calls for two tablespoons of oil, often one can be used, especially if you saute over low heat in a non-stick pan.
3. Could the ingredients be steamed, baked, broiled, or grilled instead of fried?
4. Would the dish work well without fatty meats? What could be used for flavor? (Eggplant or wild mushrooms doused with low sodium soy sauce makes a good meaty substitute.)
5. Could oil replace butter? Is olive oil appropriate?
6. If oil is drizzled over the food, (as in pizzas or Middle Eastern dishes) would the dish taste as good without it?
7. Is cheese necessary in the recipe? Can it be reduced or replaced?
8. Is cream the only possibility for thickening and enriching? (Try potatoes in soups, low-fat yogurt in vegetable purees, tofu sauces for toppings.)
9. Could salt be eliminated or reduced?
10. Could sugar be reduced or substituted?

Today we have so many more options than we did years ago. Technology has given us many new products that are lower in fat, sugar, and sodium and yet not lacking in taste. These items make substitutions simple. We now have at our disposal fat-free versions of yogurt, sour cream, salad dressing, mayonnaise, cottage cheese, ground beef, ice cream (ice milk), and cheese. We even have many low-fat products such as egg substitutes, cheese, and non-stick cooking spray. There are many tasty salt-free seasoning blends and low sodium soups and bouillon cubes. The following chart should give you some additional ideas for substituting ingredients.

If a recipe calls for...	Substitute...
Ice cream	Ice milk, frozen yogurt, sherbet
Vegetables in sauce or butter	Saute in wine or steam. Add butter-flavored seasoning, lemon, garlic, onions, herbs, or a few drops of sesame oil
French fries	Strips of raw potato sprinkled with a few drops of oil or coated with cooking spray and baked until browned
Whipped cream	1/3 cup evaporated skim milk, 1 tablespoon lemon juice, 2-4 tablespoons sugar. Chill milk, bowl, and beaters for

Healthful Hints

	12 hours. Whip until stiff peaks form. Add lemon juice and sugar.
Cream	Evaporated skim milk, undiluted, 1% milk, skim milk
Gravy	Skim or 1% fat milk, broth or juice added to cornstarch to make a cold paste. Stir in rest of liquid, and stir over heat until thickened. Add herbs and spices.
Muffins, breads, cakes	Add 1/3 less oil, and replace the fat with juice, water, skim milk, or yogurt Add 1/3 less sugar while doubling the amount extract (vanilla, etc.) Salt can almost always be eliminated except in recipes calling for yeast
Eggs	Two egg whites, 1/4 cup egg substitute, or 2 tablespoons flour, 1-1/2 teaspoons oil, 1/2 teaspoon baking powder (for baking purposes)
Pork	Tenderloin
Processed meat, bologna, sausage	Baked ham, Canadian bacon
Hamburger	Ground turkey, lean beef, cooked, rinsed and drained ground beef
Cream cheese	Farmer's cheese, low-fat ricotta cheese, drained, strained yogurt, neufchatel cheese (may need to vary according to recipe)
Oil-packed fish	Water-packed fish
1 cup shortening	3/4 cup oil
1/2 cup shortening	1/3 cup oil
1 cup butter	1 cup margarine or diet margarine

Healthful Hints

1 can condensed soup	Homemade skim milk white sauce (1 cup skim milk, 2 tablespoons flour, 2 tablespoons diet margarine)
Cream of celery	1 cup sauce + 1/4 cup chopped celery
Cream of chicken	1 cup sauce + 1 low sodium chicken bouillon
Cream of mushroom	1 cup sauce + 1 can drained mushrooms

One fear that many of us have is that by changing many ingredients we will be eliminating taste from our dishes. That doesn't have to be true. Using various spices, herbs, wine, and other flavors will add flair to your foods. Here are some well-known flavor combinations provided by the National Pork Producers Council in cooperation with the National Pork Board:

Italian Style -	tomatoes, oregano, garlic
Mexican Style -	cumin, oregano, garlic, chile
Greek Style -	lemon, garlic, rosemary, cinnamon
French Style -	white wine, tarragon
Russian Style -	paprika, onion, (low-fat) sour cream
Oriental Style -	ginger, sesame, (low-sodium) soy sauce
Indonesian Style -	peanut, lime, ginger
Caribbean Style -	lime, rum, allspice, ginger

The following is an example of recipe modification taken from the book <u>Choices for a Healthy Heart</u>:

<u>Chicken Divan</u> (original recipe)

3 chicken breasts, halved and boned
1/3 cup butter
2 10 ounce packages frozen asparagus
1 10 ounce can cream of chicken soup
2/3 cup mayonnaise
1/3 cup evaporated milk

2/3 cup grated cheddar cheese
1 teaspoon lemon juice
1/2 teaspoon curry powder
1/2 cup bread crumbs
1 tablespoon butter

Brown chicken breasts in butter. Cook asparagus according to package directions; drain and arrange in casserole dish. Top with chicken. Combine soup, mayonnaise, milk, cheese, lemon juice, and curry. Pour over chicken. Top with bread crumbs. Dot with butter. Bake at 350 degrees 25 to 30 minutes. Serves 6. 647 Calories, 865 mg sodium, 15 mg cholesterol, 48 grams fat.

Healthful Hints

Chicken Divan (modified recipe)

3 chicken breasts halved, skinned and boned
1 pound fresh asparagus
1-1/2 cups chicken stock or broth
2 tablespoons cornstarch
1/3 cup fat-free mayonnaise
1/3 cup plain non-fat yogurt

2/3 cup skimmed-evaporated milk
1/3 cup grated part-skim cheddar cheese
1 teaspoon lemon juice
1/2 teaspoon curry powder
1/2 cup bread crumbs

Brown chicken breasts lightly in a non-stick skillet. Steam asparagus until crisp-tender. Arrange in baking dish; top with chicken. Bring one cup of stock to boil. Combine remaining 1/2 cup stock with cornstarch; gradually add to boiling stock. Cool slightly. Add mayonnaise, yogurt, milk, cheese, lemon juice, and curry powder. Pour over chicken. Sprinkle with bread crumbs. Bake at 350 degrees for 25 to 30 minutes. Serves 6. 275 Calories, 400 mg sodium, 83 mg cholesterol, 6 grams fat.

Here is another example of recipe modification. The original recipe is taken from the cookbook Thoroughbred Fare Cookbook of Aiken, SC.

Cheese Cake (original recipe)

1-1/2 pounds cream cheese
4 eggs
1-1/4 cups + 2 tablespoons sugar

2 teaspoons vanilla
1 pint sour cream
1 box vanilla wafers

Lightly grease bottom of spring form pan. Crush vanilla wafers, and spread on bottom of pan. Blend until creamy the cream cheese, eggs, 1-1/4 cups sugar, and 1 teaspoon vanilla. Spread in pan. Bake at 375 degrees for 40 minutes. Cool for 10 minutes. Reset oven to 400 degrees. Blend the sour cream, 2 tablespoons sugar, and 1 teaspoon vanilla, and pour over cheesecake. Return to oven, and bake for 5 minutes. Cool 4 hours or overnight before serving. If desired, top with cherry pie filling. Serves 12. 467 Calories, 31 grams fat, 159 mg cholesterol, 254 mg sodium, 0 fiber.

Healthful Hints

<u>Low Fat Cheese Cake</u> (modified version)
by Pam Kaminski, a dentist in Charleston, SC

<u>2 cups fat-free sour cream</u>
<u>1 cup sugar</u>
1 tablespoon lemon juice
2 teaspoons vanilla
4 unbeaten egg whites

1 cup sour cream alternative (fat free)
1 cup oats
1/2 cup brown sugar
1/4 cup diet margarine

Drain cottage cheese in a coffee filter or cheese cloth overnight in refrigerator. The next day, place in blender until smooth. Set aside. Prepare crust by combining oats, brown sugar, and margarine. Press into a spring form pan, and bake at 350 degrees for 18 minutes. Cool. Combine white sugar, lemon juice, vanilla, and egg whites. Add cottage cheese and sour cream alternative. Place on cooled crust, and bake at 350 degrees for 50 minutes. Garnish with mandarin orange slices and fresh mint leaves. 143 Calories per slice, 1 gram fat, 1 gram cholesterol, 200 mg sodium, 1 gram fiber.

As you can see, by reducing fat, sodium, and sugar the recipes are more in line with the <u>Dietary Guidelines</u>. In other words, by substituting and reducing various ingredients, the recipes can be made much more healthful. By using these techniques you can do the same thing to any of your favorite recipes. No, you need not feel deprived of the foods you love. Make recipe modification a part of your healthy lifestyle. Bon appetit!

Written by: Rose Marie F. Anderson, R.D.
                  South Carolina Lowcountry Nutrition Council

Nutritional Analyses

AMBROSIA Recipe: page 348

Calories	Protein	Fat	Carbohydrates	Saturated Fat	Cholesterol	Fiber	Sodium
149	2	3	34	1.6	0	1.5	4
Kcal	gm	gm	gm	gm	mg	gm	mg

APPLE FRITTERS Recipe: page 349

Calories	Protein	Fat	Carbohydrates	Saturated Fat	Cholesterol	Fiber	Sodium
272	3	1	62	.1		1.0	6
Kcal	gm	gm	gm	gm	mg	gm	mg

ASPARAGUS WITH CHOPPED EGG & BUTTER SAUCE Recipe: page 265

Calories	Protein	Fat	Carbohydrates	Saturated Fat	Cholesterol	Fiber	Sodium
263	5	26	4	15.2	198	.6	311
Kcal	gm	gm	gm	gm	mg	gm	mg

BERRY PARFAIT Recipe: page 355

Calories	Protein	Fat	Carbohydrates	Saturated Fat	Cholesterol	Fiber	Sodium
154	5	10	18	5.0	25	1.1	67
Kcal	gm	gm	gm	gm	mg	gm	mg

BOURBON PECAN CAKE Recipe: page 358

Calories	Protein	Fat	Carbohydrates	Saturated Fat	Cholesterol	Fiber	Sodium
1154	13	73	113	15.2	178	2.0	275
Kcal	gm	gm	gm	gm	mg	gm	mg

Nutritional Analyses

BROCCOLI CARROT SUPREME   Recipe: page 270

Calories	Protein	Fat	Carbohydrates	Saturated Fat	Cholesterol	Fiber	Sodium
289	4	21	17	9.1	41	2.4	598
Kcal	gm	gm	gm	gm	mg	gm	mg

BROCCOLI AND RICE CASSEROLE   Recipe: page 269

Calories	Protein	Fat	Carbohydrates	Saturated Fat	Cholesterol	Fiber	Sodium
570	22	41	32	25.0	110	2.6	766
Kcal	gm	gm	gm	gm	mg	gm	mg

BUTTERED EGG NOODLES   Recipe: page 272

Calories	Protein	Fat	Carbohydrates	Saturated Fat	Cholesterol	Fiber	Sodium
138	2	10	11	5.7	25	.1	755
Kcal	gm	gm	gm	gm	mg	gm	mg

CARROTS AND CELERY WITH PECANS   Recipe: page 274

Calories	Protein	Fat	Carbohydrates	Saturated Fat	Cholesterol	Fiber	Sodium
228	3	22	10	2.6	0	1.2	255
Kcal	gm	gm	gm	gm	mg	gm	mg

CHICKEN IN RED PEPPER AND TOMATO SAUCE   Recipe: page 163

Calories	Protein	Fat	Carbohydrates	Saturated Fat	Cholesterol	Fiber	Sodium
948	109	48	19	8.4	36	2.9	652
Kcal	gm	gm	gm	gm	mg	gm	mg

Nutritional Analyses

CHUNKY TOMATO SOUP   Recipe: page 78

Calories	Protein	Fat	Carbohydrates	Saturated Fat	Cholesterol	Fiber	Sodium
59	1	2	8		0	.8	176
Kcal	gm	gm	gm	gm	mg	gm	mg

COCONUT PUDDING COCADO   Recipe: page 366

Calories	Protein	Fat	Carbohydrates	Saturated Fat	Cholesterol	Fiber	Sodium
614	20	47	27	24.2	462	.5	410
Kcal	gm	gm	gm	gm	mg	gm	mg

CRUSTLESS HAM QUICHE   Recipe: page 176

Calories	Protein	Fat	Carbohydrates	Saturated Fat	Cholesterol	Fiber	Sodium
286	17	22	5	11.4	158	.2	383
Kcal	gm	gm	gm	gm	mg	gm	mg

CURRIED BROCCOLI SALAD   Recipe: page 88

Calories	Protein	Fat	Carbohydrates	Saturated Fat	Cholesterol	Fiber	Sodium
102	4	7	5	4.5	16	1.5	90
Kcal	gm	gm	gm	gm	mg	gm	mg

EGG DROP SOUP   Recipe: page 90

Calories	Protein	Fat	Carbohydrates	Saturated Fat	Cholesterol	Fiber	Sodium
220	22	1	tr	tr	20	tr	289
Kcal	gm	gm	gm	gm	mg	gm	mg

Nutritional Analyses

ENGLISH TOFFEE BARS   Recipe: page 372

Calories	Protein	Fat	Carbohydrates	Saturated Fat	Cholesterol	Fiber	Sodium
607	5	40	62	15.9	95	.6	346
Kcal	gm	gm	gm	gm	mg	gm	mg

FLOUNDER NICOLE   Recipe: page 181

Calories	Protein	Fat	Carbohydrates	Saturated Fat	Cholesterol	Fiber	Sodium
75	6	2	7	.3	0	.7	69
Kcal	gm	gm	gm	gm	mg	gm	mg

GREEN BEAN SAUTE   Recipe: page 300

Calories	Protein	Fat	Carbohydrates	Saturated Fat	Cholesterol	Fiber	Sodium
115	2	9	8	5.7	25	1.4	117
Kcal	gm	gm	gm	gm	mg	gm	mg

HONEY-NUT GLAZED CARROTS   Recipe: page 303

Calories	Protein	Fat	Carbohydrates	Saturated Fat	Cholesterol	Fiber	Sodium
52	1	2	9	.7	3	.6	37
Kcal	gm	gm	gm	gm	mg	gm	mg

LEMON RICE WITH TOASTED ALMONDS   Recipe: page 304

Calories	Protein	Fat	Carbohydrates	Saturated Fat	Cholesterol	Fiber	Sodium
330	13	12	30	.4	9	.4	65
Kcal	gm	gm	gm	gm	mg	gm	mg

Nutritional Analyses

LEMON WAFERS Recipe: page 381

Calories	Protein	Fat	Carbohydrates	Saturated Fat	Cholesterol	Fiber	Sodium
35	tr	2	4	1.1	13	tr	21
Kcal	gm	gm	gm	gm	mg	gm	mg

MEATLESS CHILI Recipe: page 195

Calories	Protein	Fat	Carbohydrates	Saturated Fat	Cholesterol	Fiber	Sodium
259	13	3	45	tr	0	3.1	132
Kcal	gm	gm	gm	gm	mg	gm	mg

MUSHROOMS SUPREME Recipe: page 308

Calories	Protein	Fat	Carbohydrates	Saturated Fat	Cholesterol	Fiber	Sodium
230	6	18	11	8.0	35	1.0	361
Kcal	gm	gm	gm	gm	mg	gm	mg

OKRA BACON CASSEROLE Recipe: page 309

Calories	Protein	Fat	Carbohydrates	Saturated Fat	Cholesterol	Fiber	Sodium
79	3	3	11	.9	3	1.5	62
Kcal	gm	gm	gm	gm	mg	gm	mg

ORANGE-GLAZED SWEET POTATOES Recipe: page 310

Calories	Protein	Fat	Carbohydrates	Saturated Fat	Cholesterol	Fiber	Sodium
177	3	1	42		0	1.1	81
Kcal	gm	gm	gm	gm	mg	gm	mg

Nutritional Analyses

OVEN FRIED CHICKEN   Recipe: page 199

Calories	Protein	Fat	Carbohydrates	Saturated Fat	Cholesterol	Fiber	Sodium
466	31	30	18	16.2	134	.2	1106
Kcal	gm	gm	gm	gm	mg	gm	mg

PEACH COBBLER   Recipe: page 386

Calories	Protein	Fat	Carbohydrates	Saturated Fat	Cholesterol	Fiber	Sodium
164	3	4	31	2.4	11	.9	57
Kcal	gm	gm	gm	gm	mg	gm	mg

PARMESAN ROUNDS   Recipe: page 312

Calories	Protein	Fat	Carbohydrates	Saturated Fat	Cholesterol	Fiber	Sodium
170	6	13	8	7.3	30	tr	186
Kcal	gm	gm	gm	gm	mg	gm	mg

PEACH CRISP   Recipe: page 387

Calories	Protein	Fat	Carbohydrates	Saturated Fat	Cholesterol	Fiber	Sodium
448	4	16	75	9.8	87	.7	292
Kcal	gm	gm	gm	gm	mg	gm	mg

PINEAPPLE UPSIDE DOWN CAKE   Recipe: page 391

Calories	Protein	Fat	Carbohydrates	Saturated Fat	Cholesterol	Fiber	Sodium
491	4	15	88	8.7	113	.2	233
Kcal	gm	gm	gm	gm	mg	gm	mg

Nutritional Analyses

RASPBERRY ICE CREAM Recipe: page 393

Calories	Protein	Fat	Carbohydrates	Saturated Fat	Cholesterol	Fiber	Sodium
379	3	28	30	16.7	248	1.6	27
Kcal	gm	gm	gm	gm	mg	gm	mg

RHUBARB DELIGHT Recipe: page 394

Calories	Protein	Fat	Carbohydrates	Saturated Fat	Cholesterol	Fiber	Sodium
484	3	tr	122	.1		1.2	12
Kcal	gm	gm	gm	gm	mg	gm	mg

SAND TARTS Recipe: page 396

Calories	Protein	Fat	Carbohydrates	Saturated Fat	Cholesterol	Fiber	Sodium
414	6	32	26	15.2	61	.4	413
Kcal	gm	gm	gm	gm	mg	gm	mg

SAUTEED BROCCOLI PROVENCALE Recipe: page 320

Calories	Protein	Fat	Carbohydrates	Saturated Fat	Cholesterol	Fiber	Sodium
259	15	17	17	1.7	0	4.7	35
Kcal	gm	gm	gm	gm	mg	gm	mg

SOLE WITH BROCCOLI CREAM SAUCE Recipe: page 242

Calories	Protein	Fat	Carbohydrates	Saturated Fat	Cholesterol	Fiber	Sodium
286	28	14	6	6.9	35	1.3	217
Kcal	gm	gm	gm	gm	mg	gm	mg

Nutritional Analyses

SPICED PECANS   Recipe: page 399

Calories	Protein	Fat	Carbohydrates	Saturated Fat	Cholesterol	Fiber	Sodium
590	8	55	27	4.7	0	1.8	186
Kcal	gm	gm	gm	gm	mg	gm	mg

TOMATO-PASTA PRIMAVERA SALAD   Recipe: page 128

Calories	Protein	Fat	Carbohydrates	Saturated Fat	Cholesterol	Fiber	Sodium
55	2	1	9	.1		.6	98
Kcal	gm	gm	gm	gm	mg	gm	mg

$250.00 COOKIES   Recipe: page 403

Calories	Protein	Fat	Carbohydrates	Saturated Fat	Cholesterol	Fiber	Sodium
1004	513	2646	112	25.3	129	1.6	677
Kcal	gm	gm	gm	gm	mg	gm	mg

VANILLA ICE CREAM   Recipe: page 403

Calories	Protein	Fat	Carbohydrates	Saturated Fat	Cholesterol	Fiber	Sodium
288	5	16	32	8.6	232	.0	54
Kcal	gm	gm	gm	gm	mg	gm	mg

GLOSSARY

Glossary

A

Abaisse	A piece of dough rolled to required size
Abattis	Winglets, giblets of poultry (de Volaille)
Abricot	Apricot
Agiter	To stir
Agneau	Lamb
Algrefin	Haddock
Alguillettes	Meat or fish cut into fine strips
Ail	Garlic
Airelle Rouge	Cranberry
a la	In style, e.g., a la Francaise
a la Carte	A list of food items each priced separately
a la Mode	In the fashion
al Dente	To the bite
Allumettes	Match size cut (usually potatoes), pommes de terre allumettes
Aloyau	Sirloin of beef (contre-filet)
Anchois	Anchovy
Ancienne (a l')	Old fashioned
Anglais (a l')	English style, plainly cooked food
Anguille	Eel

Glossary

Anis	Aniseed
Annoncer	To announce (to call out orders)
Antipasto	Italian cold appetizer
Argenteuil	District in France famous for its asparagus
Aromates	Herbs, spices, and flavorings
Arrowroot	Starch obtained from the roots of the arrowroot plant
Artichaut	Artichoke
Asperge	Asparagus
Aspic	A clear jelly made from concentrated liquid in which meat, poultry or fish was cooked
Assiette	Plate or dish
Assiette Anglaise	Dish of assorted cold meats
Aubergine	Eggplant
au Bleu	Term used to describe mode of cooking fish, carp, and/or trout when live, in court-bouillon
au Four	In the oven (e.g., pommes au four)
au Jus	With natural juice

B

Baba	Small yeast-raised cake, soaked in rum-flavored syrup and topped with whipped cream

Glossary

Bain-Marie	A double boiler insert for slow cooking, when direct boiling is to be avoided. Also a steam table in which smaller pans and their contents are kept hot.
Ballotine	Stuffed boneless game or domestic bird
Bar	Bass
Barbeau	Barbel
Barbue	Brill
Barder	To cover meats with slices of salt pork
Baron	Of mutton or lamb; the saddle with legs
Barquette	A small boat-shaped piece of pastry or mold
Bar Raye	Rock salmon
Basilic	Basil
Baste	To moisten meat in the oven, to prevent drying
Baton or Batonnet	Stick (commonly denotes small stick garnish)
Batter	A liquid dough thin enough to pour
Batterie de Cuisine	Kitchen equipment
Becasse	Woodcock
Becassine	Snipe
Bechamel	Basic milk sauce (white); one of the foundation sauces
Beignets	Fritters
Betterave	Beetroot

Glossary

Beurre	Butter
Beurre Manie	Kneaded butter used for thickening sauces
Bien Cuit	Well or thoroughly cooked
Bisque	A thick cream soup made from shellfish, e.g., Bisque d'Homard (lobster soup)
Blanc	Water with flour and lemon juice (used to cook vegetables to keep them white)
Blanc d'Oeuf	White of egg
Blanchir	To blanch (meat, vegetables, etc.) by immersing in cold water, bringing to boil, draining and refreshing by re-immersion in cold water
Blanquette	Ragout or stew made of veal or lamb in a rich veloute sauce
Bleu	Blue, applied to very rare broiled meat
Boeuf	Beef
Bombes	Ice cream dessert
Bordure	Border, usually a bordure of rice (ring of rice)
Bouchees	Small puff pastry
Boudin, Noir	Blood sausage or black pudding
Bouillabaisse	A fish stew, a specialty of southern France
Bouillir, Bouilli	To boil, boiled
Bouillon	Reduce meat stock
Boulanger	Baker

Glossary

Bouquet Garni	A combination of kitchen herbs such as bay leaf, thyme, parsley tied in celery or leek, to flavor soups and sauces
Bourgeoise	Dish prepared in 'bourgeois' family style, meats served with vegetables
Bourgogne	Burgundy (wine)
Boutons (de Bruxelles)	Buttons (of Brussels), poetic menu term for Brussels sprouts
Braiser	To braise
Braisiere	Braising pan or stewing pan
Breme	Bream
Brider	To truss, to tie poultry or meat
Brioche	Yeast-leavened sponge dough
Brochette	Skewer or cubes of meat broiled on skewer
Brunoise	Vegetables cut into fine dice
Brut	Coarse
Bruxelloise (a la)	In the Brussels style (with Brussels sprouts)

C

Cabillaud	Codfish
Caille	Quail
Canapes	Pieces of toasted bread garnished and served as appetizers or snacks
Canard	Duck

Glossary

Canard Sauvage	Wild duck
Caneton	Duckling (male)
Cantaloup	Melon
Caramel	Melted sugar in a light brown syrupy stager
Caramelizer	To caramelize, to cook sugar until it reaches a brown color
Carbonnade	Braised steak
Carcasse	Carcass; the bone structure of meat or poultry without the meat on it
Carpe	Carp
Carre	Rack of veal or lamb
Carrelet	Flounder
Cartouche	A greased round of paper for covering meat dishes during cooking
Casserole	Fireproof dish, or name of dishes cooked and served in casserole
Cassis	Blackcurrant (and blackcurrant liqueur)
Cassoulet	Earthenware dish featuring beans with pork, mutton, goose, or duck
Cayenne	A very hot, red pepper
Celeri	Celery
Celeri-rave	Celeriac or celery root; a turnip-like rooted celery
Cepe	Edible fungus, a kind of yellowish flap mushroom
Cerefeuil	Chervil

Glossary

Cerise	Cherry
Cervelle	Brain
Champignon	Mushroom
Chanterelles	Mushrooms (Cantharellus variety)
Chantilly	Whipped cream sweetened with a little sugar
Chapelure	Bread crumbs
Chapon	Capon
Charcutier	Butcher and sausage maker
Charcuterie	Butcher's shop
Chateaubriand	Double steak cut from the center of the beef fillet
Chaud-froid	Food coated with cold white sauce
Chef de Cuisine	Chef in charge or executive chef
Chef de Partie	Chef in charge of shift or section of the kitchen (i.e., Chef Garde-Manger)
Chevreuil	Venison
Chicoree	Endive
Chiffonnade	Leaf vegetables shredded or cut into thin ribbons
Chinois	A cone-shaped fine strainer or sieve
Chipolata	A type of small sausage
Chou	1. Cabbage 2. Type of pastry used for eclairs, profiteroles, etc.

Glossary

Choucroute Sauerkraut, cabbage pickled with salt and fermented

Chou de Mer Sea kale

Chou-fleur Cauliflower

Chou-frise Curly kale

Chou Paste Eclair batter

Choux de Bruxelles Brussels sprouts

Clarifier To clarify or clear liquids (e.g., consomme, aspic) with ground beef, egg whites, and seasonings

Clouter Oignon cloute - onion with cloves

Cocktail Glass Stemmed glass for use with cocktails prepared with ice to chill but strained and served without ice. Held by the stem to prevent heat from the hand warming the drink.

Cocotte A small ovenproof dish

Coeur Heart, (e.g., coeur de laitue - heart of lettuce)

Colin Coal fish

Collins Glass 10-14 ounces - Mixed drinks that require a carbonated mixer in addition to its base liquid.

Commis An apprentice in the kitchen or dining room

Compote Stewed fruit

Concasser To chop roughly (commonly tomatoes)

Concombre Cucumber

Confiture Jam

Glossary

Congre   Conger eel

Contre-filet   Sirloin which faces the tenderloin

Coq au Vin   Chicken stewed in wine sauce

Coquille   1. A shell-shaped dish
2. Cooked and served in a shell

Coquille St. Jacques   A scallop

Corbeille   Basket

Corser   To flavor and enrich

Cote   A cut of meat; a piece of meat attached to the rib (Cote de boeuf)

Cotelette   Cutlet

Coulibiac (de Saumon) Salmon in brioche paste with kasha (Russian dish)

Coupe Glass   5-9 ounces - Uses include cream base cocktails or frozen ice cream drinks.

Couper   To cut

Coupes   Small bowls to serve cream or compote

Courge   Marrow

Courgette   Zucchini

Court-bouillon   Water, vinegar, and/or wine, herbs, and seasoning for poaching fish, sweetbread, etc.

Crabe   Crab

Creme   Cream

Glossary

Creme Patissiere	Pastry cream
Crepes	Thin pancakes
Crepine	Pig's caul used as casing for sausage and forcemeat
Crepinettes	Individual portions of meat, chicken or pork enveloped in crepine or breaded and sauteed or baked
Crevette (Rose)	Prawn
Crevette (Grise)	Shrimp
Croissants	Crescent-shaped French rolls
Croquette	Foodstuff, molded, breaded and deep-fried
Croustade	Pastry crust
Croute au Pot	A beef broth, popular in France, garnished with vegetables and dried crusts
Croutons	Fried pieces of bread of various sizes and shapes served as accompaniments to soups or used as socle
Cru	Raw
Cuire	To cook

Cuisine Brigade

1. Tournant .... Rounds cook
2. Saucier .... Sauce Cook
3. Rotisseur .... Roast cook
4. Entremetier .... Vegetable cook
5. Potager .... Soup cook
6. Buffetier .... Pantry cook
7. Poissonnier .... Fish cook
8. Garde-Manger .... Cold cook
9. Patissier .... Pastry cook
10. Boulanger .... Baker
11. Boucher .... Butcher

Glossary

Cuisinier	Cook
Cuisse, Cuissot	The leg of veal, beef, etc.
Cuit	Cooked
Culotte	Rump of beef

D

Darioles	Small baba mold shape
Darne	A thick middle cut slice of salmon steak
Debarrasser	To clear away
Debrider	To remove trussing string after cooking
Decorer	To decorate platters, cakes, etc.
Deglacer	To dilute roasting plaque (with wine, stock, etc.)
Degraisser	To skim off grease from stews, sauces, etc.
Demi-glace	Half glaze, brown sauce
Demi-tasse	Literally a 'half' cup; also a small cup of black coffee
Depouiller	To remove scum from surface of liquid during cooking
Des	Dice
Desosser	To bone out poultry or fish
Diablotins	Small gnocchi or croutons topped with grated cheese and browned
Dinde	Turkey

Glossary

Dindonneau	Young turkey
Dredge	To coat food with flour by rolling or sprinkling
Dresser	To dress, to decorate
du Jour	Of the day (Soup du Jour - soup of the day)
Duxelle	Chopped shallots and mushrooms cooked in butter

E

Echalote	Shallot
Eclairs	Choux pastry baked in thick fingers, filled with cream or pastry cream, and iced with fondant or chocolate
Ecrevisse	Crayfish
Egoutter	To drain, strain off liquid
Emincer	To mince, to chop as finely as possible
en	In, served in
en Papillote	Mode of cooking (particularly fish) in greased paper
en Tasse	In cup (Consomme en Tasse)
Entrecote	Steak cut from the sirloin of beef, literally "between the ribs"
Entree	In U.S.A., the main course
Entremets	Sweets, desserts
Entremetier	Cook who prepares vegetables and egg dishes
Envelopper	To wrap

Glossary

Epaule	Shoulder
Eperlan	Smelt
Epinards	Spinach
Escalope	A collop or slice
Escargot	Edible snail
Espagnole	Basic brown sauce
Estouffade	Brown meat stock
Estragon	Tarragon
Esturgeon	Sturgeon
Etuver	To cook slowly under cover with minimum of added liquid (stock, etc.)

F

Faisan	Pheasant
Farce	Stuffing or forcemeat
Farcir (Farci)	To stuff (stuffed)
Faux-filet	Boned out sirloin
Fecule	Cornstarch or flour used for thickening soups, sauces, etc.
Fenouil	Fennel
Feuilletage	Puff pastry
Filet	Fillet; a thin cut of meat, poultry, etc., or the skinless flesh of fish removed from bone

Glossary

Filet Mignon	Small steak cut from tenderloin of beef, veal, lamb, etc.
Fines Herbes	A fine mixture of fresh herbs to season meats, fish, and sauces
Flamber	To flame
Flan	Open tart
Flanchet	Flank
Fletan	Halibut
Fleurons	Small crescent-shaped puff pastry
Foie	Liver
Foie Gras	Fat goose liver
Foncer	To line the bottom dish with bacon or paste
Fondant	Thick liquid sugar icing
Fond Blanc	White stock
Fond Brun	Brown stock
Fonds de Cuisine	Basic stocks or essences
Fonds de Artichaut	Artichoke bottoms
Fondue	A cheese dish of melted cheese in which pieces of bread are dipped
Fontaine	The well or hole made in the dry flour, etc., before adding liquid to make pastry
Fouetter	To whip or whisk
Fraise	Strawberry
Framboise	Raspberry

Glossary

Frangipane	A custard-like pastry cream
Frappe	Iced
Frapper	To ice
Friandises	Small candy-like sweets, petits fours
Fricandeau	Veal braised until very tender
Fricassee	A white stew
Frire	To fry
Frit	Fried
Friture	Deep-fat frying
Fumer (Fume)	To smoke (smoked)
Fumet	Concentrated stock or essence from fish or shellfish

G

Galantines	Stuffed chicken or veal in the form of a large roll usually glazed with chaud-froid sauce and decorated for cold buffets
Garbure	A thick vegetable soup
Garde-Manger	Cold kitchen; chef who is in charge of Garde-Manger
Garnir (Garni)	To garnish, garnished, to decorate
Garniture	The garnish: starches and/or vegetables served with the main course
Gateau	Cake
Gelee	Jelly

Glossary

Gibier	Game
Gigot d'Agneau	Leg of lamb
Glace	Frozen or glazed
Glace de Poisson	Fish glaze or extract, made by reducing stock or fumet to the consistency of syrup
Glace de Viande	Meat glaze or extract, usually made by reducing meat stock to a dark, thick semi-liquid
Glacer	1. To freeze or chill 2. To cook in such a way as to acquire a shiny surface 3. To color food under salamander or hot oven
Gnocchi	Dumplings of semolina, flour or potatoes
Goblet	7-12 ounces - Stemmed type glass; ideal for beer, wine or wine based drinks like spritzers.
Goujon	Gudgeon; meat or fish cut into small strips, roughly of gudgeon size, also small freshwater fish
Grande Glass	12-16 ounces - Most commonly known for serving margaritas on the rocks (on ice) and frozen.
Granite	Water ice
Gratin	Browned surface of foods cooked in hot oven or under salamander
Gratiner	To brown a dish sprinkled with grated cheese under a salamander or in the oven
Griller (Grille)	To grill, to broil
Groseille	Currant

458

Glossary

H

Hacher	To chop finely
Hachis	Hachis de boeuf, minced meat
Hareng	Herring
Haricot Blanc	Bean (white)
Haricot Vert	French bean (green bean)
Hatelet	Decorative silver skewer used in decorating buffet pieces
Hi-Ball Glass	5-8 ounces - Most popular service glass in industry. Very versatile and used for most all mixed drinks.
Homard	Lobster
Hors d'oeuvres	The first course of appetizer, canapes served hot or cold at the beginning of a meal
Huitre	Oyster
Hurricane Glass	16-22 ounces - Polynesian or tropical type drinks or House specialty. Hour glass shaped makes for eye appealing presentation.

J

Jambon	Ham
Jardiniere	Fresh mixed vegetables cut into small dice or julienne
Jarret (de Veau)	Knuckle (of veal)
Jaune d'Oeuf	Egg yolk

459

Glossary

Julienne	Meat or vegetables cut into fine strips
Jus	The natural juice of meat, vegetable or fruit
Jus Lie	Thickened juice

K

Kromeski	A type of meat croquette

L

Laitue	Lettuce
Lamproie	Lamprey
Langouste	Spiny lobster
Langue	Tongue
Lapin	Rabbit
Lard	Bacon or salt pork
Larder	To lard, i.e., to insert strips of fat with a larding needle into lean meat
Lardons	Strips of salt pork or bacon used for larding
Laurier	Bay leaf
Liaison	A thickening or binding agent, commonly egg yolk and cream, to thicken soups and sauces
Lie	Slightly thickened
Lier	To thicken (usually with starch or egg)

Glossary

Lievre	Hare
Limande	Dab, lemon sole

M

Macedoine	Diced, mixed vegetables or fruits
Maigre	Lean. Lenten meal without meat
Mais	Maize, sweet corn
Maitre d'Hotel	Restaurant manager
Maquereau	Mackerel
Marinade	Blends of liquids and flavorings used in marinating
Marmite	Stockpot
Marmite, la Petite	A type of consomme cooked and served in a small earthenware pot
Marron	Chestnut
Masquer	To coat or mask with sauce, jelly, etc.
Medaillons	Round pieces of meat
Melanger	To mix two or more ingredients together
Menthe	Mint
Merlan	Whiting
Meuniere	A method of cooking in which the meat of fish is dredged in flour and shallow-fried in butter, served with sauce meuniere
Mignonnette	Whole peppercorns roughly ground

Glossary

Mirepoix	Diced vegetables and herbs sauteed in bacon fat used as flavoring for soups and sauces
Mise en Place	Literally 'put-in-place'; the kitchen expression for being prepared for cooking and/or service
Moelle	Marrow from a beef bone
Mollet	Soft boiled egg
Monter	The beating of cream, egg whites, etc.
Monter au Beurre	To enrich a sauce or reduction by dropping in small pieces of butter and tossing to blend
Morue	salt cod
Moule	Mussel
Moulin	Hand mill (pepper grinder)
Mousse	Applies to a sweet or savory dish prepared in molds made on a cream base
Mouton	Mutton
Mulet	Mullet, grey
Mur	Ripe
Mure	Blackberry (sometimes referred to as "mure sauvage")

N

Napper	To coat with sauce, aspic, sugar, etc.
Navarin	A brown, lamb or mutton stew
Navet	Turnip

Glossary

Noisette	Nut, or in reference to meat, a round piece of veal or lamb tenderloin; also small potato balls
Noques	Flour dumpling
Nouilles	Noodles

O

Oie	Goose
Oignon	Onion
Oseille	Sorrel

P

Pailles	Straws (pommes pailles, straw potatoes)
Paillettes	Cheese straws
Panada	A binding agent, usually for forcemeats or stuffing
Paner, Pane	To coat with bread crumbs
Pannequets	Pancakes
Panure	As chapelure - fine crumbs from dried breads
Papillotes	Cooking in paper wrapping (en papillote)
Paprika	Hungarian red pepper
Parer	To trim meat, etc.
Parfumer	To impart bouquet by addition of aromatic herbs, etc.
Parures	Trimmings, cooked or raw

Glossary

Passer a l'Etamine	To pass through tammy cloth
Pastillage	Sugar pastes used in modeling
Pate	Paste or pastry
Paupiettes	Thin flattened slices of meat, stuffed and rolled
Paysanne	Triangular-shaped slices of mixed vegetables
Peche	Peach
Perche	Perch
Perdreau	Partridge
Persil	Parsley
Persil Hache	Chopped parsley
Persille	Sprinkled with chopped parsley (parsley potatoes)
Petits Fours	Small fancy cakes or biscuits, dipped in icing and decorated
Petits Pois	Peas
Piccata	Small veal cutlets
Piece Montee	Centerpiece on a platter or buffet
Pied	Foot
Pieds de Boeuf	Cow heels
Pieds de Porc	Pork feet
Pilaw, Pilaf	A rice dish with or without meat (usually lamb)
Pintade	Guinea fowl

Glossary

Piquer	To insert small pieces of fat into lean meat, etc., with a special needle
Plaque a Rotir	Roasting plaque
Plat	Plate or dish
Plat du Jour	Dish of the day (specialty of the day)
Plie	Plaice
Plongeur	Pot washer
Pocher	To poach or cook young chickens or fish in liquid, on simmering temperature
Poeler	A method of oven-cooking similar to braising or pot roasting
Pointe	Tip (of a knife or of asparagus)
Poire	Pear
Poireau	Leek
Poitrine	Breast (Poitrine de Volaille - chicken breast)
Poivrade	Flavored with pepper
Poivre	Pepper
Pojarski	A minced cutlet of veal in the shape of cutlet
Pomme	Apple. Also used in menus and in kitchen as short for pomme de terre
Pomme de Terre	Potato
Porc	Pork

Glossary

Potage	Soup
Pot-au-feu	Rich soup with meats and vegetables
Potiron	Pumpkin
Poularde, Poulardine	Young, fat chicken
Poule	Hen
Poulet	Young chicken
Poulet d'Inde	Young turkey
Praline	Toasted almonds and nuts in caramelized sugar
Pre-sale	Lamb or mutton raised on the French seacoast. A high quality meat
Printaniere	Garnish of spring vegetables
Profiteroles	Small or medium sized balls made out of choux paste
Prune	Plum
Puree	Mashed or sieved potatoes, vegetables, fruit, etc.

Q

Quartier	Quarter; to divide or cut into quarters
Quenelles	Dumpling made of meat, poultry, fish, etc.
Quiche Lorraine	Savory flan of egg, custard and Gruyere cheese made in a thick pie dough

Glossary

R

Radis	Radish
Ragout	A rich brown stew of meat or poultry
Raifort	Horseradish
Ramequin	A savory tartlet or earthenware dish in which food is baked and served
Ravioli	An Italian pasta dish
Rechauffe	Reheated
Rechauffer	To reheat
Reduction	The result of reducing by boiling down sauces to increase the flavor and richness
Revenir	To fry quickly to color
Ris	Sweetbreads
Rissole	Deep-fried small turnover
Rissoler	To brown
Rizotto	Italian rice dish
Rocks Glass	5.5-12 ounces - Liquor or Liqueurs on the rocks (on ice) with no mixers.
Rognon	Kidney
Rognonnade (de Veau)	Saddle (of veal) complete with kidneys
Romaine	Cos lettuce

Glossary

Roquefort A 'blue' semi-soft French cheese

Rotir, Roti To roast, roasted

Rotisseur Roast cook

Rouget Red mullet

Roux Thickening agent made of flour and melted butter or other fat used to thicken soups and sauces

Royale Type of custard cut into various shapes and used as a garnish

Russe Stew pan

S

Sabayon French name for Zabaglione; dessert made of whipped eggs, sugar and wine

Saignant Rare

Saisir To sear meat surfaces in hot fat

Salamandre Salamander (a top-fired grill) for glazing or browning of food

Sale Salted

Salpicon A mixture of finely diced meat of ham or tongue and mushrooms bound in sauce

Saucisses Sausages

Sauge Sage

Saumon Salmon

Sauter Literally to jump; cooking by tossing in small amount of hot fat

Glossary

Sauteuse   Shallow pan with sloping sides

Sautoir   Round shallow heavy pan with straight walls and long handle

Savarin   Light yeast dough; usually baked in ring mold

Selle   Saddle (Selle d'Agneau - saddle of lamb)

Shot Glass   2 ounces - Liquors served "straight up." Thick walls and heavy base make this a excellent glass for shooters and slammers.

Sorbet   A water ice served between meals to stimulate appetite

Soubise   A thick sauce with pureed onions stewed in butter

Souffle   A light sponge either sweet or savory, made to order

Sous Chef   Assistant to the chief cook

Supreme   The best part of meat, game or poultry, e.g., breast of chicken (Supreme de Poulet)

T

Table d'Hote   The set menu for the day at a fixed price

Tasse   Cup, en Tasse - served in a cup

Terrine   Earthenware casserole, also a term for pate cooked in a terrine (Terrine de Porc)

Tete (de Veau)   Head (calf's head)

Thon   Tunny, tuna fish

Timbale   A straight-sided 2-inch deep dish or mold

Toddy Glass   6-8 ounces - Like a coffee mug; used for serving hot drinks like Irish coffee or hot buttered rum.

Glossary

Tomate	Flavored with tomato product
Topinambour	Jerusalem artichoke
Tournedos	A small steak from the center cut of tenderloin
Tourner	To turn, to shape vegetables or potatoes with a tourner knife; also to turn sour
Tranche	A slice
Trancher	To carve or slice
Trancheur	Carver
Travailler	To work, to manipulate or knead
Truffe	Truffle, a pungent black fungus which grows underground in northern Italy or France
Truite	Trout
Truite Saumonee	Salmon trout
Turban	Dishes molded into turban shape
Turbotiere	Turbot kettle

V

Veau	Veal
Veloute	Literally 'velvet'; a thick-textured white soup or sauce
Venaison	Venison
Viande	Meat
Viennoise (a la)	In Viennese style (breaded)

470

Glossary

Vol-au-vent	Puff pastry shell in which ragout or fricassee is served (Vol-au-Vent, Financiere)
Volaille	Poultry

Z

Zabaglione	See Sabayon
Zombie/Sling Glass	12-16 ounces - Straight walled and slender. Used when drinks call for more than average amounts of liquor. Also for service of drinks requested "tall."
Zeste	Zest, the outer rind of citrus fruit

Glossary

STANDARD BAR GLASSES

COCKTAIL
3-6 OZ.

SOUR
4-5 1/2 OZ.

CHAMPAGNE

COUPE
4-5 OZ.

TULIP
4-14 OZ.

GOBLET
4-22 OZ.

LIQUEUR
CORDIAL
PONY
7 OZ.

Glossary

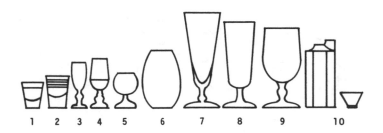

1. Shot glass
2. Special shot glass
3. Pony brandy or liqueur glass
4. Brandy glass
5. 3 oz. snifter
6. 20 oz. crystal snifter

7. 10 oz. Pilsner beer glass
8. 16 oz. footed beer shell
9. Absinthe drip glass
10. Porcelain singing sake bottle and whistling sake cup

1. 5 oz. saucer
2. 9 oz. wine glass
3. Tulip champagne glass
4. &
5. Two champagne flute glasses

6. 2 oz. sherry glass
7. 4 1/2 oz. glass
8. Wine carafe, 20 ozs.

Glossary

1. 4 oz. wine glass
2. 4 oz. wine glass
3. All-purpose wine glasses
4. 9 oz. glass
5. Grossman all-purpose 8 oz.
   lead crystal glass

6. Baccarat 10 oz. thin lead
   crystal wine glass
7. 7 oz. Roemer wineglass
8. Lead crystal glasses
9. Lead crystal glasses

1. 2 1/2 oz. cocktail glass
2. 4 1/2 oz. cocktail glass
3. 6 oz. cocktail glass
4. Waterford Irish crystal glass
5. 6 oz. sour glass
6. 8 oz. highball glass

7. 12 oz. Collins glass
8. 5 oz. Delmonico glass
9. 6 oz. old-fashioned or on
   the rocks glass
10. 7 oz. footed old-fashioned
   glass

INDEX

Index

Index

476

Index

Index

Index

Index

Index

Index

Index

Index

Index

Index

Index

Index

Index

Index

Index

Charleston Hospitality

Recipe Book Order Form

Please send _____ copy(ies)   at $24.95 each   _____

Shipping and Handling   at $3.00 each   _____

                                            TOTAL   _____

Name _____

Address _____

City _____ State _____ Zip Code _____

    ☐ Mastercard   ☐ VISA   Account # _____ Exp. Date _____

Authorized Signature _____

Mail form and payment to Johnson & Wales University at Charleston Bookstore, 701 East Bay Street, PCC Box 1409, Charleston, SC 29403. Checks should be payable to Johnson & Wales University Bookstore.

- -

Charleston Hospitality

Recipe Book Order Form

Please send _____ copy(ies)   at $24.95 each   _____

Shipping and Handling   at $3.00 each   _____

                                            TOTAL   _____

Name _____

Address _____

City _____ State _____ Zip Code _____

    ☐ Mastercard   ☐ VISA   Account # _____ Exp. Date _____

Authorized Signature _____

Mail form and payment to Johnson & Wales University at Charleston Bookstore, 701 East Bay Street, PCC Box 1409, Charleston, SC 29403. Checks should be payable to Johnson & Wales University Bookstore.

- -

Charleston Hospitality

Recipe Book Order Form

Please send _____ copy(ies)   at $24.95 each   _____

Shipping and Handling   at $3.00 each   _____

                                            TOTAL   _____

Name _____

Address _____

City _____ State _____ Zip Code _____

    ☐ Mastercard   ☐ VISA   Account # _____ Exp. Date _____

Authorized Signature _____

Mail form and payment to Johnson & Wales University at Charleston Bookstore, 701 East Bay Street, PCC Box 1409, Charleston, SC 29403. Checks should be payable to Johnson & Wales University Bookstore.

"The Twelve Rudiments of Cooking"
A Training Video by Johnson & Wales University at Charleston

Johnson & Wales University at Charleston is proud to offer a specialized training video titled "The Twelve Rudiments of Cooking." This video is created to teach the basic elements of cooking on which all culinary preparation is based. The three-segment institutional version is designed for use in high schools and vocational schools as a supplement to foodservice/home economics classes. An instructional manual is provided with this video.

The one-segment home version is designed for the culinary novice who desires additional insight into the culinary world.

Both videos total approximately 1/2 hour each and provide demonstrations of the 12 culinary techniques.

"The Twelve Rudiments of Cooking"

Three-Segment Institutional Video
(including teaching manual for classroom instruction)
Please send _____ copy(ies)   at $49.95 each   _____

One-Segment Video
(for the at-home gourmet)
Please send _____ copy(ies)   at $19.95 each   _____

Shipping and Handling   at $3.00 each   _____

                                                   TOTAL   _____

Name _____

Address _____

City _____ State _____ Zip Code _____

☐ Mastercard   ☐ VISA   Account # _____ Exp. Date _____

Authorized Signature _____

Mail form and payment to Johnson & Wales University at Charleston Bookstore, 701 East Bay Street, PCC Box 1409, Charleston, SC 29403. Checks should be payable to Johnson & Wales University Bookstore.